The Viking Achievement

Great Civilizations Series
General Editors: A. L. Basham and Christopher Brooke

THE LIFE AND DEATH OF CARTHAGE
Gilbert Charles Picard and Colette Picard

PRE-OTTOMAN TURKEY
Claude Cahen

THE WONDER THAT WAS INDIA
A. L. Basham

THE GREATNESS THAT WAS BABYLON
H. W. F. Saggs

THE GLORY THAT WAS GREECE
J. C. Stobart

THE GRANDEUR THAT WAS ROME
J. C. Stobart

THE SPLENDOUR THAT WAS EGYPT
Margaret A. Murray

Uniform with above series

BRITISH INDIA
Michael Edwardes

The Viking Achievement

The society and culture of early medieval Scandinavia

Peter Foote

Professor of Old Scandinavian
University of London

David M. Wilson

Reader in Archaeology of the Anglo-Saxon Period
University of London

SIDGWICK & JACKSON
LONDON

First published 1970
Second impression 1973
Copyright © 1970 Peter Foote and David M. Wilson

SBN 283.97926.7 (paper)
SBN 283.35499.2 (cloth)

Printed in Great Britain by
Billing & Sons, Ltd., Guildford and London
for Sidgwick and Jackson Limited
1 Tavistock Chambers, Bloomsbury Way
London, WC1A 2SG

To
Eleanor and Eva

Contents

CONTENTS

CONTENTS

ix

Acknowledgements

We have incurred vast debts of gratitude in our study of the northern countries over the years and during the preparation of this book. We remember many people, dead and alive, who have shown us great kindness and from whom we have done our best to learn. Here we can only mention a handful of names: Holger Arbman, Birgit Arrhenius, Birgit Bergfors, Martin and Charlotte Blindheim, Joseph Crabtree, Paul Foote, Olaf Olsen, Hugh Smith, Dag Strömbäck, Gabriel Turville-Petre.

Every reader will be grateful to Dr J. M. Stern of All Souls College, Oxford, and Ralph Pinder-Wilson of the British Museum, who have generously provided a new translation of the passage from Ibn Fadlan on pp. 408–11, but only we can properly estimate our obligation to Michael Barnes and Richard Perkins of the Department of Scandinavian Studies, University College London, who have read the book in proof and saved us from many slips, and to Mrs Katja Tims, secretary of the same Department, who has done much of our typing.

Copyright of illustrations

Copyright of the following is acknowledged: The late Professor H. Arbman, pl. 18 *b* and *c*. ATA, Stockholm, pls. 2 *b* and *c*, 3 *a*, 8 *a*, 9 *a*, 12, 15 *b* and *c*, 23 *b*, 26 *b*, fig. 55. Bayerisches National-museum, Munich, pl. 19 *b*. British Museum, pls. 6 *c* and *d*, 19 *a*, 25 *a*. Courtauld Institute, pl. 1 *b*. Mr S. Dahl, pl. 3 *b*. Guildhall Museum, London, pl. 26 *a*. Historisk Museum, Bergen, pl. 28. Sir Thomas Kendrick, pl. 10. Ministry of Public Building and Works, London, pl. 1 *a*. National Museum, Copenhagen, pls. 4, 14, 21, 26 *c*, fig. 41. National Museum, Dublin, pl. 24 *b*. National Museum, Reykjavík, pl. 23 *a*. Nordiska Museet, Stockholm, pl. 24 *a*. Olaf Olsen and Ole Crumlin-Pedersen, figs. 32, 33 and 34. Riksanti-kvaren, Oslo, pl. 27. Schleswig-Holsteinisches Landesmuseum, Schleswig, pl. 8 *b*. University Library, Cambridge, pl. 6 *b*. Universitetets Oldsaksamling, Oslo, Frontispiece, pls. 2 *a*, 5, 7, 9 *b*, 13, 15 *a*, 16 *f-h*, 18 *a*, 25 *b*. D. M. Wilson, pls. 6 *a*, 17 *a*. D. M. Wilson and O. Klindt-Jensen, pls. 11, 16 *a-e*, 17 *b*, 20. Mrs E. Wilson, figs. 10–31, 35–40, 42–54, 56, 58, 59.

Fig. 8 is taken with permission from W. R. Mead, *An Economic Geography of the Scandinavian States and Finland* (University of London Press, 1958; second impression 1964). Fig. 57 is adapted from Jan de Vries, *Altgermanische Religionsgeschichte* II (Zweite, völlig neu bearbeitete Auflage, 1957). This is Bd. 12/II in *Grundriss der germanischen Philologie*, published by Walter de Gruyter und Co., Berlin.

Spelling and pronunciation

The letter þ ('thorn') is pronounced like *th* in *thin*, ð ('eth') like *th* in *then*. In Scandinavian words, old and new, j is pronounced like *y* in *yes*. Readers will pronounce modified vowels as they like.

'Classical' Old Scandinavian and West Norse forms are supposed to have a conventional Old Icelandic appearance, although some effort has been made to avoid the reflection in the spelling of Icelandic developments that were not fully effected until after our period was over. Old Danish and Old Swedish forms are generally quoted in conventional normalized orthography. It will be seen that an attempt has been made to distinguish between East Norse and West Norse forms of proper names.

We are cheerfully aware that total consistency has not been achieved in any of these practices.

PETER FOOTE
DAVID WILSON

List of figures in text

Introduction

Until the voyages and colonizations of the four centuries following the discoveries of Columbus, no people from European homelands ever spread so wide in the world as the Scandinavians of the Viking Age. From Norway they settled the Atlantic islands, Shetland, Orkney, the Faroes and Iceland. The southernmost of these islands were stepping-stones which led them on to settlement and rule in large areas in Scotland, the Hebrides, the Isle of Man, Ireland and northwest England. The Icelanders went on to Greenland and the Greenlanders explored shores of the North American continent. From Denmark people came to take over the chief parts of east and northeast England and the province of Normandy in France. Danes became involved in Frisia and along the south Baltic shores. Swedes moved across the Baltic to the south and west shores of Finland, to the Slav territory around what is now Leningrad and Novgorod; they penetrated and traversed Poland and Russia to visit and attack the Byzantine Empire and towns of the Caliphate. Piracy, trade, land to plough and the pilgrim's gain: these were attractions that stirred the Scandinavian from his farm or village and carried him to Dublin or Noirmoûtier, Greenland or Seville, Baku or Compostella, Utrecht or Kiev. *Ormiga, Ulfar, Grikkjar, Jórsalir, Ísland, Serkland –* so a pair of eleventh-century Gotland merchants briskly record their journeys to the realms of Constantinople and to Jerusalem, Iceland and the Baghdad Caliphate.

Their chief lasting settlements were in the west, either in uninhabited or sparsely inhabited countries or in the lands of the Franks, English and Irish, where in the countryside they found a material culture not very different from or more efficient than their own, although in towns and courts there were greater wealth, greater social differentiation, and in some respects greater refinement. They could rapidly come to terms with native populations, and the process was greatly quickened by the newcomers' early adoption of Christianity. The smaller the numbers of Scandinavians involved, the more effective and swift the change was likely to be. The Swedes who stayed in Russia must soon have adopted Slav ways, and it is now only with difficulty that the archaeologist or philologist can detect Scandinavian origin or influence in the early Slav world. The Danes in Normandy soon lost their native tongue and in 150 years turned into the Normans whom we know best as the conquerors of England and the founders of kingdoms in south Italy and Sicily. The renowned abilities of the Normans, unattractive to many people, find no straightforward Scandinavian parallel and seem rather to spring from the grafting of Scandinavian on Frankish-Gallic aptitudes.

Early emigrants from the Scandinavian countries might keep ties with their homelands, links with families, friends and trading partners, but they had no notion of loyalty to a state or fatherland. The Viking Age saw a great mingling of peoples across boundaries and seas and it was not only the countries to which the Scandinavians came that were affected by the process. Many Scandinavians, after a time abroad as soldiers or traders, returned to their farms or joined a new Scandinavian society like that of the Icelanders. They had with them wealth of all kinds, in silver and jewels, in art and ideas, in memory of experiences that had enlarged their self-reliance and self-control. Through these people of all ranks the road was cleared for the massive innovations in religion, social organization and statehood that were largely effected in the Scandinavian countries by the end of the twelfth century.

The Norsemen abroad have often been described in English, but we mean to look chiefly at Scandinavian societies at home in the period A.D. 800 – 1200. In so doing we shall gain an inkling of the means whereby they maintained their commerce with the outside world, peaceful and warlike, on so large a scale and for so long a time. That commerce depended on many things, on the existence of stable societies fostering adaptable individuals, on ample and reliable food production, on the availability of essential raw materials, on widespread ability in the crafts necessary to provide the buildings, clothes, weapons, tools, ships, everything that made life and movement possible under Scandinavian conditions of terrain and climate – and all of these in such profusion that men by the thousand and ships by the score could be spared for ventures abroad. If an understanding of the age is to be gained,

AINLAND SCANDINAVIA

–·–·– MODERN BOUNDARIES

NORTH CAPE

WHITE SEA

HÅLOGALAND

NORRLAND

GULF OF BOTHNIA

FINLAND

Nidaros (Trondheim)

Ladoga
Novgorod

NORWAY

SWEDEN

FINNISH BIGHT

Bergen

Uppsala

SVEALAND

ESTONIA

Oslo

Birka

GULF OF RIGA

anger

Gothenburg

GOTLAND

LATVIA

GÖTALAND

ÖLAND

LITHUANIA

Viborg

DENMARK

Lund

Arkona
RÜGEN

POLAND

Hedeby

Hamburg

Bremen

GERMANY

we must also speak of religion, family feeling, social organization, justice, decorative art, expressions of communal existence in literature, games and pastimes, and the chief moments of in- dividual existence recognized by society at large – birth, coming of age, marriage, death. In these fields we may find the things that have unique value in early Scandinavian civilization, and here we may also discover the roots of the tolerance, mutual re- spect and pragmatic will to co-operate which distinguish the Scandinavian nations of today.

To do all these subjects justice would need however a library, not a book. Our account is avowedly descriptive and inevitably selective. We willingly neglect many controversial subjects but much regret that many fascinating topics, from shieling-farming to runic writing, get no more than a mention, and sometimes not that. The following description of sources – in themselves in- evitably miscellaneous – and the general bibliography, pp. 435– 448 are also necessarily concise, but we hope that in most subjects they will take the student and enthusiast straight to works where detailed and up-to-date information may be found.

Sources of information about early Scandinavia

Danish and Icelandic historians about 1200 were already in- terested in the physical remains of their ancestors' activities, and modern archaeology – in which Scandinavian scholars have been among the most eminent in the world – has produced much information about Norse life through the study of habita- tion sites, graves, fortifications, ships, weapons, tools, pottery, textiles, ornaments, cultivation-patterns, coins – and so on. Archaeology is still producing information about the Viking Age, and year by year skilled excavations reveal more of the history of this period, not infrequently with results that entail a radical re-thinking of accepted ideas about the early history of a region or group. The potential of this branch of the historical discipline is enormous.

Scholars have also been long aware of the importance of linguistic evidence in the consideration of such things as settle- ment, foreign influences, religion, social rank, trade. Place-names, for example, can tell us of the extent of Scandinavian settlement abroad and of new clearings in the forests at home, and often help us to a broad chronology of such developments. Other place-names give information about pagan cults and the gods who were honoured. Loan-words from and into the Scandinavian languages often allow conclusions of cultural significance to be drawn. Words to do with trade were taken early from Frisian, Christian terminology from English and German; a light axe was described by a Slavonic name; for a shieling in the Faroes an Irish word was used; a Norse word for 'conscience' was made by literally translating the elements of the Latin compound – these examples may suggest ways in which linguistic information can be revealing.

Direct description of behaviour and first-hand information about local and national administration in peace and war, about business and all kinds of social activity, are found in the old laws of the Scandinavian countries. Iceland had a national law, now known by the name *Grágás*, Grey Goose, extant in manuscript fragments of the twelfth century and later codices. In Norway there were provincial codes (cf. pp. 46–7) for Trøndelag, the west-coast Gulathing, and the southeast regions; these again survive in twelfth-century fragments and later lawbooks, but our know-ledge of the southeastern laws is very incomplete. There are numerous provincial law texts from medieval mainland Sweden, representing the three main regions, Götaland, Svealand and Småland (of this last we know very little). The oldest Swedish text – *Västgötalag*, the law of the Västgötar, from soon after 1200 – is also known in a revision from about a century later. All the other texts, for the Östgötar and the people of Uppland and provinces associated with Uppland, are from about 1300 or later. The *Gutalag*, the law of the people of Gotland, is largely inde-pendent of the mainland Swedish laws; it must have originated in written form very soon after 1200, although we have no manu-scripts older than about 1350. The three codes for the Danes – the Jutland, Sjælland and Skåne laws – are also known to us in thirteenth-century versions. The majority of the laws which sur-vive today were thus codified after the end of the period we are describing. There is however no doubt but that they embody many customs and regulations that are much older than the thirteenth century, and it is often possible to distinguish the relatively old and the relatively new without great difficulty. The information we have taken from the laws can be counted reliable evidence for much of the eleventh and twelfth centuries, and often it may well reflect pre-Christian realities.

There is a very large and mixed group of written sources that have to be taken into account in attempting a description of early Scandinavia. Of prime importance – but unfortunately the most meagre in extent – are original inscriptions and documents. The former are chiefly written in runes (the characters of a rectilinear alphabet, developed among Germanic peoples, particularly adapted for carving on wood or stone), and we have some hundreds of them from Denmark and Norway and some thousands from Sweden, the bulk of them from the eleventh century. They are mostly on stone monuments and formal in expression, but recent large finds of sticks with runic writing on them in twelfth- and thirteenth-century levels in excavations at Bergen show to what everyday purposes runes were put in this later period. The inscriptions include private messages, trade tallies, love poems, and letters, one of them from no less a person than Sigurd, eldest son of King Sverri. Documentary sources begin towards the end of the eleventh century, but do not become plentiful until the thirteenth. They include papal letters, charters, land-registers of monasteries and cathedrals, memorial books of religious houses, church inventories and commercial agreements.

A good deal of information about Scandinavia is found in foreign writings, Greek, Arabic, Slav, Latin, Old English and Irish. Most of these concern the Norsemen abroad, but some preserve valuable accounts of Scandinavian conditions, the best of them based on native source-men. An author's intention, political or aesthetic, his circumstances and those of the people he learnt from, his ability and idiosyncrasies, the dictates of the *genre* in which he wrote, may all require consideration before his unconfirmed testimony is acceptable. National prejudices, hagiographic commonplaces, the language barrier between Arab and Norseman, are the kind of factors that have to be taken into account. A very valuable source, for example, is the work of Master Adam of Bremen, *Gesta Hammaburgensis ecclesiae pontificum*, written about 1070, but while reading it one has to bear in mind such things as his zeal for the cause of his archbishop's primacy in the northern countries and the specifically Danish nature of much of his information.

Native Scandinavian writings must of course be approached with the same caution. They are of many different kinds and many different ages. Each kind, almost each work, poses special problems to do with period and place of origin, interpretation and significance.

We have much poetry from the ninth to the twelfth century, almost all of which was transmitted orally before it was recorded, by far the greater part of it in Iceland. We learn much about mythology from it and about men's social, ethical and religious attitudes. Much scaldic verse (p. 319) can be classed with documents and artefacts as first-hand contemporary sources of information, because it was composed on a particular, given occasion. The technique and artistry of this poetry is discussed in Chapter 10. Besides the poetry, we have an important mythological source in parts of Snorri Sturluson's *Edda*, written in Iceland about 1220.

Sermons and works of edification, though largely based on foreign sources, may contain information about the northern peoples, and they are of course first-hand witnesses of the Norse assimilation of Christianity and foreign learning. This is attested too by twelfth-century Icelandic treatises on such subjects as grammar and calendar computation, some of which display notable originality of observation. The outstanding didactic work of medieval Scandinavia is the thirteenth-century Norwegian *Konungs skuggsjá*, King's Mirror, but for the most part this is so evidently an account of the author's contemporary scene that we have not thought it proper to use it with reference to the earlier period with which we are concerned. The same is true of *Hirðskrá*, the Norwegian court regulations of the 1270s, whose provisions we have only quoted when they can be plausibly counted of twelfth-century origin.

All the Scandinavian nations have preserved medieval works by authors who describe times past or their contemporary world. They range from annals (late sources for each country) to rhymed chronicles, from Latin compendia to massive vernacular agglomerations in which a host of earlier writings may be fused into a more or less – usually less – coherent whole. Only the most important of these works will be mentioned here.

Sweden is least well served with literary sources of these kinds.

A brief *Guta saga,* Saga of the people of Gotland, is preserved with manuscripts of the Gotland Law; and lists of lawmen, bishops and kings, some with brief commentary, are appended to a version of *Västgötalag.* There are saints' lives connected with the cults of missionary martyrs and of St Erik, Sweden's royal patron. *Erikskrönikan,* a fourteenth-century chronicle in pleasing verse, unfortunately deals with too late a period to be useful for our purpose.

We have a number of twelfth-century texts written in Denmark: some brief but important chronicles, works on monastic foundations, and saints' lives. Of outstanding significance are Sven Aggeson's *Brevis historia regum Daciae,* written in the late twelfth century, and the *Gesta Danorum* in sixteen books by Saxo, called Grammaticus, finished about 1200. An Icelandic work of some independent value on the Danish kings is the thirteenth-century *Knýtlinga saga.*

Norse settlements in the British Isles are treated in the *Chronica regum Manniae et Insularum* (from 1066 on) and in an Icelandic history of the earls of Orkney, now known as *Orkneyinga saga.* This incorporates material from a life of Orkney's St Magnus, which is also known in separate forms. There are also early Icelandic writings on the people of the Faroes (*Færeyinga saga*) and of Greenland (*Grænlendinga saga*), both composed about 1200.

There are three short Norwegian histories from the late twelfth century, two in Latin, the anonymous *Historia Norvegiae,* and the *Historia de antiquitate regum norvagiensium* by a monk who calls himself Theodricus, and one in the vernacular, *Ágrip af Nóregs konunga sǫgum* (Compendium of the histories of the kings of Norway). Latin composition on St Ólaf Haraldsson (pp. 44–5) naturally began early. Writing on Ólaf Tryggvason began before 1200 with Latin works by Icelandic authors, now known only in vernacular versions. Icelandic writers were thereafter chiefly responsible for accounts of Norwegian history. The earliest collections of kings' sagas, based to some extent on older writings, came into existence in the period 1200 - 35 – these are the anonymous *Morkinskinna* and *Fagrskinna* and Snorri Sturluson's *Heimskringla,* the most extensive of them, which begins with the Ynglings in Uppsala, the progenitors of the Vestfold kings and Harald Finehair (p. 41), and ends in 1177. For the period 1177 -

1202 *Sverris saga,* Saga of Sverri, is our chief source for Norwegian affairs. It was written, largely or wholly, by the Icelandic Benedictine, Abbot Karl Jónsson, and King Sverri himself supervised the composition of the earlier chapters. The acquaintance we thereby gain with the king's personality amply compensates for any biased reporting of events.

It is evident from this brief survey that the Icelanders were intensely interested in the past of their Scandinavian kinsfolk, and Saxo in Denmark and Theodricus in Norway refer to them as authorities, especially because of their knowledge of ancient poetry. But the Icelanders were no less interested in themselves, and we have a vast amount of Icelandic historical or semi-historical literature from the early period. Ari Thorgilsson was the first historian to write in the vernacular, composing his brief *Íslendingabók,* Book of the Icelanders, about 1125 – a short and sober account of the country's history with careful citation of sources. In his time began the collection of information that was recorded in *Landnámabók,* Book of Settlements, a unique work on the colonizers of Iceland, their lands and families, known to us now in thirteenth-century and later redactions. More or less contemporary accounts of twelfth- and thirteenth-century careers and events are set down in the great compilation called *Sturlunga saga,* the Saga of the Sturlungs. There is a valuable account of the first bishops of Skálholt in *Hungrvaka,* Hunger-wakener, which serves as an introduction to the lives of St Thorlák (bishop of Skálholt 1178 - 93) and his successor Bishop Páll Jónsson (1195 - 1211). Latin and Icelandic versions of a life of Bishop Jón of Hólar (1106 - 21) came into being soon after his cult was established in 1200. Of particular interest are the accounts of miracles attributed to the merits of these native saints in the period around 1200. They give glimpses of humble life, family affection and compassion for poor and sick which seldom find a place in the histories of kings or in the tales of heroes, however realistic. Such heroic tales form the last great category of Icelandic prose composition that needs to be mentioned here, the *Íslendinga sǫgur,* Sagas of Icelanders, sometimes less appropriately called Family Sagas. These were written in the period from about 1190 to 1320, and tell exciting stories about people who lived in the period from about 850 to 1050. There are some thirty of them all told, of which probably the best known are *Egils saga Skalla-Grímssonar* (written *c.* 1215), *Laxdæla saga* (*c.* 1250), and *Njáls saga* (*c.* 1280).

As was said earlier, it is necessary to approach all these sources, Latin and vernacular, in a critical way, and some historians dismiss the Sagas of Icelanders as totally unreliable or at least as works in which fact and fancy cannot possibly be unravelled. But even the description of an event which never happened involving actors who never existed can still reveal something of a way of life and an outlook on life which may be valuable for a descriptive account of the kind we are attempting. We may be confident for instance that much that is in the sagas is relevant to the twelfth century; and sometimes we discover such basic similarity between the attitude of a tenth-century poet and that of a thirteenth-century author that underlying continuity may be reasonably assumed. It is indeed in the sphere of human conduct and its appraisal that the sagas offer us their most convincing evidence of the enduring vitality of ancient modes of thought and feeling. Sometimes, too, there is good comparative evidence – especially in long-lived customs in Scandinavia, or related practices among other peoples, brought to light by the folklorist and ethnologist – to show that factual information in a saga must in substance be ancient and authentic. The type of magic known as *seiðr*, for example, referred to by saga-writers but not practised in their time, is illuminated by knowledge of shamanistic ritual and behaviour among present-day sub-arctic tribes; descriptions of a blood-brotherhood ceremony and of precautions taken in connection with corpses and burial seem well authenticated by similar comparative study, although in a case like this last we must certainly not ignore the thick undergrowth of Christian superstition which flourished in Scandinavia and Iceland as elsewhere in medieval Europe. One must obviously use common sense in generalizing on the basis of information in sagas. It would not be unreasonable to think, for example, that a thirteenth-century description of warming milk in a vessel (which would not itself stand fire) by putting heated stones into it could just as well be true of the tenth or eleventh century – even if we had no archaeological evidence to vouch for it; or that throughout our period men hung their weapons on nails in the walls (which might otherwise be used to support wall-hangings), as we are told they did in a thirteenth-century source – even if we had no early poetry describing much the same thing. What is not permissible is to write a broad social or ethical history of the pre-Christian Icelanders – much less of the North Germanic peoples as a whole – simply by lifting chunks out of the sagas or by using them as if they contained some total picture of an old real world. As a single warning example it may be mentioned that it was once concluded that the custom of exposing new-born infants, leaving them to die in the open air, must have hit the female population particularly hard in tenth-century Iceland – because there are no old maids in the Icelandic sagas !

Societies and States

We are bound to speak of the nations and states of ancient Scandinavia as if they were entities of the kind they are today. We must, however, constantly bear in mind that, although the total geographical span of Scandinavia in Europe has not changed much, both external and internal boundaries were then irregular and in some cases very different from now. Two meeting-points are especially noteworthy: the territory at the base of the Jutland peninsula, where Danes, Frisians, Saxons and Wends mingled; and at the mouth of Götaälv, the region round modern Gothenburg on which the borders of Norway, Sweden, Götaland and Denmark all converged. We should remember too that English counties, Irish towns and Scottish islands might all be predominantly Norse, while the Isle of Man, Orkney, Shetland and Greenland are to be counted with the Faroes and Iceland as the homes of Scandinavian communities.

The period about A.D. 800, which we take as our starting-point, saw the first recorded attacks by Scandinavians on the British Isles, and the completion of the Frankish conquest and conversion of the Saxons, which first brought the Carolingian Empire face to face with a Scandinavian power. In the Viking Age that followed the Scandinavians became important in European history, notoriously as raiders, invaders and colonists, less clamorously but perhaps as influentially as merchants and middlemen. Their close contacts with other peoples had in time significant effects on internal developments in their native countries. But although their impact on the outside world in the early ninth century seems sudden, we have no evidence of any great revolutionary movement, social or economic, that had recently occurred among the Nordic peoples. The evidence is rather of a long period of steady progress. The basic settlement and utilization of the land in the different countries had gone quietly on to provide a livelhood for an ever-increasing population, although in some places the population pressure was such that only emigration would relieve it. The quantity and quality of iron-production and iron-working showed steady advance in the two centuries before the Viking Age began, and we have some inkling of the evolution in this same period of the Norsemen's ships on which their warfare and commerce were to depend. Scandinavian successes abroad in the Viking Age suggest that some kind of effective social organization existed at home, and in fact there had long since taken place a gradual extension and amalgamation of local groups under men or families whose religious and military leadership was generally recognized. These were all processes that continued through the Viking Age, a time of technical improvement and gradual social change, when the general wealth and resources of the Scandinavian countries showed enormous increase. Food production in areas where expansion was physically possible seems to have more than kept pace with the rising numbers of inhabitants, not because of new methods of farming and fishing but because of internal colonization and cheap labour in the form of slaves.

The beginning of the Viking Age coincides with the end of a period of rapid linguistic change among the northern peoples. Between about A.D. 600 and 800 the language common to the Scandinavians underwent many phonological changes, so that it became less and less like the languages of their Germanic neighbours to the south and west. These changes were on the whole effective throughout the North and then for the next three or four hundred years the rate of linguistic change was comparatively slow. Throughout our period language put no effective barrier between Greenlander and Dane, or between a man from north Norway and a man from Bornholm in the Baltic, and this community of speech was recognized in the name *dǫnsk tunga*, *vox danica*, 'Danish tongue', that was used of the language over the whole Nordic area. This emphasised a Scandinavian identity and made joint Scandinavian enterprises easy. It also decisively deepens our concept of a Scandinavian culture in the early middle ages. It must, however, be stressed that linguistic changes were only slowed down, not halted, in this period, and speech differences must gradually have con-

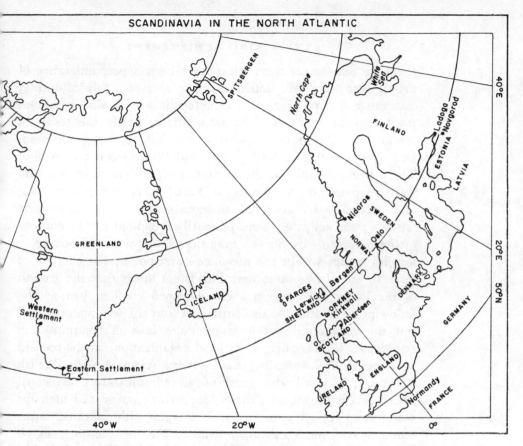

tributed more and more to the means whereby one Scandinavian distinguished himself and his nation from the others.

At the outset of the Viking Age the most effective larger unit in society was the province, *land* (D. *landskab,* Sw. *landskap*), sometimes under independent leaders, kings or earls, sometimes in a federation under the domination of a single dynasty. It is noteworthy that when some of the first Norsemen abroad announced their identity they said that they were men of Hordaland and men of Vestfold, not that they were Norwegians. Some of the Nordic provinces had sent out tribes in the Migration Age to join the more southerly Germanic peoples as they cut their way through the old domains of the Roman Empire, but for the most part they were regions that represented amalgamations of older tribal areas and groups. Regional differences remained throughout the middle ages, as they still do today, but they were never strong enough to overcome the very close similarities of language, material culture and ethnic composi-

3

tion. (In some areas there must have been a preponderance of people who were tall, dolichocephalic and of a fair colouring, but other anthropological characteristics were also common, partly genetic relics of older populations, partly the result of mixture, all the more frequent as the Viking Age progressed, with Lappish, Baltic, Slav, Celtic and West Germanic people.) The provinces existed as the territorial expressions of groups who were prepared to co-operate to ensure their self-preservation and prosperity by accepted religious and military means. As far as we can tell, they were primarily cemented by the consent of the free men – by far the majority of whom would belong to kinship groups within the province – and not by the exercise of force by one class on another. This is not to say that the growth of the larger units did not entail armed conflict, just as the following unification of the provinces into single kingdoms did, but the system did not operate under laws of conquest and oppression. Military origins of local organization can be seen in a name such as Swedish *hund, hundare* (cognate with English 'hundred', a word also used of an administrative division), which originally meant districts supplying 100 or 120 men for war service (p. 281), or in the Norwegian title of rank, *hersir,* whose first element means 'war-host'. The pantheistic religion served a public function and required public subscription, but it was not systematically organized like a church and there was no distinct class of priests. Freedom from attack, victory in war, abundant food were expected of the divine powers in return for judicious sacrifices.

The standard unit of society, whatever its larger organization, was the family. Originally this group was probably only counted through male lines, but it must early have become common to count marriage connections as part of the family as well. By the time we have detailed knowledge of Scandinavian society, in the laws from the end of our period, both sides had more or less equal standing, with only occasional preference given to the agnatic relationship. Life was focused on the family group, so much so that 'family society' is often used as a general term to describe early Norse conditions. It is however important not to be misled by the word 'family'. To most of us this means a two- or at most three-generation establishment, which younger mem-

4

bers regularly leave for careers or marriage; contacts tend to be maintained between brothers and sisters of both generations but we seldom go beyond cousins – that is, people sharing a common grandfather – in matters of 'family' concern. In early Scandinavia the nucleus tended to be larger, in as much as young men on marriage often continued to live and work on the patrimonial estate, and the whole family group tended to be much larger than today. The scope of the family can be clearly seen from a glance at the laws concerning atonement for the death of a man. Payment and receipt of this were divided among the families of the slayer and slain, the amount diminishing as the degree of kinship grew remoter. In Jutland, for example, this extended to third cousins, in Iceland to fourth cousins, that is to people who shared a great-great-grandfather and a great-great-great-grandfather respectively with the killer or his victim.

There is no doubt that an individual was less a separate being and more a limb of a larger organism, the whole family, than he is today. His responses would automatically tend to put the well-being of the family first. That demanded the maintenance of the integrity of family property and of the corporate standing of the family in the community. Profit and loss, honour and shame were all shared, and common efforts were required to achieve the good and blot out the bad. As well as sharing in communal religious observances, the family nucleus usually also took private steps to ensure divine favour. There were many divinities and there was ritual to observe at both public and domestic festivals, but there was no compulsion for an individual to establish personal relations with the gods.

Although Scandinavian societies between about 800 and 1200 were relatively stable, they were far from static. The process of amalgamation of groups into regions continued throughout the period and was completed by their coalescence into single states, united under single dynasties and fostering a more exclusive sense of nationality than had previously existed. When laws were codified at the end of our period, they still appeared as provincial laws, but those provinces were few and represented large amalgamations; and in Norway and Sweden they were soon to be replaced by national codes. As centralized monarchies were established, there were changes in military and administrative organization, and these in turn had an effect on the obligations of the different social classes and on their differentiation. Regions like Jämtland and Gotland had once existed as some kind of oligarchic republics, but the move towards centralized authority and the sole rule of kings meant that they were swallowed up early in the Viking Age. The same tendencies finally brought about the submission of the Greenlandic and Icelandic commonwealths to the Norwegian Crown in the thirteenth century.

At the centre of our period lies the conversion of the Scandinavians to Christianity. The Church came with authority, organization, single-minded servants, and a novel identification of religious and ethical imperatives. Its impact was great and affected both the concept of the state and the concept of the individual.

Family bonds were tight knit. Yet in Germanic society as a whole there had always been some loyalties which depended on the individual as an individual, not necessarily as a member of a family group. There was the loyalty of the freed man to his patron, for example, and of more especial note, there was the loyalty of the warrior to his chief, the member of a *comitatus* to his lord. The same loyalty was also fostered among the crews of Viking ships and the followers of the kings who fought to impose their rule over ever wider areas in Scandinavia and the foreign parts dominated by Norsemen. These personal ties between leader and follower played an essential part in creating the national monarchies and the aristocracies that finally came into existence with them, and they contributed to the process by which individuals were gradually released from the mesh of the old family society. This process was generally quickened by the experiences of the Viking Age, when many members of families cut themselves off as pirates, mercenary soldiers and emigrants. It was quickened still more by Christianity with its supreme concern for salvation above every earthly consideration, its demand for individual loyalty to Christ, and its negation of the natural family in priestly celibacy and monastic communities. By the end of our period in the thirteenth century the growth of towns and the existence of industry also meant that an ever larger number of people were removed from family solidarity of the old kind, which depended so strongly on continuity in the ownership and use of land.

In the period we are considering we thus have, at one end of the scale, the emergence in greater numbers than ever before of men who found themselves in the comparatively independent and isolated situation of modern individuals. At the other end of the scale, we see the development of far more remote and powerful authorities than had hitherto existed, and by means of a national administrative apparatus they combined to create, Church and State now interfere in realms of activity previously under family or local control. Self-interest and self-help had been the general rule for members of the family society in a tight circle of kinsmen and comrades, but now abstract ideals and international organizations could command men's labour and devotion. Nevertheless, the family remained a prime force in the social order, as will become clear in some of the description to follow.

Foreign contacts and influences varied from time to time and place to place in this early period. They are difficult to trace in detail, but in general they must have done much to promote and accelerate the social, political and religious changes that took place in the Scandinavian countries. It can hardly be accidental that the northern country which had least commerce with the western world in the Viking Age, Sweden, was slowest to become a Christian nation-state of the kind accepted as civilized in medieval times.

In the remainder of this chapter a sketch is given of the social and political state of the different Scandinavian countries in the Viking Age and early medieval period. The reader is warned that he will here meet more drastic generalizations than anywhere else in the book, but it is hoped that this survey will provide a framework on which the other chapters, syntheses as they necessarily are, may be disposed.

Denmark

Danish territory in the early medieval period was more extensive than it is now (fig. 3). We think only of Jutland and the islands, especially Fyn, Sjælland and remoter Bornholm, but then the Øresund was no barrier and Skåne, Halland and for long periods Blekinge also belonged to the Danish realm and, indeed, did not become the Swedish provinces they now are

DENMARK

until the seventeenth century. The Oslofjord region of Norway was also closely linked with Denmark, coastwise with Halland and across the water with Jutland; the links lay in material culture, in some linguistic features, and sometimes in political union. At the base of the Jutland peninsula the Danish boundary was gradually recognized as the Eider, but Danish influence was often paramount in Holstein, and a broad belt existed here where Danes, Frisians, Saxons and Wends merged.

The Danish territory as a whole is low-lying land. Jutland especially has many stretches of bogland and heathland, with immense sand-dune coasts; sand-drift is a constant menace. Elsewhere in Jutland and the islands there is a landscape of modest dimensions and gentle curves, now intensively cultivated but earlier with much waste and woodland, valuable forests of oak and beech. Skåne has a coastline of low cliffs and long sand beaches and spits; it is fertile country divided by long granite ridges running northwest-southeast. Eastward it merges into

8

the narrow coastal strip of Blekinge, oak-forested and rocky. Northward the long smooth coasts continue through Halland to become a stony, heathery, treeless 'skerry-fence' landscape, indistinguishable from the Swedish province of Bohuslän (once Norwegian) that lies beyond.

No one in the Danish lands lived more than thirty-five miles from the sea, most people much closer. Jutland is narrow, almost surrounded and often penetrated, in the north even severed, by the sea; the islands are small; the provinces across the Øresund are backed by forest and highland so that people look seaward with pleasure. The Danes 'live in the sea' said Ermoldus Nigellus early in the ninth century, and to thrive they had to. There were tracks in the countryside, and an ancient and imposing route, the so-called Hærvej, ran south for some 160 miles from Viborg in North Jutland, passing not far from Hedeby and giving access to the land-routes of the north European plain. But the sea and the rivers must always have been busier, and very few of the early townships owed their existence to a nodal situation for land-routes.

Fishing was important and became a great seasonal industry in the course of the early middle ages, but the essential way of life was agricultural. People grew grain and reared livestock in accordance with techniques that had largely been fully evolved by the time the Viking Age began. Settlement patterns varied from region to region, but in the many large fertile areas villages had become common by the twelfth century and must have existed in some places much earlier. Place-name study has shown that many of the more important habitations are older in origin than the Viking Age (e.g. places with names originally ending in -ing, -heimr, -leif, -staðir), but the Viking Age and early Christian period were also times of busy internal colonization as well as of emigration and settlement abroad. In this period people went on establishing homes in the countryside, with farm-names often ending in -by (Dalby, Karlby – a type of name also very common in Danish settlements in England). Many other names, like those ending in -thorp (-rup, -trup; Kragerup, Glostrup) and -rød (OD ruð; Hillerød), for example, reflect new 'breakaway' settlements and the clearing of forest land for cultivation. Agricultural methods may not have undergone fundamental changes in our

9

period, but changes certainly took place in the distribution of land ownership. Much land was in common use and this required an advanced degree of organization and co-operation, such as we observe in the elaborate rules of the law codes for sharing land, usually on a rotation system, and for its inheritance. But this organization, although it became more or less standardized through any given province, does not appear to have been imposed. It was organic and by consent, worked out between generations of heads of households.

Striking evidence of unification of interest at a national level is the organization of the country into the administrative districts called in Danish *herred* (OD *hæræth*). By an early stage in the Viking period, and perhaps earlier still, the Danish provinces were divided into such districts, each with its assembly (*thing*) and probably its cult-place. When the division was made, some sort of parity existed between the different *herreds*, and it is thought that this most probably lay in the provision of men under arms – complicated calculations have produced an estimate of about forty fighting men from each. These artificial units must be the result of a central administrative activity, although it probably represents a tidying-up of pre-existing groups – family, local and tribal – rather than a radical revision, autocratically imposed. The Danes seem to have been good at living together.

Still larger units were the *lands*, 'provinces, regions', which generally had tribal origins. Each of these had a central assembly place and some of them, perhaps all, had cult centres. The provincial laws that we have in thirteenth-century codifications are for amalgamations of these older *lands*: the Jutish Law for North and South Jutland, Fyn and related islands, the Sjælland Law for Sjælland (and for Lolland, Falster, Møen, but only from 1284 – previously these had apparently been independent in their laws), and the Skåne Law for Skåne, Halland, Blekinge, and for Bornholm after it became part of Denmark in the course of the Viking Age.

The most important class of people in Denmark in the period (as in Scandinavia as a whole, the people this book is chiefly about) were the free farmers and their sons. These recognized each other's rights of free speech on communal matters, the rights of each other's dependents, and they regulated affairs between themselves by law. As was natural, however, there were always some men, or one man, in a district who had more influence than others, whatever the cause of their prestige. In the early Christian period we see clearly the functions of local magnates and officers, allied with or part of the administrative order which ultimately depended on recognition of royal authority (pp. 123 – 7).

By the beginning of the Viking Age a single dynasty appears to have established itself among the Danes. Its leading members were called kings and they were accorded certain rights by the whole population and expected to perform certain functions. As elsewhere in Scandinavia, kingship combined hereditary and elective aspects. The candidate for the throne should be of royal blood, but he must be accepted as king by the free men at their assemblies. If he lost their favour, they could put him down, or try to. But kings in Denmark were well placed to maintain and increase their authority. They had ample means to maintain a retinue of warriors who could make their authority effective. Royal estates existed throughout the Danish lands and needed managers – they had doubtless come into being in the usual just and unjust ways, inheritance, marriage, chicanery, exaction and aggression. With ships and fighters at their disposal they could benefit directly from forays and trade abroad, and from piracy too if they were careful. Probably of especial importance was the development of trading centres, markets which with the growth in numbers of specialist workers ultimately turned into long-lasting townships (pp. 203 – 17). The king and his agents, with armed forces at their disposal, imposed tolls, sold licences, received presents, and might well be in business on their own account. They were also well aware of the general benefits that came from control of peaceful trade. At the very outset of the Viking Age, in 808, the Franks threatened Denmark's southern border and the transit trade of south Jutland. The powerful King Godfred replied with various measures, and one of his actions was to destroy a township called Reric (thought to be on the coast near Wismar) in east Holstein, a region occupied by Wends allied to Charlemagne. He brought the merchants from there, however, to settle in Hedeby (see

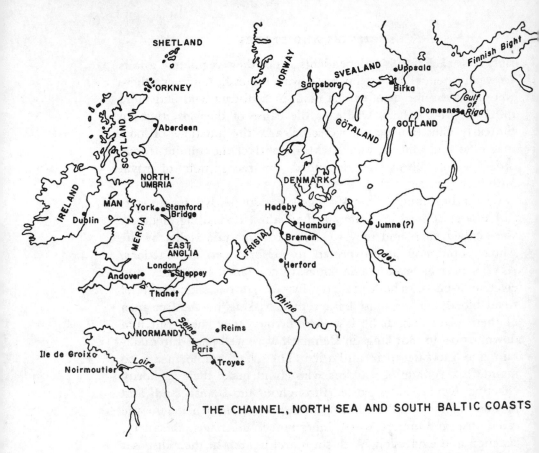

THE CHANNEL, NORTH SEA AND SOUTH BALTIC COASTS

pp. 210–3), thus apparently putting down a rival and increasing
Danish commercial potential in one go. This association between
trading centres and royal power will be observed in the other
Scandinavian countries too.

King Godfred's moves against the Frisian coasts and Frankish
settlements, and the devastation of Hamburg in 845 by ships
sent by King Horic, were acts of war, designed to fend off the
southerners and to enrich Danish commerce. It is doubtful, on
the other hand, whether the inhabitants who suffered slaughter
and slavery found them any different from Viking raids that had
no deep political purpose, and often we cannot tell either whether
an attack was a state undertaking or a private enterprise, or both.
Some campaigns against the northern dominions of the Franks
were certainly under the direction of the monarchy, but in
general we know too little about internal affairs in ninth-century
Denmark to see what connections existed between royal policy

and the massive attacks and settlements in England and France proper.

The Channel and Biscay coasts of France became familiar to many Danes in this early period. Raids were frequent and grew into great campaigns by way of the rivers, particularly the Seine, penetrating far inland, even to Troyes and Reims. Paris was a favourite target and suffered several attacks, including a prolonged siege in 885 – 6. But while the Danes proved brilliant campaigners, they failed to master some big strongholds and suffered defeats in pitched battles. They made a lot of money from booty and bribes but did not succeed in gaining territory or political control until the grant of Normandy to them in 911.

The attacks on England started in 789, but two generations pass before 'the heathen', as the English often called them, came to stay. They wintered in Thanet in 850 and in Sheppey in 855, and the aim now was conquest, not merely booty. The Danes had quick eyes for military advantage; they had speed by ship and by horse, and they sometimes disregarded oaths and truces without scruple. King Alfred and his commanders prevented complete subjugation of the country but virtually all the northern and eastern parts came under Scandinavian control. 'And in this year [876] Halfdan shared out the lands of Northumbria, and they were engaged in ploughing and in making a living for themselves.' 'And then in autumn [877] the host departed into Mercia, and some of it they shared out.' 'And in this year [879] the host went . . . into East Anglia, and occupied that land, and shared it out.' For years these men must have lived as half-farmers, half-soldiers, and those who had no permanency in land, made fighting their trade. 'Then the following summer [896] . . . the host dispersed, some to East Anglia, some to Northumbria, and those without stock got themselves ships, and sailed south oversea to the Seine.'

These widespread and lasting settlements in England were politically independent, but the colonists must have maintained contacts across the North Sea. We may assume that conquest was for the Danes the most attractive way of making a living, but not that it was the only way. Land was available in Denmark for the man who would undertake the hard work of clearing it and breaking it in – and many did this. But seventy-two hours away to the west there was excitement, as well as land ready for the plough and cheap labour, and the possibility of glittering prizes in treasure and ransom-money. Success bred expectation of success, a 'boom' mentality was fostered, and Scandinavian self-confidence in seafaring and soldiering took a long time to ebb.

The geographical position of the Danish lands demanded vigilance in every direction. In this early period the Danes took the initiative to the west, in England, and to the north, in Norway, but in the south they were under pressure. The great town of Hedeby was a rich prize, and we find that in the early part of the tenth century members of a Swedish house were in control of it, along with some part of South Jutland. Their dominion seems to have been brought to an end by Henry I of Germany who in 934 defeated the Swedish king Gnupa, took tribute from him and had him baptized. It is likely that the Danish king Gorm then completed the overthrow of the Swedish dynasty, and it may be that in his time and later the Danes, at least in Jutland, recognized Saxon suzerainty.

Saxon political influence went hand in hand with Saxon efforts to convert the Danes to Christianity. The archbishopric of Hamburg-Bremen was founded in the ninth century and at first led a precarious existence as a result of Danish attacks and prelatical rivalry. It was intended as a missionary outpost with prime responsibility for bringing the heathen Norsemen to the true faith. Various missions in the ninth century, of which the most famous was led by St Ansgar (p. 31), prepared the way for the official conversion of the Danish people about the middle of the tenth century. The source of Christian authority among them was naturally the archbishop of Hamburg-Bremen, but the Danes also had close church connections with England, and the quick conversion of the Danes settled among the Anglo-Saxons was doubtless another important factor in the early conversion of the Danes at home. We also find that rulers in early Scandinavia often preferred England to Germany as a source of priests and church practices because of the absence of political ties and of the authoritarian voice of the metropolitan of Hamburg-Bremen.

'King Harald ordered these monuments to be made in memory of his father Gorm and of his mother Thyri: that Harald who won the whole of Denmark for himself and Norway and made the Danes Christian.' This famous runic stone at Jelling (pl. 21a) was carved about 980 and we have great difficulty in understanding its proud simple statements. It must imply, however, that in his later years Harald Blue-tooth thought he had no rivals within the country and stood independent of German power to the south. The reign of his successors bears out the truth of this. For the best part of half a century the Danes were so rich and mighty that their kings could turn almost all their attention to England. At home and to the east and south they must have felt secure enough. The Danes seem to have had good relations with the Wends along the south Baltic shores throughout this time. Harald's wife was a Wendish princess, and when at the end of his life he was forced into exile by revolution, he took refuge in the famous Slav town of Jumne. The revolution that drove him out may have been led by his son, Sven Forkbeard. Sven at any rate succeeded him c. 986, and he seems to have been a military leader of genius. The wealth in men and material that the Danes could command is amply revealed by the magnificent barrack-camps at Trelleborg, Fyrkat and elsewhere (pp. 267–72). With the aid of mercenary fleets and soldiers from the other northern countries, now operating on their own account, now in combination with the 'official' forces of the Danes, large-scale attacks were made on England and France, and 'the great host', as the English writers called them, moved back and forth across the Channel and north Channel approaches. The ability to combine and concentrate large forces and maintain supplies and communications is most impressive. The leaders fought for fame and maybe sometimes for vengeance, to gain the wealth and position of the English lords for themselves; their followers doubtless had similar mixed motives, but do not seem to have been looking for somewhere to settle down and live as their ninth-century compatriots had done. They wanted glory and cash, but like as not they took the latter home with them to ensure their share of the former. 'Ulv took in England three gelds. That was the first which Tosti paid. Then Thorkel paid. Then Knut paid.' This is the epitaph of one Swedish yeoman of Uppland; it would doubtless serve for scores of other veterans throughout the North.

Sven Forkbeard died in 1014, in the midst of a great campaign in England. His men made his young son, Knut, their king, and they continued the war. For a few months Edmund Ironside and Knut were both kings in England, but on Edmund's death Knut was recognized by all. From 1018 he was king of Denmark as well. For the last years of his reign he was lord of Norway too, after Norwegian noblemen, with his support, first exiled and then, in 1030, killed King Ólaf Haraldsson.

In Knut's time the Danes must have thought well of themselves and lived prosperous lives. Knut came nearer than anybody to establishing a real North Sea empire, yet accident and the hazards of heredity brought it about that after his death in 1035 the whole structure collapsed almost at once. A mere four years later the Danes in Denmark found themselves with little choice but to accept the warlike young king of Norway, Magnús, son of Ólaf Haraldsson, as their king as well. The Norwegians must have enjoyed that. His early death in 1046 altered the situation, and Norwegian claims to the Danish throne were never again effective.

There followed a long period of rule, thirty years, under Sven Ulfsson, usually called Estrid's son, after his mother, who was Knut's sister. In Sven's time Danish attention was chiefly engaged to the south and east and from now on it is relations with Germans and Wends which dominate the external history of the Danes and to some extent dictate internal developments as well.

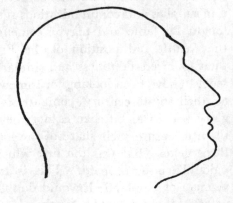

Fig. 5. Profile of Sven Estridsson, based on measurements of his skull. After Fr. C. C. Hansen.

Sven Estridsson (fig. 5) ruled from 1047 to 1074. We learn something of him and his country in the accounts of Master Adam, a German cleric of Bremen who had had long conversations with the king. He praises Sven for his capacious memory and intelligence, and he seems frank in his appraisal of the king's character. Adam's work, completed not long after the king's death, contains some passages that give unique insight into eleventh-century Danish conditions and must be quoted at length.

Jutland he describes in harsh terms: the land there is barren and except for places near rivers almost everywhere appears a desert: 'a salt land' and 'a howling wilderness'. 'And whilst the whole land of Germany is frightful with thick forests, Jutland is still more frightful, where the land is shunned on account of the poverty of its produce and the sea on account of the infestation of pirates. Cultivation is found hardly anywhere, hardly any place exists suitable for human habitation, but wherever there are arms of the sea, there the country has very large settlements.'

Of the sea between Fyn, Jutland and Sjælland he says that it is by nature stormy but that 'even if you have a fair wind, you will hardly escape the clutches of pirates'. Sjælland is a large island 'famous for the valour of its people and for the richness of its produce'; in it lies Roskilde, the seat of the Danish kings.

There follows this famous passage:

There is great store of gold there [in Sjælland], collected by sea-robbery. The pirates, whom they call Vikings and we call Ascomanni, pay tribute to the Danish king for his leave to prey on the barbarians who exist in great numbers around this sea [the Baltic]. But a consequence is that it also happens that the licence they receive to act against their enemies is often misused against their own people. So faithless are they towards each other. And as soon as one Dane has captured another Dane, he sells him as a slave, without mercy, either to a companion or to a foreigner. The Danes have much else in their laws and customs that is contrary to justice and virtue; of which I see no point in mentioning anything, unless it be the fact that if women are defiled, they are sold at once; men,

17

moreover, if they are caught in crimes affecting the royal interest or other wrongdoing, would rather lose their heads than their hides. No kind of punishment is found there other than the axe and enslavement; and when a man is condemned, then to be cheerful is an honour. For the Danes so abominate tears and lamentation and other kinds of sorrow, which we count salutary, that a man is allowed to weep neither for his sins nor for the dead who were dear to him.

These extracts from Adam can, of course, give us no idea of general conditions in Denmark in Sven's time. Of the overall aims of royal policy it is only what touches church organization that can now be seen at all clearly. Sven was dissatisfied with the authority of Hamburg-Bremen, for practical reasons as well as on grounds of prestige, and he worked consistently for the establishment of an archiepiscopal see within the boundaries of Denmark, a see whose occupant would also serve as metropolitan of the whole of the North. For a time it served his interests best to co-operate with Hamburg-Bremen, and he effected a much-needed reorganization of the bishoprics in his country. It was possible for Sven and his successors to profit from dissension between emperor and pope, generally siding with the latter when Hamburg-Bremen sided with the former. The popes came to have a high regard for King Sven, and his plans were near fulfilment when he died, but another thirty years were to pass before a Dane was consecrated as first archbishop. His see was based on Lund, a settlement turned into a township by Knut the Great, in the rich province of Skåne, where Sven himself had founded a bishopric for the supervision of the 300 churches which Adam says existed there in his time.

Thereafter the Danish Church grew rapidly in wealth and authority. Its most prominent servants, the archbishops of Lund, Asser (1104 – 37), Eskil (1137 – 77), Absalon (1177 – 1201), were members of mighty families and had prominent parts to play in state affairs. The Church's attempts to get recognition of its rights in important areas of social behaviour and legal administration – relations between the sexes, celibacy of the ordained, freedom from lay patronage, ecclesiastical courts for clerics and for some offences reserved to the Church's jurisdiction – for a time produced open conflict. It was inevitable that the Church should win on most fronts because it had both supernatural authority and vast and increasing resources in land and revenue, particularly after the general introduction of the tithe. In Denmark, as elsewhere, compromise and collaboration were achieved between Church and Crown; and whereas in the period of the Conversion both kings and priests could be largely made answerable to the main body of the farming freemen, by 1200 they were remoter powers, and an aristocratic layer intervened, whose interests were more identifiable with those of the king and great landowning churchmen than with those of the yeomen (p. 126). But in the hands of the wealthy lay the new military power, now based upon followings of semi-professional men-at-arms. The situation may be typified by what happened in Skåne, in the years 1180 – 82. There was strong opposition to archbishop and king among the farmers there. They did away with both taxes and tithes, gave the priests leave to marry and would be rid of bishops, since the priests could see to their religious needs well enough. But in the end the revolt was crushed by king and archbishop with the aid of ruthless, steel-clad cavalry, against whom the farmers had little defence.

This was a short-lived outbreak of complex origins. For the most part, the period from about 1150 onwards was internally peaceful. Diocesan and parish organization received their final form, and Danish farmers seem to have willingly spent time and money on building the solid little stone churches which now sit with such quiet confidence in the Danish landscape. Some of them still have remains of the mural and ceiling paintings which rich men must have paid for, where we find pigments used that were ultimately the exports of Spain and Sicily. Art historians point out the direct connections that then existed between Danish architecture, painting and church furniture and schools of English, French and Lombard art. The monastic foundations of this age also offer telling witness of the substantial means and piety of the greater families and of Danish integration into the world of western Christendom. In a little over 100 years, down to 1175, thirty-three houses for men and nineteen for women were established. The oldest were collegiate houses serving episcopal churches (Dalby, Skåne, c. 1066, Lund c. 1085, Roskilde *c.* 1088), and mostly in important townships. Then came Benedictine and Augustinian foundations, and then others, chiefly Cistercian and Premonstratensian, except the convents which were almost without exception Benedictine. They might have modest beginnings, even when founded by the greatest of men. Bishop Absalon of Roskilde called an old friend, William, from France to reform a small and allegedly dissolute house of canons at Eskilsø, about 1165. The Life of William tells of his initial difficulties and how his three followers got permission to return to France because they could not reconcile themselves to the short commons and sharp cold. Later the house was moved to Æbelholt and achieved great fame and possessions, not least because of the saintliness of Abbot William, who was canonized in 1224.

Sven Estridsson left many sons and he was succeeded by five of them in turn. The reigns of the first four spanned thirty years, and that of Niels, the fifth, another thirty years. The whole age was a period of comparative external peace and of internal rivalry and strife, a period when decisive steps were taken towards the transfer of power from the people to Crown, Church and nobility. We are better informed about the twelfth century than any earlier period, and we persuade ourselves that we can now see with some clarity the forces at work in Danish society and politics.

Two characters in these sixty years of Danish history exemplify the Danish situation, internal and external. Both were named Knut, both met violent deaths, both were canonized.

Knut, Sven's son, ruled from 1080 to 1086. He was a hard man who had led Viking raids on England and against the Wends in the Baltic. He was severe in maintaining the royal rights and did all he could to extend them, claiming, it seems, that exploitation of forest and sea must be paid for to the king. All voices agree that in his time the royal officials oppressed the people, and the introduction of a new tax produced a farmer's revolt in North Jutland aimed at the person of the king. Knut was worsted and retired to Odense. There he was set upon again, and he and his brother Benedikt were killed in the church where they took refuge. That church was served by the monks of the Benedictine priory there, a daughter house of Evesham, established by Knut himself, for he was a generous benefactor of churches and a zealous ally of churchmen. In 1101 Knut's body was ceremoniously translated (his relics are still to be seen in Odense) and his feast day instituted: he was revered as a saint. This meant something to his branch of the royal family and much to the Church, not least in Odense, but it is understandable that his cult did not become immediately popular.

The last of the sons of Sven to reign was Niels, who came to the throne in 1104. He had a promising son, Magnus, born *c.* 1106, but the monarchy was elective as well as hereditary, and there were others of royal blood in the running. The most important of these possible rivals was Knut Lavard, the Lord Knut, born *c.* 1096, son of Erik called 'ever-good', who reigned before Niels, from 1095 to 1103. Knut had been brought up by the leading landowning family on Sjælland and had also spent some time at the Saxon court. In his twenties he was a man who could not safely be left inactive in Denmark. King Niels gave him a difficult and dangerous task. Relations between Danes and the nearest Wendish people, the Obotrites, had varied from alliance in Sven Estridsson's time to open hostility in the period around 1100. Knut was now made lord of the march-province of Slesvig and soon freed the region from Wendish raids. Indeed, he proved so active and dashing a leader that when the Obotrites found themselves without a king, they looked to Knut and, with the consent of Lothar of Saxony, Emperor of Germany, he became their prince in 1129. He was now at one time the most prominent subject of Denmark, a Wendish ruler, and a vassal of the German emperor, with prestige and resources that naturally caused concern to his kinsmen, King Niels and Magnus. Knut seems to have been astute in his dealings with his subjects: in Slesvig he became a member of the merchants' guild, and as prince of the Obotrites he adopted some of their habits of dress.

At Christmas 1130 Knut with other great men joined King Niels in feasting at Roskilde. On 7 January 1131 Knut was on his way southward when he kept an appointment for a private talk with his cousin Magnus. They met in the open air among the leafless woods north of Ringsted. Knut was cut down on the spot. This was an answer to the question of the succession, but not one that solved anything. Civil war followed. Magnus was soon killed, in a great battle in Skåne in 1134; King Niels escaped but went to Slesvig, foolishly, for he was killed by the townsmen there in vengeance for their old guild-brother, Knut Lavard.

After a troubled generation, Valdemar, son of Knut Lavard, born a few days after his murder, became sole king of Denmark in 1157. In the first years of his reign Crown and Church fought their fight and although it ended to the Church's advantage in most issues, the monarchy also made some impressive gains. In 1165 Valdemar gave his two-year-old son Knut the title of king, and the little boy received the homage of the great men of Denmark. With this the elective element in the Danish succession was reduced to the emptiest formality, the monarchy was now hereditary and based on the principles urged by the Church of primogeniture and legitimacy (cf. pp. 140–1). In 1169 Pope Alexander III agreed to the canonization of Knut Lavard, Valdemar's father. His relics were translated to their shrine in the monastery church at Ringsted at midsummer 1170; and at the same festival the Church set her seal upon the dynasty and the person of the king with the consecration and coronation of the boy Knut by Archbishop Eskil.

In his lifetime Knut Lavard had seemed to symbolize vital problems: the problem of the succession, the problem of the Wends, and the problem of the Germans. The first of these problems had now been solved, with clerical approval and a saintly glamour lent by Knut himself. There followed a long period of stable monarchy, strengthened by alliance between Church and State, and this had far-reaching effects on Denmark's political and social life.

Danish internal strife had given the Wends and others ample opportunities to infest Danish waters and raid Danish lands. About the year 1150, for example, Prior Ketil of Viborg, while on little more than a domestic voyage, going from Jutland to visit Lund, was plundered and held to ransom by Wendish pirates. King Valdemar and his energetic kinsman, Absalon, bishop of Roskilde and archbishop of Lund, soon cleared home waters of the marauders and then took the offensive. They made many successful raids on the Wendish coasts, and captured Arkona on Rügen and forcibly converted the inhabitants as their greatest single exploit. But although this activity, and further triumphs under Valdemar's sons, Knut VI (1182 – 1202) and Valdemar 'Victory' (1202 – 41), removed the Wendish threat and enhanced the Danes' self-esteem and their sense of nationhood, they led to no permanent extension of Danish territory or influence, and Danish defeats in the thirteenth century were all the more deflating. In the long run it was German penetration in the south Baltic which proved more effective and produced lasting conquests and settlement. Danish initiative to the eastward was cramped but in this early period Danish commerce was as yet hardly threatened by the growing German rivalry. Later the Hanseatic League was to dominate the northern trade, and later still the Danish kings were to realize what power and profit their control of the Baltic approaches could give them. But as the Wendish problem got smaller, so the German problem got bigger – and indeed, it would be hard to say that it has ever been solved.

But the failure of the Danes to colonize the south Baltic shores must have been partly because they had no real incentive to do so. There must have been ample employment and profit at home, for with internal peace and freedom from attack the prosperity that depended on corn and herring suffered few setbacks, and if young men left the countryside, it was either to move to the growing townships or to join the retinues of noblemen. Certainly, one may suspect a degree of cynicism and inertia after the civil wars and perhaps there were people who doubted the value of the costly military efforts against the Wends, but there was obviously money to be made in farming and fishing and the overseas trading that continued to take the Danes afloat in the Baltic and North Sea. Plenty of sturdy self-reliance was still to be found among the Danish yeomen. Saxo tells of a Sjælland leader in the 1150s, Wetheman, who started a league of coastguards to fight the pirates. They took what local ships they wanted, but gave the owners one-eighth of their spoils; they lived simple lives, always confessing and taking the sacrament before setting sail, skippers and crews sharing equally at all times. The league started in Roskilde, but soon had support throughout Sjælland, and though they never had more than twenty-two ships at their disposal, they accounted in all for eighty-two pirate vessels.

The ordinary farmer must have been reasonably well off and proud to be a Dane. But his position differed in various ways from that of his forefather two hundred years earlier. He now paid taxes to the king and tithes to the church, and more and more farmers worked land for which they paid rent. The small farm-owner and tenant had no say in the succession to the king-ship and little influence on national affairs. The yeomen had once been the lawmakers, but now shared their powers with king and prelate, and the notion that laws were really *given* by the king and accepted gratefully by the people had gained ground. Service in the local levies might still be required, but this too was being replaced by cash taxation. Active service fell more and more on the retainers of the squires and the military caste sur-rounding the king and great men. This inevitably led to an in-flation of the privileges and self-importance of this class, although neither in Denmark nor elsewhere in Scandinavia do we find any fully developed system of graded land-tenure and service typical of feudal states in western Europe. Archbishop and bishop, cathedral chapters and monasteries, were new powers in the land, and they laid religious, ethical and fiscal obligations on the free farmers such as their pagan forebears had never known. The years through which men lived were now ordered by the fasts and holidays of the Church; men were encouraged to do good works and give alms for their souls' sake; and since material goods could be translated into spiritual benefits in this world and the next, there was some disruption in the transmission of family property and the growth of capital. Men lived in a country-side that was probably safer than in the ninth or tenth century and where justice was seen to be done more effectively, not because of better detection and arrest, but because of more rigorous and impartial punishment through royal officers. The influence of the Church's work for peace and public justice in place of armed strife and private vengeance must not be under-estimated. And in the processes of law, as witness, juryman, compurgator, and in ordinary parish and village affairs, the free farmer had much the same responsibility as ever; and prob-ably this was enough for most men's self-respect as the Danish kingdom moved into the high middle ages.

Sweden

The principal region of Sweden in early times, the part from which the whole country has taken its name, was that of the *Svear* (so in modern Swedish; WN *Svíar*, Latin *Suiones, Sueones*). They were the dominant people among the tribes settled around the lakes called Hjälmaren and Mälaren and on the adjacent Baltic coasts, the provinces Gästrikland, Uppland, Västmanland and Södermanland, and the eastern parts of Dalarna, Värmland and Närke. The heart of the area was Uppland (including Gästrikland) with Old Uppsala as the seat of the kings of the Swedes and the site of their chief sanctuary. The greater part of the region consists of low-lying plains, well forested and reasonably fertile. As general terms for this area we use Svealand, Central Sweden or Sweden proper.

South of the Svear lived another confederation of peoples called now in Swedish *Götar* (WN *Gautar,* cf. OE *Geatas*). They lived in a western group between the great lakes called Vänern (2250 sq. miles) and Vättern (800 sq. miles), in the province of Västergötland, and in an eastern group between Vättern and the Baltic in the province of Östergötland. They were cut off from the North Sea by Danish and Norwegian possessions but they controlled the upper reaches of the important Götaälv, the river which flows from Vänern to its great estuary-system around modern Gothenburg. The whole region, for which the general name Götaland will be used, is geographically less uniform than Sweden proper, but forests and fertile lands abound.

North of Svealand, in Hälsingland and Medelpad, settlement was sparse, and still more so in Norrland proper. The main settlements in Jämtland, Härjedalen and upper Dalarna, chiefly on lakes and waterways, were on important routes into Trøndelag and Østerdal in Norway; they looked as much west as east and the first two were counted Norwegian through most of the middle ages. Värmland and Dalsland were difficult forest country, march-provinces to which Norway sometimes laid claim. Between Östergötland and Blekinge on the south Baltic coast is the province of Småland, a region of higher land and vast forests. Here, in what Saxo called the 'wastes of Värend', only the comparatively small area around Ljungby and Växjö seems to have been well populated. Blekinge itself was counted Swedish by Wulf-

stan, the seafarer who gave a first-hand account of the south Baltic to King Alfred of Wessex a little before A.D. 900, but in the mid-eleventh century, and possibly before, it was looked on as Danish territory. Wulfstan also said that Öland and Gotland 'belonged to the Swedes', but these rich islands had (and retain) a character of their own.

Communication in most of Sweden was easiest by water, but many eskers (narrow pebble banks deposited by sub-glacial streams) offer pathway-ridges and they were made use of on routes much travelled in the early period. One such is the so-called Badelunda-esker, which starts near Västerås in west Uppland and leads north into Dalarna; from there an eastern branch of the esker was followed through Hälsingland into Jämt-land and so to Norway. The Eriksgata (p. 137) was another recognized route, a circuit going south from Uppsala through Södermanland, Östergötland, Västergötland and Närke and so back to Uppland. Winter weather often gave good travelling condi-tions. Climate in the early period is thought to have been not much different from that of the last half-century, and in Skåne and Halland, the coastal provinces held by the Danes, snow now lies for 40 – 60 days a year, while in Götaland and Syealand it stays for 80 – 120 days a year. Most lakes are frozen from late November to late March in Götaland, to late April in Svealand. The freezing of the Baltic, on the other hand, was less of an advantage; it lasts from a month in the southeast to 10 – 12 weeks higher up the coast. Internally the great obstacles were the bogs and forests. King Sverri of Norway and his men trekked through Värmland, Dalarna, Härjedalen and Jämtland in the spring of 1177 when the thaw added to the difficulties of the thick forests and lakes. They lived on the flesh of birds and elks, on tree-bark and withered berries from under the snow. Distances were counted in 'rests' in those days, and the average march was 6 – 7 miles, but Sverri's party made seventy-one 'rests' over not more than about 170 miles between Malung in Dalarna and Storsjön in Jämtland, with an average march of less than two and a half miles.

The inhabitants of Sweden lived chiefly as farmers, who grew corn and raised cattle. They lived on single farms or groups of farms, settlements that gradually grew from family units into

27

communal units, with joint use of local land resources in accordance with the regulations we meet in the medieval provincial laws. Hunting and fishing were important in many areas, and the products of the former could provide useful trade goods. Iron extraction, mainly from bog-deposits but probably also from rock-ore in some places, went on chiefly in Gästrikland, Småland and Dalarna, and good supplies of this metal were essential for the efficiency of Swedish food-production and Swedish arms. Copper-mining had begun in Falun by about 1100, the start of an exploitation of that region's mineral resources still pursued on a great scale today.

The Viking Age and medieval period were times of internal colonization but new land was chiefly broken in the plains of central and southern Sweden. Movement northward into Norrland and penetration of the great forests of Småland did not effectively begin until the thirteenth century and later.

A basic standard of living was ensured by home production of food, iron and timber. But many of the yeomen of Uppland and elsewhere were not merely on a subsistence diet – they were men of wealth, even opulence. Adam of Bremen said the whole land was everywhere full of foreign wares, and the richness of Swedish graves and the splendour of Swedish runic monuments represent the profits of commercial enterprise. 'He often sailed to Latvia, in dear-prized ship round Domesnes' – the headland at the entrance of the Gulf of Riga – are words on an eleventh-century Södermanland rune stone, and the lure of trade early drew the Swedes eastward. They made settlements on the south-west coasts of Finland, and sailed through the Finnish Bight to Ladoga and the Russian waterways. In the course of the ninth century they gained control over Slav communities in trading towns as far south as Kiev, an aggressive commercial expansion which may be compared with the command exercised by a Swedish warrior-dynasty over Hedeby and its approaches in South Jutland for half a century around 900 (p. 14). Of all the foreign names recorded on eleventh-century rune stones in Svealand none occurs more frequently than 'Greece' and the 'Greeks' – the usual term for the lands and peoples of the Eastern Empire – and we know too of many Swedish contacts with the Baghdad caliphate. Clearly, however, the men of Svealand had no objection either to turning an honest penny by acting as middlemen between the great international centres of Birka and Gotland on the one side and the outlying farmers and hunters of south Norrland and the Norwegian Uplands and the rich pelt-suppliers of north Norway on the other. Trade is considered in more detail in Chapter 6.

The older Västergötland Law says that it is the responsibility of the Svear (here taken to refer only to the people of Uppland) to accept or reject a claimant to the throne, and it goes on to describe how the new king is to visit the people of Västergötland, with exchange of hostages and oaths (cf. p. 137). When the Götar first recognized the overlordship of the Uppsala kings is a matter of dispute, but it seems likely that it was before the Viking Age began. Like the people of Gotland, however, the Götar retained a marked sense of regional identity, amply attested in their laws codified in the thirteenth century. In atonement for killing a man of Götaland, for example, twenty-one marks was payable, but only thirteen and one-third for a man from Svealand or Småland. In some customs the Götar were closer to the Norwegians (cf. e.g. p. 128); and in internal organization they followed the Danish system of division into *herreds* (p. 10), while in Svealand the local unit became the 'hundred' (p. 4), save in Roden, Uppland's coastal region, where the administrative unit was the 'ship-district'. The Swedish levy system (pp. 280–2) did not apply to Västergötland and much of Östergötland. These and other differences are easy to observe, but it is not easy to see the political interaction of the different regions. The Uppsala dynasty held sway over a federation which evidently provided the security needed by the majority, but Swedish control can hardly have been looked on as oppression and strong separatist tendencies cannot be detected.

We have the names of a good many kings in Uppsala and a fair idea of the chronology of their reigns, but know little of significance besides. They must have succeeded in maintaining the prosperity of their people, partly by making Uppsala a famous centre of pagan cult – where one ancient king himself played the undesirable role of sacrificial victim – and partly by promoting trade and consolidating their influence over their neighbours, chiefly the Götar. But it is not until about 1000 that we get a

Fig. 7. The scale is 1 inch to approximately
75 miles. Stavanger is about lat. 59° N, Oslo
60°, Bergen 60° 20′, Nidaros 63° 20′.
Beyond Lofoten the coast runs NE for some 300
miles to North Cape and then E and S for 190
miles to Norway's present border with the
Soviet Union.

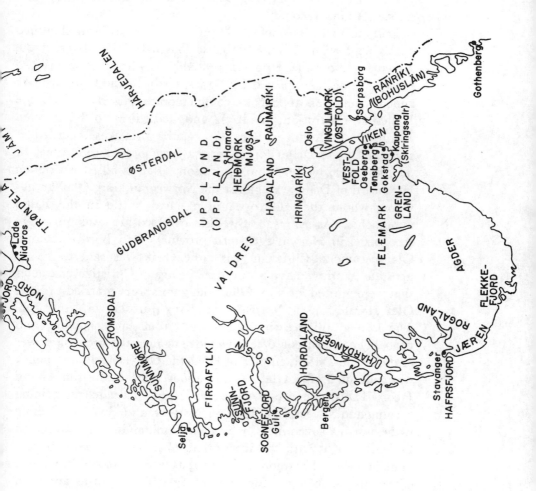

glimpse of Swedish kings in an international setting, in the persons of Erik the Victorious, his son Olaf, called *skötkonung* (WN *skaut-*, 'sheet'- or 'lap'-king – it is not known why), and his son, Anund Jacob.

Erik the Victorious defeated a man called Styrbjörn, identified as his nephew, in a famous battle fought on the plains of the River Fyris outside Uppsala probably in the 980s. Styrbjörn must have been supported by Danes, for in Skåne there are two rune stones that appear to commemorate this battle (cf. the Hällestad inscription, p. 105), and according to King Sven Estridsson, in Adam of Bremen's report, Erik was regarded as, suzerain of the Danes for at least a brief period thereafter. In 999, however, we find that Erik's son, Olaf, is allied with Sven Forkbeard of Denmark against the Norwegian king, Ólaf Tryggvason, whom they destroyed in a naval battle in the Baltic approaches. As a result Swedish overlordship was probably recognized in Norway's eastern provinces and border regions. Olaf became a Christian (his father Erik was said to be an apostate), and we have a number of coins of Christian character that were minted for him. Olaf's daughters were married to King Ólaf Haraldsson of Norway and King Jaroslav of Novgorod. The former alliance signifies a shift from earlier policy, and probably constitutes a defensive move against the growing power of the Anglo-Danish empire of Knut the Great. The same policy was continued after Olaf's death, about 1022, by his son Anund Jacob. The events are obscure, but Knut succeeded in gaining a commanding position, both in Norway and Sweden. Telling witness of his suzerainty in Sweden is found in coins struck in the early 1030s with the inscription, *Cnut rex Sv(eorum)*, by the same moneyer, Thormod at Sigtuna, as was responsible for much of Anund Jacob's own Sigtuna coinage. Blekinge was admitted to be Danish by an agreement made about the middle of the eleventh century; and at the end of that century a dispute with Norway over Dalsland, west of Vänern, was settled by the marriage of King Magnús Bareleg to a Swedish princess. National aspiration and commercial interest were not yet strong enough, however, to produce an irresistible Swedish drive to gain a western and southern seaboard.

What limited information we have about internal Swedish

affairs in the eleventh century primarily relates to the advance of Christianity in the country and reaction against it. The first mission to Birka was led by St Ansgar, first archbishop of Hamburg (later Hamburg-Bremen), as early as 829 or 830, followed by a second visit *c.* 850: his Life provides precious information about the town and about Swedish conditions (cf. pp. 208, 414). The mission achieved no abiding results and a permanent foothold was not made until the time of Olaf *skötkonung*, when a missionary bishop was established at Skara in Västergötland soon after 1000. Such an establishment was apparently impossible in Svealand at that time, but later in the century preachers were active there and elsewhere, among them the English martyrs, Eskil killed at Strängnäs but buried at Eskilstuna (which owes its name to him) and Sigurd killed at Växjö in Småland. About 1050 a bishopric was established at Sigtuna in Uppland itself. There was a strong heathen reaction in Uppland about 1070, connected with the rule of a man called Sacrifice-Sven, but it did not last long, and thereafter Christianity met no serious opposition. In that same period about 1070 Adam of Bremen described the temple and sacrificial grove at Uppsala on the basis of eye-witness accounts (pp. 389, 400), but soon afterwards the new religion's decisive victory was marked by the building of a church on or near its site (p. 418). Most of the Swedish kings from about 1000 onwards had been Christian, and there is ample rune-stone evidence to show that many of the rich farmers and magnates of Svealand also accepted Christianity in the course of the eleventh century. Even so, the public heathen cult did not disappear until nearly 1100. This stubborn competition is evidence both of the strength of the traditional religion and of the political power of the broad mass of the Uppland yeomen.

The conversion of Central Sweden was thus finally effected, but it took a long time for Christianity to spread where communications were difficult and settlements scattered. A plundering attack on the Kalmar region of Småland by King Sigurd Magnússon of Norway in 1123 could be glossed, not implausibly it appears, as a crusade; and in 1177 Sverri and his men believed that the inhabitants of upper Dalarna were still heathen. (One must, on the other hand, be wary of the scorn of one Scandinavian people for another – it has been known to lead to

33

exaggeration.) By and large, however, the twelfth century saw the peaceful extension of Christian organization throughout the Swedish provinces. About 1120 there were bishops in Skara in Västergötland, Linköping in Östergötland, and in Sigtuna, Eskilstuna, Västerås and Strängnäs in Svealand. These last four are grouped around Mälaren, at no great distance from each other, a fact which strongly suggests the intensity of the missionary effort in what was evidently the richest and most densely populated of all the Swedish regions. Parish organization and stone-built parish churches came in the course of the century, along with the first monasteries, almost all Cistercian. The primacy of Hamburg-Bremen over the Swedish Church was transferred to Lund when that archiepiscopal see was established in 1103(4) (p. 18). A visit to Sweden by Cardinal Nicholas Brekespear in 1153 did not immediately lead to the creation of a national archdiocese (as it did in Norway, p. 49). Writing forty years later, Saxo said it was because the Götar and Svear could not agree who the archbishop should be and where he should reside, and this may well be true, whatever we may think of his disdainful reference to the Swedes as 'savages still untutored in religion'. In 1164, however, the first Swedish archbishop was consecrated, with Uppsala as his seat, the new settlement near the heathen centre of Old Uppsala, to which the bishopric of Sigtuna had been moved a few years earlier, but the new archbishopric was still subject to the primacy of Lund. Shortly before this, in 1160 or thereabouts, a certain King Erik had been killed after a reign of some five years. He was soon regarded as a saint, and with the formal elevation of his relics in the reign of his son, Knut (c. 1167 – 95), Sweden acquired a national patron. In 1200 royal privileges gave the Church a high degree of fiscal and legal independence. In these respects the Swedes were not far behind their neighbours in Denmark and Norway.

The political history of the late twelfth and early thirteenth century is largely concerned with rivalry between two dynasties, one descended from Sverker, who had ruled c. 1134 – 55, the other descended from St Erik. We cannot see from what factions they drew support. The struggle for the Crown does not seem to have hindered general economic advance and national undertakings abroad. A domestic coinage was reintroduced; internal colonization continued and new mining industries were developed; trading interests led to diplomatic contacts with Saxony and England; the south Baltic coasts were fortified against the Wends; relations with the Finnish settlements were extended, and the conversion of the Finns to Christianity was undertaken to some extent in rivalry with Russian crusading moves westward in the same period. In the early thirteenth century the Swedes followed Danish example in making attacks across the Baltic in Estonia.

Adam of Bremen, writing about 1070, tells us a few interesting things about the Swedes. He comments on their wealth, contrasted with their lack of esteem for what money can buy – an idealization we need not take seriously save perhaps as an indirect indication of how rich they really were – and on the widespread practice of keeping concubines, whose offspring are accepted as legitimate (but cf. p. 117). He praises their hospitality in particular, and this may well echo the feelings of his chief informant, King Sven Estridsson, who had spent a long time in Sweden while fighting for the Danish throne. He was only one of the many pretenders and political outcasts from Norway and Denmark who took refuge and sought support in Sweden in the early period. (Saxo, about 1200, made a typical Danish comment when he said, 'No people take in exiles more promptly or spit them out again more readily.') Adam also praises the fighting ability of the Swedes, which gives them a commanding position among the northern nations.

He says they have kings of ancient lineage, but their power depends on public opinion: 'what all approve, it behoves the king to confirm.' It can happen however that the people reluctantly accept the king's ruling if it seems better than the popular feeling. The king or an appointed commander receives unquestioning obedience in time of war.

There seems no doubt but that the traditional power of the yeomen and the magnates among them, expressed above all in the 'law-districts' and their 'law-men' (p. 91), effectively curtailed the influence of the monarchy. Nevertheless, by about 1200 there are signs of the growing strength of the Crown, in alliance with the Church. Royal claims to ownership of common land and mineral finds, along with the abandonment of levy duties and maintenance dues in favour of cash taxation, are typical of the moves towards the economic and administrative independence of the national monarchy. The great men in the country and the yeomen they largely represented were bound to view the increasing powers of king and bishop with hostility, but whereas in Denmark the tension between the monarchy and leading free men had been more or less resolved by about 1200, conflict between them in Sweden continued until the latter part of the thirteenth century, when the Crown finally emerged as the strongest power with an aristocracy largely dependent on it. This slow development may be looked on as a parallel to the slow acceptance of Christianity, and is another testimony to the conservative strength of the wealthy yeomen of Sweden, backed by their traditional control of the main forms of legal and social organization.

Norway

A glance at the profile diagrams of the Scandinavian peninsula, fig. 8, will show at once how Norway and Sweden compare in terms of terrain. The western tilt of the whole land-mass makes Norway an abruptly mountainous country, with an average altitude of about 1600 feet above sea-level. Against this must be offset the chief advantage offered by its western situation – the mild and damp climate enjoyed along its Atlantic seaboard where, even in the north, the many fjords are normally ice-free all the year round and where the ice-caps that are found are comparatively very small (their area is less than one-hundredth of the total area of the country). This western seaboard provided the route from the south by which the country became generally known, the 'North-way', Norway, inhabited by 'North-men'. This name for Norwegians was used by the English in the ninth century, but it was also generally applied to any Scandinavian people. It seems to have become established as the Norwegians' own name for themselves in the course of the tenth century. The medieval Icelanders must have been maintaining an ancient habit from that same century when they went on calling Norwegians 'East-men'.

Norway (fig. 7) can be divided into four great natural regions. The border with Sweden is for the most part dictated by the long mountain range called 'the Keel' (ON *Kjǫlrinn*, Norw. *Kjølen*). West of the southern part of this lie two great valley-systems, Østerdal and Gudbrandsdal, separated from each other by a belt of high land. The waters of these valleys drain southward, finally into the Oslofjord, *Víkin*, as it used to be called, 'the inlet'. Around the head of the Oslofjord is a complex of waterways set among the most extensive lowlands of Norway, good farming land, which continues northward on a narrower

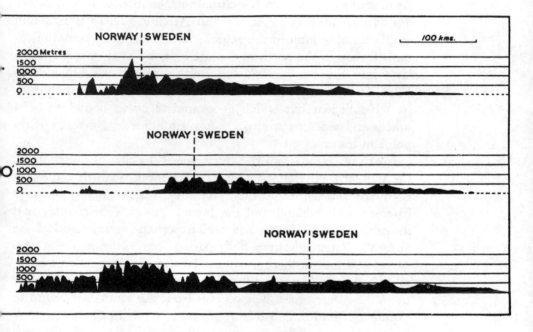

Fig. 8. Profile of the Scandinavian Peninsula. After W. R. Mead.

scale to Mjøsa, the biggest lake in Norway, and from there into Østerdal and Gudbrandsdal. The region round Mjøsa and southward is referred to here as southeast Norway. It included the medieval provinces of Ranríki, which covered the coastal strip as far south as Götaälv (the modern Swedish province of Bohuslän) and Vingulmǫrk (now called Østfold) on the east of Oslofjord, and Grenland and Vestfold on the west. North of these lay Hringaríki (Ringerike) and Haðaland (Hadeland) to the west and Raumaríki (Romerike) and Heiðmǫrk (Hedmark) to the east. These more northerly districts also formed part of Upplǫnd (modern Oppland, the Uplands), much of which remained isolated territory through the Viking Age.

Comparatively low passes lead north from Gudbrandsdal and Østerdal into the region called Trøndelag. This is the area around the Trondheimsfjord, the southern end of a large depression which runs northeastward, parallel with the coast, through Namdal, in olden times the northern limit of Norway proper. As in southeast Norway, the climate in the interior here is colder and drier, more continental than Atlantic. There is rich and ample farming land in the region, and it has good communications by sea to the north and southwest, by land through Jämtland into Sweden (p. 27) and south through the Uplands to *Vikin*. It is a neighbourhood which has the natural resources to be self-sufficient but which geographically was bound to be a junction. Its people were in a key situation in Norway's early political history.

North of Namdal lies the third major division of the country, the vast strip of territory which stretches on to North Cape and then east and south into the White Sea, where Norway now has frontiers with Finland and the Soviet Union. This country had its separate name, *Hálogaland,* which perhaps means 'land of the aurora'. Settlement here had existed for centuries but it was sparse and though there was some farming, life depended essentially on the use of natural food resources. In the centuries before the Viking Age began Norwegians from the south had begun to exploit its hunting and fishing grounds, while in the Viking Age and later some of the products of these activities made the men in control of Hálogaland some of the richest in Norway (cf. p. 40).

The fourth major region is all that lies westward of the Oslofjord-Oppland-Trøndelag axis. It is as it were one great plateau, deep scored seaward with fjords and inland with narrow glaciated valleys, often with long ribbons of deep water in them. From the middle west counties (*fylke*) of Romsdal, Sogn and Hordaland it is possible to gain access to the central and eastern valleys by way of the heads of the fjords and mountain passes or high, treeless plateaus. Connections between Sognefjord (whose head is some 125 miles from the sea) and Valdres, the district adjacent to Gudbrandsdal, were particularly close, despite a pass of 3000 feet between them. In the south, on the other hand, in the interior of Rogaland and in west and east Agder the valley-routes radiate in a southward fan; here there was little movement to north and east, and people in the Agder valleys lived isolated lives down to the last century. The western land was fertile but restricted in area, narrow strips on the shores and mountain sides and on many of the coastline's innumerable islands. But since the people mostly lived only a stone's throw from water and messed about in boats from infancy, they had little difficulty in making use of the sea as a means of escape from their predicament as an expanding population on limited soil. Emigration from these parts to Shetland, Faroes, Orkney had begun by the beginning of the ninth century; and it was to continue with larger expansion in the British Isles and the settlement of Iceland as the Viking Age progressed. It was easier, in fact, for west-coast Norwegians to make part of an Atlantic community than to become integrated with the people of the southeast. It is worth remembering that while Oslo is some 400 miles from Bergen by sea, Lerwick, Kirkwall and Aberdeen are within a 300-mile radius of it.

The steepness of the Norwegian terrain means in general that rivers are too swift to be navigable, except with frequent portages, although boats are useful on many lakes. Land routes by way of the river-valleys were used, of course, and in summer it was often relatively easy to travel inland by way of the high plateaus above the tree-line. But the main lines of communication were by sea, and coastal traffic was particularly favoured by the sheltered 'leads', the channels protected from the gale-swept Atlantic by islands forming a breakwater as much as 30 – 40 miles wide in some places. By far the longest open passage that has to be made in the 700 miles between Oslo and Trondheim is the notorious eighty-mile stretch of Jæren's exposed coast in the southwest corner of the country, between Flekkefjord and Stavanger (*Nú's brim fyr Jaðri*, 'Now there is surf off Jæren', is the warning of a tenth-century poet). Narrow waters and coastal difficulties had never been a great barrier in European history. It was the west-coast Norwegians who demonstrated that oceans need not be either.

It will have appeared from this brief description that the main regions of Norway were likely to show some social and political variety in the early period. In the southeast lived a well-to-do farming population who in Vestfold sustained princely families of outstanding wealth. In our period the most telling archaeological evidence of their existence is in the superb finds at Oseberg and Gokstad (pp. 242-9). The chief dynasty was of Swedish origin. How they maintained themselves in Vestfold we do not know, but it is undoubtedly of significance that they lived not very far from Kaupang (ON *Skíringssalr*, OE *Sciringesheal*, pp. 213-4), a great market-place of ninth-century Norway, and were in a position to control traffic in and out of the Oslofjord. Otherwise the Danes often claimed and sometimes had political supremacy in *Víkin*, particularly in Ranrike and Østfold.

In Trøndelag the population seems to have been of solid yeoman stock, a society in which it is hard to point to any outstanding princely or aristocratic element. In the course of the ninth century, however, a powerful group established itself on Trondheimsfjord, whose leading members were known as the *Hlaðajarlar*, 'earls of Lade', after their estate (now within the conurbation of Trondheim). This dynasty had originated in Hálogaland and they kept their lands and commercial interests there. We are lucky enough to have the detailed account of Ohthere, a wealthy man from Hálogaland who visited King Alfred late in the ninth century, to help us understand the way of life of the leading men in that district. Living was cheap in the north: Ohthere's small farm-stock was supplemented by a large herd of tame reindeer, which cost nothing beyond the labour of capture, and by food from hunting – he and five companions had killed sixty whales, the biggest up to 100 foot long, in a mere two days. But most desirable articles of trade were also easy to come by, in the shape of walrus ivory, ropes of walrus and seal hide, furs and feathers, which Ohthere obtained both by hunting and as a tribute from the Lapps, apparently under a fixed arrangement which presumably offered the Lapps protection in exchange. It is obvious that Ohthere's excellent products – valuable out of all proportion to their bulk so that a shipload might be worth a fortune – were only really useful if he could barter them for other necessities and luxuries: cloth, iron, flour, malt, weapons, jewellery. This trade with Hálogaland, probably chiefly maintained by way of Trøndelag in the early period, was of vital interest to the northern chieftains, and pre-occupation with its protection and development was doubtless one cause of the southward move of the *Hlaðajarlar*.

On the west coast there was a population who farmed and fished, but among them were also a comparatively large number of sea-borne warrior chieftains. They were not in a good position to maintain themselves by trade, because they had nothing much to sell (no demand for Norway's fish existed at this time), but they were in a position to take a toll of other people's commerce and able by foreign raiding both to enrich themselves with plunder and to take a share in international trafficking, especially perhaps in slaves. They applied themselves to piracy and some-times to conquest in the British Isles, particularly in Scotland and Ireland, but also held a commanding position in Norway because they sat on the coastal waters through which the traffic to and from Trøndelag and Hálogaland largely passed. The need to solve the problems posed by these gentlemen partly explains the enforced unification of Norway, against the geo-graphical odds, at an early stage in the period we are considering.

Towards 900 the young king of Vestfold, encouraged by his advisers, took it into his head to become sole ruler of Norway. His name was Harald, son of Halfdan, generally called Harald Finehair. Community of commercial interests dictated alliance with the earls of Lade, and when this combination was effected, the allies moved steadily southward from Trondheimsfjord against the chieftains of the west coast. Some of these joined them, others fought or fled, but Harald's success was constant and he finally won a decisive victory sometime in the 890s, in a naval battle fought in Hafrsfjord, just by Stavanger. Hence-forth it was accepted in principle that there should be a king over all the Norwegians, and Harald Finehair's right to rule was so firmly established that the same right was freely accorded to men of his blood for centuries thereafter. The earl of Lade was confirmed in his position of influence in Trøndelag and north-ward, though the Lappish tribute and trade seem to have been regarded henceforth as a royal monopoly. Another large increase in the king's fortune came in the shape of lands acquired by conquest or forfeiture. The wealth at the disposal of the king must have far outstripped the possessions of any of his subjects. It is noteworthy that after his final victory Harald resided on large estates in Rogaland, in southwest Norway, and left his southeastern realm to the care of others. This must have been partly dictated by strategic considerations – his ships would never be frozen in and he was well placed to meet a threat from oversea while he could not easily be surprised and surrounded – but it also clearly meant that it was worth his while to command the west-coast passage and keep close control over his new-won lands. Rogaland also has the best farming land in the west, and great landowners from this part were later to count among the most prominent men in the country.

Harald died in the 930s, aged something over seventy, and was succeeded by his son, Eirík Bloodaxe, whose queen was a Danish princess. They were not popular and were forced into exile, Eirík having two short spells of rule as king in York around 950. His younger half-brother, Hákon (modern Håkon), succeeded him; he is sometimes known as 'foster-son of Athelstan' and sometimes as 'the good'. The first name was due to his upbringing at the court of the powerful King Athelstan of Wessex (ruled 925 – 39). He returned in his teens to Norway and proved a popular ruler, especially after his attempts to convert the people to Christianity, doubtless with the encouragement of his English friends, had met with such opposition that he himself turned apostate. He suffered many attacks from his nephews, the sons of Eirík Bloodaxe, supported from Denmark, and in one of their onslaughts, c. 960, he was mortally wounded. A daughter was his only child, and the throne then passed to Eirík's sons, under the leadership of Harald 'grey-cloak'. Hákon had close associations with the earls of Lade, but Harald and his party were at odds with them, partly because of inherited hostility and partly because they wished to reduce the power of such great subjects. Their policy included, it seems, a more active interference in the far northern ventures than had been hitherto normal on the part of the king. But Harald and his brothers were in Norway as a result of Danish aid, and their uncle of Denmark seems to have expected more from them than he got. At least, we find that by about 970 Harald Blue-tooth was in league with Earl Hákon of Lade who, after he had destroyed Harald Grey-cloak with Danish connivance, undertook to rule Norway as viceroy of the Danish king. He paid tribute and fought for the Danes when the Emperor Otto II attacked Denmark, so that Harald Blue-tooth could say with some cause that he had 'won Norway' (pp. 14–5). Danish influence must have been paramount in the southeast at this time, but Earl Hákon lived in Trøndelag and in time he renounced the Danish allegiance. He defeated an impressive naval force sent against him by the Danish king, and Norway was temporarily independent again.

Hákon was a formidable upholder of the pagan cults (cf. pp. 138–9), but Christianity must have been well known to many tenth-century Norwegians, not least because of their Danish and British contacts. In 995 Hákon was succeeded by a fierce Christian, Ólaf Tryggvason, a great-grandson of Harald Finehair, an ally of Sven Forkbeard of Denmark in his attacks on England. Ólaf had become Christian and in 994 he was confirmed at Andover, with King Æthelred as one of his sponsors, not long before sailing to Norway. We know little for sure about this young man. Texts of the Anglo-Saxon Chronicle say that when he was confirmed, he vowed never to return with hostile intent to England and that he kept his word. To the Icelandic poet Hallfred (whose godfather Ólaf was) the king was 'my leader', a supreme warrior, a breaker of heathen sanctuaries, whose death left the northern lands empty and dull. To Adam of Bremen, seventy years after his death, Ólaf, though a Christian, was an aggressor against the Danes, and a man who put all his faith in soothsayings, especially in prophecies drawn from the observation of birds, so that he was called 'crow-leg' – Danish contempt and hostility have here produced a tradition that is hardly likely to be entirely just. The sober Icelandic historian, Ari Thorgilsson, writing about 1125, can simply say: 'Ólaf *rex* Tryggvason . . . brought Christianity to Norway and Iceland'; and later Icelandic prose sources are full of respectful and admiring legends in keeping with Hallfred's praise and Ari's statement. Ólaf ruled for four or five years and in that time he is credited with the conversion of Norway and Iceland, as Ari says, and of Orkney, the Faroes and Greenland. The conversion may have been superficial, but none of these countries relapsed officially into paganism after his death. If he did nothing else, he at least hastened the process by which western Scandinavians assimilated the faith and culture of Christendom.

Ólaf Tryggvason was defeated by an alliance of the Swedish and Danish kings and Earl Eirík, son of Hákon of Lade. With Earl Eirík's rule Norway's tributary position was again explicit, so much so that Knut could summon him to England in 1015 and keep him there as earl of Northumbria. When he left, a new member of Harald Finehair's dynasty appeared in Norway, Ólaf Haraldsson, like Ólaf Tryggvason an ardent Christian and with an established career as Viking and mercenary warrior behind him. In his fifteen years of rule he finished the work of conversion, established a Christian law, helped build churches and bring in priests. The districts around Mjøsa, the Uplands and the depths of Trøndelag had hitherto seen little of Norway's kings, who had chiefly lived on the west coast and been reluctant to stir far from their fleets. Ólaf's family connections were mainly in the southeast, however, and from there he made a serious and largely successful attempt to break the power of the local leaders in these parts (some of whom still had the title of 'king'), and to destroy the pagan cults. The political and religious offensive doubtless had to go hand in hand in such conservative farming societies, less affected than the coastal people by foreign trade and travel.

There were many seeds of conflict in the Norwegian situation at this time. Danish claims backed by power such as Knut the Great's were not negligible. There was tension between the exclusive demands of the new religion and the traditional hold of the pagan cults, and King Ólaf seems to have been hardest on his people in matters of faith. There was strain among the local leaders who mediated between king and people but could be assured of the favour of neither and who saw the king moving outside their select group to find the agents he needed. A political argument heard more than once in medieval Icelandic sources maintains that, if you must have an overlord, then it is better from the ordinary yeoman's point of view to have one at a distance than to have one on your doorstep. This argument seems to have been used to foster the revolt organized against King

Ólaf by magnates who looked to Knut the Great for supplies and favour. When Knut sailed to Norway in the spring of 1028, Ólaf withdrew from the country and spent two winters at the court of his brother-in-law, Jaroslav, in Novgorod. He returned with some Swedish aid in 1030, to be killed at the battle of Stiklestad (*Stiklastaðir*) in Trøndelag, shortly after entering the country by way of Jämtland and Verdal. Subsequent active intervention in Norwegian affairs by Danish regents quickly produced a violent swing in favour of the dead king. His undeniable Christian zeal and marvels connected with his death and grave caused frequent invocation of his name, with such results that a year after the battle his remains were translated and Saint Ólaf, prototype of all the princely martyrs of the northern countries, the two Knuts of Denmark, Magnús of Orkney and Erik of Sweden, came into being. He thus became a focus of Scandinavian Christian veneration and in particular a symbol that was to play an incalculable part in creating Norwegian national unity.

The death of Knut the Great in 1035 and the failure of his succession removed the threat of Danish dominion in Norway for over a century. And from about that time until the death of King Sigurd Magnússon in 1130 the country was internally peaceful as well. The stature of Norway as an independent power in the North was established by King Magnús Ólafsson, who ruled Denmark as well as Norway (cf. p. 16), and earned a deserved reputation as the victor of the Wends. He died young and was succeeded in 1047 by his uncle, Harald Sigurdsson; he is called *harðráði*, 'hard-ruler', in later West Norse sources, but the Dane, Saxo Grammaticus, said his cognomen was *malus*, 'bad'. Harald, St Ólaf's half-brother, had escaped from Stiklestad when he was fifteen and had gone to Novgorod; from there he carried on through Russia, as many other Norsemen did, to join the Varangian troops of the Eastern Emperor. He fought as an officer in a number of campaigns in and around the eastern Mediterranean, and he and his men played some part in internal strife around the imperial throne in Constantinople. He came back to Norway in 1046, rich, experienced, ambitious, and was given half the kingdom by his nephew, Magnús, succeeding to undivided rule when Magnús died a year later. Harald was aggressive but not successful abroad. He pressed his claims to Denmark with numerous attacks but won no more than booty, and his death came in battle at Stamford Bridge in Yorkshire in 1066, where he found himself because of a fundamental misunderstanding of the English situation.

Harald's aggressive maintenance of Norwegian independence was matched by his consolidation of the king's sovereignty at home. The dynasty of the earls of Lade disappeared in his day and the title of earl fell into disuse for a century. He tightened the monarchy's hold on the settlements of the Uplands, using force on occasion to make his authority clear and increasing royal property in the region by subsequent forfeitures. He forcefully maintained national independence in church affairs. The question of ecclesiastical authority in Norway was complicated by the discrepancy between the theoretical claims of remote Hamburg-Bremen and the facts of the mission field, where English workers were particularly active, though by no means to the exclusion of their German colleagues, and where, as in Sweden, Orthodox clergy might also be met. (When Harald returned to Norway he had spent half his life in the sphere of Orthodox Christianity, whose final schism with Rome did not take place until 1054.) Adam of Bremen says that Harald had declared that he did not know who was archbishop or had power in Norway except himself, an attitude that seems to have found favour with his countrymen. Certainly the Christian laws of the Norwegian provinces show in some respects a high degree of independence of canon law, and are all the more valuable as sources of social history in consequence.

The legal organization of the country goes back to the time of Harald Finehair, when the west-coast legal federation known as Gulathing was created. Its central assembly was near the mouth of Sognefjord, and in time all the western provinces from Agder in the south to Sunnmøre bordering Romsdal in the north belonged to it. In the course of the tenth century, probably in the time of Hákon the Good, the other law-provinces came into being: Frostathing Law, when the organization which already existed in the Trøndelag districts was extended to Nordmøre, Romsdal and Namdal; and *Heiðsævislǫg*, the law for the region around Mjøsa. The Frostathing Law also applied in

Hálogaland, which did not become a separate legal province until the twelfth century. In the eleventh century Ranrike and *Víkin* became a separate legal province, with a body of law probably fundamentally the same as that for the Mjøsa region, and with an assembly at Sarpsborg. This is a sign of the increasing importance of this neighbourhood, where, as well as Sarpsborg, Tønsberg and Oslo were growing settlements, and also a sign of Norwegian (as opposed to Danish) power there. For practical reasons the central assemblies of these large law-provinces were representative, not universal gatherings of all free men, as local *things* were. The representatives were nominated by the king's agents but their numbers were so large (400 in all at the Guli assembly, for example) that the yeomen remained, at least down to the mid-twelfth century, a notable force in law-making and political debate.

District organisation in Norway had in the main been effected before the Viking Age began. In the southeast there was a division into *herreds,* as in Denmark and Västergötland, and sub-division into quarters, each division, larger and smaller, with its own assembly place. In Trøndelag and on the west coast the division was the *fylki,* modern *fylke* (pl. *fylke, fylker*). This is probably oldest in Trøndelag, where the eight *fylke* are small and not subdivided, while the six large *fylke* that came under the Gulathing Law were large and had division into quarters or eighths.

The military levy system (p. 280) was also applied through the assemblies. The levy was often called out in the eleventh century, under the warlike Magnús Ólafsson and Harald the Hard-ruler, and it seems to have become generally accepted that the king had an annual right to this service. In the twelfth century it was established in Norway, as elsewhere in Scandinavia, that the yeomen should pay subsidies in lieu of levy-service, but there was no military development among the Norwegians to compare with that in Denmark, and later in Sweden, where semi-professional cavalry, maintained by local lords, began to form the main fighting force (pp. 125–6). Norway produced a class of rich landowners in the twelfth and thirteenth centuries, but they did not make a military caste, and no Norwegian aristocracy entirely comparable to that of Denmark and Sweden came into being in the early middle ages.

Norway was prosperous enough in the period 1030 – 1130 to absorb the expenses of martial kings, the maintenance of many ships, and the building of churches throughout the country (timber of course was cheap). Part of that prosperity came to depend on the new towns. Nidaros (now the city of Trondheim) on Trondheimsfjord became the chief port of the north, a nodal point for north-south and east-west routes. The shrine of St Ólaf in its cathedral attracted many pilgrims. Bergen got its own cathedral church when the bishop of Selje moved there a little before 1100, and by then the west-coast magnates had given up their piracy and gone in for land and trade. It was the Norwegian port most easily reached by English and other North Sea merchants, as well as by people from the Atlantic settlements, Iceland, Faroes, Shetland and Orkney. Later it was to become the fish-market of the western world and one of the biggest towns in Europe. Other dioceses were centred on Stavanger in Rogaland, Hamar by Mjøsa, and in Oslo, which with other towns of the southeast has already been mentioned. From the time of Ólaf the Quiet (1066 – 1093) it was usual for the king and his retinue to spend at least the winter in one of the towns, rather than on constant progress from one royal estate to another. This was another sign of the development in Norway of the concentration of supplies in towns and the money economy which active trade demanded.

It is evident that in the early period the success of the monarchy in Norway depended on alliance with great families in all parts of the country. The greatness of these families depended in the last resort on command of yeoman support, which was theirs partly because of traditional and personal loyalties, partly because of wealth to pay followers, and partly because of the control landlords could exercise over tenants. This third source of power increased in importance in the eleventh and twelfth centuries, partly because men invested in property and partly because of many new settlements (emigration was not as easy as it had been), some of which must have been tenancies on private land, while farms established on common land were looked on as Crown leases. Some changes in the composition of the leading classes must have resulted as new landowners came into prominence. At the same time there was a large-scale transfer of land

48

and income to the cathedrals and monasteries (of which a dozen had been established by 1200) by donations chiefly from the king and wealthy families. This, of course, gave churchmen a correspondingly greater say in national affairs. Land-rents were chiefly paid in produce, and trade was inevitably promoted by the need to dispose of the surplus. Fish and timber were to become the staple exports of Norway, a lot of it carried in Norwegian vessels, and the importance of Norway as a trading nation in the thirteenth century is fully attested by the extant agreements with the English Crown. The great landowners and the great merchants were one class, but the general population benefited as well, especially with the development of the rich northern fisheries.

Magnús Bareleg died in 1103 and was succeeded by three sons who ruled jointly over the country. They were not always on good terms, but they all managed to die natural deaths – the last in 1130 – unlike their nine successors down to 1184, who all met violent, some horrible, ends. This was a period of bitter civil war, between rival claimants to the throne and factions of great men, with complications caused by fresh Danish involvement in Norwegian affairs and by the independent power and policy of the Norwegian Church.

An event of far-reaching significance was the creation of a Norwegian archbishopric, after Cardinal Nicholas Brekespear came to the country in 1153. The new province, which as well as Norway covered the Atlantic dioceses from Sodor and Man in the south to Greenland in the west, was the chief result of the Cardinal's visit, but he also obtained substantial improvements in the position of the Church in Norway, including the institution of regular chapters at the cathedrals, so that bishops should henceforth be canonically elected and not royally appointed. At this time the most important powers in Norway were the Church leaders and the 'landed men' (pp. 129–30), who held the royal warrant in the countryside but who also largely represented the traditional local chieftaincies. The arrangements of 1153 had largely been organized by these groups at a state assembly in which the representation of the yeomen was little more than a token figure. By the 1160s a majority of the 'landed men' were united in their dissatisfaction with kings and pretenders of the direct line from Harald Finehair – the last one they had just killed themselves – and in their understanding that a composition with Denmark was necessary. They consequently elected their own king, Magnús, the five-year-old son of the leading man among them, Erling *skakki* ('awry' – because an old neck-wound made him tilt his head), whose wife, Magnús's mother, was at least the legitimate daughter of a legitimate king. The able Erling then ruled Norway as chairman of a council of 'landed men' and for some time as earl of King Valdemar of Denmark. Authority and legitimacy could be conferred on the new régime by the Church, and in 1163 young Magnús was crowned by the archbishop. At the same time an impressive concordat was established between Church and State that went far to giving the former all that it demanded. The king received his crown from St Ólaf, but it was delivered to him by the archbishop; the election to the monarchy was made by representatives of the people at a central assembly, but should follow rules of legitimacy and primogeniture, and in cases of disability or doubt the ultimate choice lay with the bishops. The old powers of the yeomen in their local assemblies to accept as king the candidate they favoured from the royal line completely disappeared. Norway might have settled down at this point as a model theocracy, but the stability was shortlived, for another royal bastard in the male line from Harald Finehair appeared on the scene, the most remarkable of them all.

Sverri Sigurdsson was brought up in the Faroes. At the beginning of 1177 he took command of the small band who had been trying to fight the 'landed men', and he turned these 'Birchlegs', as they were contemptuously called, into a fighting force unmatched in mobility and daring. By 1184, after extraordinary hardships and successes, he had killed Erling skakki and Magnús, his son, and was himself king of Norway. Sverri appears so much more mentally alert than anyone else we know from that time, such a curious blend of dreamer and anti-clerical (but not irreligious) thinker, that he imposes himself upon us, and we tend to have little sympathy for those who regarded him in his day as usurper and tyrant. A good many Norwegians must have felt as we do – Sverri seems to have successfully rallied many of the yeomen against the traditional leading families – but in the southeast of the country churchmen and pretenders, doubtless backed by ecclesiastical and Danish funds, never had difficulty in raising men against him. His position was in fact never secure, largely because of the unremitting hostility of the Church, which meant international difficulties and which must have affected the conscience of the ordinary people when it came to excommunication of the king, the flight of every bishop, and a national interdict. In his Church-State policy Sverri, probably for deep-seated temperamental reasons, failed to see that he could not safely or successfully act like Harald the Hard-ruler in an earlier century. Compromise between the two powers was quickly achieved after his death in 1202.

Sverri was such a remarkable man that it is hard to believe that his advent and reign did not mark some decisive stage in Norwegian history. But if there was any notable step towards the modern world in his time, it was in the unintentional increase in secularism which the deadlock between Church and Crown encouraged. Otherwise it must be said that Sverri did little more than confirm tendencies that already existed. Centralization of authority in the monarchy became more marked, because he replaced the 'landed men' with his own administrative officers (cf. p. 130). The influence of the yeomen steadily declined; it may be seen among other things in the general imposition of cash taxation and in royal nomination of lawmen in the districts who came to function as judges at the assemblies. Sverri greatly affected the fortunes of individuals but brought about no redistribution of wealth and prestige among the different social and occupational groups of his country, and in his time Norwegian fame abroad rested chiefly on fish, exiled bishops, and drunkenness. We cannot, on the other hand, be grateful enough to him for the encouragement he gave to vernacular literature, by commissioning the composition of his own saga and of a hard-biting tract against the bishops, which reveal a unique fusion of native style and foreign learning.

In the reign of Sverri's grandson, Hákon Hákonsson, 1217 – 63, Norway played an important role in European commerce and politics, and widened its realm to include the Scottish islands, Iceland and Greenland. The king and court made a solemn and successful effort to assimilate southern culture, in literature, art

51

and architecture. Sverri would doubtless have approved of most of it, though he might not have thought it had much to do with him. It is an interesting comment on his career and the times that what still lived a hundred years after his age was a recollection of the spirit of the Birchlegs, their generous fellowship and bravery, which had meant everything in the seven years of hardship and battle before Sverri's reign really began.

Iceland

It is about 425 miles from Norway to the Faroes, islands between 61° 20′ and 62° 25′ N that were visited by Norsemen by A.D. 800 and permanently settled by them *c*. 825. The Faroes were a natural stepping-stone to Iceland (fig. 2) which lies only another 280 miles to the northwest, between latitudes 63° 20′ and 66° 30′ N. The first visitors to Iceland (fig. 9) are said to have been in ships blown there by accident while on passage from Norway to the Faroes, and the first man to go from Norway to Iceland on purpose is said to have sailed by way of Shetland and the Faroes. These first sightings and visits took place in the middle part of the ninth century. They were followed by a full-scale colonization of the country in the period *c*. 870 – 930.

The only human inhabitants of Iceland before the advent of the Norsemen were Irish anchorites. The Norsemen called them *papar*, pl., an adaptation of their Irish-Latin name (OIr. *pob(b)a, pab(b)a,* Latin *papa,* cf. 'pope'). Similar Irish clergy had also been found by them in the Faroes. It is said that they left Iceland on the arrival of the Norsemen, but it is, of course, possible that some were killed or enslaved. Evidence of their settlement remains to the present in a number of place-names in Iceland, like the Papey marked on fig. 9, and one in the Faroes.

The majority of the settlers who came to Iceland at the end of the ninth century were west-coast Norwegians. A number of them were of Norwegian stock but had lived in Celtic parts of the British Isles, particularly the Hebrides and Ireland, and some had been born or brought up there. A principal reason for the emigration was the long-standing dearth of land in western Norway, but impetus was given to the exodus by political events, the warfare and oppression that went with Harald Finehair's achievement of sole rule in Norway in the years before 900

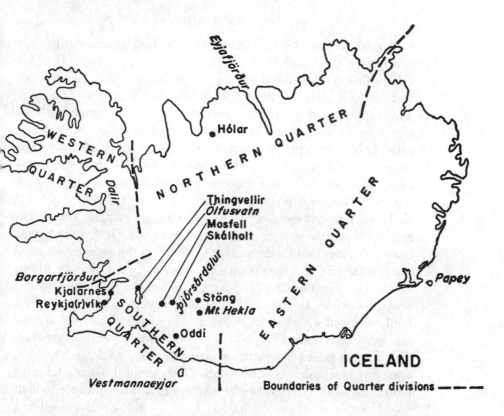

Boundaries of Quarter divisions — — —

(pp. 41–2), and successes by English and Irish forces against invading Norsemen in the years around the turn of the century. The tyranny of Harald Finehair became a popular reason in stories for the emigration of individual chieftains, but there is evidence that relations between the new colonists and the Norwegian leaders were not generally hostile. Some men are said to have moved to Iceland with the king's advice or aid; and we are told that Icelanders referred disputes over land-claims to the king's decision. A tax was imposed on people voyaging to Iceland, and this was intended as a deterrent, according to Ari Thorgilsson c. 1125, because to King Harald the emigration 'seemed to amount to a depopulation'. We can, in fact, do little more than guess at the numbers involved. A plausible estimate is that some 20,000 people came to Iceland in the age of settlement, and that the population thereafter rose to c. 60,000. A reasonable guess puts the total population of Norway in this period at 250,000, and since the Icelanders chiefly came from the southwest *fylke*, it may be that King Harald had genuine cause for concern.

The first settlers found a very big island – a little bigger than Ireland – all silent with black mountains and silver glaciers. Three-quarters of the country lie over the 1500-foot contour line; a quarter of the whole is covered now by lava or permanent ice-caps. It is a geologically young country, and there are numerous areas of volcanic activity. Hot springs and solfataras are common, and are one of the features commonly reflected in place-names, in the element *reyk-*, 'vapour'. There are fjords and natural harbours everywhere except on the south coast. The climate in general is not severe, because an arm of the Gulf Stream embraces the south and west coasts. At sea-level the average January temperature in the southwest, for example, is now only about $-1°C$. The fjord valleys are fertile and there are vast lowland areas, especially in the south and mid-west, which though often badly drained give excellent grass. The high moorlands are for the most part easy of access and offer good summer grazing. The settlers found a wealth of birds and fish, seals and whales, and huge supplies of driftwood. The ground from shore to mountain was covered with scrub birch and juniper which could not provide much material for house- or boat-building but gave fuel, charcoal for smelting (bog-iron is plentiful in some parts) and foliage that might eke out supplies of straw and hay. These woodlands were soon reduced by intentional clearing, accidental forest fires, and pasturing of sheep and goats, and with their protection gone the soil began to suffer the gradual but devastating effects of wind erosion. The place of wood as fuel was taken by peat, which is in good supply in many areas.

The first permanent settler was Ingolf, from Sunnfjord, who built his farm at Reykjarvík, a pleasant bay in the southwest, the site of Reykjavík, the modern capital. Here are low hills and gentle slopes, sea and distant horizons on three sides – in marked contrast to cramped Sunnfjord and many other districts of western Norway from which the settlers came. Ingolf took land in style – an area about as big as Harald Finehair's Vestfold – and some other major settlers are credited with very large stakes: Helgi the Lean took the whole of Eyjafjörður in the middle north and some land to the east of the fjord as well; in the west the great lady called Aud 'deep-wealthy' took land that later gave a livelihood to well over eighty farmers, and Skalla-Grím took practically the whole of Borgarfjörður. The early settlers gave land to their followers and gave or sold it to people who came later to the country. Sometimes there were fights over the ownership of land, but by and large people seem to have expected their claims to be respected, and no single company of men appears to have had either the ambition or the means to force their control on others.

The first settlers grew corn and raised cattle as they had done in Norway and the British Isles. Sheep flourished and came to provide Iceland's chief exports, wool and woollen products, especially the coarse, tough homespun cloth called *vaðmál*, and a popular kind of protective cloak (pp. 172, 174). Sheepskins, falcons and sulphur were other goods in demand abroad. The *vaðmál*, of standard width and measured by the ell, early became a unit of exchange, with a value relative to that of silver. At the beginning silver brought by the settlers was plentiful and not immediately useful, while goods were few and in demand, with the result that six ells of *vaðmál* went for one ounce (*eyrir*) of silver. The balance was altered in the course of the tenth century, reflecting both a rise in cloth production and a general increase in the price of silver, and in the latter part of our period the exchange rate rose to forty-eight ells to the ounce, dropping to thirty-six ells to the ounce about 1200. The Icelanders could feed and clothe themselves, but they lacked timber and did not produce enough corn for all the flour and malt they could use. Timber, meal and malt were consequently the chief imports, but iron, linen, fine cloth, pitch, wax, tinsmith's work, soapstone vessels, weapons and jewellery, could all be sure of a market. Some Icelanders maintained their own ships in the early period, but by the twelfth century the carrying was mostly done in Norwegian vessels. The custom was for merchants sailing in either direction to spend a winter abroad, disposing of goods and collecting payments and another cargo. Icelandic connections with west Norway and Trøndelag were always close, and with Orkney too, where corn and malt would often be easy to obtain, sometimes easier than in Norway. Many Icelanders spent some time abroad, usually in the service of great men.

The greatest seafaring venture of Icelanders in company was

an emigration to Greenland in 984 or 985. Two large areas were settled on the western side of the country where they found good grass and easy hunting; the southerly was called the Eastern, the northerly the Western Settlement. The Greenlanders later sailed to the North American mainland, but could make no permanent settlement there. They had access to timber in Labrador, but otherwise the imports they needed were the same as those of the Icelanders, and Norwegians apparently soon began to make the Greenland crossing direct without calling in Iceland. There was little commercial need for regular contact between Icelanders and Greenlanders (or between Icelanders and Faroese for that matter) and voyages between these settlements were sporadic, and sometimes accidental. In the later period Bergen became the centre at which all these Atlantic Norsemen met.

The people who came to Iceland were free men who were used to the organization of affairs at local meetings, where decisions that had binding legal force could be reached. The first generation of settlers could probably act as self-sufficient autocrats within their estates and among the people in 'client' relationship to them, but as numbers increased and isolation diminished, the need for common discussion and decision became obvious. It is said that Thorstein, son of Ingolf the first settler, established a *thing* at Kjalarnes, north of Reykjavík; and probably other local assemblies were similarly created. The settlers could not however all have had precisely the same experience of customary law and neither would their experience necessarily be appropriate in their changed circumstances. Steps were taken to create a national assembly and a national law in the 920s, on the initiative of the chieftains associated with the Kjalarnes *thing*. A man called Ulfljót was sent to Norway to learn the law on which the newly established Gulathing in Norway was based (p. 46) and adapt it to Icelandic circumstances. Meanwhile the decision was taken as to where the site of the *Alþingi*, the General Assembly, should be. They chose a splendid place on the level ground at the north end of Iceland's largest lake, Ölfusvatn. It lies on the borders of Ingolf's land and is reached without great difficulty from the most populous parts of the country, the south and southwest, middle north and middle west – men coming

56

from the east or northwest, however, could spend a fortnight or more on the journey.

Ulfljót's law provided for an open-air assembly, lasting for a fortnight each summer, which could be attended by all free men (cf. p. 86). Within the assembly there functioned a *lǫgrétta*, 'legislative court', and a *dómr*, 'judicial court'. The former was composed of thirty-six chieftains, each with the title of *goði* (pp. 132–5), under the chairmanship of the *lǫgsǫgumaðr*, 'lawspeaker', whom they elected (p. 92). He had a special place at the so-called *Lǫgberg*, 'law-rock'. Each *goði* took two advisers with him into this gathering but only he had the right to vote. Their meetings took place within a defined site, and people could watch and listen from outside. The 'legislative court' made and altered the law, granted exemptions and deliberated on matters of public importance. In the 'judicial court' cases were brought by individuals against individuals before a panel of thirty-six judges, each judge being the nominee of one *goði*.

About 965 the constitution was altered, and it is from its new form that we learn details of the local organization of law and assemblies. The country was divided into Quarters. In the East, South and West Quarters there were three fixed assembly places, each under the control of three *goðar*, making nine chieftains in each Quarter; but in the North Quarter there were four assemblies, each with three *goðar*, so that with this a national total of thirty-nine *goðar* instead of the old thirty-six was created. The balance of power at the Althing was maintained, however, by giving the title of *goði* to three new men from each of the East, South and West Quarters, so that there were now forty-eight *goðar* who sat in the legislative court. These nine new men do not, however, seem to have taken part in local assemblies as *goðar*. The local *things* met at a regular time in the spring, when matters of public interest could be discussed and where the local *goðar* nominated judges to hear cases. Quarter assemblies were also created, at which cases might be heard involving men from different *thing*-districts, but they seem to have been little used. This was because the division into Quarters was reflected in the establishment of four judicial courts at the Althing itself, and it seems as if people quickly came to regard these as the natural second stage after the local assemblies – it may be too

57

that the setting at the Althing was regarded as more neutral than at a Quarter assembly. The four courts at the Althing each had a panel of thirty-six judges nominated by the holders of the 'old and plenary chieftaincies', as the original offices (*goðorð*) came to be called. Verdicts at these courts had to be virtually unanimous and there was legal deadlock if they could not be reached. This difficulty was largely removed by the creation of the so-called Fifth Court, *c.* 1005, an effective court of last instance in which verdicts depended on a majority decision.

The Althing thus had legislative and judicial powers but there was no central executive authority. Decisions reached at the assemblies had to be enforced if necessary by the local *goðar*, aided by public opinion, but the effectiveness of such enforcement would obviously vary from case to case. In general a wronged man was expected to exact his own redress, and legal judgment in his favour did not lift responsibility from him but simply made it easier for him to put things right.

The absence of any central executive authority is in keeping with the love of independence which had brought influential settlers to the country in the first place. They seem to have been prepared to accept a system designed rather to preserve them from interference than to ensure their complete security – they had little doubt of their ability to look after themselves. In fact, in the early period economic forces and the constitution the Icelanders adopted worked together to ensure a reasonably stable and not grossly inequitable society. With the division of the first great estates there came into being a large number of well-to-do families, all of whom had very similar resources and lived in very similar style. Social balance was generally well maintained by constitutional authority spread among many chieftains, the involvement of most free householders in the assemblies and legal processes, lack of great inequality in the distribution of wealth, and the sameness of living conditions for all. Notable co-operation was also effected in ordinary communal affairs, fostered no doubt by the fact that all the settlers faced the same problems in coming to grips with life in a strange land. The great sheep round-up each autumn, for example, required organization on a district basis, and it was perhaps particularly because of this need – and related matters such as control of land boundaries and owners' marks – that the *hreppr* organization came into being throughout the country. The *hreppr* was a communal unit comprising at least twenty farmers of *þingfararkaup* status (cf. p. 86), established and regulated by laws of the Althing. As well as arranging local farming matters where joint action was unavoidable, the *hreppr* was responsible for mutual insurance and poor relief (p. 121). The organization itself is probably older than the Conversion, although these last duties were very likely laid on it after the country had become Christian.

It is true that some of the many feuds of the tenth and early eleventh centuries told of in the Sagas of Icelanders appear to reflect struggles for local domination, but even that domination seems to have largely been a matter of personal and family prestige rather than of control over sources of income that might permit the economic and political subordination of many by few. Power and influence lay in the number of one's followers, but the yeomen were not subject to the *goðar* – they were free parties to a contract with them, so that each was bound to the other by mutual agreement. Tyranny was hard to achieve, even on a limited scale. Neither was there any external military threat to enforce a concentration of command among the Icelanders, even though the king of Norway early showed an interest in the country's sovereignty. The nearest the Icelanders came to division on a national scale was over the issue of Christianity, a matter in which the Norwegian king also ominously showed what pressure he could bring to bear on these republicans. Some missionary attempts were made in the 980s, but it was the energetic King Ólaf Tryggvason who produced lasting results. A priest in his service, Thangbrand, spent one or two winters in Iceland, and among his converts were three important leaders from the southeast and south, Sídu-Hall Thorsteinsson, Hjalti Skeggjason of Þjórsárdalur (the valley where Stöng lies, pp. 156–7) and Gizur Teitsson of Mosfell. In 998 Thangbrand went back to Norway and gave a despondent report to the king, who then threatened to take reprisals against Icelanders in Norway. That same summer, however, Thangbrand's three important converts arrived in Norway and persuaded the king to let them make a fresh attempt to bring their countrymen to accept Christianity.

The following year they returned to Iceland, just in time to attend the Althing. There the situation became tense because after some argument the Christian and pagan parties declared themselves 'out of law' with each other: this refusal to recognize each others' rights was in effect a declaration of civil war. The Christians made Sídu-Hall their Lawspeaker, but he got the Lawspeaker already in office, Thorgeir, to agree to announce what the law of the whole land should be. Thorgeir was not baptized but Hall seems to have known what he was doing. According to Ari Thorgilsson, who wrote about a century after the event, Thorgeir the Lawspeaker made a telling speech in favour of the need for compromise, and spoke of the impossible situation that would arise if they had two kinds of law and religion. The preservation of legal order and peace was the main consideration he put forward, and it seems to have been well calculated to appeal to the comparatively large number of men who must have been more or less neutral in the religious question. After his speech everyone agreed that they would abide by his decision. He then formally announced the new law: everybody in the country should be Christian and people who were not baptized should now receive this sacrament; but people could sacrifice in secret if they wanted, and accepted customs to do with exposing newborn children and eating horse-meat should not be changed. There was no dissent, and the public pagan cults disappeared in Iceland. The indulgences allowed the heathen were abolished a few years later.

The conversion of the country by a legal enactment formulated by the heathen president of the General Assembly was a remarkable step. Respect for law and desire for peace were restraining factors, and there were evidently not enough zealous pagans to stand against even comparatively few ardent Christians when these were backed by the Norwegian king. Icelanders must have realized that active hostility to Christianity would soon make it hard for them to maintain relations with any part of Europe, and hardest with Norway, where their sentimental and commercial links were strongest. They must also have been aware that there was small evidence to suggest that they would suffer if they changed their faith – Norsemen in France and the British Isles, the Danes at home and now Norwegians had all

done so, and life went on much the same. When Ólaf Tryggvason
was killed that same summer, this Christian king was in battle
against Christian kings – his failure had nothing to do with his
religion.

The progress of Christianity in the years immediately following the Conversion must have been slow. It was a turbulent time
in some parts of the country, but the Lawspeaker Skapti Thórodds-
son (1004 – 30) worked strenuously for peace: he is credited
with the institution of the Fifth Court (cf. above) and he saw
that the law was put into effect even against mighty men. The
following century seems to have benefited from his efforts,
coupled it seems with the good influence of the growing Church.
A number of missionary bishops came to Iceland in the period
c. 1020 – 60, to preach, teach men for the priesthood and consecrate churches. In the 1050s the Icelanders were able to arrange
for the consecration of a native bishop, Ísleif, son of Gizur
Teitsson, one of the Christian leaders at the Conversion. Ísleif
had been educated at the school of the convent at Herford in
Westphalia – we do not know how this connection was established
– and when he came back as a priest, he looked after his estate,
married, and served his family church, until at the request of
the Althing he went abroad to seek consecration. He became
bishop in 1056 and died in 1080. He kept a school and educated
boys for the priesthood, including many chieftains' sons, but we
know little about his influence in general. He was 'never rich',
we are told, and he must have suffered from lack of resources for
entertainment of guests, alms, books, vestments, church equipment. The bishop's position was made secure, however, in the
episcopate of his son, Gizur, who was consecrated as Ísleif's successor in 1082 and died in 1118. Gizur gave his patrimonial
estate, Skálholt, to be the perpetual seat of Iceland's bishop; he
secured the adoption of a tithe law in 1096 or 1097; and he
organized the creation of a second diocese, covering the North
Quarter, which came into being when Jón Ǫgmundarson was
consecrated to Hólar in 1106. Notable advances thereafter were
the codification of a Church law in the years 1122 – 33, shortly
after the secular laws had been put into writing, and the opening
of the first monastery, a Benedictine house, in 1133 – this was to
be followed by other foundations, Benedictine and Augustinian,

in the course of the century, though the early Icelandic religious communities never became large.

Estates donated to churches were exempt from payment of tithe, and a landowner with a church naturally made his property over to the church to avoid taxation, while continuing to administer his land on the patron saint's behalf. The tithe that was paid by others was divided into four parts, one for the bishop, one for the poor, one for the church and one for the priest. Since all the churches started as the property of the men whose forebears had built them and since the churches were often served either by ordained members of the owner's family or by priests hired by them and possibly trained at their expense (cf. p. 95), it is evident that half the tithe became in fact a contribution to the estate on which the church stood. There is no doubt that diocesan and parochial services were in general greatly improved by the regular financial support given by the tithe, but the position of some yeomen and chieftains also underwent a decided improvement in that, while they were exempt from tithe payment themselves, they enjoyed a profitable residue from the tithe contributions of their neighbours. The people with money to spare seem to have begun to put it into land or mortgage loans, which increased their income and influence; at the same time there seems to have been an increasing demand for land, as a result of population growth and a surplus of workmen, and the number of people in debt or paying some kind of rent grew in consequence. The early stages of this development of a smallholding and labouring class cannot be clearly traced, but by about 1200 there was a sizeable number of poor people in Iceland. Political influence became concentrated in fewer hands at the same time, partly because economic dependence could lead to political dependence, partly because there were ruthless and ambitious individuals, able and willing to exploit the imbalance which new economic conditions encouraged. Icelanders were not unaffected in outlook by the endemic civil strife of twelfth-century Norway and the opposition between secular and clerical forces that finally came into the open there. Yet all such changes were gradual and Iceland was largely at peace throughout the twelfth century. It was an age when learning and poetry flourished, when Icelanders studied in France and England

and went on pilgrimage to Spain, Italy and the Holy Land, when the reputation of the Icelanders as custodians of the history of Scandinavia was justly established. The most important sign of the kind of strife to come was a struggle for power, with blood freely shed, in the mid-west in the 1160s and 1170s, from which the Sturlungs, the family of Hvamm-Sturla (died 1183), emerged as the dominant force in that part of the country.

Iceland's version of the general European and Scandinavian conflict between Church and State in the latter part of the twelfth century was to be found in disputes following the attempts of Bishop Thorlák Thorhallsson (1178 – 93) to remove churches and administration of property donated to churches from the hands of laymen. He met such opposition that he gave up the fight, and the issue did not again come into the open for nearly a century. Bishop Thorlák's chief opponent was Jón Loptsson of Oddi, head of a well-born family of traditional authority in the south, whose own social prestige was heightened by the fact – acknowledged in the Norwegian royal circle – that King Magnús Bareleg was his grandfather (through an illegitimate daughter). Jón can be said to epitomize the situation of the Icelandic chieftains, who since the Conversion had made the Church and its learning and literature a part of their lives, but had done so essentially on independent, native terms. Thus Jón was a *goði* and the most respected leader in the whole country; he was also a deacon and took his part in the mass. His grandfather, Sæmund Sigfússon, was the first man we know to write an account – in Latin – of the Norwegian kings; his uncle, Eyjolf, kept an important school at Oddi, where Bishop Thorlák had begun his education; while it was at Oddi in Jón's time that Snorri Sturluson, the most famous of medieval Icelandic authors, laid the foundations of his immense learning in mythology, poetry and history. Jón could see no justice in Bishop Thorlák's claim for clerical control over the churches which his ancestors had built and endowed, nor would he listen to the Bishop's admonitions to put away the concubines he kept beside his wife – one of his mistresses was Ragnheid, Bishop Thorlák's own sister.

Thorlák died in 1193 and only five years later veneration of him as a saint led to the translation of his relics and the institution of feast days in his honour. His successor was Páll, one of

Jón Loptsson's two sons by the saintly bishop's sister – an obvious victory for the native conservative interest, though there is no whisper of ironic or ribald comment about it in our sources. Indeed, Páll seems to have been a moderate and constructive churchman, but in his time and soon after his death in 1211 there flared up in several places the savage feuds, complicated by the actions and policies of the bishops in Iceland and the king in Norway, that characterized much of Iceland's thirteenth-century history. That time of trouble led to submission to the Norwegian Crown in 1262 – 4, when the Icelanders unwillingly sought that service which the Scandinavian kings had provided for their people now for centuries, the service of an umpire with loyal officers to see his decisions were kept. They did not like the bargain they made, and they came to like it less as time went on, but no real alternative was at hand.

Slaves

Rígsþula

The Icelandic poet of *Vǫluspá* about the year 1000 knew a myth which in some way made the god Heimdall the progenitor of men in their different classes: mankind is called his 'greater and lesser offspring'. This myth is figured for us in the poem known as *Rígsþula* preserved in an Icelandic manuscript written about 1350. The god is called Ríg and the poem describes how he comes to a house which he enters to find an aged man and woman sitting by the fire. These are named Ái and Edda, Great-grandfather and Great-grandmother. Ríg shares their meal, sits between them in their room and sleeps between them in their bed. He stays three nights. Nine months later Edda bears a son, swarthy-skinned; they sprinkle him with water and call him Thrall. From him are descended the race of slaves. Ríg comes to another house, where he finds a man and woman called Afi and Amma, Grandfather and Grandmother. The story repeats itself, and Amma bears a ruddy-complexioned son; he is called Karl and from him come the *karlakyn*, the race of free yeomen. A third house is visited by Ríg. Móðir and Faðir, Mother and Father, live there. Later Mother bears a son with fair hair, bright cheeks and sharp, cold eyes; he is called *Jarl*, Earl. In his youth Ríg gives him special instruction. The youngest of Earl's sons is one called Konr. To his name is added the adjective *ungr*, young. The resulting *Konr ungr* is to provide an etymology for the Norse word for king, *konungr*, and the top of the social scale is in sight. Unfortunately, the poem ends abruptly while telling of Konr ungr and his activities.

There is great difference of opinion about the age of the poem. Some scholars put it in the tenth century – and this seems more likely – and some in the twelfth or thirteenth. The information it contains about the appearance, dress and occupations of the different kinds of men is vivid and in many respects unique. It can safely be used as a pictorial source relevant to the period we are discussing, as long as it is not made the basis for statements involving comparative chronology.

Supply of slaves

The poet of *Rígspula* appears to regard the slaves as a fixed, distinctive class of remote native ancestry, but in the Viking Age and early medieval period there must have been much movement into and out of this class in Scandinavia. Human beings were probably the commonest commodity the Vikings dealt in, both as traders and raiders. Treasure in metals and jewels might easily be missed in an attack; provisions, tools and utensils might have relatively small value; but people were to be found everywhere and always had a value, ransom from kinsmen or cash from the slave-trader.

We hear the same story through the centuries. When Walcheren was ravaged in 837 'many women were led away captive', and in the ninth century many Irish prisoners were carried off 'over the broad green sea'. In speaking of the Danish depredations of 886 in France, Abbo said, 'They seize the country people, bind them and send them across the sea'; and 150 years later two Christian leaders from Norway could still attack the Kent and Essex coasts with twenty-five ships, take many prisoners and sell their spoil in Flanders. Bishop Cyfeiliog of Archenfield in Herefordshire was captured by Vikings in 917 and was ransomed by King Edward of Wessex for forty pounds in cash; it was Archbishop Ælfheah's refusal to allow ransom to be paid for him that led to his martyrdom in 1012. Redemption of Christian captives was an important object of pious endeavour and the existence of Christian slaves in the North was an incentive to Christian mission. St Rimbert in the ninth century is said to have sold even the altar vessels to buy back Christian prisoners; and on one occasion in Slesvig he gave his horse and its gear in exchange for a nun whom he met in a slave-gang there, fettered by the neck. Archbishop Unni (919 – 36) is said to have visited all the isles of the Danes, preaching the Gospel and comforting the Christians he found in captivity. Bishop Egino worked in Blekinge and Bornholm in the period 1060 – 72 and he urged his converts to use their goods to redeem captives 'who exist in great numbers in those parts'. These are the words of Adam of Bremen, the bishop's contemporary, who also tells us that Bishop Adalward received so great a gift of money from Harald the Hard-ruler of Norway (1047 – 66) that he straightway redeemed 300 captives. The laws of Gotland, Östergötland and west Norway have articles concerning the duties of kinsmen and marriage partners in redeeming captives in the hands of raiders.

Conversely, the Scandinavians did not spare each other and were themselves not spared by the Irish and Baltic peoples. Adam of Bremen says that the licensed pirates of Denmark preyed on their landsmen as well as on foreigners. It is no surprise to hear of a Swedish thrall in Iceland, a Norwegian bond-maid in Denmark. The Icelander Valgard celebrated in a poem a successful raid on Sjælland and Fyn made by a mixed force of Norwegians, Danes and Swedes under the leadership of men soon to be sole kings of their respective countries, Harald the Hard-ruler and Sven Estridsson. His stanzas include these lines: 'the Danes, those who still lived, fled away, but fair women were taken. Locked fetters held the women's bodies. Many women passed before you [he is addressing King Harald] to the ships; fetters bit greedily the bright-fleshed ones.' The writer of the Irish history called *The War of the Gaedhil with the Gaill* says that after the sack of Limerick in 967 every captive 'that, was fit for war was killed, and every one that was fit for a slave was enslaved'; and after the taking of Dublin in the year 1000 he exults that 'no son of a soldier or of an officer of the Gaedhil deigned to put his hand to a flail, or any other labour on earth; nor did a woman deign to put her hands to the grinding of a quern, or to knead a cake, or to wash her clothes, but had a foreign man or a foreign woman to work for them'. The Saxon Helmold, who did not like the Danes, tells with some pleasure that after Henry the Lion had unleashed some Wendish raiders against the Danish islands in 1169, it was reported that no less than 700 captives had been displayed for sale on one day in the market at Mecklenburg.

The numbers of the hereditary class of slaves which existed at least in some parts of Scandinavia before the Viking Age began were greatly swelled by captives in the following centuries.

With rare exceptions, there is no distinction made between native and foreign slaves in the laws, but we should remember that these are laws from the twelfth and thirteenth centuries when new supplies of slaves were rare. One exception is the Gulathing Law, which in certain cases prescribed a somewhat lighter punishment for a foreign thrall than for a homebred one, presumably because the former's ignorance was taken into account. Slaves produced slaves; but there is a difference between Denmark, Norway and Iceland on the one hand and Sweden on the other in the treatment of children born of one free and one servile parent. In the former the rule was that the child followed the mother; but in Sweden the rule was, 'Let the child always keep to the better side' (*gangi æ barn a bætre alf*) – unfortunately we cannot tell whether this was an ancient precept or a novelty. It was also possible for people to be reduced to slavery by voluntary submission or as part of a punishment for certain offences. Temporary servitude as a form of payment of debt was also known (cf. p. 120).

The slave's legal position

'Now a freeman and a slave commit a theft together, it is the freeman who is a thief and the slave shall not lose by it, for the man who steals with another man's slave steals by himself.'

'If a man's slave is killed, then no levelling oath (see p. 428) need be sworn for him any more than for any other cattle belonging to a man, should that be killed.'

'If a master kills his own slave, he is not liable before the law, unless he kills him during legally ordained festivals or in Lent, then the penalty is banishment.'

These three passages, from the laws of west Norway, Skåne and Iceland respectively, embody some of the extreme conclusions to which the nullity of a slave's legal existence as a person could lead. It has on the other hand been pointed out that the second enactment could only have been required because some people did not in fact regard their slaves merely as 'other cattle' (*annat fæ*). Conditions of life must generally have been such as to make it impossible to ignore the existence of this class within Scandinavian society, and the attitude towards the unfree was decisively, though gradually, altered by Christianity. The glimpses we have of the recognition accorded them reinforce the impression that slaves existed in large numbers, although we can, of course, have no idea of what proportion of the population they formed when their number was greatest. In Norway it was apparently thought that the labour of three slaves was necessary to run a farm stocking twelve cows and two horses. That was not a very big estate, and it may well be that stories which tell of ten, twelve and eighteen slaves in single ownership are right in that particular. On the other hand, it is obvious that slaves could not be allowed any great advantage of number, especially in isolated settlements. That slaves could and did revolt there is no doubt.

The slave then was a chattel. The ancient general rule was that if he were injured or killed, whether accidentally or intentionally, then it was only necessary to make good the loss or damage to the owner, 'restitution according to the value set on him naked', as it says in the Gulathing Law. The slave could own nothing, inherit nothing, leave nothing. His marriage had no standing and he had no authority as a parent. He could take no part in any business transaction or process of law. His only relation with society was through his master, and his master was consequently responsible for him and for any punishment to be inflicted on him. His legal non-existence naturally meant that he could not join in public assemblies or in armed levies.

Most of these intransigent rules are reflected in the laws, ensuring that in the end an owner's arbitrary will had paramount say in the treatment and disposal of a slave. At the same time, there are numerous modifications. In Iceland, for example, a man who killed another man's slave was liable to lesser outlawry (p. 383), while a slave was also awarded one-third of the compensation payable for a physical injury done to him (the other two-thirds went, of course, to his owner). It is evident that slaves elsewhere were also permitted to own, or at any rate to have the use of, goods and land. Thus, the Swedish laws make it clear that it was possible for homebred thralls to have *bo oc boscap*: a home and livestock; and slaves were permitted to do business at public markets and to make private transactions if the value involved was not more than one *ørtug* (1/3 ounce, 20 pence). According to the west Norwegian law, a thrall could make no business deal except for his knife, but some greater scope must have been permitted him for the same laws show that it was possible for a slave to make the money with which to buy freedom, doubtless chiefly by the sale of produce from a piece of land he was allowed to work for himself. In certain special cases the evidence of a slave might be accepted in a legal case: in Sweden, for example, in a dispute as to whether mother or child died first or as to whether a child was still-born or not. In Iceland the slave's legal existence was so far accepted as to make it possible for a free man to bring a case against him for verbal injury, with outlawry as a penalty. Norwegian laws allow the slave a place beside free men when it is a case of fighting off invaders; and the slave who kills such an enemy is to be rewarded with freedom.

In two law codes we find recognition of a thrall's right to take violent retribution for the seduction of his wife or daughter without himself incurring liability. In a text of the south Norwegian Borgarthing Law it says that if he finds a man in bed with her, 'he is to go to the brook and take a bucket full of water and throw it over them and bid his marriage-kinsman sleep well'. The contempt for the seducer here only matches the contempt for the thrall. But in Iceland we find this in the laws: 'A thrall has greater rights than a freeman in one matter. A thrall has the right to kill on account of his wife [*kona*] even though she is a bondmaid, but a freeman has not the right to kill on account of a bondmaid, even though she is his woman [*kona*]'. There is a joke here too, in the ambiguity of the word *kona*, but the slave's right to be treated like a man in this case is fully established, and this more liberal attitude is perhaps to be expected in Iceland where the circumstances of new colonization must often have tended to put the unfree more readily on a footing with the free. Christianity may also have helped to produce this attitude, for the great social novelty of Christianity was that theoretically it paid no attention to class status. Slaves had to be baptized and confirmed like other people, they had to be given Christian rites and Christian burial, their place in the afterworld did not depend on their position here and now. It is very likely that the number of slaves had generally been controlled, perhaps by killing the old and infirm and undoubtedly by exposing their infants to die, but now they must be kept alive and their children brought up. Unfree mothers had to be churched after they had given birth, unions between slaves should be sanctified as marriages. Progress was slow, as it often is when property is at stake. In thirteenth-century Sweden, for example, marriage between slaves was possible with the owner's sanction. In Sjælland, on the other hand, it was only between free and unfree partners that a marriage, contracted with the consent of the family and the owner, could be a legal and permanent union, while marriage between unfree partners apparently still had no legal status.

From slave to free man

It seems to have always been possible for a slave to be freed, by the gift of the owner, by the act of someone else ready to provide the purchase price, or by self-redemption. In the so-called Oldest Saga of St Ólaf, first written c. 1180 and extant in fragments from c. 1225, it says of Erling Skjalgsson, a great man in Rogaland in Norway at the beginning of the eleventh century, that apart from retainers (húskarlar) 'he also had many slaves and he made them toil until he gave them freedom. He appointed how much work they were to do to attain it; then he got himself others in their place. These men made a lot of money and often had much corn.' Whether this is precisely true of Erling or not, it would be surprising if some great landowners had not behaved in this sensible fashion. Christian views on the sanctity of human life and on charity as a duty, both of individuals and of the community, were also inimical to slavery. As an institution it was too well entrenched and too economically important for rapid changes to be brought about after the Conversion, except perhaps in Iceland, but we find some provisions in the laws which show what effect Christian efforts might have. Thus both in Trøndelag and west Norway it was for a time obligatory for the general assemblies of these provinces to free one slave each year as an act of piety. In the younger Swedish laws it is counted a crime to sell a slave who was a Christian – if sold he automatically became free. In Iceland the owner, or the owner's family, was legally bound to provide for a slave whom he had bought to work for him if the slave became incapable.

Freeing a slave involved legal formality and social ceremony. The requirements varied from country to country, with more old-fashioned practices in Norway and Sweden than in Denmark. In Jutland the laws seem to require only a public announcement of the freedom conferred, made either by the owner or his heir, but in the Skåne laws there is reference to the need for the freed man to be connected with a free family. This practice is also fully attested in the Swedish laws, a formality conveyed by the verb *ætlepas*, 'to be inducted into a family'. This was done at the assembly, and the freed man might then 'prosecute and defend on his own account and take part in oath-swearing'. In Iceland the ceremony involved presentation at the public assembly, and the freed man was connected not with a family but 'inducted into the law,' *løgleiddr*, made a member of the corporate legality of the community. This reflects the legal nullity of the slave's previous existence as well as Iceland's character as a new self-governing settlement of men of varied origins, where territorially confined and old-established families did not have the same significance in the structure of society as they did in mainland Scandinavia.

A special case was the freedom conferred on a child born of an unfree mother and a free father. It was common for wealthier men to have concubines, many of them slaves, and a free man might also have children by a slave-woman in someone else's ownership. It was the rule everywhere except in Sweden that a child took its mother's rank, but a father could liberate his unfree child, by purchase if the mother belonged to someone else (and her owner was legally obliged to sell) or by his own act if she belonged to him. If this were done while the child was still small (under three), other ceremonies connected with liberation were avoided. A *þýborinn sonr*, 'son born of slave-girl', then had freeman's rights with certain diminutions, but like other illegitimate children he had to go through a full ceremony of adoption into the family before he had equal rights of inheritance or received and paid a full share in atonement (cf. p. 5). It is in Norway, however, that we find the ritual connected with the change from unfree to free at its most elaborate. A slave might be given his freedom, or he might pay down at least half of his own redemption price, but he was not fully free until he had made his *frelsisǫl*, his 'freedom feast', or had bought himself clear, presumably by some larger payment than was otherwise required. (Norwegians undoubtedly maintained best the ancient pre-Christian notion that reverence could and should be paid to people and powers by feasting: the graver the occasion, the more you drank.) In the Gulathing Law it says this: 'Now if a freed slave wants to have control in business matters and marriage arrangements, then he must hold his freedom feast with ale made from at least three measures [of malt, probably about eight bushels] and invite his master in the presence of witnesses and give him the seat of honour and put six ounces [of silver] on scales on the first evening and offer him the "freedman's ounces".' The form laid down by the Frostathing Law is perhaps more archaic still: 'If a slave takes a tenancy or farms for himself, he must make his freedom feast, each man with ale brewed from three measures, and slaughter a wether – a freeborn man is to cut its head off – and his master is to take his neck-redemption off his neck.' We cannot tell whether the last expression describes a concrete act or is only figurative. It reminds us of the origin of the word for 'free' in Norse: *frials* from original *fríhals*, 'free-neck'.

The treatment of the man who is in process of gaining freedom or has just done so varied from society to society. The Jutland and Sjælland Laws give no indication that a freed slave is under any further obligation to his master. In Skåne a freed slave had a right to only half the atonement for death or injury payable for a free man; but his son was fully free. In a later code for Sjælland (some time after 1215) it is said expressly that a freed slave at once enjoys the right to full atonement, and this doubtless marks the very last stage of slavery in that province. In Sweden the freed slave remained in some respects subordinate to his 'patron', and his rights to atonement were also reduced. In Iceland the freed man still owed certain obligations to his previous master or to the man who gave him his freedom. The most important connection between them lay in the rights of inheritance which reverted to the patron if the slave died without an heir. If a freed slave made an attempt to circumvent this rule of inheritance, he could be enslaved again as a punishment for his ingratitude.

It is again in Norway that we find the closest regulation of this class of people. Until a freed man had made his freedom feast or found all the cash needed for his redemption, he remained closely bound to his old master. He was said to be *i þyrmslum,* which we may simply gloss as 'under obligation': *þyrmslir* are duties of respectfulness in attitude and behaviour, socially expected and legally required. A man in this situation had no freedom of movement, he owed his patron certain dues in labour for one year, he had to consult him on any business, including marriage, and he shared any atonement for injury with him. If he conspired against his former master or joined his enemies or took part in a law suit against him or 'spoke to him as if on an equal footing', then he forfeited his property and returned to servitude. On the other hand, the patron took responsibility for the freed slave's maintenance and gave him general support.

On the west coast of Norway these obligations remained in force through the freed slave's lifetime and through that of his son, as long as neither *frelsisøl* nor total redemption intervened; his grandson was fully free. In Trøndelag the subordination lasted four generations and it was only members of the fifth generation who were born free. That the class of freed men under obligation could be sizeable is shown by provisions in the old Christian Law of southeast Norway which assign a more distinguished burial place in the churchyard (nearer the church, that is) to *leysingjar,* the fully freed, and their children, than to *frjalsgjafar,* the freed men under obligation, and their children. The latter in their turn take precedence over thralls and over corpses washed ashore with their hair cut in Norwegian fashion.

The life of a slave

The usual name of a male slave is *þræll,* a word peculiar to Norse (though with a possible cognate in OHG *drigil,* 'servant') and of uncertain etymology; the English word 'thrall' is an Anglo-Saxon borrowing from Scandinavian. The common word for female slave is *ambátt,* found in all the Germanic languages in the sense of 'servant' but in them not necessarily implying servitude as it usually does in Norse. Other names for female slave, *þý, þerna,* are from the root meaning 'serve, give service';

a rarer word is *deigja,* related to English 'dough', which indicates occupation, the woman who does the baking.

Slavery is *ánauð,* 'oppression, bondage'; the corresponding adjective is *ánauðigr,* 'under compulsion, enslaved'; they are terms which may originally have especially referred to people taken as booty. The commonest generic term for the servile is the neuter word *man.* It is interpreted like Gothic *gaman,* 'fellow-man, companion', and apparently meant a member of a household or, collectively, the whole household group. In early Scandinavian it is hardly ever used of any but the unfree. Another collective word of similar import is *hjú, hjón,* which means man and wife together, the domestic group, the servants in general, but this term is used of both the free and the servile. This identification of the slave essentially as part or appendage of a whole group is in keeping with the denial of his existence as an individual human being. At the same time life within a domestic unit, especially in smaller households where segregation was hardly possible, could give a slave a loyal sense of identity with the group. Strain and antagonism between free and unfree did not necessarily exist. In Swedish laws the homebred slave is referred to as *fostre* (*fostra,* f.), 'the one fostered or reared in the home', and the name at once suggests the possibility of a closer, more personal relationship between master and slave.

The poet of *Rígspula* describes Thrall thus:

> *Forthwith he grew*
> *and well he throve,*
> *but rough were his hands*
> *with wrinkled skin,*
> *with knuckles knotty*
> *and fingers thick;*
> *his face was ugly,*
> *his back was humpy,*
> *his heels were long.*

He began to exert his strength:

> *with bast a-binding,*
> *loads a-making,*
> *he bore home faggots*
> *the livelong day.*

A girl comes along with scarred feet and sunburnt arms and a hooked nose. She says her name is Thír, which means bond-maid. She and Thrall make a match of it, live content and have children. The poet chooses contemptuous names for them, to do with their appearance, habits and work. Their sons are Brawler, Byre-man, Coarse, Cleg, Slave, Foul, Lump, Thickard, Laggard, Grey, Bent, Waller. Their daughters are She-lump, Clump, Thicklegs, Beaked-nose, Noisy, Slave-maid, Torrent-talker, Tatter-coat, Crane-shank.

From other texts we learn of the 'badges' of thraldom. Their typical dress was a simple garment of white (i.e. natural, un-dyed) wool; their hair was kept close cropped.

Slaves, of course, did the heaviest and nastiest work. The *Rígspula* poet says they built walls, dunged fields, herded pigs, tended goats, dug peat. Before the freed slave in Iceland was presented at the assembly, he was given the significant name of *grefleysingr,* 'one freed from digging'. Similarly in Norway a con-dition for freeing a 'son born of slave-girl' was that he had never put his hand 'to the rope or the spade' (*til reips né til reku*). The bondwomen saw to grinding corn in the handmill, milking, dairying, cooking, washing. They might come to enjoy par-ticular favour as concubines, nurses and personal maids. Some of the men could attain positions as overseers or bailiffs; there was the advantage that their energies and loyalties were not dis-tracted by family ties.

In general, however, slaves were despised and regarded as typically cowardly, unreliable, stupid and foul. They yielded to panic and were not in command of themselves as the proper man was; the proverb, 'Only a slave retaliates at once, the coward never', reflects this attitude towards them. Their ex-istence as a class was a constant reminder of the blessings of freedom and must have contributed to the pride of the indi-vidual free man, which in early Scandinavia was inordinately great. It was an offence to call a freeborn man a slave, and it was particularly shameful to die at the hands of a thrall. No sort of credit must be attached to the thrall for such an abomina-tion: 'If a slave kills a freeborn man, he must not be entitled his slayer' (or 'a thane-slayer' as the younger text has it) is an article in the Västergötland Law.

On the other hand, some slaves might have great ability and new captives could be of high breeding (Scandinavians decidedly favoured the postulate that heredity accounts for most things). The practice of concubinage in some circles meant that free and unfree could be closely related. Servitude was not a disability that could never be overcome. The Icelandic sagas contain stories both of slaves who behaved as they were expected to behave and of others who distinguished themselves for loyalty and bravery. Freedom was counted the greatest prize, and it might win the gratitude expressed in the inscription of the Hørning stone (North Jutland) set up about 1050: 'Toke the smith raised this stone in memory of Thorgisl Gudmundarson who gave him gold and liberty.'

The end of slavery

Christian antipathy, the falling-off of supplies, new means of livelihood offered by internal colonization and the growing fishing industry, stronger monarchical government, foreign influence, all contributed to bring slavery to an end in the northern countries. In Iceland, where new cheap slaves were hardest to come by and where the break-up of great estates early made slave-labour uneconomical, thralls disappeared in the course of the twelfth century. The retention of regulations in the laws presumably shows, however, that slavery remained theoretically possible; these were all omitted in the new codes introduced in Iceland in 1271 and 1281 under the authority of the Norwegian Crown. In Denmark the end of slave-keeping seems to have come in the first half of the thirteenth century, although we do not know the precise circumstances. It has been pointed out that the makers of the Jutish Law, promulgated in 1241, could not have regarded slavery as established either in theory or practice because they include only two references to slaves and these seem inadvertent. Similarly, the casual and indirect references in the Norwegian National Law of 1271 lead us to suppose that slaves no longer existed in Norway as a numerous class. An edict issued by King Magnus Eriksson of Sweden in 1335 says in one of its articles that 'everyone, male or female, in Västergötland and Värmland, born of Christian man or woman, may never be thrall or bondmaid or bear this name'. It is assumed that else-

77

where in Sweden slavery had already disappeared by this date.

Slavery was a recognized institution in the northern countries throughout the Viking Age and early medieval period. We may think of slaves as a class playing their part in the general economic advance made in the North in these centuries, and in particular it seems likely that the expansion of agricultural productivity depended on the existence of such a large, cheap labour-force as the thralls provided. We must also think of the greater leisure and comfort the existence of slaves conferred upon the individual free man. It is generally easier to be an expert craftsman, artist, poet, lawyer, merchant, warrior, if you do not need to dung your own fields and fetch your own fuel. The slaves made their indirect contribution to the achievement of the Vikings.

3

The Free

Dudo of St Quentin records an exchange between Rollo's Norsemen, who must have been mostly Danes, and an emissary of the Franks, himself a Dane, which is supposed to have gone like this. The emissary asks them who they are, whence they come, and what they intend. They reply: 'We are Danes, carried hither from Denmark. We come to conquer France.' He asks again, 'Under what name does your leader act ?' They reply: 'Under none, for we are all of equal authority.' Later, he asks: 'Will you bow the neck to Charles, king of France, and turn to his service and receive from him all possible favours ?' They reply: 'We shall never submit to anyone at all, nor ever cleave to any servitude, nor accept favours from anyone. That favour pleases us best which we win for ourselves with arms and toil of battles.'

This splendid piece does not mean that Dudo saw Rollo as at best the chairman of a large Viking committee, any more than the utterances here put into the invaders' mouths prevented their doing homage to Charles a year or two later. That too provided an exhilarating story in extension of the same theme. Rollo 'put his hands between the king's hands, which not his father nor his grandfather nor his great-grandfather had ever done to anybody'. He refused, however, to kiss the Emperor's foot, but when he was finally persuaded of the propriety of this act, he ordered one of his men to do so. Instead of grovelling to carry out the order, the man stooped and lifted the imperial foot to his mouth; and this naturally laid the Emperor flat on his back, to the great amusement of the company.

Fiction perhaps, but not empty fiction, either from the point of view of the house of Norman dukes for whom Dudo wrote, or from the point of view of the bulk of the Scandinavian population in early and medieval times. Freedom of speech and personal liberty were inherited from the Germanic tribal system by the greater part of the population of the Scandinavian countries. We may say that in the earlier part of our period this freedom was more of a fact and less of an ideal than was the case in the thirteenth century and later. Political and economic change brought this about, but even so, feudalizing forces never totally destroyed a sturdy range of recalcitrant and conservative farmers, whose views on the rights of men, especially when linked with the rights of the property-owner and rate-payer, build some sort of a bridge between the 'democracy' of the Viking Age and the 'democracy' of our own. There is no doubt that the exodus of Norwegians to Iceland and elsewhere in the period around A.D. 900 signified in part a refusal to accept a new régime which offered benefits only in exchange for a hitherto unknown degree of subordination.

The yeomen

The class of free farmers will be called here the 'yeoman' class. It is not an ideal term but much to be preferred to 'peasant', which is sometimes used. It must be stressed that the yeomen were the staple of society. This does not mean that they were completely undifferentiated, as we shall see, but it does mean that special groups made small minorities, and that many special groups, particularly military ones, had only temporary existence and chiefly comprised members of the yeoman class. We should remember too that a very large proportion of the population was immediately concerned with the maintenance of life by the production of food.

The poet of *Rígspula* describes how Ríg comes to the house of Afi and Amma, Grandfather and Grandmother. He found the man shaping a piece of wood for the warp-beam of a loom; his beard was trimmed, his hair cut across his forehead, his shirt was a tidy fit. The woman was spinning with a distaff, preparing to make cloth; she wore a headdress, a smock, and a neckerchief, with brooches of some kind at her shoulders. The result of Ríg's visit was the birth of a son whom they called Karl – a word implying what is quintessentially masculine, a man with proper manly attributes. The child was red and ruddy with alert eyes.

He began to grow
and turn out well,
he started to tame oxen
and make ards,
to raise buildings
and build barns,
to make carts
and drive the plough.

He marries a girl who wears an outer dress of goatskin, with keys at her girdle. A few of their sons have descriptive names: Broad, Bound-beard, Stout, Jutting-beard; but most are words used otherwise for the free, fighting man: *Halr* and *Seggr,* ancient names used chiefly in poetry; *Drengr* and *Þegn,* names that sometimes had a technical sense for men of particular status in the Viking Age and later, as we shall see below; *Hauldr,* a name used for a special and, in some areas, a superior class of yeomen in Norway. There are finally the occupational names Smith, meaning craftsman and builder, and *Búi* and *Bóndi,* denoting landowner, farmer. The names of Karl's daughters are similarly complimentary; they are words that occur, more or less frequently, as substitute-terms (p. 329) for 'woman' in poetic diction.

Bóndi, búandi is the universal term in early Scandinavia for the householder, the man who runs his own establishment – the word means the man who stays in one place and makes ready the land for use. Within the farming society free men might appear as hired hands, with or without rented smallholdings; as managers; as independent farmers on rented, leased, new or bought land; and as independent farmers on inherited 'family' land. It is to members of these last two groups that the name *bóndi* was especially applied; and members of the last group were further distinguished by appellation as *óðalsbóndi* and in Norway as *hauldr.* They formed the most important class in early Scandinavian society and will be treated first in the following.

Óðal is a name applied to land. It is to be equated with what the laws of Östergötland and Västergötland call 'family heritage' (*ætleve*), and as a technical term for inherited land bound by complex rules it has lived to the present day in Norway, Shetland and Orkney; the modern form in these colonies is 'udal'. The precise etymological sense of *óðal* is not clear, but since it is related to Frisian *edila*, 'great-grandfather', and to words represented in Norse by *aðal* 'kind, nature' and *eðli, øðli* 'nature, essence', it is possible that it indicates some degree of identification between the inherited land and the ancestors from whom the ownership was ultimately derived. It is in keeping with such a notion that although the *óðal*-estate is looked on as family land, it is in individual not corporate ownership. The owner holds it, as it were, of his forebears, not of his kin at large. This inherited land comes to be hedged about with various rules, but a basic condition was the one applied at the moment when an owner found it necessary to dispose of his estate. It had then to be offered to members of the family to which it belonged and in which the land descended. Only if they would not or could not buy it was he permitted to sell to someone else. If he neglected to offer it within the family and sold it all the same, compensation was due to his kinsmen; and in some cases the sale was not counted valid.

Men of different standing had different rights. As we saw above, the slave had none in principle and few in practice, while the freed man had limits set on his independence for a longer or shorter time, until he or his descendants joined the ranks of the traditionally free and acquired their common rights: the right to a voice in public affairs, the right to bear arms, the right to full benefit of law. But a free man's rights were also conditioned by his ancestry and wealth and to some extent – with the development of royal power – by his office. This differentiation produced a scale of money values to be paid or received as atonement in case of injury or death; and it also produced variation in a man's legal weight – what functions he could have in the judicial process and how far his oath was acceptable, alone or with others. In general, the fullest rights were only enjoyed by the freeholders on inherited land, the *óðal*-men, and when they were particularly wealthy and of proud origins, it is hard or impossible to separate them from the aristocracy we shall be talking about in the next chapter. A fundamental homogeneity of the yeoman class is indeed characteristic of early Scandinavian society, but there were gradations. It is simplest to consider them country by country.

Denmark

It is distinctive of Danish law that the atonement value set on free men is the same for everybody. This does not, however, mean that all men were necessarily content to receive the same sum, for on top of the fixed atonement an unspecified *gørsum* was required (WN *gersimi*, 'perfection; treasure, precious object'). Differences were certainly also recognized in atonement arranged by private treaty or arbitration outside the law. This extra amount was fixed by agreement and its size would obviously depend on the difference in effective power between the two parties. It has also been pointed out that men of distinguished families might often or generally be content only with vengeance, so that the undifferentiated atonement value stipulated in the laws may not have had much practical significance. On the other hand, it would not be wise to underestimate Danish passion for liberty and equality in the early middle ages.

The legal weight carried by free men did, however, vary from group to group and province to province in Denmark. Thus, it appears that originally it was only the landowning householder who could act as a juryman. In Skåne only landowners could swear oaths as compurgators in cases concerning property. In Jutland only landowners could stand surety on their own behalf if accused of theft; while in Sjælland any free man who had his own establishment, freeholder, tenant or farm-manager alike, could offer surety for himself. But throughout the country ordinary free men who were not heads of independent households were not acceptable instruments in the legal process: they could not generally act as compurgators or witnesses; and they needed the help of householders if they were themselves accused.

Sweden

In Sweden the position was generally similar. The yeoman head of a household was the full and free member of society. He and his kind had the same rights overall, the same value as an oath-swearer and witness, the same atonement in case of injury. The laws make distinctions for 'occupational' groups, lawmen, officials and bishops, but within the farming class only a single differentiation is legally noted. This finds expression in the Östergötland Law where the so-called *þukkabot* is spoken of.

This is a fixed payment made to a master if a man in his service is killed. An ordinary yeoman received three marks in such a case, but a man who kept 'his own marshall and cook and forty retainers at his own expense' received six marks. The distinction appears thus to have depended on wealth. Once the Viking Age was over, however, inheritance was the likeliest source of wealth, and such men who received a six-mark recompense can be classed among the aristocracy, even though they may not have had distinctive titles (but cf. p. 127). Grave finds and runic monuments show that large differences in wealth and esteem must have existed within the Swedish yeoman class. Rune stones, often magnificent and undoubtedly expensive monuments, could record possession of land on a grand scale. Frömund raised a stone at Malsta in Hälsingland and cut runes on it in memory of his father, Gylve the mighty: 'Gylve acquired this district and also three estates further north; he also acquired Lönnåker and afterwards Färsjö.' The sons of Finnvid owned a great farm at Älgesta in Husby-Ärlinghundra parish in Uppland; but on a rock one of them had inscribed at Nora 20 miles south of Älgesta, he can also say: 'This farm is their udal and family inheritance, the sons of Finnvid at Älgesta.' Inscriptions can also record a series of ancestors and give expression to that quickening sense of the indivisibility of the family succession and ownership of the land which the word óðal may itself originally contain. Gylve the mighty is described by his son Frömund as son of Bräse, son of Line, son of Ön, son of Ofeg, son of Thore. A stone at Sandsjö in Småland had this inscription: 'Arnvard had this stone raised in memory of Hägge, his father, and after Hära, his father, and Karl, his father, and Hära, his father, and Thegn, his father, and in memory of these five forefathers.'

Norway

In Norway we find noteworthy variations between the different provinces. The southeast laws specify only a single class of yeomen between the freed slaves on the one hand and the high officials called 'landed men' on the other. The name for the free farmer is *hauldr* (cf. its occurrence in *Rígspula*, p. 81). In the laws that applied in the west-coast regions we find that the yeoman class is split into two groups. There is the 'lineage-born house-

holder' (ár- or ætt-borinn bóndi), the freeborn head of an independent establishment not on inherited land, and the hauldr, who is
the óðalsbóndi, the free farmer on inalienable ancestral land. The
distinction between these two is made explicit in the scale of
atonement values: the hauldr is worth double the ordinary freeborn farmer. In the Trøndelag laws we find that the yeoman
class is divided into three. First is the rekspegn, the free man not
a householder, available for employment by others. Second is
árborinn maðr, the 'lineage-born man', and third the hauldr,
just as on the west coast. Here, however, the hauldr has an atonement value half as much again as that of the 'lineage-born man',
while a householder of this rank in turn took one-third as much
as the rekspegn. Apart from atonement value, the landowning
class of farmer had various privileges beyond those of other free
men: their oath was set more store by; the part of the churchyard where they were buried was closer to the church; they had
greater freedom to dispose of their goods in favour of 'sons born
of slave girls'; their wives could make independent bargains to a
greater value; they had a claim to larger shares in stranded
whales.

It is thought that the undivided class of free men found in
southeast Norway represents the ancient social norm, just as in
Denmark and Sweden. On the other hand, the west-coast
differentiation, whatever its cause, seems to go back at least
to the early Viking Age, for holdas occurs as the name of a superior
class among the Norsemen in England from the very beginning
of the tenth century. From Anglo-Saxon laws we further learn
that their atonement value is half that of an ealdorman (the
Anglo-Saxon equivalent of the Norse earl) but twice that of the
ordinary freeborn man. Whether this distinction depended on
inherited land-ownership or was adopted by members of an
invading host on the model of such a distinction is not clear.

Iceland

The distinction between hauldr and ordinary bóndi was not
exported to Iceland, although it was settled at about the time
when holdas crop up in England, and settled chiefly from those
parts of Norway where the difference obtained. The Icelanders
recognised only one class of free man, although a sense of noble

or superior family origin remained fully alive among them. There was, of course, to begin with no inherited land in the country, and later on the vast majority of the farmers were naturally all in the same position as far as inherited ownership rights went. The political outlook of the settlers was probably also inimical to the development of such overt social distinctions, just as the constitutional system they created was such as to prevent the leading families ever becoming a real aristocracy (cf. p. 58). It is interesting to note that Icelanders in Norway were granted the rights of *hauldar*. This privilege appears to date from the reign of St Ólaf (1016 – 30), however, and in that case it was most probably an advantage offered in furtherance of the king's aims to tie Iceland closer to Norway and to support the new Christian religion of the country. If an Icelander stayed in Norway for more than three years, his status lapsed to that of the ordinary freeborn man.

In terms of atonement for injury and death the Icelandic laws make no distinction of person. On the other hand, differences were certainly recognized in atonement arranged by private treaty or arbitration outside the law. But a most important distinction was made on economic grounds when it came to the exercise of the political rights of the free farmers. It was only the men whose possessions put them in the class of those liable to pay 'assembly attendance dues' (*þingfararkaup*) who had judicial functions at the assembly and who made up the members of the local administrative units called *hreppr* (p. 59). A farmer whose property did not amount to the value of a cow (or the equivalent in the shape of a boat or net) for each of his dependents and serving folk, in addition to necessary household equipment and a draught animal (ox or horse), was not obliged to attend the assembly or contribute to the expenses of those who did. Such men were not excluded from the assemblies, any more than the free men who were not householders at all, but they were not proper *thing*-men and were generally unable to serve as witnesses, jurymen or judges. There seems no doubt that the economic bar here imposed was intended to make life easier for the poorer man, a step taken all the more readily when bankruptcy only meant the sharing out of a man's dependents among his kinsfolk and, if they were lacking, among his neighbours. This is further evident from the special provision for the single-handed house-holder: for him to join the ranks of those with full rights at the assemblies, he had to have double the property just specified as the minimum. A large number of farmers remained above the dividing line, however, and there must have been some constant movement into and out of the major class with the fluctuation of individual fortunes and of general economic conditions in different parts of the country.

Managers and tenants

The general name for a farm-manager in Old Scandinavian is *bryti*, 'divider', probably so called because he was the one who doled out the food allotted to each member of the household (cf. the verb *brytja*, 'to cut up a carcase'). In early times the *bryti* seems generally to have been a slave – this is sometimes assumed in the Danish laws, for example, while as a loan-word in Finnish (*ruttio, ruttia*) the word has the meaning both of 'slave' and 'overseer' – but it could also be or become a free man's occupation. A special type of manager called *fælæghsbryti* ('partner-manager') is known in Denmark. In this case he ran a farm on someone else's land but also owned a share in the stock and equipment and took a share in the profit and loss. This type of partnership made for legal complication, which is doubtless why it figures more than the ordinary *bryti* system in the Danish laws. Employment of a manager did not necessarily imply an absentee landlord or particular wealth: someone to run a farm was often necessary where the owner was a woman or a minor or incapable for other reasons. On the *bryti* as a type of royal servant, see p. 124 below.

Some system of renting land must have been in existence at the outset of the Viking Age. In Denmark and Sweden the tenant farmer is called *landbo*, 'dweller on land (belonging to someone else)'. In Norway the same word is used alongside *leiglendingr* ('man of rented land'); in Iceland they used *landseti* ('men settled on another's land') as well as *leiglendingr*. A tenant normally paid an annual rent in kind or in cash.

The proportion of tenant farms cannot, of course, be calculated, but from the Danish provincial laws it appears that in the twelfth century the majority of the farmers in Jutland and Skåne owned their own land, while in Sjælland ownership was concentrated in fewer hands and tenancies were consequently commoner. The number of tenant farms increased greatly in the early medieval period, partly because of new cultivation of privately-owned property (it is estimated that about 2000 new settlements came into being in Denmark in the period *c.* 1000 – 1200, and they were obviously not all on no-man's land), partly because of the increase of royal holdings, and partly because of the donation of farmland to churches and monasteries. In some parts of Norway, where the area of cultivable land was severely limited, the system of inheritance brought about a constant diminution in the size of the share of land that fell to the lot of an individual heir, so much so that an ordinary family could not be maintained on one inherited portion. (Such 'land-hunger' has been counted one of the causes of the exodus from Norway in the Viking Age.) Widespread mortgaging of land resulted and it passed to the wealthy when debts could not be met. It is estimated that by 1350 only two-fifths of the land in Norway was in the ownership of the yeoman class.

A verse in the *Hávamál* (pp. 343–4) is eloquent in praise of independence, however poor:

> *Better to have a homestead,*
> *though it may be little –*
> *everyone is a champion in his own home;*
> *he may own only two goats*
> *and a rope-raftered house –*
> *but that is better than begging.*

This could doubtless refer to any age, but the development of a smallholder or cotter class was quickened by the same forces as produced the large increase in the number of tenancies by the end of the thirteenth century. It is probable that many of the slaves freed in the course of the eleventh and twelfth centuries lived on smallholdings within the bounds of a main farm, and paid rent either in kind or in labour for its use. Free men with families but no capital might do the same. A Danish term for such a man is *garthsæta* ('a man settled on – or within – the farm's boundaries'). In Swedish we find the term *hussætumaþr* and in

Icelandic *búðsetumaðr,* both of which mean a 'man settled in a dwelling on somebody else's property'; in the latter case (and perhaps in the former) the first element, *búð,* indicates the inferiority of the house he lived in, a hut or shed. As a class these people, like smallholders everywhere, were in a particularly precarious economic position; and it was only in quite exceptional times – as after the great plagues later in the middle ages – that they might find themselves in a strong bargaining position as opposed to the free farmers and landowners. But they could help themselves on by trade and good alliances.

Farmworkers and craftsmen

Individual free men would normally find employment on the family farm, but natural excess of labour in some places and dearth in others meant also that some free men would be available as hired workers. These men seem to be the *rekspegnar* of the Trøndelag laws, while Icelandic terms are *einhleypingar,* 'lone-runners', unattached men, and *lausamenn,* 'men not tied', voluntarily in service. When in employment they were called, in Norway and Iceland, *griðmenn,* 'home-men', in Denmark *innæsmæn,* 'inside-men', both names signifying their place within a household and making clear their rights and their obligations as temporary members of the established family unit. Another general term for men in service is *húskarlar,* 'house-carls', but this came to mean particularly 'retainers', of a lord or leader, and this kind of group is discussed below (pp. 100–5). Advancing specialization in arts and crafts, which went with general improvement in material standards and with the growth of towns and trade, also gave occupational opportunities to free men.

Farm work required active men as herdsmen and shepherds, especially when highland pasturing was part of the system. Others would be needed for hunting and fishing, where conditions were favourable, and for timber-felling and peat-cutting where slave labour was not available. Otherwise there was little specialization on the farm, either in outside work or in the tasks to be done inside, the preparation of foodstuffs for immediate or long-term consumption, spinning, weaving, horn- and bone-working, and the other occupations described in Chapter 5. Every farmer would be his own woodworker and blacksmith to some extent, but some men must soon have found it possible to make a living as specialists in house-building, boat-building, and the manufacture of weapons and jewellery, at least in more populous districts. The rune-stone carvers of Sweden and the poets of Iceland were also craftsmen, the former taking payment for work commissioned from him, the latter composing poems in praise of great men as a speculative but often profitable undertaking. But these men could all run a farm and sail a boat and were perfectly capable of 'holding sword or sickle and wielding up a weapon', to adapt a phrase from the Gotland Law.

PART-TIME PROFESSIONS

The law

It was important that a large proportion of the free men should have a good knowledge of the laws. Indeed, where social order depended to a great extent on agreement among the yeomen and the execution of judgment lay in the yeomen's own hands, such widespread legal knowledge was essential for peace. Learning the law by heart, discussing it, practising ceremony and rehearsing formulas must have been a large element in a boy's education, an obligation as well as a pastime. The Småland Law begins: 'Now men must go to the *thing* and hear our recital of the law; those who are present must listen and tell it to those who stay at home.' In the thirteenth-century *Gunnlaugs saga* a scene is described which is probably not untypical. Gunnlaug as a boy stayed at the home of the chieftain Thorstein and learnt law from him. One day he said, 'There is one point of law which you have not taught me: how to betroth a wife.' 'That is a small matter,' said Thorstein and taught him how to do it. Then to prove he had grasped it, Gunnlaug went through a mock-ceremony in which he 'appointed his witnesses' and became betrothed to Helga, Thorstein's daughter.

It was inevitable that some men would stand out as lawyers because of their capacious memories and casuistical insights, and their teaching and advice would be much sought after. It was common for a principal in a case to conduct his own prosecution or defence, but anyone who had doubts about his own ability

could transfer his responsibilities to someone else. The term
lǫgmenn, 'lawmen', was used of such lawyers, and it was also used
as an official title for the most skilful and best connected of them
who were called on to play important presidential or consult-
ative parts at the local, provincial or national assemblies. From
Denmark we have no record of lawmen who functioned at meetings, but there must have been Danes who preserved, created
and transmitted the laws. The Danelaw boroughs in England
had groups of lawmen who formed a kind of judicial committee,
and this system may be compared with that in Norway, where
the yeomen at their assemblies elected a similar committee of
lawmen. They would presumably consider and formulate new
legislation. In the west-coast laws of Norway, for example, there
is reference to 'that statute [concerning the levy] which has
hitherto applied and which Atli announced before the men of
the Guli assembly'. Atli must have been the chief lawman of the
legal province, possibly the same man as an Atli who was active
as leader of the yeomen in the years about 1040. Such a man
would be responsible for reciting the law and giving decisions on
points of law. These were the functions of the elected lawman
in the Swedish provinces; in addition he acted as the yeomen's
representative in dealings with king and bishop, and much seems
to have been made of his independent dignity. In the Västergötland Law it is said emphatically that the lawman must be a
yeoman's son. There is an interesting thirteenth-century list
which enumerates nineteen lawmen for this province, starting
in heathen times, probably about A.D. 1000. We see that the
office often passed from father to son, and we get some notion
of the influence for good or bad of the lawmen from the comments added to their names.

The fifth was Tubbe the marshall. He was lawman for a short
time and harsh and unjust what time he was . . . the eleventh
was Karle . . . he enquired carefully after those men who
broke the laws in our land. He punished each as he deserved,
and freed his land from evil men and monstrous deeds . . .

The Faroese thing was apparently presided over by a lǫgsǫgumaðr,
'lawspeaker', and it may be that this title was at one time in

general use in mainland Scandinavia. The reason for thinking this possible is that in Sweden, although the office-bearer was called a lawman, the name of the district in which the law was in force was *lagsagha*, 'law-saying', a name also found in parts of Norway in the same sense. It will be seen that this is the first element in the title we translate as 'lawspeaker'.

We know most about the Icelandic system. Here the National Assembly, *alþingi*, was presided over by a salaried lawspeaker, elected by the chieftains. He sat for three years in the first instance, and at each assembly in those three years he recited one-third of the laws, repeating each year that section which dealt with the conduct of affairs at the National Assembly itself. If his knowledge failed him, he had to refresh his memory in consultation with five men or more who were learned in the law (it is these who in Icelandic are called 'lawmen'). Litigation is an important theme in many of the Sagas of Icelanders; and an extraordinarily vivid reconstruction of a battle of legal wits, with expert pitted against expert, is found in the late thirteenth-century *Njáls saga*, when the author describes the to-and-fro of the great case at the Althing after the burning of Njál.

Medicine

Like the practice of law the practice of medicine could also give people a profitable and respected position in Norse society, just as in ours. The story goes that when Magnús the Good, king of Norway and Denmark, won his great victory over the Wends on Lyrskov Moor in 1043, St Ólaf, his father, came to him in a vision and told him to choose twelve men of the best descent to bandage men's wounds: 'and he said that he would obtain it from God that the power of healing would be maintained in the family of each of them'. One of them was an Icelander, Atli, and his great-grandson, Hrafn Sveinbjarnarson (died 1213), was Iceland's most famous physician of early times, well abreast of his age, it seems, in the methods he used. Our knowledge of sickness and its treatment otherwise comes chiefly from accounts of cures believed to have been effected through a saint's intercession, but no complete study of this material has so far been made. The laws also show a marked interest in wounds because the compensation payable was carefully graduated according to the nature and size of the injury, which limb was lost, and the degree of disfigurement by scar or discolouring suffered as a result. Payment to a physician is frequently an obligatory addition to the atonement. In the laws of Västergötland and Östergötland, for example, a 'full wound' is counted one that needs 'ointment and bandage, linen and doctor's fee'; and a section in the Frostathing Law reads like this:

> Now bone-payment is payable wherever a bone comes loose from a wound, though it be very small, as long as it rattles [when shaken] in a shield, then one *eyrir* must be forthcoming. One *eyrir* is to be paid for each bone up to six, but if so big a bone is removed that six holes can be bored in it, then six *aurar* are to be paid, but bone-payment is never bigger than six *aurar*. But if a wound needs cauterizing, then the 'lip-twisting' *eyrir* is payable, and the same is payable every time cauterizing is necessary. But as physician's fee one *eyrir* is to be paid every month, and two-months' worth of flour and two of butter. He who did the wounding must pay.

Hrafn Sveinbjarnarson and his forebears belonged to Christian times when men seem to have been the chief physicians, but in heathen times medical treatment was more the province of women. Lancing, cleaning wounds, anointing, bandaging, bone-setting, the concoction of herbal drinks, and midwifery (always as far as possible reserved for women) were the chief practical elements in the work, but these things were not always done coldly or irreverently – divine aid and supernatural forces, free in the air or immanent in earth and its stones and plants, had also to be pressed into service by spoken charm, acted ritual or incised rune. One stanza in the poem called *Sigrdrífumál* prays for 'hands of healing', while another says: 'Branch-runes you must know if you are to be a healer and discerning about wounds; they must be cut in the bark and on the leaf of the tree whose boughs bend to the east.' Ordinary preventive medicine lay largely in observing the right order, using the right formula, or wearing a serviceable amulet. Objects such as the last must often have been acquired from someone believed to be especially capable of lending them magic power. Practices of this kind did not disappear with Christianity, but were rather converted to Christian use. Particular stones sanctified by Christian blessing were believed to ease difficult childbirth, for example, and when a man's flesh was cauterized, it was natural for the burns to be set in the shape of crosses. Specialized and secret lore was also required for soothsaying and other forms of wizardry (cf. p. 404), and people who had such skills were doubtless often credited with influence over health as well.

Priests, pagan and Christian

These were private practitioners, as it were, in their dealings with the supernatural, but there were other people who had the official and public function of maintaining harmonious relations with divine powers. These were the priests and priestesses who performed set tasks at cult-celebrations; what little we know of pagan ritual activity is described in Chapter 12. In heathen times priestly function seems generally to have gone with a man's position as head of a community or household. This could hardly have been true of priestesses, however, but we know so little about these in pagan Scandinavia that we cannot decide what their position in society may have been. Women doubtless played a large part in domestic cults, but since in this they were probably only fulfilling the duties of senior members of households everywhere, they would not be given any special name.

We need not think that the men or women who acted as mediators between human existence and divine powers necessarily enjoyed particular personal respect for that reason. If they did their job properly, decent seasons and general prosperity should follow as a matter of course. Disaster, conversely, was the result of their neglect or error. This at any rate would be consonant with the treatment we know was meted out to priests of the Christian faith in early Scandinavia. Pope Gregory VII was moved to write to King Harald 'Hone' of Denmark in 1080, forbidding among other things the Danish practice reported to him – 'that you transfer the blame to the priests for the intemperate nature of the seasons, for pestilences of the air, and all ills of the flesh'. A good number of the priests, even on into the twelfth century, were foreigners, and such individuals who had neither property nor family in a district, and probably an

inferior command of the native language, did not count for
much. But it was especially the fact that churches were mostly
in private ownership that gave the priests so lowly a status.
Private ownership was the rule in Iceland and certainly existed
in very large measure in Norway, Denmark and Sweden, although
older patterns of lay ownership, individual or communal, had
been largely erased in these countries by the time our chief
sources came into being, towards the end of the twelfth century
and later. It is in Iceland that we find the most old-fashioned and
oppressive rules for the priest without private means who was
trained or hired for service at a particular church. The owner
of the church made an agreement with a young man, in person
if the latter was sixteen years old or more, with his guardian if
he was younger. The youth entered his household, was brought
up by him, and taught, 'beaten to the book', as it was said; and
if he could not stand it, he was put to other work and kept under
tight discipline this side injury or maiming. If a priest ran away,
it was as criminal to associate with him as with an outlaw; but
he could release himself from his situation by teaching some
other person to fulfil his priestly duties to the bishop's satisfaction. Things improved greatly with parochial organization and
a secured income for church and clergy from tithes and donations, and by about 1200 priests were usually accepted as full
members of Scandinavian communities, but even then it was
not entirely a matter of course. In the Gulathing Law it says
that the bishop is to appoint priests to churches, and if a priest
neglects his duty he is to pay a fine to the bishop, 'for we [the
yeomen] have abolished the practice of disciplining them with
blows, because we give them our daughters and sisters in marriage or let our own sons be educated as clergymen'. Here a
situation similar to that in Iceland does not seem very remote.
Saxo, speaking of the farmers of Skåne in revolt against payment of tithes and taxes in the late twelfth century, says that
they told the priests that it was they and not the archbishop
who maintained them, and threatened their life and their goods
if they did not do as they were told. On the other hand he adds
that, although some of the priests were foreigners, most were of
the same origin as the yeomen themselves, and the farmers did
not want to proceed too harshly against them. In Gotland it can

be seen that no automatic social status was conferred by priest-hood, for the laws there say that 'a priest, priest's wife and a priest's child educated for holy orders are on the same footing as a yeoman's child in respect of compensation; but a priest's child who is not educated takes rank according to that of his mother's family'.

Of course, not all priests were in the position of church-tied menials. Priests of good family or some independent means could make acceptable contracts of service and receive payment in accordance with terms laid down in the laws. The general standard of learning was doubtless not very high. We are told that Bishop Thorlák in Iceland (died 1193) feared the Ember Days because men then came to him for ordination who were badly trained and perhaps unsuitable in other ways, but he did not like to deny them because of their poverty and the recom-mendations they brought with them. Saxo tells a story of one cleric in King Sven Estridsson's following, a Norwegian eloquent in his own tongue but so unfamiliar with Latin that when his colleagues tampered with the text of the prayer for the king's majesty by changing *Dei famulus,* 'God's servant', into *Dei mulus,* 'God's mule', he blithely read it out without noticing, although the king did. On the other hand, we also know of many out-standing zealots and statesmen, scholars and latinists among Scandinavian churchmen of the twelfth century, some of humble origin, others of good or noble family. And we should not forget the important fact that the Church, in the Nordic countries as elsewhere, could offer a career to an intelligent boy, no matter his class, and almost boundless opportunities for advancement. In otherwise settled times it was especially the Church which made possible a kind of social mobility in the medieval world.

It will have been noted that celibacy among priests was not enforced in the early period in mainland Scandinavia and Ice-land – indeed, it continued to present problems long afterwards. Priests in general lived lives that were little different from lay-men. They were supposed to be clean shaven and to see to their tonsure, but they normally wore no special clothes – even Arch-bishop Asser of Lund appeared 'as rustic as a Wend' to a Saxon cleric who visited him in 1127. The Icelandic laws say priests should not wear parti-coloured clothes if the bishop forbade them. Men in orders might even carry weapons. If priests were independent, they would have to run their farms; and if they were in domestic service, they could be sent to gather sheep or on any other task – they might even be found on a raid in search of vengeance.

Gradually, as the whole Church in the North achieved economic independence, with exemption from taxation and wide legal immunities, so the man in holy orders gained in social prestige. That was finally marked in Norway and Iceland by the title of 'sir' prefixed to his name, probably on the English model – but this belongs to the thirteenth century and later.

Special Groups of Free Men

Two kinds of guilds

The Viking Age was an age of movement, especially by sea and river. Men of the North were stirred from their homes to take part in trade and piracy, soldiering and settlement abroad. A healthy, intelligent man might move from one to another of these main occupations without difficulty, but it was also natural that groups that worked predominantly as traders or predominantly as warriors should be formed, many of them only active in a corporate way on a seasonal basis. Such associations were or could be international and were not tied to land-ownership; they were divisive of family links.

Sharing capital in farming, ship-owning or trading ventures is expressed by the common Norse term *félag,* 'money-combining, partnership'; and a man who joins in such sharing is a *félagi,* whence English 'fellow'. A similar idea is probably to be found in the two names used of seemingly different groups of Norse origin in Russia, *Kylfingar* and *Væringjar* (Greek κούλπιγγοι, βάραγγοι, Russian *kolbjagi, varjagi*). They seem to go back at least to the tenth century. The best – but by no means undisputed – explanation of them so far offered connects them with the idea of associations of merchants whose members were pledged to mutual support. *Kylfingr* is derived from *kolfr,* 'stick', a token, made of wood, recognizable within the group (cf. the use of 'club' in English, a loan-word from Scandinavian, and also medieval WN *hjúkólfr* 'party, house-party'). *Væringjar*, pl., is derived from the root found in *Vár*, the name of a goddess, and *várar*, pl., 'oaths, pledges', and is consequently thought to mean a group of men sworn to aid and defend each other. This word is best known today because it became the name of an *élite* corps of mercenary soldiers in the service of the Byzantine emperors, the Varangian Guard, principally composed of Norsemen in the century from about 980 to 1080, thereafter chiefly of Englishmen and others.

The word 'guild' also came early into use to signify an association of merchants. In the first half of the eleventh century two guilds are attested by inscriptions on rune stones in Östergötland, situated not in but near settlements that became important market-towns. These guilds were probably made up of yeomen who were traders as well as farmers, the sort of people who probably account for the existence of Kaupang in southeast Norway (cf. pp. 213–4). Later in the eleventh century two rune stones were carved in Sigtuna (cf. p. 209), both of which contain references to a guild of Frisians there. The men commemorated, however, were evidently Swedes, and this perhaps indicates that what had started as a corporation of traders from Frisia had turned into a kind of 'chamber of commerce' with largely settled, local members; and this may also give us a clue to the way in which foreign models, in this sphere and others, were adapted for native purposes. Such guilds seem to have been widely organized in trading centres – we recall that King Niels of Denmark was killed by members of the merchant-guild in Slesvig in 1134 – and it is likely that they were influential in evolving forms of town-government and in creating and applying the kind of law called *Bjarkeyjarréttr* (almost certainly named after the famous Birka, pp. 205–10). This term was originally used in the North chiefly of codes for market places visited by foreign shipping, later as a general name for municipal regulations.

These guilds were merchant fraternities, and it is not until the thirteenth and fourteenth centuries that we hear of town-guilds of tradesmen and craftsmen. We do know, however, of guilds with a more general membership, not specifically merchants, that were in existence, at least in west Scandinavia, by about 1100. These were of a markedly religious character under the patronage of a special saint or saints, friendly societies organized among people of a certain social standing, respectable townsmen or substantial farmers. There is reference to a St Ólaf's guild in western Iceland early in the twelfth century; their meeting in the summer of 1119 was combined with a wedding-feast and lasted a week. A fragmentary set of regulations is extant in a twelfth-century manuscript relating to a guild in Nidaros (Trondheim), and another set, of about equal age in origin, exists for a countryside guild in Sunnhordland. Other Norwegian sources, and information about Danish and Swedish guilds, belong to the thirteenth century and later, but there is no reason to think that the early regulations are not representative.

We understand from them that it was the communal feast that distinguished the guild from other associations of people. The overt religious elements included specific prayers for prosperity and peace, but the function of the whole celebration was to promote these same objects and in this and in its atmosphere of communal fellowship it can hardly have differed much from cult-feasts of pagan times (cf. p. 402). All members had to contribute their share in provisions and, most important, in malt for the brewing. Members were both men and women, and they could bring their children with them; a boy inherited his father's place and a girl her mother's. An individual could present himself for election but could only join if the vote was unanimously in his favour. Weapons, quarrelling, abuse and wagers were banned. No member could refuse another the loan of equipment or utensils. The members were guild-brothers and -sisters, and the guild performed family functions outside the guild-meetings. Measures of mutual insurance are considered below (pp. 121–2), but some things may be noted here. A member could call up as many of his guildsmen as he liked to go with him on any mission within the *fylke,* presumably whenever he needed to make a show of strength; he had to pay their expenses. All members had to escort a dead member to the grave and contribute to the cost of requiem masses. A member who would not accept decisions reached by the guild was expelled; any one who killed his guild-brother was banished with the name of *niðingr* (see p. 426).

The artificial family relationships of the guild might come

into conflict with real ones when a guildsman was killed. The Sunnhordland regulations say this:

> If our guild-brother is killed and by a man who is not tied to us through the guild, then all members must go with the man in whose hands the case rests and give him what help we can, and those who will not go are under penalty . . . and the same applies to those who go but prove to be a hindrance, unless they are related to the killer in the fourth degree or by marriage, in that they have his mother or daughter or sister to wife: then they shall help which side they please without penalty.

Relationship in the fourth degree meant sharing a common great-great-grandparent, so the net was still spread wide (cf. pp. 4–5). All the same, the regulation does not assume that a man will automatically stand by his kinsman. It is a sign of the slow release from family bonds brought about by Christianity and new concepts of law and crime.

The hird

Germanic chieftains had picked men in their service, who formed a bodyguard and the nucleus of the armed host of the tribe. Some such groups of more or less professional warriors looked upon themselves as closed societies, which new members could only join after rites and trials of initiation.

Wealthy leaders in the Viking Age and early medieval period also had a following of able-bodied men in their service. Some of these might live in the locality and only turn out in case of need or for a summer expedition, but others formed a permanent retinue. An older name for such a group is *drótt*; cf. *dróttinn*, 'leader, lord' (used in Christian times to translate Latin *dominus* and so a usual word for Jesus). A Danish name for a member of such a body of retainers is *hempægi*, literally 'one who receives a home', but a general Norse term is the one we met earlier, *húskarlar*, 'house-carls'. This was the name given to members of King Knut's standing army in England, and its use is widely attested elsewhere – nowhere better than on the Turinge stone in Södermanland:

Kætil and Björn raised this stone in memory of Thorstæin, their father; Anund in memory of his brother, *and the house-carls in memory of their peer*; Kætilö in memory of her husband.

> *Those brothers were*
> *best among men,*
> *on land*
> *and out in the levy.*
> They held their
> house-carls well.
> *He fell in action*
> *east in Russia,*
> *the levy's captain,*
> *best of landmen.*

(On the possible sense of 'landmen' see p. 127.)

The best-known name for a band of retainers is *hirð*, a word borrowed from Anglo-Saxon *hīred* in the period around 1000. Its English meaning was 'family, household', without special reference to a lord or leader (cf. the cognate German *Heirat*). In Norse the term became restricted in time to the retinue of a king or earl, but a reminiscence of its older meaning of any band of men around a chieftain is doubtless to be seen in a phrase in the Östergötland Law where it is suggested that in earlier times a father could send his son off 'to the sea or *hirð*' to earn his living. The king's *hirð* had a separate set of rules for the conduct of the *hirðmenn*, its members. We have Latin and vernacular versions of the Danish hird-law, usually known by its name in modern form, *Vederlov*, a word which originally meant 'penalties' but which early became confused with another word meaning 'fellowship, company'. These texts are from the late twelfth century, but it was claimed at that time that they originated in Knut the Great's regulations for his standing army in England in the 1020s. We also have an elaborate Norwegian code, called *Hirðskrá*, from about 1270. There are older and newer elements mingled in this, since it is based on a code that seems to have been in existence in the twelfth century, but there is little certainty about the ultimate date of origin of the older parts.

Accounts of military organization in the Icelandic text called
Jómsvíkinga saga and in Saxo's *Gesta Danorum,* both written about
1200, have a romantic element in common and probably reflect
first and foremost the ideals and conditions of the Danish court
and upper-class military men in the time of Valdemar I and
Knut VI. They envisage strict rules governing the presence of
women in garrisons, for example, and prescribe rigid age-limits
for active service and high, hard standards of personal bravery.
They also have rules about leave of absence and the sharing of
booty. For the latter especially there must have been well-
established procedures, reflected in the technical phrase *bera til
stangar,* 'carry to the (standard-)pole' – the enemy slain and
wounded were stripped and everything brought to the chieftain's
standard where the spoil was shared out under strict supervision.
The Norwegian *Hirðskrá* also contains detailed instructions as
to how this was to be done.

Knut the Great and his father, Sven, early in the eleventh
century, must have had a well-regulated system of recruitment
and payment, and, as Sven Aggeson observed in the twelfth
century, a large army of mercenaries of motley origins would
need strict rules if order was to be maintained. Certainly, the
precision of the lay-out of the great Danish camps from about the
year 1000 (pp. 268–9) seems to typify an imposed order, which
must have extended to rules for discipline, routine duties, watch-
keeping and training. It is not likely, however, that much in the
extant *Vederlov* can have applied to Knut's *Þingmannalið* or *Tinglith,* as it is called in Icelandic and Danish sources respectively.
This force was supposed to have had 3000 men in it, but the
Vederlov seems to have been meant for the king's immediate
following.

From the brief Danish text we learn that the body of retainers
was divided into four main groups and these into smaller com-
panies. They had their own assembly at which all internal disputes should be settled. If a case against a man was proved, his
punishment was to shift his seat in the hall one place lower than
before. (Distinction was always indicated, much as now, by the
place given a man relative to the leader or host in the middle
part of a room, where warmth, light and service were concentrated.) According to Sven Aggeson, an inveterate offender was

made to sit lowest of all and everybody else could throw meat-bones at him – a pastime which figures in other stories and of which Archbishop Ælfheah of Canterbury was the victim at a Viking assembly at Greenwich in 1012. Some cases could not be settled in this domestic way. If a man attacked another member, he was driven out of the hird, 'with a niding's name' (cf. p. 426), and should leave the country. The king himself had powerful rights of process against a member of his retinue if he accused him of disloyalty or treason. He needed only the sacred oath of two other members to prove the charge against him, and even if these two were not forthcoming, the charge still stood and the accused man had to clear himself by ordeal (cf. p. 377). If he were judged guilty, his person and goods were forfeit.

The hird had its own officers. We know most about these in the Norwegian system, and it may well have been different elsewhere. The oldest of the leading positions were those of *stallari*, 'marshal', a word borrowed from Anglo-Saxon but derived ultimately from Latin *stabularius*, and *merkismaðr*, 'standard-bearer'. Both of these had, of course, military duties, and the marshall acted as the king's spokesman and as the retainers' representative before the king. By the thirteenth century, as the king's household became more of a court and less of a camp, various other dignitaries were created – plate-bearers, butler, cup-bearer, and most important of all, the chancellor, normally a cleric, who was in charge of the royal seal and secretariat.

The Norwegian kings in the eleventh century probably had an immediate retinue of ninety men, not counting menial servants. These were divided into two classes, the *hirðmenn* and a lower order called *gestir*, 'guests', whose pay was half that of the *hirð-menn*. The reason for the name *gestir* is uncertain: it may have arisen merely as a contrasting term to *hirðmenn* in its original sense of 'household men'. The 'guests' had their own leader, assembly and quarters. They acted as a kind of constabulary, doing errands for the king, executing his justice and collecting his dues. They were not likely to be a popular group, and a thirteenth-century explanation of their name says it is because they were 'unwelcome guests' in many homes.

Hirdmen were picked men and well rewarded. To join them

meant acceptance by the king and by the other members and was a great honour. A hirdman did homage to the king and swore loyalty to him and to the exclusive group he now joined. In Denmark it was possible for a man to resign and join another hird, but this possibility does not seem to have been recognized in Norway, where a hirdman remained a hirdman whether in residence with the king or not. It is interesting to find that in Norway the hirdmen out of piety maintained a hospice of their own for old and infirm members. The mutual obligation of hirdmen extended to all kinds of help and to vengeance for death, and in this way and others it resembled a guild, a similarity recognized in the Norwegian *Hirðskrá*. Guild and hird gave a similar feeling of group solidarity, a sense of security and prestige. In the hird we find a natural emphasis on *esprit de corps* and on playing the game. There is also evidence of that kind of self-regard which a masculine *élite* tends to foster, with a concomitant disdain for women and contempt for outsiders and lower orders.

But what essentially knit these men together was the personal bond they each had with their king or chieftain. The relation could be simply expressed, as in the Danish *Vederlov*: 'The king and other leading men who had a hird should show their men favour and good will and give them their proper pay. In return men should give their lord loyalty and service and be prepared to do all his commands.' The chieftain had to maintain and reward his men, and his gifts demanded a return at the proper time. 'They said to each other that the men forward should now repay the king for their mead or fine tunic-cloth' – so they are supposed to have said on a Norwegian ship as they went into battle in the twelfth century. There is moving recognition of the strength of retainers' loyalty and love for their lord in the saga of King Sverri. When the body of King Magnús, his opponent, had been found, Sverri made Magnús's men identify it, not to grieve them, he said, but to ensure that there was no doubt. 'Afterwards they went to the body and almost none could hold back his tears of those who went up and kissed his corpse.' And before his funeral, the body is again displayed and many went to look at it and came weeping away. One of Magnús's 'guests' – not one of his closest followers, that is – kissed his body and wept as he did it. 'King Sverri looked at him and said, "It

will be a long time, I think, before a man like that can be trusted".'
Stories of loyalty to the end are many, true and untrue, and this
spirit links the early medieval hird firmly with the *comitatus* of
the Germanic chieftain. It is not surprising that foreigners could
find a place in such military retinues and achieve high office in
them. They were cut off from land and family and could find
their whole being in the life of the corps and the faithful service
of their leader. The type is well known in other countries and
other periods. King Harald the Hard-ruler's marshal was an
Icelander, Ulf. When he died about 1060 King Harald is supposed to have said at his grave: 'Here now lies the man who was
most fair-minded and brave-hearted and most loyal to his lord.'
To be fair-minded and brave-hearted were ideals set up for
every man. Utter loyalty was the supreme virtue of the hirdman.
The two could conflict, and this may help to account for the
existence of the *gestir*, who were not expected to have the same
scruples as their betters.

Drengs

In the Old English poem on the Battle of Maldon, fought in
991 between men of Essex and a Viking force, the poet refers to
a Viking as 'one of the *drengs*', using a loan-word from Norse,
drengr, pl. *drengir* (WN) or *drengjar* (EN), a name also borne, we
recall, by one of the yeoman's sons in *Rígspula*. A stone just outside Hedeby was inscribed probably in that same decade; it
commemorates Erik, a ship-commander who fell when '*drengs*
besieged Hedeby'. A stone at Hällestad in Skåne honours a man
who fell in battle at Uppsala sometime between 980 and 990:
'*Drengs* set up the stone on the rock in memory of their brother.'
A stone at Bjälbo in Östergötland is from the eleventh century:
'*Drengs* raised this stone to the memory of Grep, their guild-
fellow . . .'

The word *drengr* means 'boy, youth', but these collective uses
just quoted show that *drengir*, 'lads', might especially be used to
mean the crew of a fighting ship, members of an army unit or of
a merchant fraternity. It is typical that the group relationship
takes on a family guise. The 'brother' commemorated on the
Hällestad stone was not a blood-relation but a comrade; perhaps they were all sworn brothers (p. 422).

There are many runic inscriptions in which the word *drengr* is used in the singular. In these we cannot tell for sure whether 'a very good *dreng*' means simply 'a fine young man' in general terms or 'a very fine young man who had seen active service as a member of a specific group'. The dividing line between the two might be hard to draw, of course, because any 'fine young man' in that society had to have the potential of a good fighting man. Even so, it is generally assumed that the special use of *drengr* to denote membership of a team coloured the word in its other uses. We shall see later (pp. 425–6) the range of its ethical implications.

In some cases the context seems to show that *drengr* could have a technical sense in the singular too. An inscription on a stone at Landeryd church in Östergötland commemorates a brother, 'that *dreng* who was with Knut'; and another at Simris in Skåne was inscribed in memory of Forkun, father of 'Asulv, Knut's *dreng*'. These men had been in the service of Knut the Great, possibly members of the Tinglith.

The name 'lads' must have first been applied locally to the young men who formed a ship's crew for fighting service, aggressive not defensive. They were amateur rather than professional, although this implies no reflection on their proficiency as sailors and fighters. (The village football team is the modern equivalent – an analogy one might press quite far!) The 'lads' belonged to an age-group which apparently could be readily spared from the steady summer toil of food production. The name also conveys a suggestion of the camaraderie which would rapidly develop among young men on adventurous and dangerous service, on board ship and in strange and hostile country, when self-discipline and mutual trust were essential for survival and success. A quiet farming countryside would never be quite the same again when a group of young men returned from a fighting or trading expedition, with new stories, new silver to spend, new splendours in weapons and dress, new slave-girls, new notions about the gods. Danger might also make them new friends, whose reliability and attractiveness could weigh heavy even against the traditional claims of kinsmen.

But, of course, the individual *drengs* we meet on the rune stones were mostly those who did not return. One such was

Karl from Ås in Västergötland. There his comrade Thorir raised
a stone in memory of him, 'a very fine *dreng*'; and in Jutland, at
Hobro in Randers *amt*, he set up another: 'Thorir raised this
stone in memory of Karl the noble, his comrade, a very fine
dreng.' Clearly Karl had gone to Jutland, most probably to join
Knut's fleet for the English invasion in 1016, and there he had
died and been honoured by his friend with a double cenotaph,
one in Denmark and one at home, across the sea in Västergötland. Other young men who fell far afield figure on the stones
set up by Gunnald, a magnate at Berga in Västmanland, in
impartial commemoration of his son and stepson. One says:
'Gunnald had this stone set up in memory of Gerfast, his son,
a good *dreng*, who had gone to England. God help his soul.' And
the other: 'Gunnald had this stone set up in memory of Orm,
his stepson, a good *dreng*, who had gone east with Ingvar. God
help his soul.' Gerfast had probably joined Knut's army. Orm
had gone with Ingvar to Serkland, a disastrous expedition made
about 1020 or some years later to the lands of the Baghdad
caliphate. Nearly thirty rune-stones commemorate men who
died in Ingvar's company.

Another name that is found in *Rígspula* for a member of the
free landowning class is *Þegn*, cognate with English 'thane'. In
Norse this word is commonly used of the mature man, the
veteran. It may, for example, be applied to a father in a runic
inscription where *drengr* is used of his son, and it is probably
safe to believe that it generally implied settled status as the head
of a household (and usually married).

It has been suggested that the *thegns* and *drengs* of Norse society
represented different classes in the Viking Age. The evidence for
this has been found in the fact that in the Danelaw the two
names are applied to men of different status. They were both a
cut above the ordinary but were distinguished from each other
by the fact that *drengs* normally possessed something less than
half as much land as the *thegns* did. This fixed nomenclature,
however, is probably purely English, although it may go back to
individual distinctions made between the fresh young recruit
and the experienced soldier at the time when the Danish leaders
parcelled out the conquered land.

Thegn and *dreng* are like English 'gentleman' in the variety of their connotations. They are used of free men of a recognizable but ill-defined rank; the name *dreng* may sometimes imply an occupation – as long as the Viking Age lasted – but not a career; and, as we shall see, both terms came to be applied to men with admired personal qualities that are again recognizable but also ill defined.

WOMEN, MARRIAGE AND DEPENDENTS

Women

The main tasks reserved for women were the care of small children, the preparation and serving of food, home-cleaning and clothes-washing; they were usually also responsible for milking and dairy work. The housewife was in charge of domestic staff and everything in the house; the keys at her girdle were the badges of her authority. She and her daughters made cloth, prepared clothes from finished material, and did embroidery and tapestry work. About the year 1040 a Norwegian mother had a bridge or causeway built at Dynna, Oppland, and a runic inscription carved in memory of Astrid, her daughter: 'She was the most nimble-fingered girl in Hadeland.'

Such skills must have been learnt in a girl's childhood. There was no segregation of women, though in well-to-do families a separate room might be reserved for them, and they shared in the general occupations and pastimes of the household and district. The mother and *fóstra*, 'nurse, foster-mother', must often have been important 'tradition-bearers' – of medical knowledge, for example, and the witchcraft that was more or less closely related to it, and of the riddles, poetry, stories and genealogies that made a source not only of family entertainment, but also of family pride and perhaps of family hate. We know of one or two women in Norway and Iceland who were themselves poets.

When the Church brought formal education to the North, it was unusual but not impossible for a girl to benefit from it, though she would have to come of a well-to-do family to have the leisure for it. About the year 1110 a girl called Ingun was a pupil at the cathedral school at Hólar in north Iceland, as bright as any of the boys. Having learnt Latin she then taught it to others, and she corrected Latin books copied at the school by having them read to her as she sewed or did tablet-weaving or other handiwork.

A woman had no political rights and her only part in the judicial process was as a witness in a few exceptional cases (cf. for example, the text about the Norwegian legitimation ceremony on p. 118). In Iceland she could not act as a *goði,* even though it was technically possible for her to own a *goðorð.* She could not bring a case at law unless a man undertook the prosecution on her behalf. In early times it may not have been possible to proceed against a woman as an individual – a husband was certainly responsible for the actions of his wife – but this was not so in the twelfth century, although the rules varied from place to place. In Iceland, for example, women could undergo ordeal, and the laws countenance the possibility of outlawry and execution as penalties for women.

Originally it seems to have been the general rule that a daughter did not share in the family inheritance as long as she had brothers to take it over; and a daughter had to be an only child to pay or take atonement for her father. To some extent, however, the daughter's dowry (p. 113) must have been thought of as equivalent to a share in the heritage. Exclusion of women from inheritance was law in Iceland, Norway and Sweden down to the end of our period, but in Denmark this was changed so that a daughter received half a brother's portion. Danish historians towards 1200 thought the change went back to the time of Sven Forkbeard (died 1014), but we have no way of verifying this. The Danish system spread to the rest of Scandinavia in the thirteenth century. As a curiosity it may be mentioned that late medieval and subsequent records show that in the small south Swedish province of Värend daughters and sons had equal rights as heirs, a practice contrary to all the other Scandinavian rules and one which the promulgation of a National Law for the whole of Sweden was not able to eradicate. Opinion is divided as to whether this custom was of antique origin or a comparative novelty, but it remains a notable example of the degree of independence that could exist within the different regions of the northern countries.

In Denmark and Sweden women remained theoretically under

tutelage at all times. In Norway and Iceland an unmarried girl was under the authority of a legal guardian (usually her father), and if she had property of her own, it was in the charge of another person (usually but not necessarily her guardian) until she reached a certain age (twenty in Iceland, for example). She could take charge of it herself after that, but still needed the consent of her guardian before undertaking any major financial transaction. A married woman was under the authority of her husband and had, at best, very limited freedom in the private disposal of anything that belonged to her or in buying or selling on her own account (not more than to the value of half an ounce of silver in any one year in Iceland, for example; in Norway wives of superior yeomen had greater personal rights in such matters than those of ordinary yeomen, cf. p. 85). A widow came nearest to legal independence in that she could have charge of her own property, no matter her age, and administer that of her children; she also had more say in arrangements that might be made for another marriage.

In a formal, legal sense women do not seem to have counted for much in what was essentially a man's world. The subordination of women could doubtless be harshly maintained, but there is also much evidence to show that in general they were respected and might have much personal freedom. This was probably more so in pagan than in Christian times, and was likely to be more marked in a new settlement like Iceland and in Viking colonies abroad than in the settled farming society at home. The report of al-Ghazal, the Muslim ambassador from Cordova to Vikings, probably in Ireland, in 845, particularly stresses the frank and independent behaviour of high-ranking Norse women, something which was presumably in striking contrast to what he was used to. Women in their widowhood could certainly be rich and important landowners, as may be seen for example from the rune stones and good works such ladies were responsible for in eleventh-century Sweden; and about 900 one of the leading settlers in western Iceland was the matriarch, Aud the Deep-wealthy, who took possession of vast lands and portioned them out among her kinsmen and dependents. In the tenth century a woman called 'the red girl' was the leader of a group of Vikings in Ireland; and there are other legends of fierce and imperious women that must certainly have some basis in reality. Some women might be 'peace-weavers', promoting concord and reconciliation, but the proud, vindictive woman who urges her menfolk to bloodshed figures more often in story and gives rise to the proverb, 'Cold are women's counsels'. Some women we know in twelfth- and thirteenth-century Iceland show that she was no figment of the imagination. The actions of the legendary Brynhild and Gudrun, without whom the web round Sigurd's tragedy would not have been spun, never ceased to fascinate and perplex the men of the North (pp. 349 – 50).

Outstanding women, real or legendary, must have done something to lift the status of women in general. But that status must have been essentially maintained by the intelligent and active farmer's wife, of good stock, sure of her position and powers, a type we often meet in the Sagas of Icelanders. She improved her husband's reputation and ran the household in his absence or after his death. As we have seen, the Viking Age took many men away from their homes, as merchants and fighters, some of them never to return. The initiative and independence of their womenfolk must have been fostered by the responsibilities they were left with. The Fläckebo rune stone in Västmanland, Sweden, was set up shortly after 1050 by the yeoman of Hassmyra in memory of his wife, Odindisa; one sentence in the inscription reads: 'No better mistress will come to Hassmyra, to look after the farm.' Odindisa, capable and valued, may stand for all the Norse women of her kind.

RELATIONS BETWEEN THE SEXES

Marriage and divorce

A girl was, as it were, a part and a possession of the family as a whole; her reputation affected the abstract honour of her kinsmen and would be reflected in the concrete value she represented in the marriage bargain that would ultimately be struck for her. Attentions paid to a girl by visits, conversation, poems in her praise, were severely frowned upon, although it seems to have been thought only natural that a girl should be prepared to accept them. If a proper proposal of marriage did not follow such courting, blood-vengeance might be sought by her father or brothers. The making of a verse in praise of a girl was punishable in Iceland, for example, with outlawry – partly because of the publicity poetry received but partly perhaps because of the spell-binding effect that verse was sometimes feared to have. Other sexual transgressions, from those that offended modesty to fornication and rape, were forbidden by law and subject to harsh penalties.

Nevertheless, we have plenty of love-poetry from Iceland and love-charms, and even a twelfth-century runic stick from Bergen with a trite line that could figure in a modern song: 'I should like my girl to be like you'. Even expression of love by women is not unknown in the Icelandic stories, nowhere more charming than in the story of Thordís, daughter of Gudmund: she caught sight of her lover approaching the farm and said: 'Now there is much to be made of the sunshine and south wind, when Sǫrli rides through the gate.' There is ample evidence, even occasionally in the laws, to show that the realities of the sexual situation were recognized. The power of *inn mátki munr*, 'the mighty passion', was admitted even by the poet of some of the *Hávamál* verses (pp. 343–4), who did not trust women ('Praise a wife when she has been cremated . . . a virgin after she has been married'), but knew both what deceivers men were and what fools love could make of them. Or there is this descending catalogue of fines imposed in the Gotland Law for touching a woman: take her wrist or ankle, pay four ounces; touch her elbow or her leg between knee and calf, pay two and two-thirds ounces; take hold of her shoulder or just above the knee, pay one and two-thirds ounces; touch her breast, pay one ounce; but if you touch her higher still above the knee, 'that is the touch dishonourable and is called the fool's clasp; no money is payable for that – most women put up with it when it goes that far.'

Among the Germanic peoples marriage had essentially been a business contract between two families. Christianity radically changed attitudes towards it and few traces of its earlier commercial nature remain in the provincial laws of Denmark and Sweden. In Norway and Iceland, on the other hand, it is evident that, in spite of some innovations, the old system prevailed until well after 1200. Laws and other sources from these countries give us a clear picture of the kind of legal form, commercial bargaining and customary ceremonial that had once been the norm throughout Scandinavia and, indeed, further afield.

The prospective partners were expected to be of similar status in birth and means, though it could happen that a girl was *gefin til fjár*, 'married for money'. The first step in the business was a proposal made to the girl's legal guardian. If he favoured it, the girl's consent might be sought but it was not necessary – in heathen times she had no escape from marriage, but in Christian times she could plead a wish to take the veil. There was then a formal betrothal ceremony, sealed with a handshake before witnesses between the guardian and the suitor or his representative – the girl herself had no part in this. At this meeting the *brúðkaup* – a word that came to mean 'marriage' in general but is properly 'bride-bargain, bride-price' – was fixed by arrangement of the size of the *mundr,* the sum paid by the groom, and of the *heimanfylgja,* 'the accompaniment from home' or dowry of the bride. For a wedding to be legal and children legitimate the *mundr* had to be paid – in Iceland it was a minimum of eight ounces of silver, while in Norway twelve ounces was the minimum and called 'the poor man's price' at that. In the distant past the *mundr* had probably stayed with the bride's family, though what it represented is not certain. It was probably not a purchase-price for her person, as if it were a slave that was being bought, but rather a gift that bore some relation to her notional value within the totality of people and property that constituted her family; when she left her family, that totality was preserved by the money paid as *mundr*. Be that as it may, the situation in our sources is that the *mundr* is a sum which was transferred to the bride and treated as her property – that is to say that, if she and her husband had children, it made part of their inheritance, but if they did not, then it reverted to her kinsfolk. The *mundr* probably matched in some degree the dowry, which was a customary payment, not an obligatory one. Rules about it differed, but it usually remained the wife's property and could, for example, be reclaimed by her family in case of divorce. The groom was further obliged to add a fixed percentage to his wife's dowry, and a present, variously called a 'bench-gift' or 'bride-veil-fee', was expected from him on the morning following the wedding-night.

The wedding itself took place within a set time after the

betrothal. It took the form of a feast usually at the bride's home, but it could be held at the man's house or at the house of some prominent connection. The feast culminated but did not end in the bedding of bride and groom; parties might go on for a week or even a fortnight. There were religious ceremonies connected with the wedding in pagan times, particularly designed to ward off evil influences and to promote fertility; and drinking played an important part both in ritual and in secular merry-making. In Christian times bans had to be called, proof that the marriage was not within the forbidden degrees might have to be produced, and it became customary for the couple to be blessed at the church-door. The term *brúð(h)laup*, also common as a general word for 'wedding', means 'bride-run(ning)', and seems to have been used originally of the procession of the bride to the feast, if it was not at her house, and particularly of her journey to her new home.

A wife's adultery was a serious crime, so much so that some provincial laws gave a husband the right to kill her and her lover out of hand if they were caught together. A man, on the other hand, was not penalized if he kept a concubine or had children outside marriage. Divorce was naturally much affected by canon law, which allowed annulment in some cases and separation without the possibility of remarriage in others, but the sources preserve some evidence of an older, native system under which it was only necessary for a formal declaration to be made before witnesses by either husband or wife for divorce to be legally effective. The procedure seems to have been simple, but the financial ties between husband and wife were probably harder to loosen and might well lead to trouble. But the ideal was undoubtedly the faithful wife who stood by her husband to the end. Here the thirteenth-century Icelandic saga-writers bear chief witness, but the loyalty they admired was no novelty. The author of *Njáls saga* gave it an everlasting symbol in Bergthóra who, as she refused to leave her husband's side to escape from their blazing farmhouse, said: 'I was given young to Njál, and I have promised him that one fate shall fall on us both.'

Legitimate children

The only sort of population control that could be exercised in early times was by allowing unwanted members of society to die. This may sometimes have happened with the sick or old, while every time a child was born, a decision had to be made as to whether it was to be reared or not. The decision rested with the father, and if the child was legitimate, he would doubtless normally accept him as a member of the family, although children seriously deformed were usually put out to die, a practice allowed even in Christian times. Once the child had been given suck, he could not be killed without penalty. The child was given a name, and even in the heathen period this seems to have been accompanied by sprinkling the baby with water and giving a gift (another present was given when the first tooth was cut). Choice of a name was important, because name and personal qualities were felt to be interdependent. Sometimes the names went from generation to generation in an alliterating series (Agni, Alrek, Yngvi, Iǫrund, Aun, Egil, Óttar, Adils, Eystein, Yngvar, Ǫnund, Ingiald, Olaf were successive kings of the Uppsala dynasty, all with names beginning with a vowel); sometimes names were chosen on the so-called 'variation' principle – a ninth-century Norwegian Végeir had sons Vébjǫrn, Véstein, Véþorm, Vémund, Végest and more children with names of the same kind. Sometimes the name of a dead kinsman, grandfather or uncle, was chosen for a new son, and there is some evidence to suggest that a transfer of character, even re-birth, was believed to go with the name. Biblical names and saints' names came gradually into use after the Conversion, but without replacing older native names, including many that were compounded with names of heathen gods, especially Thor. The earliest recorded instance of the use of Jón, from Iohan(nes), the commonest of all Christian names in Scandinavia, is from about 1040. Other foreign names were sometimes adopted, both in pagan and Christian times. The most famous is probably Magnús, in use among Norsemen in Ireland in the tenth century but made popular on account of Magnús the Good, born in 1023, son of St Ólaf of Norway. Magnus was known early as a saint's name, but it was believed by the early Icelandic historians, rightly or wrongly, that King Magnús's name was modelled on the cognomen of Charlemagne, Carolus magnus.

In Christian times it was baptism which gave the child the

right to live and made him a member of Christian society, as the laws required. The exposure of children other than the badly deformed could not be allowed by the Church, although a concession to the Icelanders when they accepted Christianity was that they should be allowed to control their population by putting children out to die in the way they had been used to; the concession was removed a few years later.

The authority of a father over his children was complete. The treatment they received would obviously vary from the harsh to the indulgent. It is clear from many stories that people liked to see signs of manliness in a child, and this meant chiefly admiration for the obstreperous and defiant boy. Children were often fostered in another family, often by a man who stood in some kind of 'client' relationship to the child's father. 'One-fourth depends on the fostering' was the extent to which the Icelandic proverb acknowledged the influence of upbringing and environment. Princes might also be brought up at a foreign court. The best known example is that of Hákon, son of King Harald Finehair of Norway, who spent some of his childhood and youth at the court of Athelstan of Wessex. Ties between foster-relations could be as strong as the closest blood-ties, or stronger, as is suggested, for example, by a runic inscription on a cross from Kirk Michael in the Isle of Man. It was commissioned by a lady in memory of her foster-son and the inscription ends with the words: 'It is better to leave a good foster-son than a bad son.'

The laws made fifteen or sixteen the age of majority in all the Scandinavian countries, but there are some signs that in an earlier period boys of twelve were accepted as full-grown members of society. The question of the legal responsibility of a boy was treated differently in the different countries and provinces. In Trøndelag, for example, a boy of eight or under was not chargeable with an offence, and his father or guardian was responsible for what he did; on the west coast of Norway, the age was twelve or under; but in both these places from those ages to fifteen, the age of majority, a boy was liable to pay and to receive half the full atonement. The offences of boys under age in Sweden were counted 'accidental', while in Iceland if a boy under twelve killed somebody, he could not be outlawed but his family had to pay full compensation.

Illegitimate children

An illegitimate child was one born outside marriage or before marriage. Subsequent marriage did not legitimize, although the rule of canon law which says that it does had been introduced in some parts of Scandinavia by the time the laws were codified.

Unwanted children would be chiefly the offspring of slaves and those born out of wedlock. When an illegitimate child was born to a free woman, it was doubtless also presented to the father, if that were possible. If he were not at hand or if he refused to acknowledge the child and it could not be proved to be his, then the responsibility for it rested with the mother's family, and it was for her father or guardian to decide what the fate of the child should be.

Questions of marriage and illegitimacy were much the concern of canon law, and the native customs of Scandinavia were soon affected by it. Even so, the laws show that the Church's ruling in such matters was by no means fully accepted even in the thirteenth century. Again the different provinces and countries have rather different customs.

Normally an illegitimate son had no right of inheritance as long as legitimate heirs existed, but in Denmark and Sweden a father could declare his paternity at the assembly, 'proclaim him a member of the family', and give him gifts. By this act the son became entitled to a share in the inheritance, though still under strict rules, and doubtless to a share in the joint responsibilities of the family, such as those of atonement and the maintenance of destitute kinsmen. In Iceland the laws appear to recognize no means of legitimation, and they restrict the gift a father could give an illegitimate son to twelve ounces. There is a story in the thirteenth-century *Laxdæla saga* about Hǫskuld and his favourite son, Ólaf, born to him by an Irish princess who had been his concubine (it is supposed to have happened in the tenth century). He cannot make him an heir but he can give him gifts, with his legitimate sons' consent. He abides by the letter of the law by giving him twelve ounces – of gold, eight times the value of the silver ounces intended by the laws.

It is in Norway, however, that we find the most colourful legitimizing customs, which seem to be as old-fashioned as those to do with freeing a slave (pp. 72–3). The ceremony for 'induction into the family' (*ættleiðing*) is described thus in the Trøndelag laws:

> That is a full induction into the family when a father leads his son into the family with the agreement of those who are his nearest heirs. Ale from three measures [of malted grain, probably about eight bushels] is to be brewed and a three-year-old ox slaughtered. The hide is to be flayed from the right-hand hind leg above the knee and a shoe made from it. The father shall make the son who is to be led into the family step into that shoe. The father [when he himself steps into it] is to have in his arms those [legitimate] children of his who are under age, but his grown-up sons shall step into the shoe themselves. If he has no legitimate sons, then those men who are nearest to the inheritance after him are to step into the shoe. The man [being inducted into the family] is to be put in the lap of men and women. Women may bear witness equally with men that a man was fully inducted into the family [by this ceremony], as may also the shoe into which they stepped, if it is preserved.

The Gulathing Law has an essentially similar description, more circumstantial in some respects, less so in others. It includes the formula to be uttered by the father: 'I lead this man into the property I give him, into payment and gift, into bench and seat, into compensation and atonement-ring, and into every right as if his mother had been bought with a purchase price' [i.e. legally married, cf. p. 113]. This formula is in an authentic native style (a series of alliterating phrases that unfortunately cannot be given in similar style without undue violence to the English), and a still more archaic impression is made by the phrase 'lap of men and women' in the Trøndelag laws, *rekka skaut ok rygja*, where the words for 'men' and 'women' are ancient terms otherwise found almost exclusively in poetry.

People in need

The incapable, the destitute and the unfortunate were theoretically the sole responsibility of the family, but it was bound to happen sometimes that no family existed or that other members of the same family were already helpless. Society at large had then to be concerned with such people, and might find it necessary to decide what responsibility individual members of a given family had to aid their kinsfolk. Some recognition of communal interests of this kind must have existed in pre-Christian times, but the advent and growth of Christianity, with its emphasis on good works, gradually brought about a greater acknowledgment of the need for charity as a social duty. Information about these matters comes almost exclusively from the laws, in codes which were made 150 to 250 years after the conversion of the Scandinavians to Christianity. On the other hand, it is right to stress that they are not much more than a century or so later than any sort of full-scale organization of dioceses and church finances in the different countries, and it was only with such organization that Christian ideas of care for the impoverished could be given any notable practical effect in legislation. There were strong conservative forces to be overcome: the yeomen were decidedly reluctant to give away their own, especially when there was any chance that the idle or feckless might benefit from the gift. There is no doubt but that many of the laws were ancient when they were codified, while in other cases comparative study may reveal older conditions behind innovating statutes.

In Denmark and Sweden the term *flætføring* (Sw. *flätföring*) was used of a man who, voluntarily or of necessity, gave up maintaining himself and found someone else to look after him. It has been suggested that the verbal phrase behind the term, which means 'moving onto the floor', was originally applied to the action of the head of a household when he gave up his independence and moved himself from his central seat to a bench among ordinary members of a home. Another and perhaps better explanation is that it means moving onto somebody else's floor, i.e. into somebody else's home. Normally the *flætføring* went to one of his kinsmen, but if none could or would take him in, he could go to someone outside the family, although steps were then usually taken to safeguard his property for the benefit of his natural heirs. Treatment of such a man varied from place to place, partly in accordance with his status and capital. At one extreme we find an antique system in the laws of Östergötland by which the so-called 'voluntary thrall' surrendered all personal rights in return for lifetime maintenance. In Skåne, on the other hand, we learn of more modern arrangements by which a man could divide up his wealth among his heirs but keep a portion for himself and then make a private arrangement with one of his kinsmen for his keep and protection. He retained his personal rights in case of injury done to him, but had to share any atonement awarded to him with the man who now cared for him.

Destitute people were first the responsibility of their family, and the laws stipulated the sequence in which kinsmen should act to help them. The Icelandic laws say this, for example:

A man must first maintain his mother. If he can manage more, then he must also maintain his father. If he can do better still, then he must maintain his children. If still better, then he must maintain his brothers and sisters. If better again, then he must maintain those people whose heir he is and those he has taken in against promise of inheritance. If yet better, he must maintain the freed man to whom he gave liberty.

If a man cannot maintain his mother and father, he must approach his nearest kinsman who has the means and offer to work as his slave in order to pay off the loan necessary to keep his mother and father alive. If maintenance by the family was impossible, the responsibility lay with the farmers of the *hreppr* (p. 59), sometimes with the inhabitants of larger regions, the *thing*-district or Quarter or even the whole country.

In west Norway a bankrupt man should go with two-thirds of his children to his kinsmen and his wife with the other third to hers. They should then pass on from kinsman to kinsman according to the degree of their relationship and their respective means until every member of the family had found someone to keep him. There is a strange provision in the laws of the same region covering the case of freed slaves who became destitute: 'A grave is to be dug in the churchyard and they are to be put in it and left to die there. The patron [the man who gave or gained them their freedom] is to take out the one who lives longest and maintain him or her thereafter.' Presumably such people would already have to be helpless with hunger before they could be treated in this way, and it has been suggested that the idea behind exposing them in such a public and much-visited place was that it would generally stir someone to take pity on them. Let us hope so.

Poor relief and mutual insurance

Paupers were a common burden and the community did what it could to prevent any increase in their numbers. Kindly and generous men must have existed in pagan times, but we only know of poor relief as public policy in Christian times, and it is difficult not to attribute it mainly to the Christian prescription of alms-giving and good works as a means to salvation. Certainly, it was the introduction of the tithe and of gifts of food (looked upon as food saved because of the obligatory fasting ordained by the Church) which made organized poor relief possible. One-quarter or one-third of the tithe went to the poor and the food-gifts were turned into annual donations that were also distributed among the poorer families. The foundation of hospitals and alms-houses also sprang from private or public piety.

In Iceland we meet a well-regulated attempt to help the un-fortunate and protect the community by a scheme of mutual insurance within each *hreppr* (p. 59), laid down as the law of the land. If a man lost a quarter or more of his cattle through disease, the other farmers in the *hreppr* made good half his loss. The other eventuality covered was loss by fire of three farm-buildings, the living-room, kitchen, and pantry in which women prepared food – all rooms where the use of fire was inevitable. (If a man had a 'hall' – *skáli* – as well as a kitchen, he could specify in advance which of these he wished to be covered by the compensation.) A church or chapel on a man's farm was also included, doubtless because of the obligatory use of candles there. These buildings and their ordinary contents – everyday clothing, food, church vestments in daily use, the best bell if there was more than one – were to be valued if destroyed by fire, and the local farmers paid half the loss. In any one year members of the *hreppr* were not to contribute more than 1% of their total wealth in payment of this kind of compensation. Neither was the same man to receive insurance payments more than three times.

Similar provisions are not found in the other Nordic laws, but the guilds had arrangements for mutual aid, at least from the twelfth century onwards. Thus the statutes for the Sunnhordland guild mentioned above (p. 99) say that the guild took responsibility for damage to a member's house, 'in which he feeds his household and his guests', and to his byre; if his corn-barn burnt down, each member gave him a measure of corn if it happened before Christmas, half a measure if it happened after Christmas; if his hay-barn was burnt, his stock was divided up among the other members and kept by them until new grass was available; if a merchant among them suffered a loss of three marks or more by robbery or shipwreck, each member gave him a measure of corn; and finally, if a guild-brother was in captivity, all the members had to contribute to his redemption.

Life in twelfth-century Scandinavia must often have been harsh for the poor and incapable, yet it cannot be said that conditions then compare unfavourably with those of later centuries in Europe as a whole, before the great social reforms of the last hundred years or so. Indeed, in some respects, things were better in the earlier period for then the natural duty of the family to stand by its own members, firmly maintained from heathen times, was strongly enforced by law as well as graced by Christian charity, while, later, family cohesion became less and less an obligatory matter.

4

Authority and administration
Chiefs and kings

There were superior men in every locality who, for reasons that were doubtless shifting and are today inevitably obscure, held central positions in community affairs. They were of good birth but not necessarily connected with families of kings and earls. Before the law, they were like other yeomen; their style of life may often have been richer, but poorer men among them might well find that reputation of ancestors and individual good sense could also compensate for lack of means.

Preservation of internal peace and external power depended on the organization of law and military force. Both the legal and military systems depended on co-operation among the free men; but warfare, unlike law, required swift and authoritative decisions. Command in threatening times was the function of the leading men and their wartime authority naturally spilled over into times of peace. Steps to keep that authority in bounds might then be taken by the yeomen who could use the law to limit the scope of a leader's influence.

Such local chieftains were in existence when the Viking Age began, and they continued to exist more or less independently of the royal power. But the kings also had their officers and servants in the districts, and by the end of the twelfth century a merger of the two sources of authority is under way, with gradual encroachment of royal power on local hereditary positions. Where the merger was more or less complete, a new class was born, an aristocracy dependent on the monarchy and seldom representative of the local yeomen. But in these things there are great differences between the northern countries.

Denmark
In Denmark the local military leader was called the *styræsman*,

'helmsman', a term generally used of a ship's captain. There were from one to four such leaders in each *herred*. Each was responsible for building and maintaining the ship used by the local levy. Dues were contributed by the local men, but a *styræsman* probably needed private means to maintain his office. According to the Jutland Law the position was a hereditary one but could only fall to the lot of a son or brother. If neither existed, the office fell to the king, who nominated a successor. This royal right to fill the vacancy is doubtlesss a novelty; it would earlier have been left to a local decision.

If the *styræsmæn* acted in concert they could have great influence. In 1074 and 1104 it seems to have been the leaders of the levy fleet assembled at Isøre in north Sjælland who decided the election of the Danish kings, Harald 'Hone' and Niels respectively.

But the *styræsmæn* were not the only magnates in a given *herred*. Others would stand out and take the lead with them at the assemblies. They were referred to as *hethwarthæ mæn*, 'men worthy of honour'; and they may have been called *landmæn* (or in West Norse *landsmenn*), 'land-men, men of land', prominent landowners, like the man commemorated on the stone at Skivum in northeast Jutland, 'best and first of the land-men in Denmark'.

Most districts, in time all of them, contained royal property, run by a steward (*bryti*, cf. p. 87 above). His duties included the reception of the king's income from other people in the locality. In earlier times this consisted of traditional gifts of supplies for the king's maintenance, but by about the end of the twelfth century this had been replaced by a standard tax (*stuth*, 'support'). The steward's duty was further extended to the claiming and collecting of what was due to the king – his share in fines or atonement, for example, paid in cases settled in the courts – and he became the king's executive officer in the district as well as administrator of the king's estate. He got a new name, *umbuthsman*, 'agent'. His task was to see that the king's interests were not ignored at any stage, and his personal status improved as his official responsibilities grew. On the other hand, limits were set on his function to make things fairer for other men. In the twelfth century he could not act for other people in lawsuits; and he could only claim compensation due to the king after a private individual had established a case in the courts against an offender. We may compare the restrictions placed on the activity of 'landed men' in Norway, p. 130 below.

Even among the magnates a few families might stand out as pre-eminent, and these tended to be closely associated with the monarchy and allied to it by marriage. The highest such families might possess the title of *earl* (cf. pp. 135–6).

We know of two especially important families in Denmark in the period *c.* 1050 – 1250, one from Jutland, descended from Thrugot Ulfsson, prominent under Sven Estridsson and father-in-law of King Erik Ever-good, the other the 'White' family from Sjælland, descended from Skialm the White, who died in 1113. From the former family came Asser and Eskil, who between them held the archiepiscopal see of Lund from 1104 to 1177. From the latter family came Archbishop Absalon and his successor, Anders Suneson, who together held the see from 1177 to 1228. The progress of European civilization in Denmark and the country's fame owed perhaps more to the accidents of health which gave these four great prelates so long a tenure as chief officers of Church and State than to any other cause.

From the time of Harald Blue-tooth in the tenth century down to the death of Sven Estridsson in 1075 there was for the most part strong monarchical rule in Denmark. The *styræsman* with his ship's crew of forty local men made a unit in the national military force called the *lethang*, 'levy' (cf. p. 280). Once England had been lost, however, about 1040, a century and more passed before any large-scale Danish attacks across the sea were made, and by then military conditions had greatly changed. The most important military nucleus in Denmark itself was the king's immediate retinue, the hird, which does not seem to have been large, and because internal conditions were generally peaceful, great men probably did not keep many retainers in their service. Rivalry among the sons of Sven Estridsson, however, and open civil strife during and after the reign of Niels (1104 – 1134), until the final succession of Valdemar in 1157, produced conditions which led to a multiplication of private forces and to a novel interest in fortification as well. A more numerous and more specialized class of men-at-arms came into existence. The importance of these increased under Valdemar I and Knut VI, partly because of general changes in military requirements and partly because of their campaigns against the Wends. The Danish levy had produced men who were oarsmen and foot-soldiers, stoutly armed but not mobile or heavily protected out of their ships. The Danes now needed cavalry, first and foremost to keep on a par with the Saxons to the south, but they also found they could use cavalry to good effect in their south Baltic expeditions where combined operations by ships and horsemen added speed and thrust to their attacks. The ordinary yeomen continued to provide the rowers and reserves, but cavalry, expensive to maintain and requiring more training than the ordinary militia, was chiefly provided by 'private' soldiers who could afford the outlay. The king came more and more to rely on his own hird, the hird of the archbishop and bishops, and the men-at-arms in the private following of men of means – most of these were or became members of the hird and they brought their retainers, few or many, with them. The socially momentous step was then taken of recognizing the contribution made by such men to the commonweal – men who 'risk their necks for the peace of king and country', as it says in the Jutland Law of 1241 – by exempting them from taxation and giving them a share in royal revenues. This leading military group must have been of mixed origins to begin with – families traditionally in royal service, rich yeomen and yeomen's sons, soldiers of fortune, foreign as well as Danish. (It was out of their crudeness and vitality that the great Danish 'heroic' ballads of the thirteenth century were to spring.) But in time all these settled down to share the same prejudices and enjoy the same privileges, as an aristocracy thrust between the ordinary yeomen and their rulers. At first they were not independent of the monarchy, as the magnates of the old order had largely been, but gradually their self-consciousness as a class, their supra-local interests – resulting from landowning, fostering and marriage outside a single locality – made them into a power with sectional interests not necessarily consonant with those of the king above them or the yeomen below them.

These developments belong in their final stages to the thirteenth century but grew inexorably from twelfth-century conditions. It was then a great irony that in Denmark and Sweden the word that came to be used of this privileged class was *frælse*, corresponding to Latin *libertas*, 'freedom, immunity', but formed from the native adjective *frials*, 'free', derived, as has been mentioned, from an original compound *frī-hals*, 'free-neck', the word universally applied in the northern countries to men not in servitude. This name was now particularly applied to an upper class and the class of free yeomen was correspondingly depressed. What had once been a broad range of landowners and fighting men had now split into two: a small group of landowners and warriors who were distinctly more free than a large group of farming tax-payers, among whom the number of tenants was rising and the number of freeholders falling.

Sweden

A development similar to that in Denmark took place in Sweden, but it belongs to a slightly later period, and we cannot trace the change in detail, not least because we know very little about internal organization in the Swedish provinces in the period before the thirteenth century. In general it is reasonable to suppose that there was, as in Denmark and Norway, a dual source of local authority in the persons of local landowning magnates and of king's stewards. The former must have been men like those mentioned in the laws of Östergötland, able to maintain forty men at their own expense, or those we meet in a good many rune-stone inscriptions, men like Gylve the mighty in Hälsingland and the sons of Finnvid in Uppland (cf. p. 84). Their influence depended on wealth and on tradition. They would have most say in the local assemblies, in the selection of the province's lawman, and in the election of the king or in ratification of his election. In Väster- and Östergötland there were so-called *hæraðshöfþingiær*, '*herred*-leaders', who acted as legal officers both at the assemblies and in their districts.

The famous Turinge inscription in Södermanland, quoted p. 101, refers to the dead man as 'best of *landmen*', and another inscription from the same province speaks of 'land-born men'. These terms have been interpreted, like the two instances of *landmen* in Denmark, as 'magnate, prominent man of land', and possibly the equivalent of *lendr maðr*, 'landed man', in Norway, a title used specifically of a man granted land (or income from land) by the king along with a sort of lord-lieutenant's responsi-

bility in a district. The Swedish and Danish evidence is too slight
to allow a certain equation of land-man and 'landed man' to be
made, but in Västergötland, which stood in a number of respects
midway between Norway and Sweden proper, we do find
references to people with precisely the same title as these Norwegian officials. In the older Västergötland Law it says that in
disputes over land 'a bishop's rights of testimony are above
those of the king, a landed man's rights above those of a bishop,
and a yeoman's rights above those of all of them'. (The yeomen
in the last resort made the law, and here they give themselves
an advantage to help protect their interests against the encroachment of superiors. We may compare the Västergötland requirement that bishops and lawmen should be yeomen's sons, and the
restrictions placed on officials in Denmark and Norway, pp.
124–5, 130.) In the later law of the province it says that if a
'landed man' claimed in a dispute that he was a yeoman, he had
to prove it with twelve compurgators, 'but no man is a landed
man unless his father is a landed man'. This suggests that, although
the title of 'landed man' remained, it bore no relation to administrative realities.

Royal administration in Sweden is especially connected with
farms that have the name *Husaby*. Upwards of sixty are now
known, most of them in the Central Swedish provinces. The
place-name is also not uncommon in Norway, particularly in
the south of the country, and it occurs, though rarely, in Denmark. It seems likely that the Norwegian examples are accounted
for by old political connections with Sweden, but remembering
the part played in name-giving by fashion and accident, it
would not be wise to think that the name had just the same
significance in its every occurrence.

A Husaby farm was Crown land, part of the official inheritance of the Uppsala kings. Such a farm was run by the
king's *bryti*, steward or bailiff. The farm would lodge the king
and his retinue on their progress through the country. The word
hus, 'buildings', the distinguishing element in the place-name,
is thought to refer to the larger or more numerous buildings that
would be required for the accommodation of the king and his
men; and it may also cover the storehouses in which the pro-
vender contributed by the local farmers for the king's main-

tenance was kept until he came to eat it or dispose of it. In some districts at least the *bryti* came to have a share in the local administration of law, like the *umbuthsman* in Denmark. It may be added that the royal farm would make a natural centre for the gathering of the local levy and for organization as a stronghold, just as it would also make an attractive object of attack for invaders and marauders.

Norway

We do not know much about the inland districts of Norway in the early period, rather more about the west coast and Trøndelag. In these latter regions we find local leaders with the title *hersir* (pl. *hersar*). The word's first element is *herr*, 'military host', and the name probably first signified the man who took command when the men of the district were called out for war. The title was hereditary and remained well known, but it seems to have disappeared from administrative use in the course of the eleventh century. About 1200 Icelandic historians equated the rank of *hersir* with that of *lendr maðr*, 'landed man', and officers with this title, who existed in all the regions of Norway, seem to have replaced the *hersar* well before that time. This replacement did not necessarily mean a change of people, for it is likely that the old *hersar* often became 'landed men' – they represented a traditional authority in the districts which the kings would want to make use of.

As we saw earlier, the 'landed men' held land and with it authority from the king. They were his sworn liegemen, they took precedence in the hird, and their superiority was recognized by higher sums awarded them in atonement for injury and death and by other privileges. It was not a fully hereditary position but represents a halfway stage between the old local chieftain and the new royal servant. The son of a 'landed man' had the rights of a 'landed man' as long as he could reasonably expect a grant of land and authority from the king – up to the age of forty, that is. If no grant was forthcoming, his rights became the same as those of the superior yeoman called *hauldr* (pp. 84–5).

In the twelfth century 'landed men' appear as king-makers and men of wealth and pride – 'gold necks' and 'big bucks' are the unfriendly names applied to them by King Sverri and his men. It is clear that they and their families were the leading social and political element in Norway at this time when the monarchy was divided and weakened. We do not, however, know how many 'landed men' there were – an estimate of between 50 and 100 is vague but safe. The reign of Sverri and his thirteenth-century successors provided comparatively strong monarchical government, and in this time the number of 'landed men' was greatly reduced. Their title remained and was regarded as the equivalent of 'baron' in England, but it had less administrative significance than hitherto.

The laws enumerate some restrictions on 'landed men' that are clearly intended to safeguard the ordinary yeomen. Thus, a 'landed man' was not allowed to enter a court where a case between ordinary men was being heard; and he was allowed to join the *lǫgrétta* – in Norway the committee at the assembly which discussed points of law – only with the express permission of the yeomen. If a 'landed man' broke the law against the yeomen in Trøndelag by using violence against any one of them, then the men of two counties (*fylke*) were under legal obligation to rise up against him.

The kings of Norway had their private estates here and there in the country. Each was in the charge of a steward, commonly called an *ármaðr*, a word which probably meant originally 'messenger, representative'. In the early period *ármenn* were often slaves, but the personal status of such officers improved with the prestige and power of the central monarchy; the office was held by free men, and their authority came to extend over more matters than the superintendence of royal property. There was no automatic hereditary transfer of such stewardships and this was obviously to the royal advantage.

By 1200, as was mentioned above, the number of 'landed men' was reduced, and the functions they had performed were now those of the local official called *sýslumaðr*, a vague term meaning something like 'functionary' but often translated, not inadequately, by the word 'sheriff' (as of an English county). He had a territory to administer but was a royal appointment, not a local representative; men of the rank of *lendr maðr* might become *sýslumenn*, but the term is originally distinctive of official function, not class. The *sýslumaðr* can be looked on as a kind of amalgamation of *ármaðr* and *lendr maðr*. The system was to royal advantage because the kings now had much better control over their great men than before. It probably had an adverse effect on the position of the yeomen in the long run, because there were fewer grounds than formerly for the identification of the local leader's interests with theirs.

Jämtland and Gotland

Both these regions came comparatively late under the control of kings: Gotland under Sweden, and Jämtland first under Sweden and later under Norway. They preserved a high degree of yeomen independence throughout the early period, evidently with an effective balance of power among the landowners. But as soon as the king's right to call out a levy or impose a tribute was recognized, local officers to act on the king's behalf became necessary. They would normally be local magnates, and it is in any case obvious that the king's point of view would count for less in such provinces than in others that were nearer to him and less homogeneous than these in population and traditions. There are some notable men mentioned in the Saga of the Gotlanders, but we know little about great men in Jämtland. There is however a famous rune-stone inscribed about 1050 by Östersundsbro, Frösö, which reads: 'Östman, son of Gudfast, had this stone set up and this causeway made and he caused Jämtland to become Christian.' This provides a parallel on the one hand to the great Jelling monument of King Harald Blue-tooth of Denmark (pp. 14–15) and on the other to the Icelanders' acceptance of Christianity by a single legal act (p. 60), and offers a tantalizing glimpse of the social state of the Jämtland farmers and of the position among them of Östman, son of Gudfast.

Orkney, Shetland and the Faroes

We know little about the leading men in these Atlantic islands. In Orkney there was a hereditary dynasty of earls (p. 136), and the important yeomen had the distinctive name of *gœðingar*, 'men endowed with or possessed of goods'. It is probable that most or all of these were related to the earls, but that in other respects their position was comparable to that of 'landed men' in Norway. There was hardly room for many such in the islands. Their responsibilities included the maintenance of ships and beacons as part of the defensive system. Orkney was, of course, particularly vulnerable, because of the proximity of the often hostile Scottish mainland, and the military functions of the *gæðingar* were all the more important in consequence.

Shetland and the Faroes, on the other hand, had no levy organization that we know of. By the end of the twelfth century they were run by *sýslumenn* of the Norwegian king, but they had been tributary to the Norwegian Crown long before that. It is likely that in the early period the king left the superintendence of his interests to some individual leader from one of the traditionally important families in the islands, a man who would doubtless be a member of his hird and under vows of personal loyalty to him.

Iceland

Iceland and Greenland remained politically independent from the time of their discovery and settlement until late in the thirteenth century. We know little of Greenland beyond the fact that it was a republic of farmers, doubtless with oligarchic tendencies, as in Iceland. We know much more about Icelandic conditions.

Iceland managed without a central administration and a national leader. An essential reason for the Icelanders' successful neglect of monarchy or earldom was the country's remote position: aggression directed against the island was as impractical as aggression mounted from it. No military organization was thus necessary and no hereditary commanders could extend their authority from military to civil spheres. The Icelanders consequently paid out less than most Scandinavians in the way of taxes and gave none of their time to national service in armed levies. What dues they owed, they normally owed on a local scale, and there was no need for centralized agencies to collect payments. The first need for any such organization came with the creation of the two bishoprics and the introduction of a tithe-law (pp. 61–2).

There was no national leader, for the Lawspeaker (p. 92) could hardly count as such, but there were local chieftains. Each of these had the title *goði* (pl. *goðar*), a strange name which means 'priest', a man in some special relationship with gods, divine powers. The chief function of the *goðar* in Iceland was secular, but the only recorded instances of the word outside Iceland refer to two men in Denmark who lived one in the ninth century, and one in the tenth (p. 396); in both cases the name seems to refer primarily to the man's priestly function.

The first *goðar* in Iceland were members of the families recognized as outstanding (doubtless not all for the same reasons) among the settlers who arrived in the period *c.* 870 – 930. These same families did not all retain the office throughout the period down to 1200, but a good number did. The existence of such leaders and the nature of the relationship between them and the rest of the free farmers were fundamental elements in the code of laws agreed on for the whole population some time in the 920s. Down to *c.* 965 there were thirty-six *goðar,* a neat number which may have come about accidentally, but which is more likely to have been produced by negotiation and compromise. About 965 there were constitutional changes which provided for thirty-nine *goðar* in the country, plus nine others with the same title but with functions limited to the deliberations and procedures of the National Assembly (pp. 56–8).

A *goði* had few special rights accorded him by law, and atonement payable for him was the same as for any free man. He did, on the other hand, have specific duties, and he had to be at certain places at certain times – if he neglected his responsibilities he could be prosecuted and fined and deprived of his office. The *goðar* acted in groups of three at the local assemblies, one of them 'hallowing' the assembly at the outset and so functioning as a priest. They were in general charge of proceedings at these meetings, and they nominated the judges, probably twelve apiece, who sat in the court of law which was set up at them. At the National Assembly the *goðar* sat in the *lǫgrétta* – here the legislative assembly – each with two free men who acted as advisers. They also nominated judges to sit in the four judicial courts that were organized at the National Assembly after the 965-reforms, and in the so-called Fifth Court on its introduction soon after 1000. One of their number, the chieftain from the family of Ingolf, Iceland's first permanent settler, had the privilege of 'hallowing' the National Assembly. He had the ancient title of *allsherjargoði,* 'priest of all the host'.

The function of the *goði* at the National Assembly was thus legislative but not directly judicial. Execution of justice was, however, in part his responsibility, in so far as he had to preside over the formal confiscation of an outlawed man's property. Execution was normally left to private initiative, but a *goði* might be expected to take action against someone looked on as a public enemy.

All free men in Iceland had to be 'in *thing* with' a *goði*, a relationship entered upon by mutual consent and guaranteeing mutual support. In the early tenth century a man could engage himself to any *goði* he liked, but after the 965-reforms, *goði* and *thing*-man had to live in the same Quarter-division. To be an effective *goði* the leader needed men who were ready in the last resort to fight on his side. The number and quality of his followers would depend on tradition, in his family and theirs, but particularly, because of the element of choice in the contract, on his personal popularity. It would pay a leader to be complaisant, energetic and generous. His performance would doubtless be judged most critically in the terms he could get for his supporters, not in the cases that came to the courts (where penalties for given offences were firmly laid down in the laws), but in the many disputes that were settled out of court by agreement and arbitration.

The name of the office of *goði* is *goðorð*. Its flexible and personal nature was recognized in its legal definition as 'power, not property' – it consequently could not be valued for tithe purposes. It could, however, be inherited, bought and sold, and divided. In the last case the owners were supposed to take it in turn to function as *goði*. Conditions of this kind make it still harder to think of the *goðorð* as conferring any kind of single-handed autocratic power on its owner.

We do not know how the population of free farmers was divided up among the 36-39 *goðar*. Some were certainly more powerful than others, but shifts within the oligarchy must have taken place as the generations changed and personalities and circumstances altered. Generally, a reasonable balance among them must have been maintained, and, as will have been seen, there were various checks in the constitution that made it extremely hard for any one leader to make headway on his own.

Probably in the eleventh century, however, and certainly in the twelfth, the *goðorð* became concentrated in the possession of only a few families, and this meant that in time most of the *goðar* acting at the assemblies were little more than nominees. This is symptomatic of Iceland's time of troubles in the thirteenth century, which ended with submission to the Norwegian Crown's demand for tribute. By the end of that century the *goðar* had disappeared and were being replaced by *sýslumenn* and governors appointed by the Norwegian king.

Earls

The primary meaning of the word 'earl', Norse *jarl*, was 'a distinguished man', but by the ninth century its application in Scandinavia was almost entirely restricted to men of high rank, who might be independent rulers or subordinate only to kings. Our knowledge of earls in Denmark and Sweden is slight. Indeed, the word itself is not directly attested in early Danish sources, although the title must have existed among the Danes. In the early tenth century, for example, there were earls among the Danes in England, where, as is well known, the Norse title finally ousted the Anglo-Saxon title of *ealdorman*. In the twelfth century the title of duke (*hertugi*) and count (*greve*) were used in Denmark on the German model, especially for those men, usually members of the royal family, who had charge of the march-provinces of Halland and Holstein. Västergötland appears to have been ruled by an earl in the tenth and early eleventh century, but thereafter, although the office doubtless continued, we know no one with that title under the Swedish kings until just before 1200. The principal officer of state in Sweden at that time was Earl Birger, and the title continued in his family into the thirteenth century.

Earls are better known from sources concerning Norway, but there remain a good many obscurities about their origins and functions. This is partly due to the fact that we know the name 'earl' both as a dynastic title and as a title conferred by a king on an outstanding ally or major commander. There were two long-lived dynasties of Norse earls, one in Norway and one in the colonies. The first, the *Hlaðajarlar* (earls of Lade), had a hold on north Norway, from Trøndelag northward, from at least the end of the ninth century, and at times they ruled virtually the whole country (cf. pp. 43-4). The line lasted into the eleventh century, and then for about a hundred years there was no earl in Norway, until the title was revived in 1159 and occasionally given to great men thereafter. The second, the Orkney dynasty, was founded about 900 by a grim humorist called Turf-Einar, son of the Norwegian earl of Møre, and it survived throughout the period we are dealing with. The Orkney earls acknowledged the overlordship of the Norwegian king but were virtually independent; as was natural, they could not avoid involvement in Scottish affairs. Norwegian colonies elsewhere in the British Isles were mostly ruled by kings.

We are also told by the Icelandic historian, Snorri Sturluson, who wrote about 1220, that when Harald Finehair (p. 41) gained power over all Norway, he made a tidy arrangement by which he appointed an earl in each *fylke*, with at least four *hersar* under him (p. 129). Later, however, he says that some of King Harald's many sons drove these earls away and made themselves masters of their income. Snorri may have been influenced by knowledge of the English system, but an ancient piece of evidence which suggests there is something authentic in his account is the poem *Vellekla* (p. 365) composed about 990, in which the poet says that Hákon Hlaðajarl (died 995) ruled over the land of sixteen earls. This answers rather closely to the number of *fylke* on the west coast of Norway, from Rogaland in the south to Hákon's hereditary power in Hálogaland in the north, including also the eight *fylke* of Trøndelag. However this may be, it is clear that earls could not long have played a part in national administration, and there would indeed hardly be room for them. There were plenty of king's sons and grandsons about, and they preferred to be kings themselves.

In the laws an earl figures in the hierarchy on the same level as a bishop. He is midway between the 'landed man' and the king, with a wergild twice the former's and half the latter's.

Kings

The Germanic word 'king', Norse *konungr*, has as its basic meaning 'man of noted origin'. The prime significance of descent, suggested by the etymology, is fully borne out by the nature of kingship in the northern countries in the early period. The main features of Germanic kingship remain unaltered. Kings were drawn from a particular family, and within that family any man in the direct male line, legitimate or illegitimate, young or old, was eligible. A choice then had to be made and this choice rested with the people – the free yeomen and their leaders. Often, of course, the choice might be obvious, or the election might be engineered, for a king was likely to be interested in finding the man to succeed him. It may be that the title of 'king' was used fairly freely in early Norway and among Viking bands, but, as far as we know, it was always necessary for the name to be conferred upon a member of a particular family in a formal, specific way. A man was 'given the title of king', 'accepted as king', 'judged to be king', always by a group of ordinary men acting, or claiming to act, for all their kind. Thereafter the elected king and his people, through these same representatives, bound themselves by mutual oaths. The two sides of the bargain are put like this in an early text: 'the yeomen had great strength and great support to offer to the king, power to maintain his dignity; and in return the king was to provide princely service and leadership in difficulties and battles.' This election, acceptance and hailing of the king was normally done, or repeated as soon as possible, at the major provincial assemblies. Thus in Denmark the new king appeared at the assemblies at Viborg (Jutland), Lund (Skåne) and Ringsted (Sjælland), and probably in early times made a further progress as well. In Sweden the new king was first accepted at the assembly at Mora äng, ten miles southeast of Uppsala, where there seems to have been a ceremony which entailed lifting the king up onto a boulder. He then made his progress through the country by the recognized route called *Eriksgata*, probably best interpreted as 'the road of the only-mighty', and appeared at other assemblies, where the oaths of mutual trust were again sworn by him and the leading men of each province.

Once a king had been made in this way, he took over the official wealth of the monarchy – in Sweden this was called the 'Uppsala-wealth'. There might be some immediate treasure in silver, goods, horses, ships, but essentially his resources lay in land, stock and buildings on estates scattered over the countryside. A new king would naturally remember close kinsmen and friends in appointments to offices, but it was a very rudimentary administration that he had in the early period and continuity was essentially provided by the hereditary leaders in the districts.

The king derived his special nature from his paternal ancestors but his real powers were firmly regarded as lent him by the people. St Rimbert in the ninth century said of the Swedes: 'For it is the custom among them that all public business depends more on the unanimous will of the people than on the royal power'; and his words are echoed by Adam of Bremen 200 years later. The old Frostathing Law says: 'No man shall make an attack on another, neither the king nor anyone else. And if the king does this, then an arrow-message shall be sent round all the [eight] *fylke*, and he is to be sought out and killed if he is found. And if he escapes, he is never to return to the country.' The king was subject to the law, not above it.

The king had one function: to maintain and, if possible, improve the 'honour, safety and well-being' of his people. This he could do by defending his people against human enemies and by successful aggression. This made him responsible for public safety, and the organization and conduct of war. These activities were bound to involve him in law-making, in adjudication and in the execution of legal decisions, but a king cannot originally have had independent legislative and judicial functions. The other important way to ensure continued prosperity was by procuring the favour of the divine powers. A king represented the whole people in relations with neighbouring chiefs, for example, and he had the same intermediary function in their dealings with the gods. He had to play his part in prescribed ritual, and special circumstances might require religious initiative on his part. In pagan times successful war could also have a religious aspect, while after the Conversion, Christian ideas of how a king should behave gradually prevailed, at least in theory.

We get the clearest idea of a pagan leader's relationship with the gods in the poem called *Vellekla,* composed about 990 (see p. 365), in praise of Earl Hákon, ruler of virtually all Norway at that time. As a warrior, Hákon killed his enemies and so swelled Odin's supply of seasoned fighting men; he came to power *at mun banda* – with the good will and to the pleasure of the gods. Twice the poet says that the divinities 'steered' Hákon, directed his course. The earl protected the sanctuaries and, as a result, the beneficial gods turned to the sacrifices, and the ground grew as it used to. As for the good works of a peaceful Christian king, we have a rare catalogue in the words of self-praise put into the mouth of King Eystein of Norway. He lived at the beginning of the twelfth century, but this passage is from *Morkinskinna*, written a century later.

Up north in Lofoten I established a fishing station so that poor people might make a living . . . and I built a church there and provided a living for a priest, and put money towards church-building in a place that was up to then practically heathen . . . In Trondenes I also put up a church and endowed it . . . there was a route from Trøndelag over the Dovre mountains, people often died of exposure there and had hard journeys – I built a hospice there and endowed it . . . Off Agdenes there was a bare coast and no harbours, and ships were always being wrecked there, but now a harbour has been built and a good berthing-place for ships, and a church put up as well . . . then I had beacons made on the mountain-tops . . . I also had the palace made in Bergen and the Church of the Apostles and a staircase between them . . . I also had St Michael's Church built and established a monastery there. I also arranged the laws so that all men might have justice in their dealings one with another . . .

There has been much discussion as to whether the pre-Christian northern peoples regarded their kings as sacred, as if they themselves partook of the nature of the gods. It seems certain that they did not go so far. It does seem clear, on the other hand, that they regarded kings (or in some cases earls) as a special kind of human being – because of their descent, because of traditional attitudes of awe and loyalty, because of their position as mediators between men and gods, and doubtless because some kings were exceptionally able and imperious men, with riveting powers of personality. The Vikings probably had as little notion as we have of the true source of the vitality that was believed to exist in the royal line. Descent from gods was often claimed (Earl Hákon is called 'offspring of divinities' in the poem *Vellekla*, for example), but this certainly did not make the king's person sacrosanct. But although kings were not regarded as incarnations of divinity, it does on occasion seem to have been believed that in some way they were personally responsible for the fecundity in crops and beasts evident in their reigns, as if the gods favoured them not only for what they did but for what they were. This would explain some stories that tell of people's reluctance to part with bodies of prosperous rulers – the best-known one, but doubtless apocryphal, is told by Snorri about the ninth-century Norwegian king, Halfdan the Black, whose corpse was quartered so that four provinces might each have a part. It might also account for the interest displayed in the deaths and burial places of earlier kings – the latter were evidently sites that needed to be treated with care. Some kings, on the other hand, were made to suffer for bad seasons and other disasters, either by rejection and exile or by death. In the latter case, the king might be offered as a sacrifice to the gods – no higher effort to placate them could be imagined. It seems likely that the position of the king as high priest, symbolic or real, must also have played a part in effecting the conversion of the Vikings to Christianity. Individual Danes and Norwegians might become Christians, but it was only when kings accepted the new faith that it then became established among the whole people, to the exclusion of other beliefs. If people had been used to thinking of the king as perhaps their most important link with the divine powers, it was natural that they should follow his lead when he was baptized. The traditional connections between kingship and public cult may also help to explain why the great national saints of Denmark, Norway, Orkney and Sweden are kings and princes who died at the hands of their own people in the early Christian period of the eleventh and twelfth centuries.

Christianity had a profound influence on kingship. The Church wished to regulate royal succession in accordance with the principles of legitimacy and primogeniture. It was further claimed that the king's authority was derived from God and that without the sacramental sanction of the Church, in the form of unction and crowning, a king was not a king. All this was directly opposed to the native Scandinavian tradition, which looked for descent in the direct male line, irrespective of age and legitimacy, and demanded election of a king by the people. The Church prevailed, but it took two centuries. Evidence of its success falls just within our period. In 1170 in Denmark the child Knut was crowned king in his father's lifetime, and his succession was thus ensured without reference to the possible claims of an illegitimate elder brother and without reference to the assemblies of the people. In Norway the same stage was reached with the accession of Magnús Erlingsson in 1162, a boy whose mother was a king's daughter but whose father was not a king's son, and with his coronation a year or two later. The superiority of the religious power was recognized in the concordat achieved betwen Crown and Church at this time, given expression in the coronation oath and in various statutes from this and later years.

The idea gained ground that the nation was a unity within fixed boundaries in which only one proper king could exist at any given time. With this went the notion that the whole country was the king's patrimony, so that anything not in individual or family ownership automatically fell to the king. Knut Svensson apparently tried to lay claim to Danish woodlands before 1100, and royal annexation was later extended to waste land, to foreshores and coastal waters and rivers, as well as to treasure trove and the forfeit goods of outlaws. Kings also had vested interests in the development of commerce generally and markets and towns in particular: they provided order and safety but exacted tolls, controlled the coinage, and often owned land within the privileged area. The yeomen had from early times contributed to the living expenses of their king, and they had turned out for military service under his leadership; the latter might also entail labour in the building of fortifications. It gradually came about that a king was felt to be owed by his people a complex of dues for civil and military needs, most of which had been translated into cash taxes by the end of our period. This general increase in the king's wealth, influence and authority was supported by the teaching that it was the duty of a Christian subject to be obedient to his lord.

In pagan times the king had been a kind of umpire in legal matters, but he came more and more to be looked on as the first source of law and as the supreme judge, another development aided by the Christian view of a king's duty to maintain religion, virtue and justice and to punish wickedness and vice. With the idea that the country as a whole was the king's there came the idea that the peace of the country at large was his peace. A crime against an individual was thus also a crime against the king, since it was his peace that was broken; and in cases where a man was killed or injured it may have been thought that the king had lost something in the way of notional service from his subject who had suffered. The king should consequently have a share in the compensation that was paid. The precise origins of the king's rights to atonement in this way are obscure. All the mainland Scandinavian laws acknowledge his claims, but in Denmark and Norway especially there are signs that the recognition of the king's rights is still a comparative innovation, and in a number of disputes of a personal kind, for example, the Danish laws make no award to the king in specifying the compensation to be paid.

The idea of treason, disloyalty to the king, as the most serious of crimes also developed with changing ideas about the king's status and the subject's responsibility. Disloyalty to the group at the local or provincial level had, of course, always been known and punished, but in earlier times the king was owed personal fidelity only by those who were his sworn retainers and he was not officially concerned with the man who in some way acted against the interests of the people – this was the affair of the yeomen at their assemblies. In the Danish laws there is no recognition of any kind of lese-majesty, although naturally it is all-important in the court law, the *Vederlov* (p. 101). In Swedish laws, on the other hand, we meet a number of offences characterized as *epsörisbrot*, 'sworn-oath offences'. These are crimes which, while unpunished, mean that the king has failed to keep the oath he swore on his accession to maintain peace, and they are thus a standing reproach to him. The king's oath necessarily covered all his people, so statutes concerning such offences were in fact national, not provincial in scope and tended to put the king in a supreme position of legal authority. The new doctrine was also to give the king a menacing increase in political and executive power, since death and the confiscation of property were the usual penalties for such crimes.

The early kings lived with their followers and had little privacy. It was required of them that they should be generous with food and drink, clothes and weapons and other gifts – 'shield-flingers', 'bracelet-givers', to use the terms of poets. They should maintain their own and their people's honour against outsiders, hold their lands in a vice-like grip, as Egil Skalla-Grímsson said of King Eirík Bloodaxe in the tenth century. Peace and prosperity were valued – and there are legends about great and good kings, in whose just days the land grew fat. At the same time, it is typical that of all the Norwegian kings least seems to have been remembered about Ólaf the Quiet, who reigned in peace from 1066 to 1093, while most was remembered, or made up, about the mighty missionary Vikings, Ólaf Tryggvason and Ólaf Haraldsson, who ruled for less than twenty years between them.

The king had to lead. It was an advantage if he had a good voice and a forceful style, for he would often need to speak in public. (We may note in passing that the finest oratory preserved in all the literature of the Norse middle ages is by King Sverri of Norway, witty, mordant, impassioned.) He had to be a fighter, more daring or more crafty than other men; and he had to be hard, for he lived face to face with his followers and fought hand to hand beside them when the time came. Not least, he had to be cheerful, able to inspire and buoy up his men: 'he threw off his war-gear', 'the joyous prince joked with his men', is how a contemporary poet described King Hákon the Good as he cast aside his coat of mail and encouraged his companions before battle in the 960s, both actions a telling summary of these essential qualities looked for in a king.

We know very little about early Swedish kings, more about kings of Denmark through Adam of Bremen and Saxo. We know most about the Norwegian kings and Orkney earls, in some cases through their own poetry, but chiefly in poetry made about them and in the prose of twelfth- and thirteenth-century Icelandic historians. We have, for example, few portraits that are as completely authentic as this near contemporary one of Magnús Erlingsson at the time of his death in 1184:

King Magnús was easy-going and light-hearted; much after the fashion of young men, a great one for drinking and girls.

He enjoyed games and liked to be better than everybody in agility and dexterity. His physical strength was also above the average. He was generous, but he would have his own way, and he was eloquent in speech. He was boldest of all men in battle. Much of a dandy and showy in his dress. He was rather tall, a muscular man, slender waisted, with well-proportioned and shapely limbs. His face was handsome save for some irregularity about the mouth.

King Magnús went into his last battle dressed in a tunic of fine cloth, half white and half red, carrying a famous sword called Fish-spine. We saw earlier what love he inspired in his men (p. 104). He was twenty-eight when he died. We must remember that, although some of the early kings, like Harald the Hard-ruler and Sven Estridsson, grew into grizzled statesmen, many of these kings died young by our standards. The great Knut of England and Denmark became king when he was about sixteen and was under forty when he died. King Hákon the Good of Norway ruled for some twenty years and fell in battle when he was not much over forty. Ólaf Tryggvason was killed when he was about thirty; Ólaf Haraldsson, king and martyr, was about thirty-five, while his son, Magnús the Good, died of disease when he was twenty-three and left a great reputation. Magnús Bareleg was nearly thirty when he died in a raid on Ireland in 1103. It was this Magnús who is supposed to have said, 'A king is for glory, not for long life.' He may have been rash and wrong-headed, but those words strike an authentic note which cannot be ignored in any consideration of kingship – indeed, of life – in the Norse period.

5

Daily life

From archaeology and from the Icelandic literary sources it is possible to quarry a lot of evidence about daily life in the North. The picture recovered from our sources is certainly incomplete. The untidiness, the smell, the fuggy cold and the smoky interior of a house of the Viking Age are difficult to apprehend; yet such physical factors would have had as much effect on the minds of the Scandinavians as the poetry and stories which were told in the halls of the chieftain. In this chapter we can only consider the externals of life, we cannot produce a complete picture of the happiness or misery of the individual Scandinavian.

The basic economy

The economy was based on agriculture and on hunting and fishing. Only merchants and administrators, and the people involved in providing for their needs, lived in the towns, and then probably for only part of the year. For the vast majority of people everyday life was lived in the country; they worked on farms and on the sea and were often – particularly in western Scandinavia – relatively isolated. People would travel to market, to parties and games, to family gatherings or ritual feasts, and such journeys would provide their main social contacts. During the winter months, however, some sort of isolation would descend on most communities and many people would be worried as to whether their provisions would last through the winter. In many places their life would be a constant battle against semi-starvation, cold and disease. Entertainment was at a premium: the embroideress, the craftsman and particularly the story-teller would never starve, for they were the people who illuminated the winter months and helped make life tolerable. For the rest, games, feasts and the recollection of past events were all that would cheer those involved in the dreary round of farm-life in the dark northern winter.

This gloomy picture is not a completely true reflection of life throughout the Viking world. In Denmark, for example, the single farm was less isolated from its neighbours than in the northern valleys and communication was easier. In Iceland the first settlers were fairly rich and owned a good deal of land and doubtless led a reasonably comfortable life; but to many people in Norway and Sweden the family economy would be cut to the bone.

One great difficulty in understanding Scandinavian society of the Viking period is a lack of knowledge of the poorer classes (cf. pp. 118–22). In the literature we receive an impression of a 'middle-class' society. We know something of the slaves, of the hostages and of the family servants, but only rarely, as in the *Hávamál*, do we catch a glimpse of the smallholder and his family. In the chapter which follows this slant towards the richer members of society must be continually borne in mind.

Economic life is naturally conditioned by local ecology – climate, soil, solid and surface geology, geographical position, height above sea level and many other physical factors must be taken into account when attempting to reconstruct the past. In an area as large as Scandinavia it is impossible to make very many specific statements about the basic economy of the Viking Age. Generally speaking, however, the further north the settlement the less cereal crops were grown and the more important animal husbandry became. In the far north a hunting-fishing economy would be supplemented by a few cattle or sheep (cf. p. 40), but even such judgments may have to be modified, for fragments of ploughs of alleged Viking date have been found in Troms, 200 miles north of the Arctic Circle. In the coastal regions, fishing would be an important factor in the daily life of the people. Where mountain pastures were available, the farmer might move his animals to the higher ground for summer feeding. In Iceland the economy was mainly pastoral, in the Danish islands it was based on mixed farming, with a bias towards grain production.

In all areas hunting and fishing were important. Game was relatively plentiful and the lakes contained plenty of fish and, if not, could be artificially stocked; an eleventh-century inscription from Li, Oppland, Norway, records the stocking of a lake, Rausjøen, thirty miles west of Lillehammer: 'Eilif Elk carried fish into Rausjøen.' Fish-hooks and floats of wood as well as hunting or fishing baskets have been found on inland sites and indicate the importance of this side of the economy. Delicious sea-birds – puffins and guillemots, for example – were netted. Duck, ptarmigan and other birds were lured or shot. Eggs were taken from nests. Reindeer, elk, bear, red deer, rabbits and hares could all be hunted, depending on the area in which the huntsmen lived. Whales were stranded or – as today in the Faroe Islands particularly – driven by fishermen into the inlets and killed there; seals were hunted. Offshore fishing with net and line produced food which could be dried or salted away for the winter months or traded at the nearest markets. Despite the opportunities for supplementing diet by hunting, local famines were common, especially in years when the crops failed. Such shortages, which are often recorded in literature, may be put down largely to inefficient techniques of food storage and even of husbandry.

Although food was the primary object of hunting and fishing, many raw materials were produced as a result of the chase. Bone and antler were used for making knife-handles, combs and spindle-whorls; and the raw material was sometimes traded over great distances – reindeer antlers, for example, were brought to Lund from the far north of Scandinavia. Furs had an obvious value and were one of the chief exports of Scandinavia – the skins of seal, walrus, bear and reindeer would be in great demand, as were such products of the skins as ropes. Walrus ivory was of great value and objects made of this material, presumably imported from the north or from Greenland, are found throughout northwest Europe. Oil for lamps and feathers for bedding were both by-products of the huntsman's skill.

Despite the importance of hunting and fishing, the economy was firmly based on agriculture. Cattle, sheep, horses and goats were bred for both meat and milk; pigs were common in south Scandinavia. Remains of chicken and other domestic fowl rarely occur in archaeological finds, but they are mentioned in the Eddaic poems and other sources; geese seem to have been particularly common. The cattle were smaller than those with which we are familiar today, but animal husbandry was well advanced; in Iceland, for example, measurements of bones from settlements of the Viking Age have shown that the beasts were at least as tall as, if not taller than, later medieval Danish cattle. Further, there is some evidence that farming in this period was more intensive than it had been previously. It was during the Viking period, for example, that Norwegian farmers developed to the full the practice of transferring their stock to the mountain pastures during the summer months. Burials in these mountain settlements (Norw. *sæter*) begin in the Migration Period but become more common in the Viking Age, and it is probable that this farming practice did not start until the seventh or eighth century.

In certain hill areas of the Atlantic colonies shieling sites were developed for sheep-farming. In the Faroe Islands it is probable that this practice was copied from the Celtic world, since the Norse word *ærgi* (borrowed from Irish or Gaelic, cf. Ir. *airghe*, Gaelic *airgh*, 'shieling') only occurs in northwest England and the Atlantic islands but not in Iceland. Since the *sæter* obviously developed in Norway in a period before there was any real contact with the Celtic world, it is possible, therefore, that the function of the *sæter* and the *ærgi* differed in some way. Excavation in the Isle of Man on such sites has not produced any conclusive dating evidence earlier than the twelfth century, but the excavator, Peter Gelling, postulates a Viking date for some of the recorded examples.

Throughout Europe at this time, as the pastures became exhausted in the autumn, the cattle were carefully sorted and the weaker ones were killed off in order that the available fodder should last through the winter months. (It has been calculated that a cow would eat 2500 kg. of hay during the Icelandic winter.) The slaughtered animals were dismembered and then smoked, pickled or dried to fill the larder. Sheep and goats, being hardier, could survive the winter, although in Iceland they might be taken indoors overnight or at the height of a storm.

It is difficult to generalize about the crops that were grown, because the physical evidence is so sparse and is scattered over such an enormous area. Only in south Scandinavia, in Denmark and Skåne, is the evidence capable of reasonably clear interpretation, and only here has any concerted work been done on the problem of vegetable remains. Grain was, of course, cultivated throughout Scandinavia; indeed, literary sources and finds of such tools as querns demonstrate that it was grown in northern Norway and Iceland. Carbonized and waterlogged grain (from settlement sites) and bread (from graves) tell us something of the kind of cereals grown. Rye was becoming more popular at this period, but it is impossible to say with any certainty how much more important it was than oats or barley. Other cultivated crops included peas, hops and cabbage. (Cabbage was probably introduced in the Viking Age, since its name, *kál*, is a loan-word from Frisian or Anglo-Saxon.) Wild fruit added to the diet, apples, cherries, plums, sloes, elderberries, blackberries, strawberries, raspberries, blueberries and hips have been recorded; wild garlic, angelica and wild leek are also documented, as are hazelnuts and walnuts; acorns are occasionally found on Viking sites and may have been used for making bread. Seaweed may also have been collected for food or fodder. Some of these fruits and vegetables could have been cultivated, or at least cared for; Norwegian laws, for example, have references to angelica-, cabbage- and leek-gardens. Flax for making linen was also cultivated.

Settlements and houses

It is usually said that in Denmark villages were the normal form of settlement, while elsewhere in Scandinavia settlements took the form of single farms. One site which shows the inadequacy of such a generalization is at Vollmoen on Engeløya, in Norway, where sixteen houses surrounded a central oval area, which measured 30 x 60 mm., but this site, which is typical of a number found in Nordland and in Rogaland, may be of much earlier date. Again it could be argued, for instance, that what is in effect a village of the Migration Period has been excavated at Vallhagar on the Baltic island of Gotland, and there can be no reason to deny the existence of villages in Sweden during the rather later period covered by this book; indeed, a fortified settlement of some size at Eketorp in Öland (see pp. 263–4), which, after a period of desertion, was in permanent use from the beginning of the eleventh century, argues definitely in favour of such a conclusion. Intensive search, together with the reconstruction of medieval land utilization, has, however, failed to reveal any satisfactory evidence of Viking Age villages in Gotland; indeed, only one Viking Age farm has been excavated on the island. In Iceland, Greenland, and to a certain extent in Norway and Sweden and some of the colonies, evidence for scattered single farms is better documented. On the other hand, at least three settlements excavated in Denmark must certainly be classed as villages of the Viking Age. One of these lies under the Viking fortress at Aggersborg in Jutland (see p. 270). Another is the village at Hagestad in Skåne which seems to have housed a small fishing community. The third and best-documented village is at Lindholm Høje in Jutland which is discussed below. Generally speaking, however, many scholars would accept that the villages of the Viking Age in Denmark lie under the present villages. This cannot, however, be altogether true, for preliminary investigation of some deserted villages suggests that the Danish 'village' must sometimes have consisted of a community of separate farms and was not necessarily a nucleated settlement set round a green or along a street – this for example is the case at Borup Ris.

The most thorough investigation of a Viking village was that undertaken at Lindholm Høje on the northern shore of the Limfjord in Denmark. In some respects it seems rather advanced, for it may well have had a trading function, as it certainly had a manufacturing function (remains of a metalworking industry were discovered on the site). The village dates from the eleventh century and partly overlays an earlier Viking Age grave field. It died as a settlement c. 1100, perhaps because of the effect of drifting sand, perhaps because of the silting up of the fjord. Most of the houses uncovered here had at least two building periods and the mass of post-holes is difficult to interpret, but at least four different forms of house have been recognized. The most unusual form was a square courtyard house, but at least one long house with bowed sides was found, as well as long houses of rectangular ground plan and some twenty-five huts with sunken floors. The courtyard house is unique in Scandinavian civil settlements of the Viking period, although groups of houses arranged in this fashion occur at the great Danish military sites at Trelleborg, Fyrkat and Aggersborg (fig. 41). The Lindholm house is the earliest example of a type of courtyard house which was common, but not universal, in south Scandinavia up to the present century. Unfortunately, all that survives is the ground plan, and it is impossible to determine the use of the different units of the building.

The buildings with sunken floors found at Lindholm are of a type known all over western Europe throughout the first millennium. They occur elsewhere on Danish sites of the period, for example, in the towns of Aarhus and Hedeby, in the pre-camp village at Aggersborg and in the village at Hagestad in Skåne. The houses were rectangular, mostly between three and five metres in length; they had upright supports for the ridge pole at the gable ends and the roof came down to ground level on either side. At Lindholm – as at many other European sites – a good number of them contained implements connected with weaving and they are often described as weavers' huts, but evidence elsewhere suggests that they were used as ordinary dwelling houses by poorer members of society. The presence of weaving implements in such houses is explained by the fact that weaving was the commonest independent activity of the ordinary cottager.

Long houses with curved walls are also found throughout Germanic Europe. The earliest example of a Scandinavian house of this form occurs at Trælborg, near Kolding, Jutland, and dates from the fifth century. Such houses are encountered in most of the Viking areas, but have not yet been found in Sweden. They are best documented in the great eleventh-century Danish camps (pp. 270–1) and are so typical of these camps that they are often described as houses of the Trelleborg type, after the most famous of them. At Trelleborg (fig. 10) these

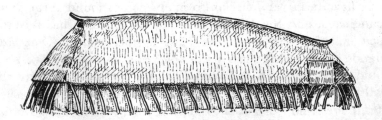

Fig. 10. House of the Trelleborg type, based on a number of reconstructions by Olaf Olsen.

houses, about thirty metres long, were constructed of halved tree-trunks, set together in upright rows, the curved face being placed externally, as in the stave-churches of south Sweden and Norway (see fig. 59). Elsewhere other building techniques were used – particularly common are wattle-and-daub structures and houses with walls of turf set on stone foundations. At Trelleborg the roof was carried on the walls, which are supported at the top by external posts set at an angle to the wall, producing an effect rather like the later medieval flying buttress – their position in certain cases implies the use of wall-plates (horizontal beams at the top of the wall). Rooves were perhaps shingled (i.e. covered with small wooden plate-like tiles), perhaps thatched, perhaps covered with turf or with thin flat stones overlaid by turf. The curved wall produced a curved roof ridge. Some idea of the outward form of the building can be gained from a number of house-shaped objects: a casket or shrine, once in Cammin Cathedral in Poland, the model house on the head of a pin from Klinta on the Swedish island of Öland (pl. 2c), the ornament on the earliest Scandinavian coins, pictures on Gotlandic stones, and a series of English tomb-covers, known as 'hog-backed' tombstones (pl. 10). These last, which are presumably meant to represent the house of the dead, often take the form of a house with a shingled roof. At Trelleborg the houses were divided transversely to produce a large central room flanked by two smaller ones; the large room had benches along each wall and a long central hearth. The doors were in the long sides at either end and were apparently entered by a porch. The houses at Trelleborg, Fyrkat and Aggersborg were, of course, built for a military purpose (see p. 270), but their external appearance must have been very similar to many houses found throughout Scandinavia and the Viking colonies. An example has recently been excavated on Unst, the most northerly of the Shetland Islands, while in the Faroes examples of such houses have been found at Sørvágur, Kvívík and Fuglafjørður (pl. 3b). Here the walls were of turf on stone foundations and, as on many such sites, there is no trace of the external posts found at the Danish camps or at Lindholm Høje. The roof was supported internally by two rows of posts, the base of the post usually resting on a large stone and not buried in the ground; there were benches along the sides, but no evidence of internal walls. At the Braaid, in the Isle of Man, the long walls of a house of this form were apparently of turf and the gable walls of timber. Small details like these differentiate the houses from site to site, from country to country, but basically the form was the same and in some areas apparently persisted until the thirteenth and fourteenth centuries.

One unsolved problem concerning the houses of the Viking Age, and particularly those of the Trelleborg type, concerns the form of the roof timbering. There are as many arguments as there are types of roof and in view of the many imponderables – we do not even know whether the Scandinavians normally used a tie-beam or not – it would be unwise to enter into a discussion which can only produce a series of unfounded generalizations.

A common form of Viking house is the long house, sometimes known as a hall-house, with straight sides. Such houses, which are found in all parts of the Scandinavian world both at home and in the colonies, have ancient origins and are encountered throughout the Germanic area. The details of construction are very like those of the curved-sided houses (without the external supports found in the camps) – sometimes, indeed, the corners are rounded giving a similar general appearance to the latter's ground plan. Some of these long houses are very grand and were beautifully constructed. At Westness in Orkney, for example, a house measuring some 30 x 8 m. awaits excavation. It has been compared with 'Earl Sigurd's Hall' on the nearby island of Birsay, which has been excavated and dated to the tenth or early eleventh century. Much of 'Earl Sigurd's Hall' has been eroded by the sea, and it is consequently difficult to interpret the whole complex and the hall in particular, but it must originally have been nearly as large as the Westness house. The walls are of turf (2 m. thick) with an external facing of carefully-placed flagstones. Less imposing long houses of this form are the basis of many of the more elaborate farm complexes of the Viking period. Such a complex is that excavated at Ytre Moa, Årdal, Sogn, Norway, where the ruins of six rectangular houses have been investigated. The houses were scattered haphazardly about the site without being connected to each other by common walls. The investigation is not yet completely published but it seems reasonable to suppose that some of the structures functioned as farm buildings, although it is clear that not all the buildings were contemporary and that the two dwelling houses so far discovered were occupied at different times – one replacing the other after a fire.

The farm complex itself has been most thoroughly examined in one of the southern Icelandic valleys – Þjórsárdalur. From *Landnámabók* we know that Þjórsárdalur was settled in the first stages of the colonization of Iceland at the end of the ninth century and it seems likely that it was thoroughly settled by the end of the tenth century. About 1104 an eruption of the volcano Hekla devastated the buildings and fields of about twenty farms in this area. The ash from the great eruption covered the valley and it has lain waste ever since so that the excavators, who tackled a number of sites in the valley in 1939, had a unique opportunity of recovering details of the daily life of a farming community during the first centuries of the colonization. Not all the available sites were excavated, but attention was concentrated on Skallakot, Stöng, Snjáleifartóttir, Ásláks-tunga fremri, Skeljastaðir and Stórhólshlíð; in 1960 a further site in the area – Gjáskógar – was excavated with similar results. It should be realized that many of the conclusions of the excavators of 1939 were based on the hypothesis that the eruption of Hekla took place in 1300. The revised dating to *c.* 1104 enables us to make much more sense of this important investigation.

Excavation showed that the basic hall-house of the settlement period was first split up into separate rooms, then extended by the addition of small rooms at the rear which opened out of the hall, and then extended again by the addition of a living room at one end of the main building. These changes took place in the course of two centuries and the process of change must have begun shortly after the period of initial settlement, when it was realized that the large hall or a complex of scattered buildings was hardly suitable for the Icelandic climate. A comparison of the description of the Flugumýrr farm, drawn from the account in *Íslendinga saga* of its burning in 1253, with the excavated sites has enabled scholars to understand the different purposes to which the various rooms were put (explained in fig. 11). From this description it appears that the main hall was divided

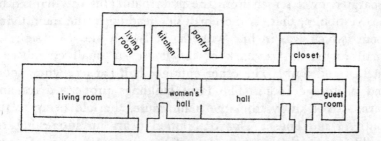

Fig. 11. Reconstruction of the Flugumýrr farm, based on the description in Íslendinga saga.   After Roussell.

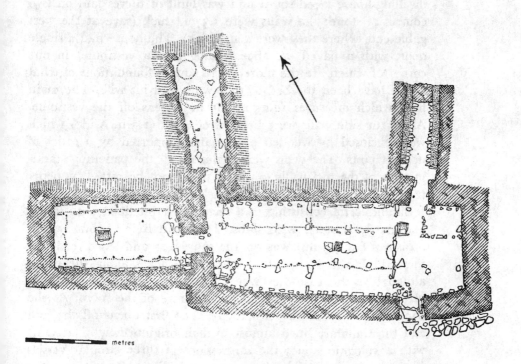

Fig. 12. Plan of the farmhouse at Stöng, Iceland.

into two unequal portions; the smaller one, for the women, being separated by a screen from the main hall. This was flanked by two vestibules, that on the north side leading to the main living room (which was in line with the hall) and also to a series of small rooms at the back of the house – a small chamber, a kitchen and dairy. The other entrance hall led to a guest room and a storage room. The farm buildings proper – byres and barns – stood away from the main house, the fold being to the south of the house. This description bears an interesting resemblance to the ground plan of the excavated sites of 1939. The lay-out of the excavated sites demonstrates the casual nature of the planning of the building; rooms were apparently added as the need arose, with little regard to appearances.

Typical of these farm complexes is that at Stöng (fig. 12) which stands on a small rise in the heart of the valley. The main dwelling-house faced south and was built of turves laid on two courses of stone; the walls were 1.3 m. thick (save at the west gable end, where they were 2 m. thick). The house had a single door, with a paved entrance leading into a vestibule, in one corner of which are the more-or-less square foundations of what might have been the bed of the owner and his wife. The main hall (which measures 12.25 x 5.85 m.) opens off the vestibule. Along the side walls were benches of earth (1.5 m. wide) which were enclosed by wooden planks and supported by a series of upright posts. The walls were wainscotted, the panelling standing free of the turf walls so that it would not be rotted by penetrating damp. There was a long central fireplace of typical Icelandic form, consisting of a rectangular pit lined with stones and partly covered with slabs. The main living room (which measures 8 x 4.3 m.) was on the same axis and led directly off the hall. It was wainscotted and had benches along the walls, although in this case they were only 50 cm. in width. The fireplace consists of a stone box in the centre of the room. At the back of the house were two rooms. The first opens off the hall and the walls are lined almost to their original height (1.1 m.) with a volcanic stone; the impressions of three circular vessels (1.44 m. in diameter) in one corner indicate that it was the dairy. The second room, opening off the vestibule, was, according to the excavators, perhaps used for storing meat – other scholars suggest that it was a lavatory. To the east of the house was a building presumably devoted to storage and, a little further to the east, the byre. Although incomplete, the byre is an impressive building with a series of upright stone slabs which form stalls on either side of a paved central alley which could easily be cleaned when the byre was mucked out. Standing apart from the rest of the complex was a small building with a sunken fire-box which must be taken to be a smithy. Among the equipment found on the floor was a large stone (presumably an anvil), a basin to hold water for quenching the metal, and a small quern which it has been suggested was used for making a red dye from volcanic ash.

Such a farm was probably typical of Iceland in the Viking period – similar houses have been excavated elsewhere in that country – but that the type was not confined to Iceland is demonstrated by the presence of a similar complex at the Norse site of Birsay, Orkney. The earlier type of dwelling, in which the buildings had not come together to form a house with more than one or two rooms, can probably be seen at the Icelandic settlement of Hofstaðir (because of its simplicity of plan and because of its name, *hof*, which means 'a building used for cult purposes', this was at one time considered to be a temple, cf. p. 398). Hofstaðir has a large hall and only one or two ancillary rooms.

We must, however, turn to other colonial areas for a really substantial and well-published Viking farm complex. A site at the southern tip of the mainland of Shetland, romantically named Jarlshof by Sir Walter Scott, has provided us with a typical farm of the Viking period at a place which has a continuous history of habitation from the prehistoric period to the middle ages. The original ninth-century house at Jarlshof was about 23 m. long and divided into two rooms – a hall and a kitchen. The walls were curved, and the hall had stone-faced benches on either side. Except for the east gable the house was stone-built. At the end of the eleventh century a byre was added at one end. About a century later the main dwelling was abandoned and a small long-house was built at the opposite end of the byre. Some distance to the northwest were the associated buildings – a bathhouse (a simple building for a steam bath like a modern *sauna*), stables, barn, smithy and other buildings, all separate from each other. A complex like that found at Jarlshof must have been common in Norway and the British colonies, and perhaps, even, in Sweden.

In concluding this short survey of the main physical features of Viking houses it should be said that the available evidence does not really help us in solving general problems of settlement patterns in the Viking Age. No clear picture of these is likely to emerge until much more archaeological work has been done.

Specialized buildings

Apart from certain types of farm buildings and work-hops (discussed elsewhere) two main kinds of structure should also be mentioned – the boat-house and the mill.

The importance of the sea to the Vikings cannot be over-emphasized. They took care of their boats and during the winter they were kept in boat-houses (*naust*). The ruins of some hundreds of these houses are scattered along the shores of Norway and, although some of them date from the Migration Period and many of them belong to later times, some at least are of Viking date.

Lying in isolation near the shore they have one open end and walls curved like those of the houses found at Trelleborg (fig. 10). A Norwegian example dating from the Migration Period, at Killingsviken, Leirvik på Stord, Sunnhordland, had a line of stones lying where the keel would rest. There were no internal post-holes in this building – so here at least the roof rested directly on the wall. The significance of buildings of this form in the general history of Scandinavian houses is controversial, but their existence cannot be ignored.

In farms in most parts of Scandinavia and the Viking colonies grain was ground by hand in querns with a circular upper stone and an eccentric handle. Richer families might use quernstones of imported Eifel lava. In the centre of the upper stone was a hole through which unground grain was poured. Children were sometimes given model querns (examples having been found, for example, at Jarlshof and on Unst) – a sure sign that corn-grinding was an everyday occupation.

In centres of greater population, however, water-mills were introduced towards the end of the Viking Age. They appear in

Norse as *kvern* or *mylna* (a loan-word from OLG, ultimately from Latin *molina*) and later in the middle ages they often figure in legal documents. In 1161, for example, the monastery at Tommarp, in the rich agricultural province of Skåne, owned five mills on the local river, one of which was a fulling-mill. What may well be an example of an early eleventh-century mill has been discovered in the town of Lund. When it was first published it was interpreted as a bath-house, but Egon Thun has pointed to the very close parallel between this building and water-mills elsewhere. Very little remains of the structure; only a square floor and a long water channel, which Thun presumes to have been used to direct the water to turn the wheel. A large area of alluvial mud in the area was perhaps deposited as the result of damming existing watercourses to provide a regular supply for the mill.

The evidence at Lund is thin, but does seem to demonstrate the existence of water-mills about a hundred years before the earliest records of mills in documentary sources. A rather later water-mill has been discovered recently at Borup Ris in Jutland, dated by the radio-carbon method to 1150±100 years. It probably had a horizontal wheel, but we must await Axel Steensberg's publication of this important monument which, he hints, may have been preceded by earlier mills of which only faint traces of the dams survive.

Furnishing

Houses are built as shells in which people can live, and their decoration and furnishing play an important part in the enjoyment of life. The ground plan which the archaeologist uncovers enables us to reconstruct the shell; to furnish it one must turn to casual finds and literary description. Eating, sleeping and sitting about were the main activities provided for. From literary sources we know that tables were, on special occasions, set up on trestles along the front of the benches which lined the walls, but smaller tables must also have been in everyday use. One such table survived in a tenth- or eleventh-century grave at Hørning in Denmark; made of oak with a moulded frame below the top, it stands on four legs, and is only 30 cm. high and 50 cm. across. Whether this was a normal piece of furniture or whether it was especially constructed for use in the grave is unclear: there is however some evidence that furniture was generally not very high, and this is borne out by some of the surviving chairs (fig. 13). Benches were built along the long walls of the house, forming an integral part of the structure (see p. 156). The central section of one bench was the rightful seat (*ǫndvegi*) of the owner of the house, conventionally but misleadingly called the 'high-seat,' in English; the guest of honour sat opposite the host. The 'high-seat' was flanked by the 'high-seat' pillars, the appearance of which cannot be surely reconstructed. They were probably not an integral part of a house because on more than one occasion settlers took these pillars from Norway to Iceland and it does not seem likely that they would have pulled down their houses to get at them. On sighting the new land they threw the pillars overboard and built their new house near the place where they were washed up, a practice which indicates in some measure the symbolic importance of such objects (cf. p. 400).

The benches also served as beds and would presumably be covered with furs and skins, perhaps even with woollen blankets. Richer people would have a separate bed-closet, perhaps built into the structure of the house – as possibly at Stöng (see p. 156); such bed-closets were partitioned off from the rest of the house and could be closed by a door with an internal fastening. Movable beds are also found among the furnishings of the rich boat burials, but it is not known whether these were only used by travellers. Eiderdown-type bed-coverings were found at Oseberg, a down-filled pillow is recorded from a Danish grave at Mammen, Jutland, while mattresses were found at Tune, Norway. Bedding and feathers are specifically mentioned as part of the booty taken after the sack of Dublin in 1000. The various members of an ordinary household would sleep all over the house; the kitchen with its tempting fire was, for example, a recognized sleeping-room. It is clear from the literature that by the thirteenth century separate huts or houses were also used as sleeping quarters and, although these have not been found on single farm sites, we might assume that some of the huts with sunken floors found on more populous sites fulfilled this function. Chairs have been found in the Norwegian boat burials and in the excavations at Lund (fig. 13); from Lund also comes a three-legged stool.

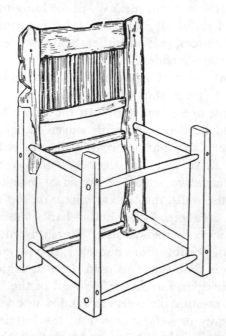

Fig. 13. Reconstruction of a chair from Lund; height of back 75 cm.
Kulturhistoriska Museet, Lund.

Storage was always a problem; cupboards were unknown and
many objects – particularly weapons – would be hung on the
walls of the houses, while some things – clothes for example –
would be kept in chests. A tool chest was discovered at Mästermyr in Gotland and a number of chests have been found in Norway. Some were fastened with built-in locks, but barrel-shaped
padlocks, which are often found on settlement sites, must also
have been used to secure private property. Keys of bronze and
iron – the badge of the housewife – are commonly found on
Viking sites. Cooking utensils of soapstone, pottery and metal
could be piled on the floor, or on rough shelves; buckets, wooden
storage bins and tubs would also be treated in the same way,
while at Stöng we have seen how tubs for sour milk and whey
were let into the floor. Food was stored in various ways: on
shelves, buried in the ground, or (where there was sufficient salt
in the atmosphere) merely hung up to dry on the outside walls

of the house; some fish and meat would be hung indoors and we may presume that fish-drying sheds (*hjallr*), mentioned in thirteenth-century sources, existed earlier. Some food would certainly be stored in larders outside the house.

An important piece of equipment in most houses would be the upright loom (see p. 169) which, when in use, would presumably lean against one of the walls. In the richer houses some of the walls would be decorated with woven hangings. Generally these would be plain, but in wealthy houses richly decorated tapestries, like those found at Oseberg (narrow strips of cloth which depict narrative scenes of heroic or religious character) were hung on the walls, displayed perhaps on top of plain hangings on special occasions. Other houses had wainscotting decorated with elaborate incised carving. Eleventh-century Icelandic panels (pl. 23a), possibly from churches, survive to give us some idea of the linear style that was used. In a description of the interior of a Norwegian farmhouse we read of the 'newly-planed' panelling: this presumably refers to sanded wooden walls which would give a grey or yellow colour to the interior of a house. Painted fragments of decorative woodwork from the royal burial mounds at Jelling and Gokstad and from an eleventh-century stave church at Hørning, Denmark, demonstrate that such wooden carvings were not always left colourless; furniture too was occasionally painted.

The floors were of stamped earth – often strewn with reeds – and must have collected a great deal of dirt, whilst the atmosphere in the main rooms cannot have been improved by the smoke, which would billow around the rafters, ultimately finding its way out through a hole in the roof. One might suppose that in some cases the fire was laid in an iron fire-basket, of which an example has been found at Mästermyr in Gotland in association with the tools mentioned above. Such a practice must, however, have been rare; more normally the fire was laid within a kerb or a trough in the centre of the floor (as at Stöng, see p. 156) and the word *langeldar* (literally 'long fires') indicates its long narrow shape. The fire on the main hearth was always kept alight and was the focal point of the house. Fire was struck with flint and steel (or a stone containing iron pyrites) in tinder; both often occur in graves. The woodstack was placed outside the house and at one of the medieval Icelandic sites a circular hole in the lava shows the shape of the stack in a farm buried by a volcanic eruption. The fire also provided illumination, but lamps of soapstone filled with oil were common. Two types of lamp are known; a simple, open bowl, sometimes with suspension loops, and a bowl set on an iron spike which could be stuck upright in the floor. Candles were presumably only available in rich households (one was found in a royal grave at Jelling, for example) and, later, in churches. Tarred billets of wood were used as torches, presumably outside the house. If windows existed they would have been very small and either covered with shutters at night in the winter or 'glazed' with translucent membrane or polished horn; such lights could probably only have occurred in wooden houses, not in those built of turf or stone. Towards the end of the Viking period, however, properly glazed windows are recorded in Denmark; a round-headed window from an eleventh- or twelfth-century stave-church from Framlev, near Aarhus in Denmark, does not, however, have any indications of glazing. In Iceland the first recorded mention of glass in a church occurs in the late twelfth century.

Food and cooking

One of the most important rooms or parts of the house was undoubtedly the kitchen. It was warm here and the lazy spent the day round the fire under the feet of the women who were preparing the food. The food to be cooked was grown on their own farms or bought in local markets; only spices and wines were imported in any quantity.

The diet was based on dairy produce and on fish and meat – either wild or domesticated – *Rígspula* records how in even the poorest household the guest was offered soup and stewed veal. The meat must often have been boiled as a stew in a cauldron on the fire, but meat was also spit-roasted (the Norse word *steikja*, to roast on a spit, whence English 'steak', is related to the English word, 'stick'), but it may also have been boiled in pits filled with water which was heated by taking stones from the fire and transferring them to the pit. Experiments by Michael O'Kelly on the basis of Irish prehistoric evidence have shown that 100 gallons of water in a wooden-lined pit could be brought to the boil by this means in a mere 30 – 35 minutes. A 4.5 kg. (10 lb.) piece of meat could be cooked in 3 hours 40 minutes. This method was in use in Iceland, as in Ireland, until the sixteenth century. Another cooking method involved packing warm stones round meat in a hole in the ground and covering it with earth; the meat, in the words of one Danish archaeologist, was thus 'partly roasted and partly stewed in its own juice'. At Jarlshof fish – ling, saithe and cod – were cooked in an oven heated with small warm stones. Meat and fish were also eaten raw, dried, pickled in brine or whey, salted (especially from the twelfth century onward) and possibly smoked; and there is evidence from Iceland and Norway of the production of sausage-shaped puddings from intestines stuffed with lard, blood and meat. As is the custom nowadays in Iceland, dried cod was eaten with butter. Salt was obtained by boiling sea-water (or even seaweed) and collecting the deposited crystals; foreign salt became an important article of trade in the twelfth century and later. Other seasoning was undoubtedly used, mostly, one presumes, herbs and spices, like juniper berries, which were available locally (at Oseberg, cummin, mustard and horse-radish were found). Members of the onion family, especially garlic, were very popular. More exotic spices were probably imported from the Near East.

In preparation of meat dishes various utensils were used. In some households the roasting spit was formed of iron, either in the form of a fork or of an iron rod, sometimes with an elaborate handle (fig. 14). These could be turned by hand or rested on forked sticks over the fire. Wooden sticks were doubtless also used as spits. Cauldrons (cf. pl. 5) for stews were made of iron sheets riveted into a bowl-like form, or were more simply made of a single iron sheet. Although the thin metal bronze bowls,

Fig. 14. Roasting spit from Søreim, Dale, Luster, Sogn og Fjordane, Norway. Historisk Museum, Bergen.

commonly found in Scandinavia, were probably used for washing rather than for cooking, soapstone bowls were certainly so
used. The cauldrons had a curved base and a twisted iron handle
which enabled them to be suspended from one of the roof beams
or from the apex of a tripod. Another implement used in cooking consists of a spiral strip of metal with a long handle (fig. 15);
this may have been used as a kind of gridiron over a fire.

*Fig. 15. Gridiron for cooking from Nordgården, Sparbu, Nord-Trøndelag,
Norway.* Universitetets Oldsaksamling, Oslo.

Milk was used in various forms, for butter and cheese, and as
a drink. But mostly it was separated into curds and whey or
buttermilk – products which were variously treated. Both butter
and cheese were made from unskimmed milk, the butter was
sometimes heavily salted and could be stored for a fairly long
period of time; a fragment of a churn (the head of the dash) was
found in the Lund excavations. Whey was also used as a pickling
medium and milk was a popular drink. Liquid dairy products
were stored in tubs from which they were ladled with a handled
vessel of wood, bronze or soapstone.
One alcoholic drink was mead, of which the base was honey.

Beer was made from malted barley and hops (although the latter can only have been used late in the period) and there is some indication that fruit wine was made, although this was almost certainly only used for sacramental purposes. True wine was imported and was a great luxury. The Vikings seem to have been men of some thirst; their parties – though probably rare save in the most prosperous circles – were alcoholic in the extreme and, because of the impurities contained in the drink, they must have had the most frightful hangovers. The dangers of drink are emphasized in *Hávamál* (see p. 326), but on the other hand the alcoholic celebration of important events was a social, even a religious, obligation (cf. p. 402).

Grain was of course used for purposes other than the manufacture of drink. Unleavened bread made from rye, barley and even peas was an important element in the diet. From a Viking grave at Ljunga, near Söderköping in Sweden, came a ring-shaped roll of bread about 6 cm. in diameter and 1.7 cm. thick, made of coarsely ground peas with a good admixture of the bark of pine and a bit of sand which must have come from the quern stone. In the Birka graves a number of small oval rolls of carbonized bread of similar size were found, but the type of grain used is unknown. The introduction of the bread-oven is held by some to be coincidental with the introduction of the baking of rye bread, but this is hardly susceptible of proof. The earliest surviving bread-oven was found in eleventh-century levels at Lund; it was domed and may have been part of a communal bakehouse used by all the inhabitants of the area – but this is a late and probably atypical example. Beech oven-rakes were also found here. The normal method of baking was to use the hot ashes of a fire, over which the dough was cooked probably on the long-handled, small, flat, circular pans which are fairly common in Viking Age grave-finds. These pans may have rested on the flat covering stone of fireplaces like that found at Stöng.

Two phrases from *Rígsþula* are always quoted in any discussion of Viking Age bread: *økkvinn hleifr, þungr ok þykkr, þrunginn sáðum*, 'coarse loaf, heavy and thick, stuffed with bran', and *hleifar þunnir hvítir af hveiti*, 'thin loaves, white, of wheat'. The rich could afford better quality grain and better ground flour. The flour ground in a mechanical mill, like the admittedly late example from Lund, or in the imported lava querns (see p. 201), would obviously be finer than that roughly ground from contaminated grain in a hand-quern made of local stone. Both kinds of flour were obviously used in Scandinavia, since some flour was certainly imported into Norway and Iceland in the later part of the period.

As we have seen, vegetables and fruit obviously played a part in the diet. Although peas and beans were cultivated, most vegetables would be gathered wild. It is not known whether they were always cooked or whether they were sometimes eaten raw.

Meals were served twice a day; one meal (*dagverðr*, 'day-meal') fairly early in the morning, after the initial farm work had been done, and the other (*náttverðr*, 'night-meal') in the early evening, when the day's work was over. At meal-times both master and servants, having washed their hands, sat in the hall at a long table or at a number of small tables; in wealthy houses table-cloths might be used. The food was eaten from wooden platters, often of rectangular form, but might also be served in wooden or soapstone bowls or metal pots. Meat was cut with a knife and most people carried a short-bladed knife in a sheath at their waist. Spoons of horn or wood were used for eating stews and porridge. Drink was consumed from cup-shaped vessels of wood or from drinking-horns, which were made, as their name implies, from cattle-horns; they were often, but not always, mounted with a metal tip and their mouth was bound with a strip of sheet metal, which was sometimes elaborately decorated. It was impossible to stand the drinking-horns upright and they must have been held or passed on if they were not drained each time by the drinker, a custom perhaps implied by one of the most famous legends of the god Thor who was challenged to drain a horn, the end of which, without his knowing, was out in the sea. In rich houses imported glass vessels would also have been used (in two Edda poems a glass vessel is referred to as *hrímkalkr*, literally 'frost cup'); like the drinking-horns these would often not stand upright. The drink would probably be served from buckets or bowls with ladles: some beautifully-made and elaborately-ornamented utensils of this sort – a few imported from Britain – have been found which can only have been made for use at table.

Weaving

Other than cooking, the most important domestic craft was weaving. In the humbler houses the loom must have overshadowed the ordinary furniture and, though it may not have been set up throughout the year, it may well have dominated the life of the female – and even the male – members of the household. In Scandinavia the commonest woven cloth was wool, but linen was also produced. To most women – and some men – a good deal of life was given up to spinning, to the manufacture of cloth and to the final preparation of garments or hangings.

The wool was first shorn or plucked from the sheep or goat, then roughly cleaned of burrs and coarse dirt and, finally, graded. Next it was combed with a pair of short-handled wool combs, each of which had the teeth set in a wooden bar at right-angles to the handle. The teeth consist of long iron prongs (about 10 cm. long) with hooked terminals. The carded wool was then attached to a distaff, an object of which no specimen survives; it is, consequently, impossible to say whether it was a long stick, which could be held in the girdle, or a short stick which was held in the hand or the crook of the arm. The wool was then teased out onto a shaped stick or spindle, weighted with a spindle whorl of stone, clay or metal, which was set spinning. The drawn fibres were fed onto it from the distaff. When the spindle reached the floor the yarn was rolled onto the spindle and the process started again. Spindle whorls are one of the commonest objects found on early medieval sites and one must imagine that nearly all the members of the household sat spinning in the winter months – even men and boys.

The yarn was then removed from the spindle and wound either into a ball or, if the wool was to be dyed, into a skein on a frame or reel. Two reels were found from the Oseberg ship-burial (fig. 16): they have a pair of curved bars of wood joined in the same plane by a transverse bar (roughly 40 cm. in length) which served as a grip. The skein was then wound from corner to corner, the curved ends of the bars allowing it to be slipped off when the required length had been wound. A more elaborate reel was also found at Oseberg: known as a swift, it consists of a pair of crossed bars with movable pegs near the terminals. This rotated horizontally on an upright spar so that the wool could be wound round the four pegs. The finer wools were dyed with vegetable or mineral dyes – red, green, purple, yellow and brown – and this process often took place in the skein, as can be seen from the final products. We must also presume that some cloth was dyed after it had been woven and fulled. Local dyeing was, however, not very successful – there was always a demand for finely dyed cloth from abroad.

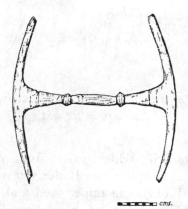

cms.

Fig. 16. Reel for winding wool from Oseberg. Viking Ship Museum, Oslo.

The wool was then woven on an upright warp-weighted loom (fig. 17). The only loom to survive – again from the Oseberg burial – is atypical and one must reconstruct the early medieval loom on the basis of examples found in modern peasant communities, from pieces of equipment which survive in archaeological contexts and from the study of nomenclature. The loom basically consisted of two uprights of wood joined at the top by a bar of circular cross-section. To this were attached the warps, which were weighted at the bottom by soapstone weights or baked-clay rings to give tension to the wool. The warps were divided by a rod into two sheds. The loom was laid at an angle to the wall and probably fixed to it. In this way the warps not held by the shed rod would hang vertically, the other warps remaining in the same plane as the loom. The lower warps (or shed) were tied by loops to a heddle bar (or a number of heddle

169

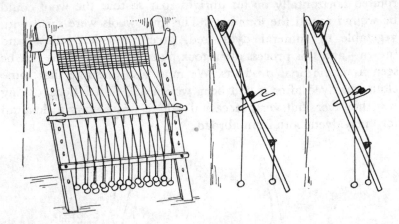

Fig. 17. Diagram of a warp-weighted loom showing the main features described in the text.

bars in the case of twill) which was in front of the upper shed; when this bar was moved towards the weaver the lower shed could be drawn through the upper shed and the weft laid. By releasing the heddle bar the lower shed would then return by gravity to its original position. The weft was kept straight by a weaving baton – a long flat piece of wood or whale-bone, shaped rather like a sword. Various other tools were used for the same purpose; bone combs and rods (known as pin-beaters), which could deal with recalcitrant threads or help in weaving complicated patterns, are often found. It is probable that no shuttle was used in this type of weaving, rather a skein or ball of wool was passed from side to side.

After the cloth was cut from the loom it was, sometimes at least, shrunk in water to thicken it and obliterate gaps and fulled with some alkaline material of detergent property to reduce the dirt and oil content. Fulling was not, however, universal and many of the textiles from the Birka graves for example, were not treated in this way. A fulling mill is indicated by the name *Walkemølla* recorded in twelfth-century Skåne.

This account of the process of preparing cloth is highly simplified. There would be many variations from the norm, but the basic method described here must have been used through much of the Viking period. The method of preparing flax, for example, was different, but the process of weaving linen was similar. The method of starting and finishing pieces varied, and borders and braids were sometimes produced by tablet-weaving. By this process the warp passed through holes in the corners of a number of small rectangular plaques of bone or wood, which were then juggled by the weaver to produce various types of highly complicated step, meander or animal patterns. At Oseberg, for instance, some fifty-two such plaques were found in the burial.

The atypical loom found at Oseberg poses another problem. It is technically described as a two-beam vertical loom. It has two lateral posts, joined by transverse posts at top and bottom and stands on its own feet. Marta Hoffman notes the suggestion that it might have been used for weaving figured fabrics, like the elaborate examples found at Oseberg, but carefully states that its actual use is unknown. It is even possible to suggest that it is not a loom at all, but a stretcher used for embroidery.

The importance of cloth is illustrated by the fact that in Iceland it was a recognized form of internal currency (see p. 55) and was the staple Icelandic export. In the Viking Age, however, we have no evidence that it was anything more than a cottage industry. A fairly large amount of cloth survives from the Scandinavian Viking Age. It is mostly found in graves and rarely occurs in large pieces. One of the largest finds, from Oseberg, is not, however, properly published. Two main weaves predominate – plain (or tabby) weave and twill. Basically, plain weave consists of single wefts over single warps alternately, while in twill weaving the wefts pass over one warp and under two or more warps, to produce an effect of diagonal lines. Both these weaves are found, but it is difficult to identify them with any certainty in the literary sources. Other forms of weave are known, based, for example, on various tablet braids, but are incidental to the main stream and ill documented archaeologically.

One of the commonest terms for cloth in Norse is wadmal (vaðmál). The word, which means 'cloth measure', can be found as a loan-word in Middle English and early German, which indicates that the material itself was exported. The strict regulations regarding its manufacture and size in medieval Iceland reflect not only its importance as a currency, but also its importance as a standard export. No piece of surviving cloth can be definitely defined as wadmal; when the word appears in literature in the post-Viking era, it is defined as a twill. We may, however, safely assume that it was a fairly coarse cloth.

Cloth was also imported in great quantity into Scandinavia. Obviously luxury cloths – like patterned silk and Anglo-Saxon embroideries – are easy to identify as imports, but it is not easy to decide whether some of the fine woollen and linen textiles found were imported or manufactured within Scandinavia. That linen was produced in Scandinavia itself is indicated, for example, by the presence of linen beaters in the Oseberg grave. But just as little is known about the actual physical appearance of cloth woven in Scandinavia, so, unfortunately, very little is known about the physical appearance of cloth woven in contemporary Europe. It is thus difficult to say whether some of the extremely fine twills found at Birka and other sites were, as has often been suggested, imported. However, cloth of finer quality than that found in Scandinavia is well documented in Europe in the post-Viking era, and this, together with the recorded instances of the import of cloth in twelfth-century sources, suggests that some of the twills of uniformly high quality found in Viking graves are imports – perhaps some of them may be the Frisian cloth, so famous in early medieval literature in western Europe.

Embroidery was a common occupation; silks, coloured wools and even filaments of precious metal were used. Needles of iron, bone and bronze, sometimes in cylindrical needle-cases, are of quite common occurrence and it has been suggested that the gold and silver thread was inserted with tweezers. To this type of embellishment were added certain simple lace-making techniques.

Various embellishments could be added during weaving. Tablet-woven strips were used as borders and an interesting technique of manufacturing shaggy cloaks has been found in Viking contexts in the Isle of Man, the Western Isles and Iceland. This pile-weave (ON rǫgg, f., rǫggr, m.) is executed by laying short lengths of wool in the shed or tying them round the warp threads. When woven, the short lengths of wool appear as tufts. The garment produced had the appearance of a shaggy fur. It was an important Icelandic export, but it was also made in Ireland and elsewhere.

Dress and adornment

Although cloth was used for sails, hangings, tents and awnings, much of the cloth produced was – like the shaggy pile-weave just mentioned – used in making clothes. Archaeology is of little help in this field, providing only a few representations of human figures, a mass of jewellery and fragments of cloth. For knowledge of the dress worn by the Scandinavians we must primarily consult literary sources. Men commonly wore a shirt and under-breeches (which could be ankle-length) of wool or linen. They wore stocking-breeches, or ankle-length trousers, which could be wide and baggy, or knee-length trousers with hose from ankle to knee. Stocking-breeches might be of wool and be worn with shoes, but might also be of hide or fur, when shoes would not need to be used. Shoes would be worn over bare feet with ankle-length trousers and with hose; the latter was normally gartered to the leg with bands. Trousers were kept up with a sash or belt. Over the shirt a tunic was worn – red and leaf-green seem to have been favourite colours – with a belt around the middle. The sleeves were sometimes laced at the cuffs or decorated with tablet-woven braids or gold thread. Purse and knife were normally attached to the belt, but sometimes a knife was carried on a cord round the neck. If a sword was worn, it was usually carried in a scabbard suspended from a baldric over one shoulder. Both belts and baldrics were fastened with buckles, and were often embellished with bronze or silver mounts. There were various kinds of hats: hats with floppy brims, tight-fitting caps of wool or other material, a fur hat was called a 'Russian' hat; some men might prefer to wear a helmet – not much more elaborate than a close-fitting metal bowl – or a fillet of ornamented silk or linen. Gloves, finger-gloves and mittens, were used, of wool or fur. The common outer covering was a cloak, which might be cowled. Poorer people, boys in service and slaves, for example, might make do with a kind of simple blanket with a hole cut in it for the head, which did duty both as tunic and cloak, but we also hear of cloaks of the finest cloth richly coloured, with decorative borders right down to the hem. They were fastened at the neck with a pin, or by a tie or strap which went round the neck. A long, trailing robe might also be worn by wealthy men, more for ostentation than protection, it seems, since such a robe could be made of silk. For outdoor wear in dirty weather the *rǫggvarfeldr* (the shaggy cloak, cf. above) or sleeved coats of hide or fur were usual.

Women wore a woollen or linen chemise, sometimes pleated, with short sleeves or no sleeves at all, and probably some wore drawers. They wore hose, kept up with ties, and all of this was under a long dress with a belt round the middle – with knife and purse hanging from it, and keys too if she were the housewife or housekeeper. Among the wealthy the sleeves of the dress might have a train, be wide or long and stiffened in some way. Women, in the early Viking period at least, usually wore two or three brooches. An oval brooch (pl. 3a) high on either side of the chest with, say, a trefoil brooch between them. A festoon of beads or pendants, of glass, amber or even of precious metal, was often suspended between the two outer brooches. Brooches of other forms were also used; circular brooches, elaborate bowed brooches, derived from the ancient safety-pin type, and ring brooches of British inspiration, were among the most popular kinds. In the early Viking period a piece of looted ecclesiastical metalwork might be adapted as a brooch by a Viking for his wife and throughout the period foreign jewellery was often worn. The rich – both men and women – would wear metal collars and bangles of silver and gold. Many women would have a neckerchief or shawl. Unmarried girls wore their hair loose, perhaps with a band across the head, but married women usually wore it gathered up into a knot at the back of the head and covered by a head-dress, tall and curving or tall and pointed. The cloak was long and trailing and could not have differed much from that worn by men. People slept in their underwear or naked.

Shoes are occasionally found during excavation. An important collection of eleventh-century footgear has been recovered during excavations in Lund. There were two main types (fig. 18). The uppers of the first type usually consist of one or two fairly large pieces of leather, with slits along the upper edge for lacing. The uppers are sewn together at the back or side, have a pointed heel and a slashed ankle piece. A simple embellishment is added to some shoes of this classs in the form of a sewn or tooled line from toe to ankle. The second type of shoe has a rounded heel and lace-holes reduced to two or four slits. The ankle-piece is sometimes slashed. Calfskin shoes with the fur still on are mentioned in literary sources.

An ankle-boot from Oseberg, perhaps 200 years earlier in date, is made of two pieces of thin goatskin – a sole and an upper. The sole is almost symmetrical, without bias to left or right. The boot has a lace, 140 cm. long, which passes through holes in the opening and is bound round the ankle. Laces were usually of leather and might have tassels.

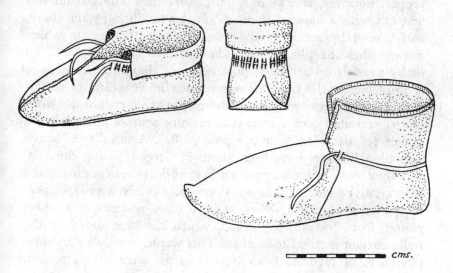

Fig. 18. Shoes from eleventh- and twelfth-century levels in Lund, Skåne.
Kulturhistoriska Museet, Lund.

Agriculture

Of the agricultural implements of the Vikings, the most important – the plough – is least well documented. People are unlikely to bury whole ploughs with the dead – and, even if they did, much of the implement was made of wood and would have rotted away – but shares are occasionally found in graves, as in one near Vanaja Kirkeby on the Baltic island of Åland. Shares are also found on settlement sites, as for example at the military camp of Trelleborg in Denmark, but coulters of definite Viking date are unknown, as are such wooden parts of the plough as the mould-board.

It is probable that two types of plough were used by the Vikings. The first type, the ard (arðr), is a common prehistoric object and, as it is documented in Scandinavia until quite recent times, there seems no reason to suppose that it was not known there in the Viking Age, for the word was certainly used. The function of the ard was to break up the surface of the ground by passing a downward-directed point through the earth. It was pulled by one or more draught animals and guided by a man. The plough proper, however, is a more sophisticated tool. The ground was first cut with a coulter, then undercut and lifted by the share, and turned by means of the mould-board (the feature which distinguishes the plough from the ard). Although there is no really satisfactory archaeological evidence that this second type of implement – the plough – was present in Scandinavia at this period, its existence may be inferred from the fact that the word (plógr) certainly occurs in twelfth-century sources and probably earlier (cf. the verse from Rígspula, p. 81). A number of heavy iron plough-shares have been found in alleged Viking contexts, and they seem to have appeared first in Scandinavia during the Migration Period. The heavy share may imply a plough, perhaps even one with a wheel, and we have evidence of a wheel plough from Navndrup, Jutland, which has been dated by the radio-carbon method to c. 1220. This would hardly be the first plough to be made in Scandinavia; in the later Viking period, at least, the heavy plough must have been known.

Physical traces of ploughing are rarely found. At Lindholm Høje, Jutland, however, a considerable area of furrowed land was uncovered during excavation (pl. 4); its appearance suggests that a heavy plough was used. Plough marks were also discovered under the Viking burial-mound at Cronk Moar in the Isle of Man. These are, for the moment, the only evidence of ploughing from Viking sites and one cannot generalize on this basis, especially in view of the fact that the Manx ploughing may have been carried out with a Celtic implement.

The study of field systems in Viking Age Scandinavia is as yet in its infancy. The energetic work of Axel Steensberg has, however, enabled scholars of various disciplines to map the field systems dating from between 1000 and 1200 at Borup Ris in Jutland. Unlike most of the medieval field systems so far mapped in Europe (and observed, but not dated, in Denmark) the fields at this village site are placed at right-angles to the contours. The fields are well marked by long rows of stones which had been cleared by the farmers from the elongated strip fields which they had ploughed. The fields vary in width, the original home-field of one farm, for example, having a width of about 48 m., although most only measure between 12 and 15 m. This seems to be a planned field system laid out at one time, but the site cannot as yet be considered typical of Denmark, or even of the area. This is the first step in a programme of field examination which we hope will considerably improve our knowledge of Danish agricultural practice in the early medieval period.

No harrow is known of Viking Age date, although this implement is well documented elsewhere in western Europe in the tenth and eleventh centuries and may, indeed, be mentioned in *Atlakviða* (pp. 350–4), a tenth-century poem. Spades were made of wood and are recorded from such large burial mounds as Gokstad, Oseberg, Tune and Jelling. They had a step for the foot on either one or both sides of the shaft, and often had a slightly convex edge. Both spade (*páll*) and shovel (*reka*) appear in the laws; the *páll* is distinctly a narrow pointed implement. There is apparently no evidence in Scandinavia for an iron spade-shoe (to strengthen the edge of the blade) although such objects are common in contemporary western Europe. Single-ended picks for loosening earth and grubbing up roots are recorded from Norway, whilst ironshod hoes of various forms are well documented archaeologically. On the west coast of Norway, where fields were often small and corn-growing was difficult, it was quite common to cultivate a field with a spade rather than with a plough.

Harvesting implements were the sickle, scythe and leaf-knife, all of which had a wooden handle and an iron blade. All three objects are commonly found in Viking contexts. The earlier sickles have the tip of the tang bent over at an angle so that it could be hammered into the handle and then bound with twine or an iron band. At a later period the blade was riveted to the handle. There are two main types – one with a straight blade and the other with a curved blade. Many straight-bladed sickles have saw-toothed cutting edges, but this feature rarely occurs on the curved-blade sickle. The scythe blade is normally straight – little more than an elongated version of the straight-bladed sickle – between 40 cm. and 70 cm. in length. Occasionally the blade is slightly curved, but more often it has an in-curved point, a slender blade and an obtuse hafting angle; the form of the handle is not known. The leaf-knife, used for cutting foliage for fodder, has a long, broad, slightly-curved blade, terminating in a small beak. It was hafted in the same way as the sickle. All these implements were sharpened with short whetstones, which are found quite commonly. Hay-making implements – pitchforks and rakes – have not been recognized in archaeological contexts and were presumably made of wood.

Carpentry

In Scandinavia wood was the natural medium for most manufactured objects, and the ability of the Viking woodworker is amply demonstrated in the major finished products of his art which survive – the ships and churches, for example, which are discussed in Chapters 7 and 12 below. These were not the only products of the carpenter's skill: houses, shacks, household utensils, agricultural implements and innumerable other structures and objects were made by either skilled or unskilled craftsmen. The soft woods of northern Scandinavia and the hard woods of Denmark and south Sweden provided an inexhaustible source of raw material for the carpenter's craft.

The tools which were used in the Viking Age would – with a few exceptions – occasion little surprise in the hands of a modern craftsman. They are well documented in Scandinavian sources and only a few tools – the pole-lathe and plane, for example – have not been found. The former is testified, however, by turned wooden objects of Viking date; while the plane, which exists in more or less contemporary European contexts, was used by the Vikings, for the word for it, *lokarr*, is in fact a loan-word from Old English and is used in a tenth-century Icelandic poem.

The complete equipment of a carpenter is best illustrated by the contents of the tool chest from Mästermyr in Gotland. The fact that tools of another trade (metalwork) occur in this find is

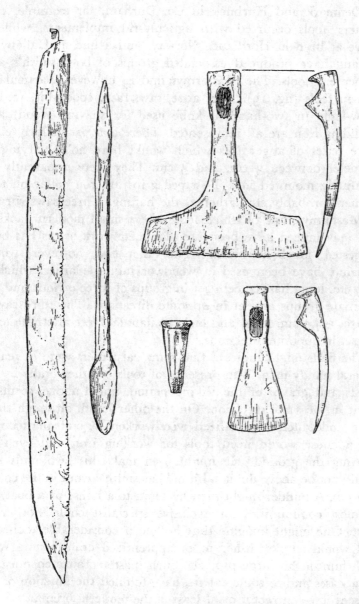

Fig. 19. Saw, spoon-bit, wedge and adzes from Mästermyr, Gotland.
Scale: ¼. Statens Historiska Museum, Stockholm.

paralleled elsewhere in the Viking period. At Skovlunde Mark in Denmark and Hurbuck in Co. Durham, for example, carpenters' tools occurred with agricultural implements, while a grave at Bryn in Hordland, Norway, and a find at Halleby in Jutland have produced associated groups of both smith's and carpenter's tools. The Mästermyr find is, however, particularly rich in tools (fig. 19). Axe, adze, saw, rasp, spoon-bit, wedge, draw-knife (a two-handled knife used for shaving wood) and moulding iron are all represented. There is a particularly elaborate series of auger bits which would bore holes varying in diameter between 3 cm. and 5 cm. They were apparently all separately mounted in a T-shaped grip: an iron collar on four of them probably strengthened the hafting. Three saws survive at Mästermyr, one of which looks like a small modern hacksaw and may indeed have been used for metalwork or, as has been suggested, for boneworking. The other two, however, would certainly have been used in woodworking: the larger, which is 58.5 cm. long, has its teeth set in groups of three or four and the alternate groups are set in opposite directions. The third saw is shorter (34.5 cm. long) and lacks its handle. Here alternate teeth are set in opposite directions.

The finds might indicate that some carpenters were in reality general handy-men. The presence of tools of other crafts in the chests and graves of the Viking period, noted above, seems to point in the same direction. On the other hand, although there were undoubtedly specialized woodworkers, a craftsman building a house would need tools for working iron and even for clearing the ground. He might even make his own nails and would not be above doing a bit of blacksmith's work in the course of a job. A builder might turn his hand to a house or a boat, for in most communities an exclusive specialist could not easily exist. One might imagine that he had a considerable tool-store and would employ itinerant or apprenticed craftsmen to work with him on his large projects. Such master craftsmen must, in some cases and to some extent, have fulfilled the function of the present-day contractor or at least of the modern foreman.

The specialist in house-building and boat-building did, however, certainly exist. The story of the expert builder of Ólaf Tryggvason's great ship, the Long Serpent, is told elsewhere (pp.

250–1). In Iceland we hear of several expert house-builders and carpenters. One of them was Thórodd Gamlason who built the first cathedral church at Hólar, soon after 1106. (It is said that, as he worked, he followed the lessons of the boys in the bishop's school there and learnt a lot of Latin.) Later on in the twelfth century we hear of Bersi Dagsson, 'a most skilful carpenter', who was engaged to panel the walls of an anchoress's cell as a means of thwarting a plague of mice.

Whatever his social or political status – and it is extremely difficult to gain any knowledge of the carpenter from literature – the surviving results of his work are an impressive monument to his achievement. The sheer physical labour of providing the raw material is also worth remembering. A tree, when felled, had first to be split with wedges and then adzed into shape – all apparently without the benefit of a large saw: the humbler craftsman would probably have to start with the standing timber, a long way from the final mortice-and-tenon joint of the finished piece of furniture.

The metalworker

The fact that, by the manufacture of weapons, a man's life and heroic prowess were laid in the hands of the smith, made the blacksmith's task almost glamorous. Did the hero Sigurd not own a sword so sharp that when held still in the river it cut through a strand of wool allowed to float with the current against its edge? Was not the legendary Wayland a smith, and did not Thor carry with him a hammer – the chief tool of a smith? Scandinavian literature teems with references to smiths, either as weapon-makers or as jewellers. Some of the richest graves discovered in Scandinavia are those of iron-workers, and iron as a raw material was undoubtedly of great economic importance.

The most dramatic archaeological illustration of the wealth of the smith is given by a tenth-century smith's grave from Bygland, Morgedal, Norway. The inventory is fantastic: four swords, four spearheads, seven axes, two shield-bosses, nine knives, thirteen arrow-heads, fourteen rattles and eight bits as well as the following smiths' tools (fig. 20): two tongs, a number of heavy hammers, two light hammers, an anvil, four fullers, a pair of metal shears, a nail-iron, a draw-plate for making wire, two files, a ladle, a mould for silver-bars, a large bar which may have been used in the manufacture of axes, what may be the binding of a pair of bellows, as well as some raw material and a lump of slag. Other objects of minor or domestic importance can be added to this list.

Iron itself was freely available in the form of bog-ore, deposited in the peat over long years. But as O. Arrhenius has demonstrated, it was also mined before the twelfth century. Abundant timber provided fuel for smelting. It is possible, however, that the Scandinavians were not altogether satisfied with the quality of their own iron production for there is ample evidence of the import of fine weapons – sword-blades particularly – into Scandinavia (cf. pp. 273–4). It is odd that, in this iron-rich area, we know so little of their extracting processes.

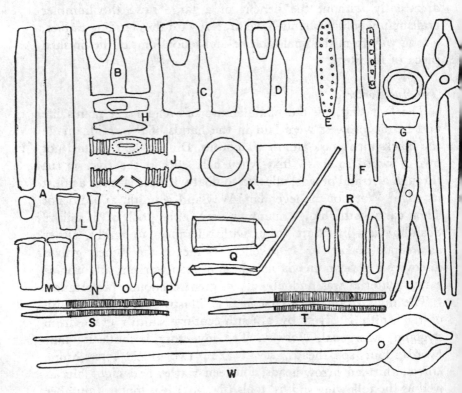

Fig. 20. Some of the tools from the smith's grave from Bygland, Morgedal.
Universitetets Oldsaksamling, Oslo.

Recent excavation has cast doubt on the generally-held view that until the seventeenth century iron was always extracted by firing the ore in a pit (bowl furnace). Although bowl furnaces have been found on sites such as Sör Amsberg and others in Dalarna, Sweden, examination of large lumps of slag of the Roman Iron Age found in Denmark and of five slag pits at Drengsted suggests that the ore and fuel were placed in a pottery chimney (known as a shaft furnace) over a pit covered by a plug of straw. Air was received through holes at the base of the chimney and the slag fell to the bottom and eventually into the pit beneath. Although there is no Viking Age evidence of it, this method was common in Europe until the seventeenth century, although bowl furnaces were also used; it was a most efficient method and one that, once introduced, may well have continued in use in Scandinavia.

The basic reduction process of iron from ore, in whatever form of furnace was used, can be simplified in the formula:

$$Fe_2O_3 + 3CO \longrightarrow 2Fe + 3CO_2$$

The carbon monoxide was provided by charcoal burning in air. The ideal temperature for this process is between 1100° and 1150°C – a temperature easily obtainable with charcoal, but more difficult with ordinary wood. The furnace would be fired for about twenty-four hours with charcoal: heated or crushed ore was then added and the temperature would soon rise to a level at which the bloom – the spongy iron – could form. Depending on the amount of iron needed, firing was continued for as much as a day. After cooling, the bloom was taken from the furnace and freed from lumps of slag. The bloom was then reheated and hammered on an anvil, to get rid of included slag and other impurities, and shaped into bars of raw material.

It is unlikely that the smith normally extracted his own metals; we must assume that his work started with the purchase of bars of raw material. His method of work was no different from that of the modern smith; his tools as we have seen were similar and he could forge sophisticated objects and fine steel. One particular decorative treatment is mentioned in the literature. A passage like that from the twelfth-century *Krákumál* –

stakk á storðar lykkju	I thrust into the serpent
stáli bjartra mála	steel of bright patterning –

must refer to the results of the technical process of pattern-welding, which gave the blade of a sword a marbled appearance. It was carried out by welding together bars of iron, twisting them and drawing them out to form a laminated structure which, when polished (and perhaps etched with acid), would appear as a series of twisted light and dark bands along the blade; the pattern was irregular because of the inclusion of slag and scale. A hardened steel edge was then welded to this central bar. Such a weapon would not only be decorative but also strong and flexible: the technique was known throughout the Germanic world, but it is not thought to have been introduced into Scandinavia before the Vendel period. It is sometimes incorrectly described as 'damascening', but this process was not known in the Viking North.

The products of the jeweller form one of the most obvious archaeological remains of the Viking period. The jeweller's tools are, however, rarely found. Again the find from Mästermyr in Gotland has produced some of them – a punch, tongs, what may be a soldering lamp, a lead stamping pad, spatula, hammers and draw-plates for making wire. Crucibles and moulds, slag and raw material, are however quite commonly found on Viking settlement sites (see p. 210). Matrices for producing impressed patterns on thin sheets of metal are also occasionally found and are normally made of bronze. A drawing tool for making filigree wire was found among other jeweller's tools at Birka; made of soft iron, it has seven holes which are reinforced with hardened steel plugs.

Little is known concerning the source of the jewellers' metals. Silver and gold must have been imported, either as bullion or coin; but copper was mined in Sweden. The only direct evidence of mining comes from peat with traces of minerals, which can only have been mined, from near the Stora Kopparberg mine at Falun in Dalarna. Radio-carbon examination of the peat level dates it to the late Viking Age. The copper mined here was alloyed with other metals – lead and tin for example – which were probably imported from Germany, although it is just conceivable that they were mined from Scandinavian lodes. Zinc was another metal used as an alloy to produce brass, and this must also have been imported into Scandinavia – probably already alloyed. Much of the metal used was obviously scrap, but some of the surviving ingots are so pure that they must be considered the products of mining operations.

The early literary sources suggest that the blacksmith might also be a jeweller. The most famous and least reliable of these sources concerns Vǫlund or Wayland, who made gold rings and iron swords, worked silver and bone and set jewels (cf. p. 347). But if we ignore such a legendary tale and turn to the later historical sources, it is clear that the jeweller was a specialist – a conclusion supported by finds from metalworkers' workshops at Ekerö, Hedeby and elsewhere. On certain occasions the work of the jeweller and the blacksmith overlapped, as, for example, when iron was encrusted in a decorative fashion with other metals, such as bronze, brass and silver. Such encrustation was very popular in the Viking Age, particularly on the hilts and shafts of weapons (pl. 7) and on riding equipment: its use on spurs survived into the post-medieval period. The method used by the Vikings was probably similar to that described by the twelfth-century German monk Theophilus in his book *De diversis artibus*:

When you have smoothly filed a spur, put it over a burning coal fire until it becomes black and, after it has cooled down, hold it in the left hand and turn the wheel [of an elaborate cutting machine] . . . and incise it outside along its length and then twice along its breadth . . . With the small shears cut small pieces of silver . . . lay them on and rub them . . . until they stick fast . . . put [the spur] over the coals until it again becomes black . . . and polish it with a long tool made of very smooth steel and fixed in a handle . . . Heat it again and polish it vigorously with the same tool.

The method described here applied not only to silver, but also to copper and brass, which were used, together or separately, to build up a polychrome glitter on the black iron.

This love of glitter is seen in all Viking metalwork. The brooches and other ornaments, mass-produced though they often are, clearly demonstrate this, and much of the technical effort which went into the manufacture of this jewellery was expended to this end. Multi-faceted, cast and impressed surfaces, elaborate filigree wire ornament and skilfully applied punch-marks on plain surfaces, were the chief means used to achieve it. The technical methods of the Scandinavian jeweller cannot have been very different from those used by the craftsman-jeweller of today. Although accurate evidence concerning them is wanting, their achievements can still be admired and their methods imagined.

Other industrial processes

In this chapter we have described the main products of the Vikings and the evidence for their manufacture, but other industries, the production of bone and antler objects, for example, were also of importance. Combs, knife-handles, weaving tools, toggles, as well as fine caskets and gaming pieces, testify to the skill of the craftsmen of this industry. At Birka there was a considerable bone and antler industry, one of whose most fascinating products are antler mounts for swords, found both in a finished and unfinished state.

Another notable industry, which is mentioned elsewhere (p. 194), was the quarrying and manufacture of objects of soapstone. This became of very great importance in the late Viking Age, when spindle-whorls, loom-weights, net-sinkers, moulds and crucibles were produced, as well as vessels. The importance of the industry is emphasized by figures produced in 1952 by Arne Skjøldsvold for Norway: at that time 652 soapstone vessels were known from the Viking Age, as compared with fifty pottery vessels. Most of the vessels (pl. 5) are more or less hemispherical in shape, rarely ornamented, but often beautifully worked with a rippled interior. Some were marked by their makers or owners at the rim, and the pride revealed by this detail reflects their importance.

Pottery became increasingly important as the Viking Age progressed. Little is known of the technical details of the potter's trade, but by the end of the Viking period sophisticated wheel-turned pottery was being produced in Scandinavia, based on prototypes which were mainly derived from Germany and the south Baltic. The relative unimportance of pottery in the material culture of Viking Age Scandinavians seems to the archaeologist to be one of the oddest features of their cultural pattern. At a time when the whole of the rest of Europe was practically covered with a layer of broken pots, hardly any is discovered in the North. The soapstone industry could hardly provide all the requirements of the population, and this lack of material must be taken as an indication of the importance of the carpenter's trade, for the cooking utensils, storage vessels and table-ware must largely have been made of wood.

An important craft involved the preparation of leather and, later, of vellum. The professional tanner probably appeared during this period, but we have little information concerning him. Preparation of leather would be an essential home industry and much of the tanning was probably carried out on the farm.

Pastimes

Occupational conditions often allowed and climatic conditions often imposed a good deal of leisure. The Norsemen had many pastimes, for indoors and outdoors, winter and summer.

Adam of Bremen said that Sven Estridssoṅ was an obedient son of the Church in everything except in indulgence in feasting and women – and the latter weakness he regarded not so much as a personal fault as an inborn propensity of the Danish nation, one which the Swedes shared with them. A twelfth-century clerical writer, on the other hand, condemned the drunkenness and consequent brawling and bloodshed of the Norwegians in Tønsberg and Bergen, while an Icelandic homilist of the same century says: 'In this country lasciviousness is made game of in conversation, just as drunkenness is in Norway.'

Drink and women as bought entertainment were naturally the pleasures of the better-off, common in the towns but less so in the countryside. They were not much frowned upon, although moderation was a virtue acclaimed by pagan and Christian alike. The Church fought against sexual laxity but made slow progress.

In the homes and at parties much pleasure depended on the spoken word. People made and recited poetry, swapped verses, sometimes competed in scurrility; they asked riddles, made comparisons between men, more or less formally, or played a similar game in which the virtues of a chosen object or person were enumerated; they made up stories, repeated old ones, and by the end of our period, read aloud from books.

Games with dice and boards and pieces were played between pairs. Chequer and peg-boards have been found in Norse graves, both at home and abroad. Chess became known in Iceland in the twelfth century, and must have been known in continental Scandinavia before that. Some of the best Norse pieces of sculptured figures of men and women are among chessmen of the twelfth and thirteenth centuries found in the Hebrides and Sweden.

We know almost nothing about Norse music – the harp was played and it was counted a fitting accomplishment for a gentleman – three men who we know were able to use the instrument in the eleventh and twelfth centuries were a Norwegian king, an Orkney earl and an Icelandic bishop. Forms of fiddles and pipes were also known. Dancing certainly existed, probably generally performed to verse-singing (love-songs exchanged between men and women are said to have been dance accompaniment in Iceland about 1100), and this was probably derived from pre-Christian forms. In the course of the twelfth century the general European ring-dance became established. Various kinds of 'hobby-horse' games, with miming and mummery, were known; some of them had probably had pagan ritual significance. Jugglers, clowns and acrobats might be found at the courts of kings and were itinerant in the more populous areas of Denmark and Sweden. They were regarded with a contempt made explicit in the so-called 'Players' statute' in the older Västergötland Law:

If a player is struck, that is always invalid [i.e. there is never any redress]. If a player is wounded, one who goes with a fiddle, and with viol or drum, then a wild heifer is to be brought to the raised middle of the assembly place. Then all the hair is to be shaved off its tail and the tail greased. Then the player is to be given newly-greased shoes. Then he is to hold the heifer by the tail and the heifer is to be lashed with a sharp whip. If he can hold it, then he shall have this fine animal and enjoy it as a dog enjoys grass. If he cannot hold it, let him have and put up with what he got, shame and hurt.

It is hard to think that this statute was ever put into execution more than once in Västergötland, if that.

Outdoor occupations were especially for the young and active, but some were games for audiences too. Hunting, fishing, rowing, sailing, swimming (with competition in endurance under water), running, jumping, wrestling, ski-ing, skating, were all enjoyed as pastimes. Tests of physical strength were common – Iceland is strewn with great boulders all alleged to have once been lifted by Grettir the Strong, the famous outlaw of the eleventh century – and rock climbing and other trials of endurance and agility were practised. Ólaf Tryggvason's legendary performance is the most vivid – he could walk forward and aft on his great warship *outboard* by stepping from oar to oar as his men rowed! (Saxo tells the same story of King Harald *gilli* of Norway, who died in 1136.) Training with weapons was essential for the free man, fencing with sword and shield, throwing spears and stones, shooting with bow and arrows. In the last sport, for which the Norwegians were particularly famous, competitions with prizes were organized.

Games which drew audiences were especially some kinds of ball-games, played chiefly in winter on flat frozen surfaces – we know that both bats and balls were used but the rules are not entirely clear; horse-racing; and horse-fighting. There was undoubtedly wagering on the results. Horse-fighting was particularly popular (and remained so long after the middle ages in some parts of Norway). Stallions were marked out as likely fighters and bred up accordingly. The usual practice was to tether mares at the edge of a marked-out area and then goad two stallions against each other within sight and smell of them. We hear a good deal about the sport in Icelandic stories because quarrels and fights often resulted among the owners of the horses.

The chief games of children were doubtless those in which they imitated grown-ups, sometimes by play-acting, often with wooden weapons, model boats, clay-built farmsteads. They rolled or threw anything ring-shaped or ball-shaped, including snowballs at their elders – one twelfth-century nobleman in Nidaros was believed to have mistaken the whiz of the axe that killed him for the whiz of a boy's snowball.

189

And anyone, big or small, could be happy with a knife and a bit of wood. There is the story of St Ólaf of Norway, who sat in his seat one Sunday and whittled a piece of stick. This was noticed as a breaking of the sabbath by his young attendant, who gently and tactfully pointed out: 'Tomorrow is Monday, my lord.' The king gathered the chips and burnt them to ashes in the palm of his hand. What pastime he permitted himself then we are not told.

6

Trade and Towns

The trading connections of the Vikings demonstrate the far-flung extent of their contacts. It was the Vikings who extended the existing eastern trade-routes through Russia from the Baltic to the Arab world; they it was who traded with Byzantium and North Africa, with Lapland and with England. Silver and gold poured into their homeland; silks, furs and wine formed part of their stock-in-trade. But the very glamour of these world-wide connections sometimes causes scholars to ignore the problems of internal trade. The great marketing centres dealt not only with merchants and slave-traders from the whole of Europe, but also with local farmers and itinerant craftsmen. The traces of iron-smelting and soapstone-working found at Kaupang, the antler comb industry found at Lund and the leather-workers' material found at Hedeby reflect not only international but local trade. The farmer and his wife were just as likely to buy iron objects and soapstone bowls at such a major market as Kaupang to which they brought their own produce, as were Frisian and German merchants to buy the rare furs and ropes which were also obtainable there. The prosperity of Scandinavia presumably depended as much on internal as on external trade.

Local marketing

Few traces of this local trade remain, but the occasional distribution pattern of a group of objects along a valley may tell of humble tinkers or cheapjacks, who, passing from market to market, from source of supply to place of sale, would stop to tempt a farmer's wife with jewellery or a length of linen on the way.

An archaeologist has no difficulty in identifying exotic things found in Viking graves – a coin from Baghdad, for example, or a reliquary from Ireland – but he finds it extremely difficult to

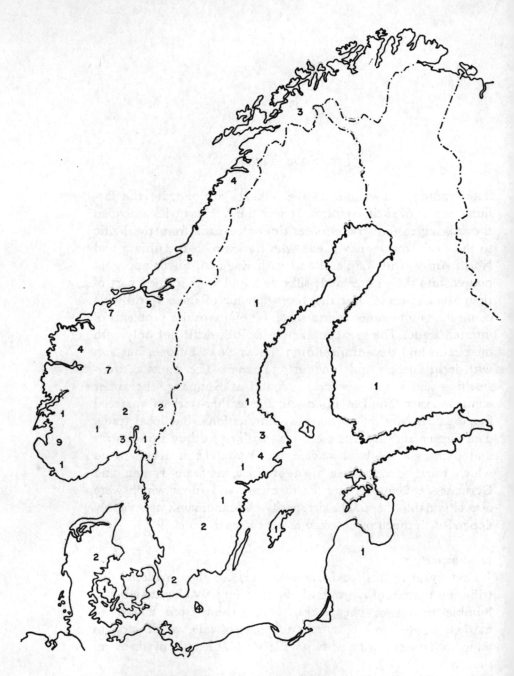

Fig. 21. The distribution of oval brooches of Petersen Type 27 as recorded by Paulsen in 1933. The numbers indicate the examples recorded in each province.

say whether a brooch found in Trondheim was manufactured in the region of Bergen or Lund. However, certain trends of internal trade can be recognized. In Norway, for example, throughout the first millennium of our era, there was a considerable iron industry and it is now possible to recognize some products of that industry outside Norway. In certain Swedish provinces, in Dalarna and Gästrikland, for example, a fair number of swords of a Norwegian type have been found – surely brought here as a result of trade. This can be contrasted with the situation in other Swedish provinces, where such objects are uncommon. The same two provinces have also produced a fair number of objects made in the lands on the south coast of the Baltic Sea. From such finds it can be postulated that the routes of these regions were important lines of mercantile communication between east and west Scandinavia.

It is more difficult, however, to decide the pattern of trade and the routes used when we consider objects found in substantial numbers. One of the commonest antiquities of the Viking Age is the oval brooch; it occurs in a number of different forms which have been subdivided by the Norwegian archaeologist, Jan Petersen, into distinct types, based on details of form and ornament. Let us take one of these types – no. 27 in Petersen's series (pl. 2a): when the last recorded figures were published in 1933, 81 examples were known from Norway, 27 from Sweden and 10 from Denmark. Such figures might lead us to the conclusion that this was a Norwegian type and that brooches of this form found elsewhere were imported. But such a supposition could be misleading, for very few of the surviving brooches come from a common mould; the brooches must, therefore, be seen as products of a number of different workshops, perhaps scattered throughout Scandinavia. Apart from a marked coastal distribution (fig. 21), there is no significant geographical concentration of these objects. The highest number of finds of this type from any single province is from Rogaland in Norway where fourteen examples were found in nine graves – hardly an adequate sample on which to base a theory concerning trade or area of origin.

The evidence, therefore, is often contradictory and difficult of interpretation. The traditional archaeological method of plotting artefacts on a map and indicating broad lines of trade is practically useless when we deal with Viking brooches and many other objects. Internal trade is, however, clearly demonstrated by one or two phenomena.

First of all a number of rune stones bear inscriptions recording the building of a bridge or causeway, or the presence of a ford. Although these objects may be classed as 'good works' and were doubtless primarily erected to help people make their way to church, they must also be seen in a commercial context as marking well-known routes. Similarly, place-names with the elements WN *kaupangr* (EN *köping*) and *torg* can be taken as evidence of trade. It is not without interest that these elements are loanwords; the former equivalent to the English element Chipping (OE *cīeping, cēaping,* as in Chipping Sodbury); the latter from Slavonic, appearing e.g. in Russian *torgŭ,* 'market place', whence it was borrowed into Finnish to give, for example, the name of the east Baltic port of Turku.

The presence of metalworkers' workshops in certain towns is indicative of trade – largely for the home market. In the great town of Birka there are traces of jewellers' workshops and an example of such a workshop of immediately pre-Viking date has recently been excavated at Helgö in Sweden; such centres of production certainly existed elsewhere. Both Birka and Helgö were centres of trade and it must be presumed that most of their products were made for the home market and were bought by the local inhabitants. In days when metal brooches were more important than buttons, trade in articles such as these catered for something broader than the luxury market.

Evidence of internal trade of a semi-industrial character is occasionally found. In Norway, for example, a considerable industry was based on the manufacture of objects of soapstone – particularly bowls (pl. 5). This industry was so important that for much of the Viking period no pottery was made in Norway; vessels of soapstone and wood took the place of pottery and were traded throughout the country. Such a specialized industry could only have been supported on the basis of a major internal trading network.

Trade in iron was important. The raw metal was extracted (see pp. 182–3) and beaten into bars – possibly those in the rough shape of an axe with a shafthole which are found in considerable numbers in Norway (pl. 9b). These bars were presumably threaded on a rope and carried by pack-animal to the individual smithy, where they were fashioned into tools and weapons. The physical weight of this raw material presupposes a body of semi-professional merchants organized to carry it, some of whom may well have specialized in such a material. Food must also have been a medium of local marketing. Barley, fish, meat and other foodstuffs were probably brought to local markets by farmers and fishermen. Livestock and cloth would doubtless also be bought and sold at the same market.

Much of this internal trade must have been carried out by barter. Goods would change hands at the local market and only be converted into silver coin or bullion by the itinerant trader dealing in manufactured goods who had to travel from market to market and back to his source of supply. Coins were used, however, by the Scandinavians and are discussed below.

Foreign trade

The really glamorous facet of the mercantile activity of the Viking period is the international trade which leaves such an indelible impression on the archaeological material. In recent years some historians have criticized the validity of the archaeological evidence for trade in the first millennium of our era. The importance of the external trade of the Carolingian Empire, for example, has been minimized and the exotic objects and coin hoards, used by archaeologists as evidence for trade, have been related to payments of a political character, piracy or other theft, gifts between rulers, or compensations under Germanic law. To a large extent archaeologists themselves have been to blame for this misconception in that they have tended to point to extreme luxuries – a peacock in a Norwegian royal burial or a lizard-skin purse at Birka – as evidence of trade and have neglected the more common and significant objects, which are most likely to have been carried by merchants. In examining foreign goods found during excavation one must evaluate their function in order to distinguish between a gift, a curio, or an object of merchandise. We must distinguish between an Irish shrine which was looted and an Eifel quernstone which was traded.

The tendency to consider the Vikings only as pirates has obscured an important facet of their political and economic life. While piracy was an element in their initial impact outside Scandinavia, the really important feature of their foreign relations ultimately concerned emigration and conquest. Once they had settled in a foreign country, they were likely to maintain economic ties with their original homeland as well as develop them with their new neighbours. At this stage they began to shrug off their piratical past and trade became of paramount importance. Once the Vikings had settled in a new land they quickly became acclimatized to its political structure and with their adventurous background became competent traders.

An important medium of exchange was silver, which itself

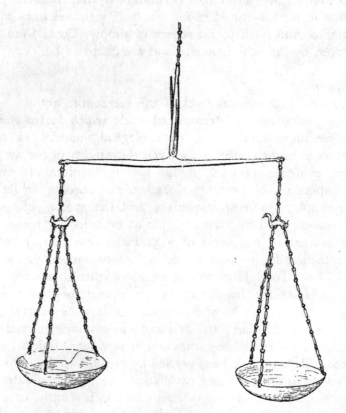

Fig. 22. Scales from Jåtten, Hetland, Rogaland, Norway. Scale: c.⅓.

may well have been one of the chief imports into Scandinavia. The Vikings, like most people of contemporary Europe and western Asia, used silver as a standard of exchange. Although coins were struck within Scandinavia from the beginning of the ninth century onwards, it was not until about 975 that there was large-scale minting in the North. The Vikings were, however, well aware of the idea of coins of standard weight, and used imported coin in their normal trading activities. The large number of deliberately cut coins – hacked in half in the markets – shows, however, that they tended to judge coin as bullion and not by its face value. Not only did they cut coins into pieces, they also cut jewellery and ingots into fragments to make up a weight which was satisfactory to each side of the bargain. Weights based on the various standard coinages – Arabic, Byzantine, Anglo-Saxon and German – are occasionally found, as are scales (fig. 22) which were used to weigh coins and bullion. It might be postulated that the occurrence of cut coin is indicative of international trade because within the country of origin a coin would – once a firm standard had been achieved – be accepted at its face value, while abroad it would not. This has, however, little relevance within Scandinavia itself where, as we have said, coins were not produced in any quantity until *c.* 975.

The weight of coins of different countries was often remarkably similar, although various difficulties – such as the alteration of the silver content – make generalization dangerous. Taking, however, the standard average weight of the Arabic *dirham* as 2.97 gm., it can hardly be coincidental that the average weight of the Anglo-Saxon penny was 1.46 gm., or very nearly half that of the standard eastern coin. But, although it is often said that the weight of the Carolingian *denier* approximates to that of the Anglo-Saxon penny and the half-*dirham*, this is only true of the period after the reign of Louis the Pious. It is significant that the debasement of the Carolingian coinage in the late ninth and early tenth century, to a weight approximating to a half-*dirham* or an Anglo-Saxon penny, is chronologically coincident with the first payment of a danegeld by the Franks to the Vikings.

In the late Viking Age a standard system of weights was developed on the basis of 1 *mǫrk* = 8 *aurar* = 24 *ørtogar* = 240 *peningar*. The last element was the standard silver coin. The relation of these weights to the pre-Viking Scandinavian system of weights, based on an *eyrir* (singular of *aurar*) of about 26.8 gm. (approximately one ounce), is difficult to calculate, for in the Viking period this was reduced to about 24.5 gm. There is some evidence that the Vikings adapted their metrological terminology to the existing European and Islamic standards and there are certainly Scandinavian finds which are based on European or Arabic standards (pl. 9a). It must be presumed that silver was used by weight as a medium of trade and we can perhaps assume that such coins as were undoubtedly used by the Vikings had some relation to their own system of weights. This is emphasized in many literary sources where arm-rings of silver and gold are described by their weight. Arm-rings are frequently found in hoards (pl. 9a) and this convenient and ostentatious form of wealth was presumably often used by traders.

That the Vikings used coins from western Europe and the Arab world is well attested by the following table which records the approximate number of coins dated between 800 and 1100 found in Scandinavia. This of course omits the coins minted in Scandinavia in the late Viking period, of which quite a large number survive (6,600 for example from Denmark).

	Arabic coins	Anglo-Saxon coins	Frankish/German coins
Norway . .	400	2,600+	2,500+
Sweden . .	52,000	30,000	58,500
Denmark . .	3,500	5,300	9,000

Generally speaking the Muslim coins (silver *dirhams*) are the earlier element (first appearing in the North towards the end of the ninth century), but about 970 there seems to have been a crisis, perhaps owing to the mid-tenth-century development of the silver mines in the Harz mountains, and western coins and coins from the western part of the Caliphate begin to predominate in the Scandinavian hoards. The same feature is reflected in the coin finds of the great trading centre of Birka. Perhaps the easternmost trading route through Russia began to lose its importance, certainly Birka loses its pre-eminence at this time, and the weight of trade shifts to Gotland and the Polish routes across Europe. Generally speaking, the Viking Age Scandinavians seem to have had no fixed monetary system for any long period within their homeland; their trade must have depended primarily on barter, with precious metals forming a standard of exchange by weight. In Icelandic and Norwegian sources, for example, the woollen cloth wadmal (see p. 55) may be reckoned by the ounce, referring to a value by weight of silver. Archaeologically the same fact is demonstrated by the large number of Scandinavian hoards which contain fragments of ornaments and plain rings of precious metal as well as coins – in Gotland alone (the richest area for coin hoards) more than 2,300 ingots and pieces of hack-silver have been found. One might suggest (and it is to some extent borne out by literary evidence) that the Vikings accepted coin at its face value in its country of origin (whether as settlement of trading debts or as political blackmail) but in their homelands they relied purely on its bullion value. Silver must be seen therefore as a valuable import into Scandinavia as well as a medium of exchange.

The Scandinavians did, however, develop their own coinage. Its use is difficult to determine but it must be an indication of trade. The first Scandinavian coins appeared in Hedeby in the early ninth century, their weight based on that of the Carolingian coinage. Minting continued until about 850, when (possibly owing to the rising price of silver in the Caliphate) it seems to have slowed down to a trickle, only to revive gradually during the first half of the tenth century. It is not known where these coins were minted; it is reasonable to suppose that they were produced at Hedeby, a thesis supported by their distribution, but there is no direct evidence for such an assumption. Towards the end of the tenth century, under Sven Forkbeard of Denmark, Olaf of Sweden and Ólaf Tryggvason of Norway, coins were produced in Scandinavia which were based in design and weight on those of Æthelred of England. From this time forward there were national coinages in Scandinavia, although the standard weight varied considerably.

The Scandinavian settlers of Britain quickly developed their own coinage. In the Danelaw, where the invaders were first exposed to the monetary economy of England, Guthrum was probably minting coins of English type in the years between 886 and his death in 890. This ephemeral coinage was the forerunner of the large number of coins produced by Vikings over the next two generations in the Scandinavian areas of England. In Ireland there was apparently no demand for coinage until the last years of the tenth century, when a high-quality coinage based on that of the English kings was produced in Dublin (pl. 6).

Other objects of trade leave little or no trace in the archaeological material. Slaves, furs, ropes, fish, honey and timber (probably the chief exports of Scandinavia), woollen cloth, salt and spices, wine and silks (probably the chief imports) were certainly traded by the Vikings, as we know from literary sources of both Scandinavian and foreign countries. Only occasionally, however, do we find physical traces of them. Remains of wine-jars (Bardorf ware and *Reliefband*-amphora) and fine wine jugs (some inlaid with white metal, pl. 2b) demonstrate commercial relations with the wine-producing areas of the Rhineland, probably with Mainz which was at this time one of the leading trading centres of Europe.

Of the great Scandinavian fur trade, which must have been one of the major sources of income for Viking merchants, little remains other than casual mention in Arabic, Scandinavian, German and Anglo-Saxon literature and traces of marten and beaver skins in graves at Birka. Of his voyage of exploration round North Cape, Ohthere, the Norwegian from Hálogaland, said:

> Chiefly he went there, as well as to see that land, to get walruses, for they have a noble bone in their tusks . . . and their hide is very good for ship's ropes . . .

Ohthere must have been typical of many Scandinavian fur traders in the Atlantic. One such who is mentioned in Icelandic sources was a Norwegian called Skinna-Bjǫrn (the name means pelt-Bjǫrn), who had been to Novgorod. In this town he had presumably dealt in the beaver, black fox, sable and squirrel which are mentioned by such Arabic authors as Ibn Horradadbeh (died 849) and Ibn Rustah (after 922) who tell of Scandinavian traders in Russia. A valuable product of Greenland was fur – indeed, the breakdown of the Greenland economy in the later middle ages can perhaps in part be ascribed to the opening up of the Russian fur trade to the European market and the decline in demand for the furs of the North.

Another important export from Greenland was walrus ivory, which, together with ivory from the north of Norway, kept the greater part of western Europe supplied until the re-introduction of elephant ivory in the thirteenth century. Objects of horn were probably exported, as objects of iron certainly were. The Arab authors Ibn Horradadbeh and Ibn Miskawaih mention the importance of swords in the eastern trade, but how many of these may have been of German or Frankish origin is unknown. It is possible, however, that iron was imported into Muslim countries from the North in ingot form. In the west finished iron objects may have been imported from Scandinavia, as is suggested by the story of a request from Knut the Great for three dozen Norwegian axes. On the other hand, sword blades and complete weapons were also imported into Scandinavia from Europe, especially from the Rhenish area. Some of the Anglo-Saxon swords frequently found in Scandinavian graves must be considered as booty; but the many sword blades bearing the names of German smiths and mounted with a hilt of Scandinavian workmanship must surely represent trade. Soapstone vessels were undoubtedly exported from Norway to Germany, Iceland and the Faroes, and possibly to the British Isles. Shetland had at least one soapstone quarry of its own and may also have traded in its products. Traffic in livestock may have been of some importance to the Danish economy; some perhaps were traded for the lava querns from the Eifel and glass and weapons from the Rhineland which are often found in Scandinavia.

At this period there was, however, little need for international trade in northern Europe in staple foods and the absolute necessities of life. With the exception of a substance like salt, there was probably a reasonable abundance of food and clothing in the Viking homelands. In Iceland the kinds of food produced were limited (cf. p. 55) and there are records of Icelandic import of meal and malt from Scandinavia, but the Icelanders were comparatively rich. There would be a tendency for the Vikings to import objects which were more or less luxurious. At this period, when transport – even by sea – can hardly have been cheap, long-distance trade must have been largely conducted in luxurious and light goods – silks, spices, weapons, semi-precious stones (like jet, which was imported from England), and wine would presumably be ideal. Although the lure of the Caliphate must have been strong – where slaves varied in price between one hundred and six hundred *dinar*, according to training – slaves were probably handled only in small numbers by the Viking trader who would normally pass them on to a middleman.

Within the western Atlantic area Icelandic cloth achieved some fame. It was sold in bolts or made up as cloaks, some of which (*vararfeldir*, literally 'trade-cloaks') could be described as a standard of legal tender. The great shaggy cloaks called *rǫgg-varfeldir* (whose manufacture is described on p. 172) were an important export of the Icelanders at this time, although Iceland was not the sole source of their supply (cf. p. 173). The practically treeless condition of Iceland created a demand for timber and it might have been this factor which gave an initial impetus to the trade in timber which later, in the twelfth and thirteenth century, was to become and then remain one of the staple exports of Scandinavia. There is no reason why the export of timber to England should not have started in the Viking period, but of this there is no evidence.

In the course of the twelfth century the character of Scandinavian trade changed. The growth of the north German and Polish towns created a demand for food, some of which was provided from the North. Grain was exported from Denmark, Baltic herring was in great demand, and fish began to be an important element in the Norwegian economy, dried and salted fish being exported as the cod fisheries of Lofoten were brought into being. The demand for fish was increased with the conversion of Scandinavians and Wends to Christianity in the eleventh and twelfth centuries, and because the Church's fasting rules became firmer in this period. It is in the late twelfth century that we first hear of imports to Norway of corn, flour and cloth from England, which probably began to supply malt at the same time. The boy kings Hákon Hákonsson and Henry III exchanged letters in 1217 which, although providing us with the earliest surviving formal agreement concerning Anglo-Norwegian trade and the rights of merchants, probably only reflect previous arrangements of a similar nature.

Markets and towns

Commerce on such a scale demanded large trading stations. Out of these, in the ninth century, grew the first Scandinavian towns, through which passed much of the east-west trade of Europe and a great deal of the north-south trade as well. In the towns traders met to line their purses, fill their ships or load their pack animals under the protection of the local king's representative and, in some of the towns, foreign merchants in the late Viking Age banded together to form national guilds for self-protection (see p. 98). Here were gathered specialist craftsmen who made material for other markets – jewellery, leather goods and combs, for example. Most of the towns were defended by banks and palisades or isolated from attack by natural features. They are among the most remarkable phenomena of the Viking Age.

HELGÖ. The great Mälar Lake, which reaches into the rich central area of Sweden known as Svealand, has always been one of the major routes into the heart of Sweden proper, and in the Vendel and Viking period it formed the means of access from south, east and west to the royal seat of Uppsala. In this lake, well protected from the Baltic pirates, there grew up a series of towns of which Stockholm is the latest and largest (fig. 23). To the international markets in this area came merchants from all over the Baltic and from even further afield. The first of these trading posts was Helgö (its modern name is Lillön, in the parish of Ekerö – it is often loosely referred to by the parish name), once a small island in the lake, but now – because of the lowering of the water level – joined to the mainland. Excavation since 1954 has revealed the first of a series of house sites, some on terraces on the rocky slopes above the shore, and some on the flatter, low-lying shore on the landward side. The settlement was apparently founded in the fifth century, but had begun to lose

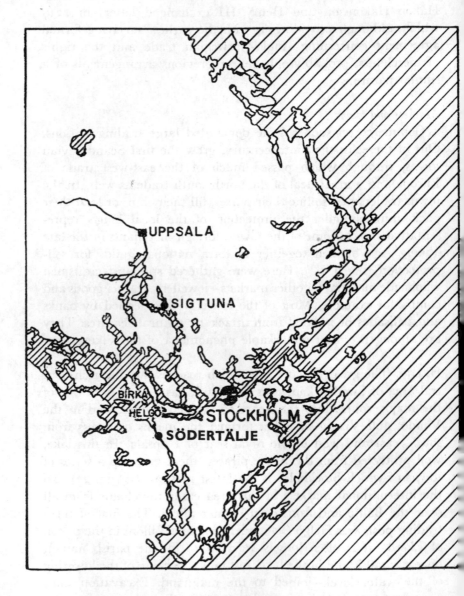

Fig. 23. Map of Mälaren showing the positions of the early towns and trading stations.

its importance in the late eighth century, when the town of Birka was founded nearby. The rectangular houses found on the terraces were in some cases associated with small sheds which were used for industrial purposes. Most of the finds of this very rich site are not relevant to this study because they are much earlier than the Viking period, but the imports of glass, pottery and metalwork indicate lively contacts with the continent of Europe, with Germany, Poland and the Baltic states, as well as close relations with Finland and more tenuous links with the Mediterranean and Britain.

Wilhelm Holmqvist and Birgit Arrhenius, the excavators of the site, see Helgö as the precursor of the Viking town of Birka, which lies a few miles away. They believe that Helgö was the main trading centre of the Baltic in the period before Swedish traders opened up the Russian routes about 800. The cramped and gradually silting harbour at Helgö was inadequate for the increased number of ships, some possibly of greater draft than those previously encountered in this area, which came to Mälaren as a result of the explosion of trade at the beginning of the ninth century. The merchants consequently had to look elsewhere for accommodation. It is interesting that the Swedish settlement on the southern shore of the Baltic at Grobin, near Liepāja (Libau) in Latvia, also began to decline at the same time. Perhaps the disappearance of this enigmatic colonial settlement (military strong-point, trading station, or whatever it was) was also connected with the change of emphasis in the direction of Swedish trade towards the richer lands of Russia.

BIRKA. Birka, on the small island of Björkö (literally Birch Island) a few kilometres from Helgö (fig. 24), lies on the main line of communication between the kernel of the kingdom of Uppland, at Uppsala, and the sea. Its existence as an important town is mentioned in contemporary European literature in Rimbert's late ninth-century biography of St Ansgar, the apostle of Scandinavia, while shortly after the final decline of the town Adam of Bremen, writing c. 1070, also records certain details of the town's appearance. Birka according to these sources was a walled town with a fortress, governed by a representative of the king, and with a *thing*.

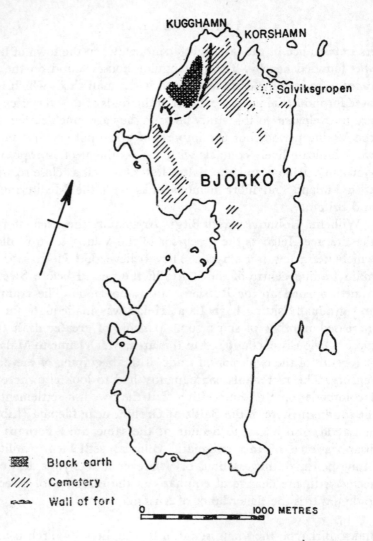

Fig. 24. The island of Björkö showing Birka, with the fort to the south and the three extra-mural harbours.

The exact location of Birka was for a long time in dispute, but after the first excavations on Björkö in the seventeenth century few people doubted its identification. The excavations on which our knowledge of the town largely rests were carried out intermittently between 1871 and 1895 by Hjalmar Stolpe – one of the greatest nineteenth-century field archaeologists. Stolpe's investigations were mainly confined to the vast grave-field which lay outside the walls of the town and the material he found provides one of the richest quarries for the archaeological interpretation of the Viking Age. Our knowledge of the town itself is slight. Excavation by Stolpe and others in a limited area has produced a certain amount of archaeological material but little knowledge of the actual appearance of the town's buildings and layout. Its major physical features are clear (pl. 8a and fig. 24), although a drop in the water-table since the Viking Age has greatly altered the topography of the island of Björkö and the defensive features of the town.

Dominating the site is a fortified outcrop (pl. 8a), the strongpoint of the town, which probably served as a refuge for the population in time of danger; it is defended on the landward side by a massive stone and earth bank and on the seaward side by formidable cliffs. The line of the bank is cut in three places by gates. Excavation inside the fort has produced little general information, but it is suggested that it was garrisoned by troops who would keep watch since the bare smooth rock at the top of the fort affords a wide view over the lake and the approaches of the town. Below the fort, to the north and slightly separated from it, lies the site of the town itself. This meadow-like area, now dotted with birch and juniper, was once a thriving market, thronged in the summer months by traders from the whole of Scandinavia, from the realm of the Carolingians, from Russia, from Arab states of Asia and from Constantinople and other parts of the Eastern Empire. In its streets walked Ansgar, the apostle of Sweden, rubbing shoulders with the merchants and with members of the household of the pagan king of Sweden. Here was all the noise of workshops, animals and creaking carts, curses in twenty languages and prayers to a dozen gods. All this was enclosed by a bank which nowadays stands to a height of two metres. This defensive work, which was originally much higher and probably capped by a wooden walk, has six openings and it has been suggested that these openings indicate the position of wooden towers – it seems unlikely that they would all be gateways. In the centre of the 29-acre enclosure is the area of ancient settlement – the *Black Earth* – so called on account of the colour of the soil in the area (a 2-metre accumulation of overburden due to human activity). The extent of the *Black Earth* has not yet been completely revealed, but it is possible that, as in Roman and later medieval towns elsewhere in Europe, trades like that of the blacksmith which involved the use of fire were carried on under the shadow of the wall, and not in the midst of the houses, to avoid the risk of general conflagration. Unfortunately only about one-thirtieth of the total area of the town has been excavated and little, for example, is known of the houses. Dried clay, apparently the skimmed surface of a log-cabin type of block house, has survived, suggesting the presence here of a Slav type of building of a form at present unknown elsewhere in Scandinavia. Structures of wattle and daub are also attested, but whether they were of houses, sheds, screens or fences, it is impossible to say.

The town was primarily a port. On the sea-front are the remains of substantial oak piles which presumably formed part of the staging of the jetties and quays and perhaps of a protective harbour wall, but there were also two natural harbours to the north of the town, Kugghamn, 'cargo-boat harbour' (the first element is borrowed from MLG *kogge* or Frisian *kog(ge)*), and Korshamn, 'cross harbour'. To the east of the town was a remarkable artificial harbour, now known as Salviksgropen, with an 80 m. long basin which would form a very well-protected dock. This can only have been constructed at the height of the town's prosperity and may be related to a number of artificial terraces – sites of buildings – which can be observed on the ground in the area outside the town but which have not yet been excavated.

Birka was not only fed by ships; during the winter, when the lake was frozen, the ice would form an easy means of access by sledge. The large number of bone skates found in the Black Earth reflects the importance of winter movement to the inhabitants.

Birka lived by trade. Rimbert in his description of the town talks of the two groups of people who lived there – the *populi*, permanent residents, and the *negociatores*, merchants – and the activities of this second group are reflected in the finds from the great grave-field outside the walls of the town and round the fort. Nearly 1200 of the 2000-odd graves have been excavated.

The coins, weapons, pottery, glass, silks (the last found in forty graves) and other personal possessions buried with the dead show contacts with Britain, the Carolingian Empire, the Caliphate of western Asia, Russia, the Lapps and with the neighbouring Scandinavian kingdoms.

Sex	Arabic coins	Non-Scandinavian European coins	Scandinavian coins	Byzantine coins
men	40	1	–	–
women	44	12	36	2
double graves	20	1	1	1
not known	27	3	1	–

Table of coins found in Birka graves (after B. Malmer).

The grave finds also indicate the date of the town. The earliest graves can be dated to about 800, and as some later graves are found under the rampart itself, it appears that the rampart was not built until the early tenth century. The latest graves seem to belong, to judge by the coins found in them, to the last quarter of the tenth century, and it is usually presumed that the inhabitants moved from Birka to found the nearby town of Sigtuna somewhere between 950 and 975. At the same time it should be said that Sigtuna did not take over the main body of the Birka trade – it seems more probable that this went to the island of Gotland which had become a more popular entrepôt for the Baltic merchants. Adam of Bremen tells us that by about 1070 there was practically nothing to be seen of the once great town of Birka. But it did not disappear dramatically, for there is no evidence of any great sack of the town. It simply fades gently out of history, the last datable find being a hoard of coins and arm-rings which was presumably deposited in the Black Earth in the 960s.

Like Helgö, Birka also had manufacturing industries: metal-workers' moulds, silversmiths' hammers, an iron for drawing filigree wire, crucibles and a certain amount of raw material were found in the excavations. But the evidence is much less convincing than that provided at Helgö, no doubt because of the less thorough character of the excavations. Some of the most interesting of the moulds – one for instance, which was used for making copies of an oriental pendant – demonstrate the eastern contacts of the town's craftsmen. Another important industry was horn-working. A great quantity of raw material (pieces of elk- and reindeer-antler) and finished and half-finished products were found within the town, demonstrating a comb-making and sword-furbishing industry. Whetstones were also manu-factured here.

HEDEBY. Contemporary with, and comparable to, Birka was the great town of Hedeby (Haithabu) on the eastern side of the neck of the Jutland peninsula (fig. 40). As it is seen today its appear-ance is not unlike Birka, with a semi-circular wall and a similar fort outside it (pl. 8b). It covers a bigger area than Birka, but must have fulfilled a similar function. The early history of the town is obscure – beginning perhaps as two or three minor settlements – but it seems to have started to function as a trad-ing station about 800 (see p. 11).

It has long been known from historical sources. The Anglo-Saxon chronicler, Æthelweard, for example, writing in the late tenth century, described it as a town, 'which is called Sleswic by the Saxons and Haithaby by the Danes'. Earlier the tenth-century Arab traveller, at-Tartusi, visited what may have been this place and was unimpressed; it was 'poorly off for wealth and goods'. But the actual site was not recognised until the Danish archaeologist, Sophus Müller, identified it at the end of the nineteenth century. Excavations were started at Hedeby at the beginning of this century and have gone on intermittently to this day under the leadership of German archaeologists from Kiel and Schleswig. The pattern of its history is now beginning to emerge. The fort lies to the north, on an eminence. Roughly rectangular in form, its highest point is about 26 m. above sea-level. Its walls do not survive to any great height, but excavation has revealed at least two building periods. No traces of occupation have been found in the fort and it must be assumed that it served as a refuge in time of war. Although it may date to the pre-Viking period, a Viking date is quite possible, in view of the remarkable coincidence of plan with that of Birka and of its position in relation to the town itself.

The town (pl. 8b) lies on the edge of the Haddebyer Noor, an inlet of the Schlei (fig. 40). Its semicircular rampart rises to a height of between 5 and 10 m. and encloses an area of about sixty acres; it had four openings and was continued northward into the water in the form of a palisade. The date of the wall is not clear, but an early bank of turf and sand faced with timber and probably capped with a timber breastwork must date from the end of the ninth century. This was later strengthened. Through the centre of the enclosure ran a brook, only a few feet wide, its sides reinforced with wooden piling. The brook must have provided a convenient source of fresh water for washing and other domestic purposes. The original town-centre flanked this stream but the inhabited portion of the town perhaps did not entirely fill all the fortified area. The reason for the large enclosure is unclear. It has been suggested that the wall delineated a free-trade area with its own privileges; but it is possible to consider this area as storage space or as room for temporary merchant camps, and part of it was certainly used as a cemetery. It is likely that much of the walled area would give the impression of a large open-air market in which the merchants' wares were displayed on stalls or laid out on the ground – a practice which would take up a great deal of room. The merchants who came to sell their wares, the ships' crews and the peddlars, lived almost certainly in tents or shacks in the area round the permanent settlement. Even if the sailors slept on board their ship to protect their stock-in-trade, they would cook their food on shore, for shipboard life was very cramped and even on the shortest of coastal trips the crew doubtless preferred to sleep ashore. The enclosure itself served to protect a rich centre from concerted attack by ambitious political leaders or pirates.

In the main part of the town a considerable number of wooden houses have been traced by excavation. The earlier houses in particular are well preserved. In the old centre of the town were a series of quite substantial rectangular houses, measuring on average about 15.5 x 6 m. Some had walls of wattle and daub, but more commonly they were found to be of stave construction (i.e. made up of tree-trunks split lengthwise and placed side by side vertically in the ground with the curved surface on the out-side – cf. fig. 59). They were set in plots bounded by wattle fences and occasionally had outhouses and often a well. The houses were built with their gables towards the timber-paved street and set back a little way from the street. We know little of their internal structure; usually they had a central hearth and a roof thatched with reeds. As the houses fell into disrepair they were rebuilt on the same plot. The houses towards the west were mostly small huts, between 3 x 4 m. and 4 x 5 m. in size, with sunken floors and wattle walls and a fire-place in one corner. They were built at a later stage in the history of Hedeby, prob-ably for the poorer element of the population.

The finds from the town are similar to those at Birka. Here again weights and scales and exotic objects indicate the trading character of the community and, as has been shown, there is a strong probability that coins were minted here. The finds in-dicate that the closest trading connections were with Germany and the Baltic, but material from all over western Europe has been excavated here. Among the objects found on the site were a number of agricultural implements, but more important in-dications of Hedeby's internal economic function are finds which indicate minor industries – iron-smelting, bronze-casting, weav-ing, bone- and horn-carving, glass-making, and even a pottery which produced ceramics of a type commonly found between the Rhine and Elbe. Analysis of the animal-bones show that the commonest meat, after beef, was pork and venison, while finds of seeds indicate that barley, wheat and hops were used in the town, while wild fruit, hazelnuts, strawberries and other fruits and berries were gathered by the inhabitants.

There were several grave-fields at Hedeby. While not having so many well-furnished graves as Birka they tell a similar tale, save only that Christian influence was strong at Hedeby and made its mark in the tenth century – with the result that fewer people were buried with grave-goods in the pagan manner.

The material from the cemeteries, together with that from

the excavations in the town, enable us to build up a chronological picture of the development of Hedeby. The first settlement on the site was a little to the south of the later rampart, between the southern gate and the water's edge. The dead of this period were buried in a cemetery to the southwest and seem to be chiefly of Frisian origin. About 800 a settlement grew up in the centre of the area which was later surrounded by the rampart, with a cemetery a little to the west. At about the same time a smaller settlement and cemetery were established between the fort and the rampart. The two outermost settlements disappeared in the course of the ninth century and the central settlement was extended. The central cemetery was enlarged as was also the southernmost cemetery. The graves become almost completely Scandinavian in character. The first fortification was probably raised in the late ninth century and was reinforced in the course of the tenth century as the volume of trade increased. At the same time the pagan grave-fields were neglected and a more-or-less Christian cemetery, which ultimately held about two thousand bodies, was begun in front of the southern gateway.

A thick layer of ash and charcoal in the central area represents the final destruction of the town by fire just before 1050. Whether this fire was accidental or whether it was the result of the sacking of the town, either by the Wends or Harald the Hard-ruler of Norway, is unclear. This was the end of Hedeby and in its place, a few miles away, the modern town of Schleswig was founded as its successor. It must be emphasized that this account of Hedeby is provisional. Recent work, as yet unpublished, will surely modify our description and interpretation of the site.

KAUPANG. Kaupang in Vestfold, Norway, lies on the shore of a now shallow bay set between rocky hills. In the Viking Age, when the sea-level was six feet higher, it formed a comfortable natural harbour, protected from attack by a string of islands and shoals. Excavations have been carried out in this area for more than a century and have been continued systematically since 1956. The thick *Black Earth* deposit here, comparable to those at Birka and Hedeby, show that it was a settlement of some size and the excavations have demonstrated its connections with western Europe. The place-name Kaupang enshrines the original function of the settlement as a market, while its geographical location seems to indicate that the town was *Sciringes heal(h)*, a place mentioned in one of King Alfred's additions to his translation of Orosius's *Historia adversus paganos*.

The excavations have not yet been published and only a very general picture of the site is available. There is no trace of a bank or palisade round the settlement area, but at the shore was a stone-faced embankment with a pair of jetties. Behind the embankment were found traces of houses, some of the larger examples having slightly curved walls. As at Birka and Hedeby industry flourished – traces of both metal and soapstone industry have been found. Imported objects uncovered inside the town include Rhenish pottery and glass. There are two grave-fields outside the town, Lamøya and Bikjholberg. The former has produced about 140 graves, most of them cremation burials with few grave-goods; the grave inventory does, however, include European pottery and a Carolingian sword-blade bearing the smith's name Ulfberht, well known from other European finds. The richer grave-field at Bikjholberg contains a large number of burials, mostly in boats or coffins, and the excavations there have produced a fair quantity of west European, Scandinavian and Hiberno-Saxon material.

The graves have been interpreted as those of farmer-merchants. To judge from its grave finds, Tjølling, the administrative division in which Kaupang lies, was one of the richer areas of Norway during the Viking Age (cf. p. 40). It formed the commercial hinterland to the port and market of Kaupang, and its inhabitants became prosperous as a result of this outlet for their products and by their position as middlemen. Kaupang was obviously not as rich as Birka and Hedeby; it has much more the character of a local market-town with international connections – probably one of a number of such towns in Scandinavia.

Gotland and the later towns

These three towns – Birka, Hedeby and Kaupang – are the earliest known towns in Scandinavia, but there are a number of other sites which might well provide similar results if they were thoroughly excavated. High on this list is Västergarn in Gotland. The island of Gotland seems to have become extremely rich in the tenth century, probably indeed the centre of Baltic trade. This wealth is adequately demonstrated by the large number of hoards of silver found on the island. Visby, the present capital of Gotland, may have been founded in the Viking Age, but it is quite possible that the original chief port of the island was Västergarn, a little to the south of Visby, where a wall and traces of *Black Earth*, similar to that found at Birka, have been observed under the drifted sand. The beaches of Gotland would have been ideal landing-places for the shallow-drafted Viking ships and there may have been no real need for a town in the island; but a major market would have been desirable, and Västergarn may have fulfilled this function.

Other towns seem to have developed, like Sigtuna, at a later date, some at least as cult places, administrative centres and episcopal seats. Skara, Lund and Södertälje in Sweden, Slesvig, Ribe, Aarhus, Viborg, Aalborg, Roskilde and Ringsted in Denmark, and Oslo, Bergen and Trondheim (Nidaros) in Norway, are all of Viking Age origin and archaeological evidence has been found to demonstrate their ancient status – particularly at Lund, Sigtuna, Aarhus and Oslo. But all these towns, with the possible exception of Sigtuna, are so overlaid by their modern successors that excavation is difficult. However, the wholesale re-development of the ancient centres of Lund and Aarhus has enabled a concerted archaeological survey of these towns to be attempted. Successive seasons of excavation at Lund have revealed a town, which came into being about 1020, with a number of early churches, including the stone cathedral started *c.* 1080 and richly endowed by Knut Svensson in 1085. Lund was a royal town and a cathedral city, but its streets were narrow and its houses (as far as we know at the moment) were mainly of wattle and daub, although buildings of other structural form have been found. One large building, 16 m. in length, has been found; but its original use is as yet unknown. The finds are generally poor, although occasionally relieved by richly ornamented woodwork or even luxuries like silk. But few imports have been found and the town seems to have functioned as a local market. It supported a considerable bone industry, which might have been of more than local importance. There is also evidence in Lund of a remarkable pottery industry, closely in-

fluenced by that of the Slavs of the south Baltic lands. This industry may have provided pottery for the region but it was of
little consequence in international trade. Other industries and
trades – bronze- and tin-working, shoe-making, weaving, woodworking and so on – are well represented, but there is no evidence that they were of any importance outside the town and
its immediate surroundings. Lund – although a royal foundation
with a mint – must have been fairly typical of the normal market-
towns of Scandinavia.

Aarhus in Jutland was perhaps closely related in function to
Kaupang in Vestfold and may indeed have formed one of the
main ports of the Danish-Norwegian trade. The Viking town
there was built on a gravel outcrop in the centre of the modern
town – 3 m. below present ground level. It was surrounded by a
palisaded rampart and its ships could be drawn up on a sandy
shore. It apparently came into existence in the tenth century and
has had a continuous history ever since. The economy was
similar to that at Kaupang, dependent on trade and small industries and the rich agricultural hinterland of Jutland. Excavations close to the wall have revealed a number of small houses
with sunken floors and a central hearth. Presumably these are
equivalent to those found in the poorest parts of Hedeby, providing space only for sleeping and cottage industry. The finds
are objects of reasonable quality and suggest that the people who
lived here were certainly not slaves – one can perhaps see them
as free craftsmen. Although only these poorest houses have been
excavated, casual finds suggest that, as at Hedeby and Kaupang,
there were larger houses and richer families living here.

Excavation of the ancient wharf at Bergen, Norway, a town
which was traditionally held to have been founded by King
Ólaf the Quiet about 1070, has revealed something of the growth
of an important mercantile centre at the end of the Viking
period. The earliest wooden-built houses lay directly on the
gently sloping foreshore. The first two of a series of fires which
destroyed this area took place in 1170 (or 1172) and 1198 and
the necessary rebuilding started a process of consolidation of the
area to form a quay by means of staging which extended into
the harbour and allowed the ships to tie up alongside. Long
merchants' houses were built on the quay, with their narrow

ends towards the sea and small passages between them. It is calculated that by 1170 the consolidation of the wharf had already extended at least 30 m. out into the harbour on a hard bank of rubble and rubbish some 4 m. thick contained by baulks of timber. The origins of this town are obscure, but Asbjørn Herteig, who has so brilliantly excavated this fascinating and complicated site, suggests that it was already a fishing village before the official foundation of the town by Ólaf the Quiet. What is clear from the archaeological evidence is the immense amount of foreign trade carried on through Bergen, chiefly revealed by the vast quantity of continental and English pottery of the eleventh and twelfth century. It reflects the imports mentioned by King Sverri in a speech made in Bergen in 1186, when 'wine in Bergen was no dearer than beer', when honey, flour and cloth were the main goods brought from England and when in exchange for wine the Germans took home butter and dried fish. We are brought into touch with individual traders by labels of wood carved with runes which record the ownership, and sometimes the value, of some of the goods traded from this port.

Norse towns abroad

In the colonies, also, the Vikings founded and defended their towns. The great ports of Ireland – Dublin, Cork, Limerick, Waterford and Wexford – owe their existence to the Vikings. Founded as fortifications in an alien country they became international markets. Dublin – a small settlement of Celtic origin – was occupied by the Viking Turgeis in 836 and fortified c. 840, and only later became famous as a centre of trade. Its international character is hinted at in Arabic, Norse, English and Irish sources. It was an important administrative centre and the *thing* met on a mound which was still to be seen in the seventeenth century, when it was referred to as 'the fortified hill near the College'. Excavations at High Street in Dublin are beginning to uncover an important industrial area of this notable Viking city: the finds are rich, as is to be expected when we consider the geographical situation and royal status of the town. Brendán Ó Ríordáin, the excavator, kindly tells me that the houses were constructed of wattle panels supported by posts and had stone-lined hearths in the centre of the floor. Evidence of bone-working,

weaving and leather-processing has been uncovered. The economic and administrative importance of Dublin is also demonstrated by its coinage. From about 995 the Dublin Vikings issued
their own coins (pl. 6c, d) and, despite a debasement at an early
stage of the mint's history sufficient to make these coins unac-
ceptable outside Ireland, English coins were, for nearly a hundred
and fifty years, of relatively small importance in the local monetary economy. The earlier history of Dublin as an important
settlement is illustrated by a pagan Viking burial ground at
Islandbridge, Kilmainham, outside the walls of the town. The
grave-goods are largely Norwegian in character and of ninth- or
tenth-century date. Unfortunately only a small part of the
cemetery has been properly excavated so we cannot even guess
at the total number of graves, but we may suppose it to be comparable in size with the cemeteries at Hedeby or Kaupang and
no less rich.

In England the Vikings took over existing towns and converted them to their own use and we may assume that they did
the same in Normandy. Finds from some of these towns, notably
York and Rouen, show the strength and wealth of this Viking
settlement, as does the important coinage of the Viking kings
of York and of the Five Boroughs – Stamford, Nottingham,
Lincoln, Derby and Leicester.

The archaeological evidence, however, is very slender. Only
one structure – a wharf at York – can be associated with any
certainty with the Viking period, for the rest we rely on casual
finds – swords, ornaments, brooches and pieces of sculpture.
One has to turn to the Baltic and to Russia for further evidence
of the foundation of towns and trading stations by the Scandinavians. Indeed it was in the south Baltic (fig. 25) that the
earliest colonial towns were founded. What might be a town of
this group, known as *Truso*, is mentioned by King Alfred in his
description of Wulfstan's voyage; it was apparently situated on
one of the mouths of the Vistula, probably behind the Zalew
Wislany in the Gulf of Danzig. From Wulfstan's description it
could be anywhere between Danzig and Kaliningrad (formerly
Königsberg) and although Elblag (formerly Elbing) is favoured
as the site of this town, no real evidence for the identification
exists, save for a small cemetery with Viking elements which has

been found in Elblag itself. Recent research would identify the
village of Druzno as Truso, but excavations here have only just
begun and are as yet inconclusive. Alfred is the only author to
mention Truso and he seems to accept it as a native Baltic town. It
is unlikely to have been in any sense under Norse control.

Alfred describes the land east of the Vistula as having many
towns, each with its own king; while Rimbert in his Life of St
Ansgar says that Kurland had five towns and mentions two by
name, *Seeburg* and *Apulia*. The latter is probably the modern
Apuole in northwest Lithuania, while the former has been
identified as Grobin, near Liepāja (Libau) in western Latvia.
Here, near a large fort which has produced pottery and objects
of central Swedish type, Birger Nerman has excavated three
large cemeteries. One of these contained more than a thousand
cremation graves, closely comparable with those found in seventh-
and eighth-century Gotland; the second cemetery was similar,
but the third contained objects of Central Swedish origin. The
Gotlandic people who settled here have been considered traders,
and the men from the Mälar region soldiers and warriors. Grobin,
like certain other places in Latvia, was apparently a town under
Swedish control and seems to have been maintained as a trading
post and military strong-point for the extensive eastern trade
along the Vistula. Its collapse between 800 and 850 coincides
with the growth of the Russian towns of Staraja Ladoga and
Novgorod and the eastward shift of trade, a shift reflected in
Scandinavia by the growth in importance of Birka and Gotland.

One other Baltic town should be mentioned in this context.
Wolin, at the mouth of the Oder, near Szczecin (Stettin), has a
history which goes back to about 900 and is identified with the
Jumne which Adam of Bremen describes as the largest town in
Europe. It was apparently a Slav town but was frequented by
Scandinavians and people from Byzantium and Germany. Adam
records that there was much northern merchandise in the town
and this statement is supported by finds in Wolin, where a fair
number of Scandinavian objects have come to light and where,
in the centre of the town, even remains of ninth-century houses
of Scandinavian stave-construction have been excavated. Wolin
probably controlled the trade along the Oder into central Europe
and was certainly of importance in relation to the Baltic trade.

The problem of the Viking presence further east in Russia is a complicated and controversial topic. Scholars have tended to side with one of two factions; the first firmly believing in the importance of the Scandinavian element in the founding of Russian towns and of the Russian state itself, the second discounting this influence almost completely (these two schools of thought are labelled in technical literature by the unfortunate terms 'Normanist' and 'anti-Normanist'). The problem is aggravated by the diversity of languages of the historical sources – Norse, Greek, Russian, Arabic – and by the still greater diversity of the languages in which they have been discussed. No one can master all the arguments and all we can hope to do is to give as balanced a view as possible. We are conscious that we write as western Europeans with less knowledge of the eastern sources and more of the northern and western point of view.

Northern influence in Russia was primarily mercantile. The Scandinavians came to Russia in search of trade and any political power and control which they gained there was incidental to their main purpose. Evidence for this trade rests on archaeological and literary sources, and discussion of the validity of this evidence is at the basis of the Normanist controversy. It is an undoubted fact that there were Swedish Vikings in Russia from the first half of the ninth century onwards. They came first as traders and later as mercenary soldiers, and their leaders played an important part in the foundation or consolidation of the city states of early medieval Russia. A number of towns are associated with the Vikings and some of them may have been founded by them: at one time or another, between the ninth and eleventh centuries, the Vikings controlled, for the purposes of trade and military power, the towns of Staraja Ladoga, Novgorod, Kiev, Izborsk, Bjeloozero, Chernigov, Rostov and the precursor of Smolensk. On the basis of these towns they developed and controlled the north-south commercial routes through western Russia from the Baltic to the Black Sea (fig. 25). Some of these towns may have been founded by the Scandinavians, some may have been settlements fortified and developed by the Scandinavians; but it is likely that by means of these towns the Vikings, for some time at least, controlled the rich route to Byzantium along the Dnjeper. To the Scandinavians of the eleventh century,

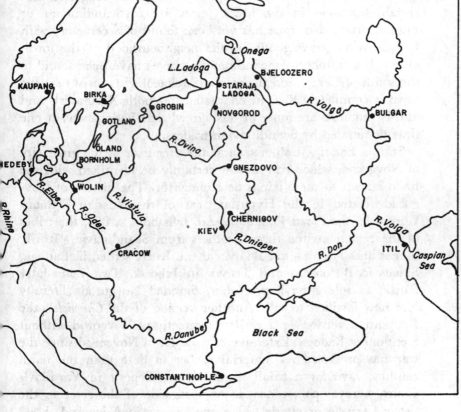

Fig. 25. Scandinavia and east Europe.

Russia was 'the land of towns' (Garðar, Garðaríki); the Slavonic word for a fortified place, *gorod* (as in Novgorod), is ultimately the same as ON *garðr*, but we do not know for sure whether the one is derived from the other.

The town of Staraja (=old) Ladoga (in Scandinavian sources known as Aldeigjuborg) was situated on the left bank of the river Volkhov, some 12 km. from its outlet into the south of Lake Ladoga; it is thus connected by water with the Gulf of Finland and the Baltic, by way of the River Neva. The site of the town covers an area of 9000 square metres and is enclosed by a strong bank of earth. Excavations in the town itself have produced little material that is definitely Viking, but it has been suggested that certain buildings in the lower levels are of Scandinavian or Finnish origin. No trace has yet been found of a cemetery with Scandinavian grave-goods in the neighbourhood of the town, although a number of Scandinavian graves have been found to the south of Lake Ladoga. Russian archaeologists insist that the town is completely Slav in character, but both Normanists and anti-Normanists are more or less agreed that Ladoga was at one time dominated by Scandinavian traders.

Staraja Ladoga is often seen as the precursor of the great city of Novgorod, which can almost certainly be identified with the town known to the Vikings as Holmgarðr. The history of Novgorod related in the Hypatian text of the Russian Primary Chronicle, the *Povest Vremennykh Let*, tells how, c. 860, the tribes of the region invited three brothers from Scandinavia – Rurik, Sineus and Truvor – to rule over them. Rurik settled in Ladoga, Sineus in Bjeloozero and Truvor in Izborsk. Two years later Rurik, as sole surviving brother, founded Novgorod (literally 'the new fortified town'). Another version of the *Chronicle* – the Laurentian version – places Rurik directly in Novgorod without mentioning Ladoga. Extensive excavation in Novgorod since the war has produced no material earlier in date than the tenth century, save for a small ninth-century deposit in Yaroslav's Court, a royal palace on the opposite side of the river to the present *kremlin* or citadel. The excavations in Novgorod, however, were mainly on the *kremlin* side of the river, so that the area where on topographical grounds one would expect the early city to be found, remains largely unexcavated. This low-lying area, surrounded by a stream, would be an ideal site for a Viking town; the *kremlin* on the opposite side of the river would correspond to the forts at Birka and Hedeby. Novgorod must be reckoned a major Viking trading-post and, despite the arguments of the anti-Normanists, it is difficult to discount the very specific entry in the Russian chronicle, written only two hundred and fifty years later, that Scandinavian princes came to rule in the region. By the tenth century there was a large Slav cultural element in the town, as is shown by the houses and small finds, but this element was balanced by considerable Viking influence in the political and commercial sphere. An inscription on the eleventh-century Swedish rune stone from Sjusta, Skokloster, Uppland, is interesting in this context in that it records that a Swede, Spjallbude, 'died in Holmgarðr in Ólaf's church'. Here is not only an eleventh-century Scandinavian dying in Novgorod, but also a record of an early church-dedication to St Ólaf, the Norwegian saint killed in 1030, who had family connections with Novgorod and had himself been there (p. 45).

Two other towns are important in relation to Viking commercial activity in Russia, Smolensk (or its precursor) and Kiev, the centre of the ancient Russian state. The evidence for the importance of the former is based on an extensive grave-field at Gnezdovo, west of the present town. This is one of the largest grave-fields in Russia; it extends over an area of about 250 acres and consists of nearly four thousand small mounds, most of which enclose cremation burials associated with a fair amount of material of Viking origin. Unfortunately Russian archaeologists maintain that only two of the 700 burials so far excavated 'were undoubtedly burials of Norsemen'; these people, they allege, 'were in Russian service'. In fact, there are a fair number of Scandinavian objects of late ninth- and tenth-century date – by 1913 they had already found twenty-four oval brooches – as well as a number of objects which were made in the Smolensk region under Scandinavian influence. The grave-field, taken together with an area of *Black Earth* like that at Birka found in the neighbourhood, suggests that Gnezdovo was one of the main trading stations in Russia, having its outlets to the Baltic by way of Novgorod and Ladoga and the headwaters of the Volga, and to the Black Sea along the Dnjeper by way of Kiev. The evidence available suggests that throughout the ninth and part of the tenth century it was controlled by the Scandinavians: as was the view of such distinguished Russian archaeologists as Ravdonikas and Spitzyn.

Kiev was the most important town of medieval Russia; it was the centre of the Russian state in the middle ages and was one of the great entrepôts of Europe, having links overland – by way of Cracow, Breslau, Prague, Pilsen and Regensburg – with Mainz, the hub of west European trade, with the Black Sea and the silk route, and to the north with the Baltic. It is impossible to describe Kiev as a Scandinavian town, although it was for certain periods under Viking rule and it has produced a certain amount of archaeological material of Scandinavian origin, particularly in the graves of the 'necropolis' of the old town. Excavations here, as in other Russian towns, have produced no convincingly Viking type of house, but as the same is true of many Irish towns, which were certainly Viking foundations, it would be unwise to give undue weight to this negative result. Like the other Russian towns Kiev has produced a great deal of evidence of settled craftsmen, particularly metalworkers who, although strongly influenced from Constantinople and eastern Europe, occasionally adapted Scandinavian ornamental traits.

The trade-routes

The trade-routes of the Vikings can to some extent be reconstructed from literary sources. The accounts given by Ohthere and Wulfstan to King Alfred tell us something of the traders' voyages in northern waters:

> Ohthere said that the province he lived in was known as Hálogaland. Nobody, he said, lived further north than he did. There is a mart in the south of that land which is called *Sciringes heal* [Kaupang, cf. pp. 213-4]. He said that one might sail thither in a month, if one anchored at night and each day had a favourable wind, and all the time should sail along the coast . . . From *Sciringes heal* he said he sailed to the mart known as *æt Hæþum* [Hedeby] in five days; it lies between the Wends and Saxons and Angles and belongs to the Danes. When he sailed thither from *Sciringes heal*, Denmark was to port and open sea to starboard for three days, then for two days before he came to Hedeby he had Jutland and many islands to starboard.

> Wulfstan said that he went from Hedeby, that he was in Truso in seven days and nights and that the ship was under sail all the way. Wendland was to starboard, and to port was Langeland, Lolland, Falster and Skåne, and then Burgenda-land [Bornholm] was to port and they have their own king. Then . . . Blekinge, Möre and Öland and Gotland to port, and these provinces belong to Sweden. And as far as the mouth of the Vistula we had Wendland on the starboard.

These passages mention some of the important routes of Norwegian coastal waters and the Baltic. One may presume from the description that Wulfstan was familiar with the sea-route to Birka, for two of the islands he mentions north of Bornholm – Öland and Gotland – are not visible from the south Baltic and they, and the province of Blekinge, which he mentions in the same breath, must have been familiar to anyone sailing along the east coast of Sweden to Gotland or Birka. Ohthere and Wulfstan between them document the coastal routes of western Norway, the route from Kaupang to Hedeby and that from Hedeby to Truso. The Hedeby-Birka sea-route we may take for granted – it is well documented in Rimbert's Life of St Ansgar.

In the east the Dnjeper route through Russia is described in the Russian Primary Chronicle:

> A trade route connects the Varangians with the Greeks [the people of the Byzantine Empire]. Starting from the Greeks, this route proceeds along the Dnjeper, above which a portage leads to the Lovat. By following the Lovat, the great lake Ilmen is reached. The river Volkhov which flows out of this lake enters the great lake Nevo [Ladoga]. The mouth of this lake [R. Neva] opens into the Varangian Sea [the Baltic].

It is along this route that most of the Russian towns discussed above are found. The Dnjeper portion of this route is described by the Byzantine Emperor Constantine Porphyrogenitus in chapter nine of his handbook *De administrando imperio*, in which he tells of the hazards encountered in the tenth century by the people he calls the *Rus* on their way from Kiev to the mouth of the river; how they passed the series of rapids partly by carrying their boats and partly by off-loading them and steering them through the shallower rapids. This was a rough journey, lasting at least six weeks, with trials including not only the passage of seven rapids[1] but also attacks by hostile tribes on the lower

---

[1]Constantine gives us the names of these rapids in Slav and 'Russian' (i.e. Norse); the latter are Essupi, Oulborsi, Gelandri, Aïfor, Baruforos, Leanti, Strukun. A Scandinavian explanation can be provided for all of them, although there is controversy over the precise interpretation of some. (Even the most conservative anti-Normanist will agree that at least three of them are of certain Scandinavian origin.) *Oulborsi*, the Greek transliteration of the 'Russian', i.e. Norse, name of the second rapid, is thus EN *(H)ulmfors*, 'island foss', with dative singular ending; *Gelandri* [sic], the name of the third, is identified as the present participle, EN *gællandi*, 'the yelling'; and the fifth name is a similar form, *Leanti*, from EN *(h)leiandi*, 'laughing'.

reaches of the river. But this was not the only eastern route used by the Vikings.

One chronicler called the Dvina (which empties in the Gulf of Riga) 'the route to the Varangians', and he was well aware of the Volga route, which he mentions in the same passage but does not associate with the Vikings. The direct route to the Baltic by way of the Dvina from the head-waters of the Dnjeper was obviously of great importance, as witness the large number of hoards and finds of coins of the Viking Age in Latvia:

			Find places	No. of coins
Arabic coins	.	.	52	767
Western coins	.	.	36	1500
Byzantine coins	.	.	7	13
Silver bars	.	.	41	199

Even more coins have been found in Estonia (Professor Moora records some 10,000 coins and fragments of silver). The considerable trade between the Baltic states and Sweden is shown, particularly in Gotland, by the large quantity of Baltic objects found in Viking Age cemeteries of the tenth and eleventh centuries in this island.

An important eastern route of the late ninth and the tenth centuries was that along the Volga from the Caspian, either to Novgorod and Ladoga or to Bjeloozero and Lake Onega, by way of the Bulgars' market place at Bulgar near Kazan, where the fur-traders from the Perm forests came westwards along the Kama. From there the Caspian traders could easily reach Baghdad and touch part of the 5000-mile silk-route to China. It was in this area that the Vikings came into contact with the Arabs, some of whom, like Ibn Fadlan, give us the first thorough descriptions of the Scandinavians abroad (see pp. 407–11). The Khazars (basically a Turkish tribe of Jewish religion) controlled the lower Volga and the area between that river and the Don, with their capital, Itil (Atil), on the Volga (fig. 25); their strength enabled

them to levy tolls on the merchants, as did the Bulgars further
north. Despite these taxes the Scandinavians would find it worth
their while to travel to the Caspian region; for here, even more
than in Kiev, they would meet with the world's traders, particularly Jews, whose commercial activity spanned Europe and
Asia and reached into Africa. For those who were not really
traders, there was plenty of plunder available here and sizeable
Scandinavian fleets were raiding in the Caspian in the late ninth
and early tenth centuries.

A handful of objects illuminate this easternmost route: a
Scandinavian sword found near Kazan, a Swedish pin from
Tjemchai in Kirov, and even a few graves from Bjelimer in the
same province. Further to the southwest, in the province of
Vladimir, a greater amount of Scandinavian grave material has
been recorded. Such material – though not exactly plentiful –
demonstrates that this route was used by the Vikings and along
it may have travelled some, at least, of the vast quantity of
Arabic silver coins found in Scandinavia and some of the silks
and other oriental objects found in Sweden. The importance of
this route should not be underestimated merely because it is not
backed by the authority of the chronicler's description of 'the
route of the Varangians'. Indeed, Peter Sawyer has suggested
that the contacts of the Kiev *Rus* with Byzantium may have been
exaggerated at the expense of other routes. While such a statement should be treated with caution, the Mainz-Kiev route
certainly continued to Bulgar and much of the silver of Kiev may
have come from the Volga.

Although the archaeological parrot-cry *ex oriente lux* is particularly apposite when applied to the Swedish Vikings, trade
with, and by way of, central Europe must not be forgotten.
Holger Arbman pointed out that there is some archaeological
evidence of a trade-route through Poland, along the Vistula to
the Dniester and the Black Sea. This route would cross the great
Mainz-Kiev route and would also afford access, together with
the route along the Oder from the trading post at Wolin, to
Cracow and even the Moravian Empire, which was at its richest
and most powerful in the ninth century under Rostislav, Svato-
pluk and Mojmir I. Was it perhaps by this central European
route that the late tenth-century Viking sword called the sword

of St Stephen, now in the cathedral treasury at Prague, reached Bohemia, and was it by this route (rather than by the Rhine and the Danube, or direct from Kiev) that some southern warrior received a decorated Viking spear which he lost in the Danube at Budapest? The Viking presence in these regions is demonstrated by a late ninth- and early tenth-century cemetery found at Lutomiersk, near Lodz, in central Poland, the cultural connections of which are almost equally divided, as far as its grave goods are concerned, between Sweden and Hungary. Objects from Poland which can be paralleled in the Kiev region suggest a westward shift in the interests of the eastern traders after 960 – 70, with the full development of Wolin. This shift may be due to the sudden growth in importance of the western silver mines or, as Peter Sawyer suggests, to the political activities of the Kievan princes in north Russia which interrupted the flow of traffic between the Volga and the Baltic. Whatever the case, there can be little doubt that the central European route was of some importance to the Scandinavian economy, but its true value is imponderable.

The route along the Oder and Neisse, which was presumably used by the Vikings, would bring Scandinavia into contact with western Europe through east Germany, but for most Vikings the road to western Europe was undoubtedly by way of the North Sea and the Atlantic. The trader from Kaupang, Ribe and, later on, Bergen and Trondheim would follow the coast to the mouth of the Rhine. From the hinterland of this river Scandinavia received much of the exotic pottery, glass, weapons and jewellery found in northern contexts – inconsiderable remains of trade, but certain indications that such a trade existed. Some of this material undoubtedly came to Scandinavia as a result of the great raids and campaigns in the course of which the Vikings reached Paris and Trier and sacked monasteries and towns deep in northern France and Germany. Between 841 and 844, for example, Quentovic, Rochester, Rouen and Nantes were ruthlessly sacked and another raid took some Vikings as far as Seville. Much booty and ransom must have been taken to Scandinavia after raids such as these, but raids could easily develop into trade, as is demonstrated by the fact that for some time in the early ninth century the great port of Dorestad near the mouth of the

Rhine was controlled by Scandinavians under Rorik, who was virtual ruler of the Low Countries (throughout this period the centre of one of the richest areas in Europe). By the middle of the tenth century, however, there were fewer and fewer raids on western Europe and, in the more or less stable conditions which ensued, the Vikings had ample opportunity to develop their western trade.

In the west the trade-routes were the sea-routes. Although the Vikings were capable of sailing for days out of sight of land (pp. 255–6), they preferred to navigate by visual contact with the shore, as witness the voyages of Ohthere and Wulfstan (p. 224). They apparently sailed direct from Ireland to Iceland or from Norway to Greenland with the same confidence as along the coastal shipping lanes of the Baltic. By ship they traded in the North Atlantic, the North Sea, the Mediterranean and across the Baltic. They sailed down the rivers of Europe and, in Russia, accomplished strenuous portages (although there is some evidence that they did not always carry their ships from one river to another, but changed to locally built boats at certain specific places).

It should not, however, be forgotten that the Vikings, with carts, sledges, pack-animals, by ski and on foot, also travelled overland (see pp. 256–62). Scandinavia was not, as we have seen, without roads. One which was extremely important was the road which stretched the length of Jutland and was already in existence long before the Viking Age (p. 9). Hoard finds along this track indicate its use throughout the Viking Age, and its closeness to Hedeby and the gate, the Kalegat, where it passes through the Danevirke on its way to Germany (fig. 40), suggest its importance as a trade-route.

Piracy

Traders and raiders may not have always been easily distinguishable. The first Vikings to arrive in England were greeted as traders, but the local magistrate who went to meet them on these terms died as a result of misreading the situation. Piracy was a real risk on all trade routes. Quick profits in movable wealth and slaves must have tempted many to brigandage.

There are a number of indications of piratical activity in the archaeological and historical sources. The large number of hoards in Gotland reflects a society particularly susceptible to attack from the sea; occasionally perhaps as the result of major political action, but also probably because of individual piratical initiative. Most hoards must originally have been buried as a precaution against sudden attack, and the fact that they were never retrieved must generally mean that the expected attack came.

Piracy was always a major threat in the Baltic. Rimbert records that Ansgar was captured by pirates on his first voyage to Birka (c. 829) and that he and his merchant companions were lucky to have escaped with their lives. Later, in the twelfth century, there are records of Wends (from Pomerania and north Poland) raiding the Danish islands and Konungahella, an important township on the Götaälv. In Adam of Bremen and in the sagas we read of Vikings carrying out acts of piracy against their own kind – a tale of the biter bit!

The control and administration of trade

It has been suggested that the deliberate foundation of Hedeby by a Danish king and the intimate connections between Birka – and, one might add, Helgö – and the royal seat at Uppsala (witness Ansgar's second mission) demonstrate that the ninth-century kings of Scandinavia exploited the wealth of the towns. Indeed in the accounts – which we have no reason to doubt – of the foundation of Hedeby by Godfred one gains an impression of something rather like the much later medieval town-plantation in France and England for tax-farming purposes (see p. 11). More explicit evidence of this royal interest in towns is demonstrated further east by the kings and princes whom we have seen to exist in towns in Kurland and in the Russian trading posts. One of the obvious benefits to the ruler would be the control of the mint, always an important source of royal revenue. Although it is not proved, there is little doubt that coins were minted at Hedeby. Viking kings were certainly willing, even eager, to issue coin, as is demonstrated in the western colonies, where coins were certainly minted, for example, by the Viking kings of York and Dublin.

Customs duty is documented in the twelfth century. About

1125 Icelanders were paying tolls (*landaurar*) in Norway which they regarded as ancient in origin and a little later references to Danish dues occur. There seems little doubt, however, that the Vikings were familiar with the idea at an earlier date, even if they had only met it on the Volga, and it is inevitable that some sort of toll would be introduced in relation to any recognized market.

There is evidence at both Birka and Novgorod of a mayor or governor, presumably a royal official, who controlled the administration of the town. Birka, according to Rimbert, had a *thing*, or assembly, which was presided over by the governor: in Ansgar's time this man was called Herigar and he was also a counsellor of the king. At Birka there was apparently also a court for the settlement of law-suits and there is some indication that this court may have been held in a special building. Birka obviously had a fairly sophisticated administrative machinery and this must also have been the case elsewhere.

The merchants apparently banded together in national guilds, the further to protect their persons and their pockets (see p. 98). We must presume that guilds of Scandinavian merchants existed in western Europe in towns controlled by non-Viking authorities; but of this we have no evidence before the twelfth century. The merchant was an international figure who needed protection in foreign markets; in the days before consular representation, an organization like the national guild afforded some measure of protection, even of encouragement, to the traders.

The towns used by the Viking traders, and even the towns in their own lands, were very much international communities. Although the proportion of stolen property and money which appeared on the market was probably high, trade was an important factor in the Viking economy. The activity of the Vikings, whether as raiders and pirates or as traders, stimulated the general European economy and their adventurous voyages opened up new markets and produced fresh materials in which trade could be carried on.

7

Transport

Ships and boats

The ship has become the accepted symbol of the Viking. Without it the Scandinavian achievement could not have come about. The fast, skilfully-built, sailing ships from the north circumnavigated Europe, adventured into the Mediterranean, were seen on the Black Sea, brought explorers to America; they carried traders along the great rivers of Russia, mercenaries to Byzantium, settlers to the British Isles, colonizers to Iceland and Greenland and raiders and pirates to all parts of the western world. By their enemies these ships were hated and envied, copied and improved. By the Vikings they were regarded as the symbol of power and a companion in death. In one account of the Danish King Sven's invasion of England (1013) a chronicler gives a splendid picture of the departure of a Viking fleet:

> When at length they were all gathered, they went on board the towered ships, having picked out by observation each man his own leader on the brazen prows. On one side lions moulded in gold were to be seen on the ships, on the other birds on the tops of the masts indicated by their movements the winds as they blew, or dragons of various kinds poured fire from their nostrils. Here there were glittering men of solid gold or silver nearly comparable to live ones, there bulls with necks raised high and legs outstretched were fashioned leaping and roaring like live ones. One might see dolphins moulded in electrum, and centaurs in the same metal, recalling the ancient fable . . . But why should I now dwell upon the sides of the ships, which were not only painted with ornate colours, but were covered with gold and silver figures? The royal vessel excelled the others in beauty as much as the king preceded the soldiers in the honour of his proper dignity . . . Placing their confidence in such a fleet, when the signal was suddenly given, they set

out gladly, and, as they had been ordered, placed themselves round about the royal vessel with level prows, some in front and some behind. The blue water, smitten by many oars, might be seen foaming far and wide, and the sunlight, cast back in the gleam of metal, spread a double radiance in the air . . .

But ships were more than a symbol of power and wealth, they were the most important means of transport in northern Europe — and in many places essential means of communication. Roads, while not unknown, were often little more than tracks and generally were of much less importance for communication than rivers, lakes and sea. This is especially true of Norway where the geological structure of the country made the coastal waters the natural means of social and commercial intercourse, a fact which is stressed by the community of culture along the whole length of the Norwegian coast from Kirkenes to Kristiansand – towns about 1600 km. apart as the crow flies.

Our knowledge of Viking ships is derived from a number of sources. Primarily it comes from surviving ships, or portions of ships, the most important being those found in the graves at Tune, Oseberg and Gokstad in Norway, and the group of ships found in Denmark during the mammoth underwater rescue operation at Skuldelev in Roskildefjord. But to these important physical remains can be added information from a fairly large number of boat-graves from each of which only a few facts emerge. Mostly they come from Norway (where some five hundred examples have been recorded), but they have also been found in Sweden and Denmark (where only three boat-graves

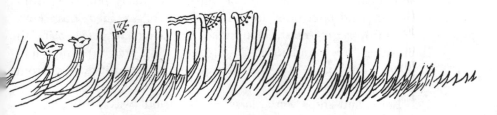

Fig. 26. Representation of a fleet carved on a piece of wood from Bergen, Norway. After Herteig.

have been found) and in the Viking colonies, particularly the British Isles, but also in Iceland, France and Russia. A second, and vital, source is provided by the contemporary and detailed representations of ships, complete with rigging, found on memorial stones in the Baltic island of Gotland (pl. 12) and by rough scratchings on various pieces of wood in Norway (fig. 26). Thirdly, we have descriptions in contemporary Scandinavian poetry and western European literature and in the laws and sagas of a somewhat later time. Lastly, for the performance of one such ship, we have the log of a copy of the Gokstad ship which sailed the Atlantic to be a Norwegian exhibit at the Chicago World Fair of 1893.

Ship-building and sea-faring produced a highly specialized nomenclature in the northern languages, and one thing which shows the superiority of the Scandinavians in these activities is the number of nautical words that other people borrowed from them. Such loan-words are found particularly in Irish, Scottish Gaelic and French and to a lesser degree in English. Among words borrowed into French, for example, are: *beitiáss* (tacking-spar), *brandr* (curved gunwale fore and aft), *festr* (mooring rope), *húnn* (mast-top), *hǫfuðbenda* (shroud), *rif* (reef in sail), *stag* (stay), *skeið* (type of vessel), *veðrviti* (weather-vane). In Irish we find, for example, *berlingr* (boom), *byrðingr* (type of vessel), *hlunnr* (ship's roller), *karfi* (type of vessel), *kjóll* (ship, keel), *knǫrr* (type of vessel), *lypting* (poop-deck), *segl* (sail), *skúta* (type of vessel), *stag* (stay), *stýri* (steering-oar), *þopta* (thwart). Foreign words of a similar kind taken into Norse are very few in comparison and seem to belong either to the very beginning or the very end of the period 800 – 1200. The chief early ones are *akkeri* (anchor), *bátr* (boat), *kuggr* (cog, kind of ship), most likely borrowed from Frisian; and later ones, from Low German, are *búza* (buss, kind of ship), *mastr* (mast, alongside the native *tré*, *viða*, *viðr*, all meaning 'tree', and *siglutré*, 'sail-tree'), and *prámr* (pram, small boat). The name *langskip*, 'longship', comes ultimately from Latin *navis longa*.

Boats and ships were classified in various ways, and the different types were not always kept distinct. The smallest vessels were defined according to the total number of oars, e.g. *sexæringr*, 'six-oared boat', *tolfæringr*, 'twelve-oared boat' – the latter is the largest to be described in this way – probably because these boats were not too big for one man to take a pair of oars. Larger boats (where one man could not take a pair of oars) with between 12 and 32 oars (the largest of this sort we know) could be defined by specifying the number of rowers on each side. The biggest of this sort and larger kinds still could be identified by the number of paired rowing-places they contained; such a place was called a *sess*, and a ship can be called, for example, a *fimtánsessa*, 'fifteen-bencher', and so on. According to the Gula-thing Law, the smallest ship that could be 'counted by benches' was a *þrettánsessa*, 'thirteen-bencher', i.e. one with twenty-six oars. The standard levy ship all over Scandinavia seems to have been the 'twenty-bencher', though some smaller ones might be included and there were bigger ships with 25 or even 30 and more rowing-benches (cf. p. 237). The lateral space between the rowing-seats was called *rúm*, 'room, space' – it might have a distinguishing name such as *austrrúm*, 'baling room' – and each *rúm* was divided into 'half-rooms'. It was thus possible to describe a ship by the number of *rúm* in it. In a cargo vessel meant for sailing, not rowing, this would presumably be the same as the number of frames (*rǫng*, pl. *rengr*), which offers yet another way of describing the size of a ship. The Gotland Law says that a harbour-watch should be kept on any ship that was of 13 frames or bigger – the minimum size here seems approximately that of ships nos. 1 and 3 from Skuldelev which have 14 and 11 or 12 frames respectively (p. 253).

Different categories and sizes of ship had different names, but again the distinctions are not always clear. The simplest sort of craft was the dug-out and its descendants. It had the name *eikja*, derived from *eik*, 'oak-tree', and was in common use as a ferry on rivers and lakes. (A number of other names are known that were originally applied to the dug-out, but they survive almost exclusively in poetry.)

The word *bátr* is used of a ship's boat, sometimes also called *eptirbátr*, 'boat in tow'. Few families on the coast could have been without a boat of some kind. In Gotland borrowing an unattended boat was put on a level with borrowing an unattended horse, and this suggests how generally available they were.

The word *skip* is used of almost any independent vessel, not necessarily very large by our standards. The chief names for ships and some of the chief features by which they were identified are as follows.

Vessels designed chiefly for carrying cargo were the *ferja*, 'ferry', and the *byrðingr*, which probably got its name from its high-boarded bulwarks, which allowed goods to be piled up between them. The chief ocean-going vessel was the *knǫrr*, a word of uncertain etymology, but probably containing a reference either to the tough wood of the stem or to the creak of the timbers in a sea. This is the 'dear-prized ship' found in a verse attributed to the tenth-century Icelander, Egil Skalla-Grímsson, and again on a Swedish rune stone from the eleventh century (quoted p. 28). It was the sort of ship that went with Ingvar on his expedition through Russia to Serkland (cf. p. 107), and it was in such vessels that the regular sailings to Iceland and Greenland were made. Names of foreign origin for merchant-ships are the *búza* and *kuggr* mentioned above. A general term for merchant-man is *kaupskip*, trade vessel.

General-purpose vessels, after the fashion of the pinnace of later times, were the *skúta* (related to *skjóta*, 'shoot'), primarily built for speed and mounting up to thirty oars; and the *karfi*, with 12 to 32 oarsmen, the class to which the Gokstad and Oseberg ships probably belonged (cf. pp. 248–9). The origin of the name *karfi* is disputed, but since none of the suggestions throws useful light on its construction or purpose, the matter is of no importance here. It appears from a late Norwegian text that the name could be used of a ship fitted out for the levy but smaller than the longship.

The longship was the real warship, with at least twenty benches. One common sort was called *snekkja*, a word that means something thin and projecting (cognate with English 'snag'); it was doubtless especially used of craft with a high length-beam ratio (cf. Skuldelev ships 2 and 5 and the Ladby ship, pp. 252, 249–50). It is noteworthy that in the twelfth and thirteenth centuries it was particularly used of the Swedish twenty-bench levy vessel and of the ships used by the Wends. According to a report that seems reliable, Wendish war-ships in the 1130s carried forty-four men and two horses. A big longship was called a *skeið*, which may mean either 'that which cuts through the water' or 'a piece of wood long and sword-shaped': either description would be appropriate. The biggest warships of all were called *drekar*, 'dragons', probably because of their ornate prows.

We do not know many names for ships in the early period. Famous ones like *Ormr inn langi*, 'Long Serpent', *Visundr*, 'Bison', *Trani*, 'Crane', must have had figureheads to match their names. A fast sailer is given the name *Stígandi*, 'Strider', because 'it hauls the sea under it so fast'. By about 1200 saints' names and place-names were common elements in ship-names.

The terminology of boats and ships in the Viking and early medieval period is, as can be seen, extremely complicated and here we have only tried to sort out the main terms. It has been shown that it is often difficult to apply a particular descriptive name to a particular vessel, but size often provides a rough criterion for a ship's nomenclature. The dimensions of a vessel might also be a criterion of purpose: warships would tend to be long and light with a large number of oars to give speed and manoeuvrability; but many vessels, while built for a specific purpose, could be adapted without much difficulty for other purposes. There is no doubt that in the twelfth century ships with thirty or more pairs of oars were used; but were ships of this size used at an earlier date? In recent years certain scholars have argued that they were not. Most of the arguments of the protagonists of this last theory can be questioned. For example, contrary to their statements, there is a continuous series of literary references to ships of this size between 995 and 1262; the gap between 1061 and 1182 which was alleged to exist can be filled by a reference to a merchant ship of 27 *rúm* visiting Iceland in 1118 (see p. 256). Again, the technical difficulty of scarfing a keel, an argument raised against the physical construction of such a long ship, has been discounted by Olaf Olsen in his preliminary work on the Skuldelev ships, where he has shown that this was well within the Norsemen's capabilities. However, really long vessels of thirty pairs of oars (over 30 m., and perhaps nearer 40 m., in length) can only be considered exceptional – they would almost certainly never have been used in Viking raids, for example. Such a large number of oars would only be used to propel a warship, which needed the greater manoeuvrability and auxiliary speed which could be provided by a **large** number of rowers. The merchant ship could not be measured in such terms (see p. 253) because the few oars provided forward and aft were only intended for work in harbour or enclosed waters. There is no reason, however, why some merchant ships should not have been as large as the longest warships. The vessel wrecked in 1118, which has just been mentioned, was a merchantman.

Survival

It was common practice, particularly in Norway and Sweden, to inter the dead in boats or ships. The tradition is longstanding in Scandinavia and is a familiar characteristic of certain coastal parts of the Germanic world in the pre-Viking period – the most famous example being the seventh-century Anglo-Saxon ship-burial at Sutton Hoo in Suffolk. The idea of a voyage to another life is persistent in the legend and myth of many European countries, and glimpses of similar beliefs can be discerned in Germanic literature of northwestern Europe at an early date, as in the Anglo-Saxon epic *Beowulf*. In some cases the boat was burnt with the body in it and a particularly rich ship cremation of the Viking period, detectable by the clench nails used to fasten the planks (strakes) of the ship together, is that from Myklebostad, Nordfjord, Norway. Occasionally the rite is mixed. A grave excavated at Tune in Norway, for example, contained cremated human bones within an unburnt ship. A considerable number of inhumed ships have been recorded and even though most of them have naturally rotted away in the earth, their plan can be recovered by careful excavation in favourable soil conditions, as has been most remarkably achieved at Ladby in Denmark. In poor soil conditions (in shallow, acid soils like those in the island settlements of western Britain) even the most careful excavation can only reveal the shape of the vessel and a few clench-nails. However, certain vessels have survived almost intact in barrows in Norway because it happened that they were laid on a patch of blue clay and were well sealed in a mound. The three chief examples of such accidental preservation have been found on the shores of the Oslofjord, at Tune, Gokstad and Oseberg.

With the development of skin-diving the idea of underwater exploration in search of archaeological remains has become familiar to millions. Most of this work has been done in the Mediterranean, but the cold waters of Scandinavia have also yielded their share of wrecks of ships, some of which date from the Viking Age. An important find is at the Viking town of Hedeby where the remains of at least two vessels, possibly sunk during the sack of the town in the eleventh century, survive under water save for a few salvaged parts. The most exciting find, however, is undoubtedly that from Skuldelev in Denmark, where the energetic efforts of Olaf Olsen and Ole Crumlin-Pedersen have raised five wrecks from the bed of Roskildefjord. They were sunk there as block-ships in the eleventh century to seal a known channel and to hinder possible attack from the sea. The Hedeby and, more particularly, the Skuldelev finds demonstrate how our knowledge of Viking vessels may increase greatly in the future.

Some ships or fragments of ships have been preserved in bogs, like the remarkable prow which so closely resembles that of Wreck 3 at Skuldelev found in a peat-bog on the Isle of Eigg (fig. 27). When a complete vessel is found in such circumstances

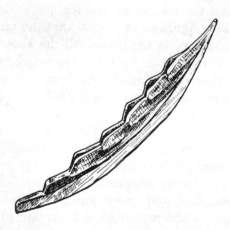

Fig. 27. Stem-post of a ship from the Isle of Eigg. National Museum, Edinburgh.

239

it can often be interpreted as an offering of a religious nature; however, when unused fragments are found in a bog it is perhaps better to regard them as having been placed there in order to harden or mature the wood. Other vessels have been found in ancient harbours, as in the Swedish port of Kalmar. It can be seen that the survival of vessels is completely accidental, but a sufficient sample remains to enable the naval historian to make certain judgements with a fair degree of accuracy.

The origin of the ships

We may safely assume that by the beginning of the Viking era the Scandinavians had developed sophisticated sailing vessels. There is, however, no indication that they were unusual in outward appearance to the inhabitants of the lands which they attacked; for, although the first Viking raids occasioned surprise to the western annalists, the chroniclers give no picture of a major technical departure from the design of ships already familiar in western Europe. There is some indication in western sources that the vessels were more efficient than those commonly seen in the North Sea, but even this is equivocal.

Probably the most important element in the genesis of the Viking ship was the adoption of the sail. Finds of ships in Scandinavia between the end of the Roman period and the beginning of the Viking Age seem to suggest that the sailing vessel was rare, if not unknown, in the north. All the known ships of this period in northern Europe were rowing vessels, some of which (like the seventh-century English boat from Sutton Hoo, Suffolk, which was approximately 27 m. in length) were of considerable size and complexity. As long as there was no sail, there was little need for a keel, for the keel's function is to provide further purchase by the hull on the sea: with the development of the sail, however, the form of the vessel had to change to allow for the greater strain due to the pressure of wind on the sail.

The chronological and geographical origin of the sail in northern waters is obscure: masted boats are attested in both archaeological and documentary sources in British and Atlantic waters during the Roman period and one may assume that they continued to be built in the Migration Period, perhaps by the Frisians. The idea of the sail was familiar in Europe and cannot have escaped the eyes of the Scandinavians, who, despite the absence of archaeological evidence, may have used sailing ships long before they developed the superlative vessels of the Viking Age that we know at first hand. Nevertheless, one may perhaps use the archaeological material as the basis for a hypothetical discussion of the development of the Viking ship. A boat – one of two found in a bog at Kvalsund, Møre, Norway – although not datable by associated finds is typologically earlier than the Viking ships from Gokstad and Oseberg and is usually dated to the seventh century. It is a rowing boat, 18 m. long, clinker-built of eight strakes partly lashed, partly nailed to natural-grown frames. It is the first northern vessel to be found with a proper keel, albeit of modest proportions, and it has a steering oar on the starboard side. While there is no sign of a step for the mast, the keel and steering oar may indicate that the design of the vessel was based on that of a sailing ship, for such features also occur on larger Viking ships. If the dating of the Kvalsund vessel is correct – and unfortunately this is by no means certain – it might give an indication of Scandinavian familiarity with sailing ships before the Viking Age.

Otherwise, among the boats found in Scandinavia which can be securely dated to the pre-Viking period, there is no definite sailing vessel. Boats from Nydam and elsewhere, although often of considerable size (the largest Nydam ship, for example, is 23.7 m. overall), are all rowing boats and, although some of them have lateral steering oars, the lack of a formal keel, in all but one case (the pine-built ship from Nydam), suggests that they could never have been under sail. Whether the finds which survive are typical of the North in the early centuries of the first millennium is difficult to say. It is possible, for instance, that while sailing vessels were in use for ocean passages, the ships and boats that survive merely exemplify vessels used in coastal and inland waters and in the Baltic. It is often forgotten that Viking boats designed solely for rowing do survive. One example, from Fjørtoft, Haram, Sunnmøre, Norway, with a length of ten metres, neatly answers to the description of a *tolfæringr* (twelve-oar boat) and has no trace of a mast.

The Viking ship

In order to consider the construction of the Viking ship it is best to start with the best-documented and most seaworthy of the surviving examples – the ninth-century Gokstad ship (figs. 28, 29, 31). The construction of this magnificent vessel enables us to understand the skill and attention to detail of the Scandinavian ship-builder. She is 23.3 m. overall and 5.25 m. amidships. The height from keel to gunwale is 1.95 m. Her dead weight (unloaded) has been calculated at 9 tons: when fully loaded with crew and equipment she would probably have weighed 18 tons. It is difficult to estimate the exact draught of the vessel, which to a certain extent would depend on ballast and load, but when she was fully loaded with all her equipment and a crew of seventy, the draught would probably only be about 90 – 95 cm.

The ship (fig. 28) is built of oak, except for the decking, mast and yards, which are of pine – as are the oars. The most important member of the ship is the keel, which is of T-shaped cross-section. It is scarfed where the stem and stern posts join the main keel timber. These posts are incomplete, but probably rose to a slowly curving tip like that found on one of the Skuldelev vessels (fig. 34). The hull is built up of overlapping strakes. The strakes were first nailed together and then lashed to the frames

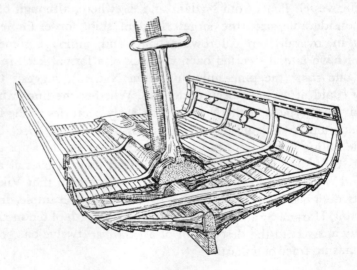

Fig. 28. Section through the Gokstad ship.

by means of pliable spruce roots through holes in cleats left free standing when the plank was smoothed (a feature not found at Skuldelev, see below, p. 253). The Norse term *súð*, 'overlapping planking', properly means 'sewing' or 'suture', and is related to the technical name for the means of fastening timber to timber in a boat, *saumr*, which also means 'sewing' (cognate with the English word 'seam'). This must originally refer to the use of lashing to secure the strakes, as in the Gokstad ship, but later it was generally applied to the method of attaching the planks by nails of wood or metal. (*Saumr* in its modern forms is a general term for metal nails in the Scandinavian languages.)

The two lowest strakes of the Gokstad ship were attached to the keel by nails. The tenth strake from the keel on the water-line (ON *meginhúfr*, 'main-plank') was rather heavier than the others and the strakes above this were fastened by wooden pegs to naturally-grown, roughly L-shaped, knees attached to cross-beams which tied the ship together and incidentally helped to support the decking, which was not nailed down. The cross-beams were supported in the centre by upright members which rested on the frames. The two topmost strakes, however, are not attached to these knees, but to top frames. The strakes are skil-fully scarfed along the length of the vessel, and the third strake from the gunwale on each side bears sixteen circular oar-holes, each hole having a small slot through which the blade of the oar could pass. When under sail, the oar-holes were closed by a wooden cover, which swivelled on a nail. The iron nails, used to fasten the strakes to each other, were clenched over a washer inside the vessel. The strakes were caulked with wool-yarn and tar – a process carried out as the ship was built, although some re-caulking was done after the ship had seen some service. The vessel was made more waterproof by a coat of tar.

A bar was attached inside the gunwale to which the shields of the crew would be tied when the vessel was at anchor. The bar does not run the whole length of the ship. Sixty-four shields were found with the Gokstad vessel, two to each oar hole. The mast was seated in an elaborate housing fastened to the ribs. This is some 3.75 m. long and contains a socket with a rounded bottom. At deck level the mast passes through a mast-fish, which is some 5 m. in length. It is fairly clear that this member had split as a result of the strain on it when the vessel had been under sail; it has been repaired by iron bands. The mast could be lowered or raised at will, and, when in an upright position, was locked in place by a billet of oak – the mast-lock. We have no evidence of the details of the rigging of this particular vessel. In fact it is possible that the rigging was very simple (fig. 29). Representations of ships on the Gotlandic picture stones indicate that there was probably a forestay, as well as shrouds from the mast to the sides of the ship aft. Linguistic evidence supports such a supposition since we know the words for stay (*stag*) and shroud (*hǫfuðbenda*) belong to the Viking period, when they were borrowed into Old French for example. There appears to have been no fixed anchorage for these ropes (although on one of the Skuldelev vessels the forestay passed through a hole in the prow)

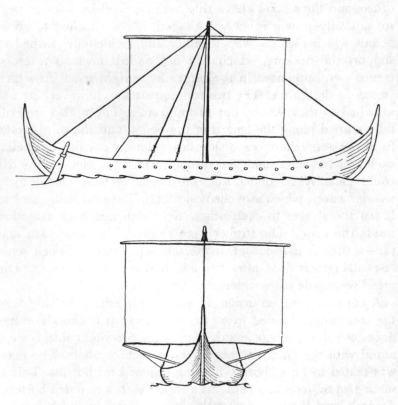

Fig. 29. Suggested rigging of the Gokstad ship.

and we must suppose that they were fastened through holes in the knees. There is no evidence for a backstay, which might well be unnecessary in view of the strong seating of the mast; on ships depicted on the Bayeux tapestry both forestay and back-stay are clearly shown, but this may have no significance for Scandinavian vessels.

The forestay would be of use in erecting the mast which was presumably lowered when beached and when the ship was being used for any length of time in inland waters. When stowed, the mast would be laid across crutches which stand well above the deck and which presumably also served to carry the oars when the vessel was under sail. The crutches would also support an awning when the ship lay at anchor. Ropes at this period were made of bast or hemp, and records survive of walrus- or seal-skin ropes, which were probably made by cutting the hide in a spiral round the body of the creature.

The mast of the Gokstad ship is incomplete. It is of pine and has in the past been reconstructed at a height of about 13 m. Recent suggestions, however, have reduced this height to about 10 m. It is further argued that the short mast with the smaller sail would have lessened the need for special shrouds or ballast, and it is consequently possible that the Viking vessels may have been lighter and faster than has hitherto been assumed. Fastened to the mast by means of a knee or a loop of rope or horn was a yard some 13 m. long, to which was attached a rectangular sail (probably not more than 11 m. across). We learn from literary sources that sails were often striped. The method of reefing is obscure, for although traces of what may be reefing ropes sur-vive, there is no general agreement as to their use. Åkerlund, however, has suggested that a series of lines were passed through loops on the sail and the sail could then be shortened by pulling on the lines which were fixed to the bottom of the sail (fig. 30), an argument supported by the evidence of the Gotlandic picture stones (pl. 12). Sail could also be shortened by lowering the yard. An under-yard may have been used for sailing before the wind, but two 8 m. spars found in the grave were almost certainly used to spread the sail in a slight wind. They fitted into sockets in blocks fastened to the ship's sides just forward of the mast, the other end being attached to the clews (lower corners) of the sail

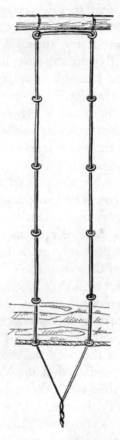

Fig. 30. Suggested method of reefing the sail of a Viking ship.

(fig. 29 bottom). One of these spars could be used to hold the sail towards the wind, but it would be difficult to control in gusty weather. A spar used for keeping the sail close-hauled was called a *beitiáss*. The first element of this word comes from the verb *beita*, 'beat into the wind, tack'; the second means 'spar, beam'. It appears that the sail was controlled by two ropes attached to the clews of the sail, which could be made fast in the after part of the ship. These sheets could be called *aktaumar* (literally 'driving reins'), although we do not know whether this name was universally applied to them. They perhaps ran in the manner shown in fig. 34, but more likely were attached to the gunwale

246

in a less elaborate way. There is for example a passage in the thirteenth-century *Laxdœla saga* which says of a man who was steering a boat, described as a ferry, that he 'had the *aktaumar* around his shoulders because there was little room in the boat; it was chiefly loaded with chests, and the cargo was piled up high'. It may be noted that there were twelve or thirteen people on board, including a child, but they were only on a short coastal voyage.

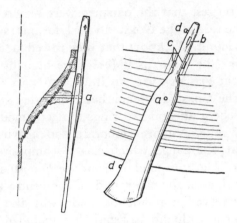

Fig. 31. The steering oar of the Gokstad ship.

The ship was steered by what looks like a large oar (fig. 31) attached to the starboard side and the aftermost frame by means of a tree-root or withy (*a* in fig. 31) which passed through the rudder itself, a large wooden block, the side of the ship and the frame. The gunwale above this fixing point is strengthened by the addition of a heavy plank; this plank and the block formed a firm fulcrum for the rudder which was turned by a straight tiller (about 1 m. long) inserted in a socket (*b* in fig. 31) in the steering-oar. The steering-oar, which extended below the keel, could be raised when the ship was run up on land by swivelling it on the withy, after unfastening the strap that fixed it at the gunwale (the strap-holes are marked at *c* in fig. 31). The decking of the ship is slightly higher in this place to form a platform for the helmsman, the chief and his entourage.

247

By the use of the rudder and with the help of the sail a considerable manoeuvrability could be achieved; but the vessel (although she could sail close to the wind) could not, of course, sail into the wind. When head-winds were encountered the sail would be lowered and a favourable wind awaited. If no great distance had to be covered the oars could be used in such circumstances. The method by which the vessel was rowed is obscure; the oars are between 5.3 and 5.8 m. in length with a narrow blade. The oar-holes are only about 40 cm. above the decking, which would suggest that the oarsmen were seated – presumably on chests in the case of the Gokstad vessel, for no traces of rowing-benches were found. We know that they rowed facing aft.

The anchor – the word itself (*akkeri*) is thought to be a very early loan from Frisian – was an important part of the vessel's equipment. The Gokstad anchor had a wooden stock and iron flukes, the Oseberg anchor had rings to accommodate the cable and the buoy rope. A more elaborate and heavier anchor has been found at Kaupang, which has a composite iron-bound wooden shank. The iron anchor from the Danish ship-burial at Ladby had a ring on the stock and in the centre of the crown, and a well-preserved iron anchor chain was also found there. Other equipment with the Gokstad ship included a gangplank with foot-holds, casks and tent-posts; these last could possibly have been used on board the vessel when she was hove to, and perhaps even when she was under sail.

The great characteristic of this vessel is her elasticity and lightness of weight (see p. 242). The fact that the frames were attached to the strakes by withies made the vessel less rigid than a nailed ship; fewer ribs were needed and she was, therefore, lighter. The elasticity was commented upon by the master of the replica which sailed the Atlantic in 1893 who observed that the ship undulated with the waves; the bottom and keel would rise and fall by as much as 2 cm. and the gunwales twist as much as 15 cm. out of true. The ship was fast, achieving 10 knots with ease and sometimes more.

The Gokstad ship was certainly not a warship, but as she must have been owned by a chieftain or prince, we should perhaps classify her as a general-duties vessel. Her admirable seaworthiness fitted her for duty as a merchant vessel and in time of war, or in the course of a raid, her shallow draught and great speed would be adequate for any emergency.

There can be little doubt, however, that the ships from Oseberg and Tune are best considered as *karfar* (see above, p. 236). The Oseberg ship, with her elaborately carved stem (pl. 11) and detailed embellishment, is exactly the sort of vessel which should be considered as the property of a chieftain who would use her in coastal waters. While she is much less stable and suitable for ocean-going than the Gokstad vessel, she gives an impression of what ships like those in the description quoted at the beginning of the chapter really looked like. Here are no golden dragons and gilded weather-vanes, but the richness of the carving with its coiled serpentine prow is some measure of the elaborate attention which was lavished on the vessels belonging to the Viking leaders. Some of the vanes described by the chronicler survive elsewhere (e.g. fig. 53), having been re-used on churches, for example; pictures of them also survive in various contexts, as in the lively sketch found during recent excavations at Bergen (fig. 26).

The ships portrayed on the Gotland picture stones are undoubtedly warships, crowded as they are with warriors fully armed and ready for battle (pl. 12). These pictures surely demonstrate that, although the warships may have been larger than any of the surviving Viking Age ships, they must have been very similar in appearance to the Gokstad vessel, perhaps decorated in a fashion comparable to that encountered on the Oseberg vessel. They were perhaps decorated with iron embellishments at the prow as were the Ladby and Île de Groix ships or with gold nails such as Archbishop Absalon used on a great dragon-ship in the twelfth century.

The Ladby ship at any rate was certainly a warship. Her measurements are best set out in tabular form in comparison with those of the Gokstad ship.

	length	beam	length-breadth ratio	no. of strakes	gunwale to keel
Ladby	about 21 m.	2.75 m.	7.20 : 1	7	0.65 m.
Gokstad	about 23 m.	5.25 m.	4.50 : 1	16	1.95 m.

On the basis of these measurements she can only be considered a warship of almost canoe-like proportions. Although she probably had a mast it would be difficult to sail her because of her shallow draught. This type of warship could have been used in the coastal waters of the Baltic and it might be possible to compare her with similar boats of the Viking period found in the Swedish graves at Valsgärde in Uppland, which are as yet unpublished. It can also be compared in many respects to one of the Skuldelev wrecks, no. 5, which was about 18 m. long but had only half the beam measurement of the Gokstad ship and lower sides. Such vessels were, however, very different from the warships made for use in the North Sea and in Atlantic waters; they must be considered Baltic craft and it is not without interest that a vessel from Danzig-Ohra seems to be a Slav copy of such a warship.

The Atlantic vessel, the true 'Viking ship', was, as we know from literary sources, often larger; it had taller sides than any surviving vessel, sides which were built so that they would tower over their adversaries in battle. There are indications that in the average fleet there would be only one really enormous ship, with more than thirty pairs of oars. The most famous ship of this class is undoubtedly the Long Serpent, reputed to be of 32 or 34 *rúm*, built by Ólaf Tryggvason, close to Nidaros (Trondheim), probably in the winter of 998. It made a deep impression on contemporary poets. A story of its building was first recorded by Oddr Snorrason in Iceland about 1200, and on the basis of this Snorri gives the famous account which follows:

The winter after King Ólaf came from Hálogaland, he had a great vessel built at Hladhamrar, which was larger than any ship in the country, and of which the frames are still to be seen there. The length of keel that rested upon the grass was seventy-four ells[1]. Thorberg *skafhǫgg* was the name of the man in charge of making the stem and stern of the vessel; but there were many others besides – some to fell wood, some to shape it, some to make nails, some to carry timber; and all that was used was selected very carefully. The ship was both long and

[1]This sentence, which makes the ship's length *c*. 37 m., only occurs in one late manuscript, but the statement seems reasonable.

broad and high-sided, and strongly timbered. While they were planking the ship, it happened that Thorberg had to go home to his farm upon some urgent business and he remained there a long time. The ship was planked up on both sides when he came back. That same evening the king went out, and Thorberg with him, to see how the vessel looked, and everybody said that never was seen so large and so beautiful a ship of war. Then the king returned to the town. Early next morning the king returns again to the ship, and Thorberg with him. The carpenters were there before them, but all were standing there and doing nothing. The king asked why they were like that. They said the ship was spoilt and that somebody had gone from stem to stern, and cut one deep notch after the other down one side of the planking. When the king came nearer he saw it was so, and immediately said and swore that the man who had thus damaged the ship out of envy should die if he were found out, 'And the man who can tell me who it was will have great rewards from me' . . . Thorberg says, 'I will tell you, king, who did it. I did it.'

The king says, 'You must restore it all to the same condition as before, or your life shall pay for it.'

Then Thorberg went and smoothed the ship's side until the deep notches had all disappeared. Then the king and all present declared that the ship was much handsomer on the side which Thorberg had cut, and the king asked him to shape it so on both sides and gave him great thanks for the improvement. Afterwards Thorberg was the master-builder of the ship until she was finished. The ship was a dragon, built after the manner of the one the king had captured in Hálogaland; but this ship was far larger, and more carefully made in all her parts. The king called this ship the Long Serpent, and the other the Short Serpent. The Long Serpent had thirty-four benches (rúm) for rowers. The prow and the stern were covered with gilding, and the freeboard was as great as in ocean-going ships. This ship was the best and most costly ship ever made in Norway.

The Long Serpent with a length of about 37 m. was longer than any other ships recorded in the literature. There seems no reason

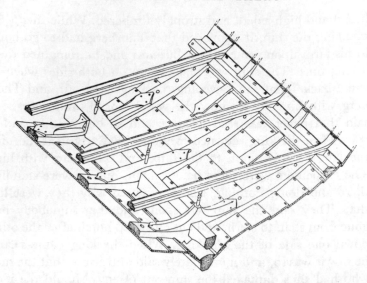

Fig. 32. The construction of Skuldelev 2. After Olsen and Crumlin-
Pedersen.

why this should not have been the length of the vessel, but it
would be wise to bear in mind that warships could vary enor-
mously in length and form.

The nearest we come to a vessel of this size and form is the
early eleventh-century Wreck 2 from Skuldelev (fig. 32). She is
an oak vessel and was very fragmentary when recovered. She
must have been about 28 m. long and not more than 4.8 m. in
beam – a length-beam ratio of about 6 : 1 (midway between
that of Gokstad and Ladby). She was a lightly-built ship with a
very worn keel showing that she was often pulled up onto land.
It has been estimated that she would have carried between fifty
and sixty warriors.

The five Skuldelev ships raised from the bed of Roskildefjord
in 1962 provide us with much knowledge of tenth- and eleventh-
century shipbuilding[1]. Two Skuldelev ships have already been
mentioned, but Wrecks 1 and 3 are of particular interest in that
they provide undoubted examples of merchant vessels. In most

[1]It should be noted that all the Skuldelev measurements and drawings used here
are provisional, based on the preliminary report of Olaf Olsen and Ole Crumlin-
Pedersen (see Bibliography).

respects they exhibit the normal characteristics of the Viking ships as typified by the Gokstad ship. They are 16.5 m. and 13.5 m. long respectively; but their beamier proportions, greater freeboard and heavier timbers demonstrate their function beyond question. No. 1 has a length-beam ratio of 3.5 : 1, no. 3, 4.2 : 1.

The most substantial vessel was thus Wreck 1 (fig. 33). She was built of pine (with prow, stern and keel of oak) and the main object of the builder was to provide a solid and roomy hull suitable for traffic in the Atlantic and North Sea. She had fourteen frames and was decked fore and aft; she had an open hold amidships. She could be rowed from a small number of oarholes above the decking, but would normally run under sail. Like all the Skuldelev vessels the strakes were not lashed to the frames – trenails (wooden pegs) were used instead. The well-preserved Wreck 3 was much lighter (fig. 34). It was built of oak on eleven or twelve frames, with eight strakes on each side. She has an elegantly curved but plain prow, the lines of the strakes being carefully continued in the carving on this member. Like Wreck 1 it has an open hold amidships with a volume of 10 cubic metres to the gunwale (Wreck 1 had a hold-volume of between 30 and 35 cubic metres). She drew about 1 m. of water when loaded, compared with a loaded draught of 1.5 m. for Wreck 1. She was a sailing vessel and, like Wreck 1, had oar-holes only fore and aft. The mast was stepped in the keelson and was supported by shrouds fastened to cleats outside the gunwale – an extraordinary feature which would suggest that the vessel was used only in Baltic waters, where there was no significant rise and fall of the tide to carry away these important attachments when moored alongside a quay or jetty.

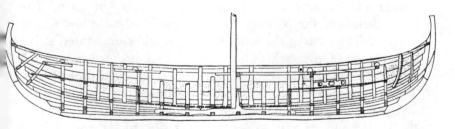

Fig. 33. Skuldelev 1. After Olsen and Crumlin-Pedersen.

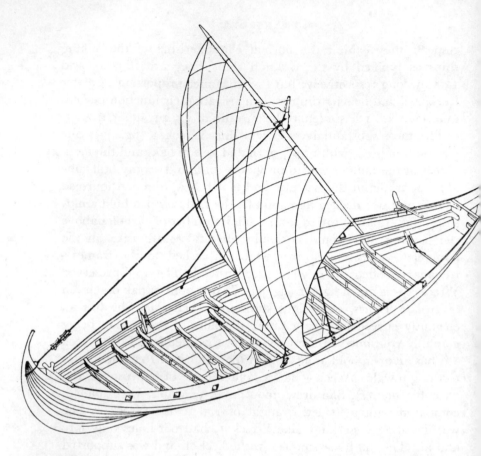

Fig. 34. Reconstruction of Skuldelev 3. After Olsen and Crumlin-
Pedersen.

The *karfi*, the *bátr*, the *langskip* and even the *kaupskip* are, as
far as can be seen from the surviving examples, remarkably
similar in structure and – to a certain extent – in form. The
basic design of the Viking ship was modified to allow for its
purpose. The form of the long, narrow, shallow-draughted Baltic
warship, or of the *karfi* (which would best be used round the
Norwegian fjords and skerries) varied only in length-beam ratio.
There were many common factors – shallow draught, high prow
and stern, clinker building. Bertil Almgren has suggested that
the Viking success was to some extent due to the use of light
shallow-draughted vessels which enabled the raiders and traders
to sail up rivers, to cover fair distances by portage, and to

draw up on sandy beaches, where heavier vessels were unable to venture. He has also demonstrated how such vessels could be used for the transport of horses for military purposes – as happened in the Baltic in the twelfth century: the short distance between keel and gunwale would allow the animals to scramble out of the vessel without much trouble. He points out also that the ships had greater speed, were not dependent on sail alone and were able to land anywhere.

It is a cliché that the Scandinavians were skilful sailors. To a large extent their navigation was carried on within sight of land, but quite often they would have had to cross miles of open sea, and would need navigational aids. There is no reason to suppose that the sailors of the Viking Age knew magnetic compasses. Their navigational equipment seems to have been fairly simple, although a recent flight of fancy has suggested that the Vikings used a stone which polarized light as a navigational aid. Such an object may have been the *sólarsteinn* referred to in various sources, but we have no specific description of its navigational use, although a passage in one text may imply such knowledge of the properties of a crystalline stone as would allow one to determine or estimate the position of the sun in dirty weather with its aid. Basically the Vikings used simple, rule-of-thumb, celestial navigation – based, for example, on the Pole star and, obviously, on the sun. They also undoubtedly used observation of such creatures as whales and birds as navigational aids. Fulmars, for instance, might give northing or southing and smaller sea-birds – puffins and common guillemots, for example – would not stray too far from land at certain times of the year. It has been suggested that by the use of a simple bearing-dial (of which a mid-fourteenth-century example has been found in Greenland) together with azimuth tables (like those drawn up early in the eleventh century by the Icelander, Oddi Helgason, Star-Oddi), a sun-compass of very fair accuracy might have been achieved by Viking sailors. By this means the navigator rights the bearing-dial at the known azimuth of the sun for that latitude at dawn or sunset and the helmsman steers by this and by the direction of wind and sea. The Norsemen may have had a fair idea of latitude (they certainly had none of longitude) and followed a principle documented in the later medieval period, whereby it was customary to sail to the latitude of a destination and follow this parallel until land was sighted. That this was general practice has, however, recently been questioned. Presumably, however, for voyages along well-known routes, say from Iceland to Scotland, they could obtain reasonably direct bearings and sail by them perhaps with the aid of a simple traverse board. In one text of *Landnámabók* we read these directions for sailing to Greenland:

> From Hernar in Norway one is to keep sailing west for Hvarf in Greenland and then you will sail north of Shetland so that you can just sight it in very clear weather; but south of the Faroes so that the sea appears half-way up the mountain slopes; but on, south of Iceland so that you may have birds and whales from it.

Such a passage shows that the author of this notice knew about sailing by dead reckoning, by the observation of natural phenomena, and possibly even by latitude sailing, for both Hernar and Hvarf lie roughly on latitude 61° N.

At all times however the sea held danger. We are told many times of sailors blown off course, lost at sea, shipwrecked or returning to port because of lack of favourable winds. We read in *Kristni saga*, 'On Good Friday [1118] a merchant ship was driven ashore under Eyjafjöll, spun in the air and landed, bottom up; it had 27 *rúm*.' It is recorded that of twenty-five ships which left Iceland for the colonization of Greenland only fourteen reached their destination, all the rest were driven back or lost. In coastal waters pirates added to the other dangers, but the lure of trade, conquest and new land apparently transcended all the hazards of seafaring.

Land transport

Although there is a lot of documentary evidence of overland travel in the Viking Age, detailed description of the means of transport and the material remains of them are so few that it is possible to say little more than that horses, two-wheeled carts, four-wheeled wagons, sledges, skis, skates and pack-animals were used. People travelled widely: for trading, to go to meetings of the local or national *thing*, on warlike errands, to go to pagan feasts or to Christian churches, to parties and to family events. In summer the wealthy would travel by horse and the poor on foot; in the winter (if they had to go anywhere) skis, skates or sledges would be the obvious alternative. Merchandise would travel mainly by pack-animal, sledge or in some places by cart (there is a reference in the Gotland Law to the carrying of produce in carts) when there was no alternative route by water.

The horse was an animal of great importance and was common. Even so, it was valuable and the eleven horses buried in the Ladby burial mound must represent a sacrifice of some importance. The horses of the period were small by modern standards, rarely, if ever, achieving a height of fourteen and a half hands (150 cm.). Occasionally, when horses are buried in a man's grave, the bridle is found in position at the horse's head and many pieces of riding equipment survive in the Viking graves. The bits are usually undecorated but the bridles themselves (fig. 35) were often very showy, embellished with rich mounts (pl. 16 f-h). Saddles are rare. An incomplete saddle of beech

Fig. 35. Reconstruction of the bridle from the Borre ship-burial (cf. pl. 16 f-h).

wood was found at Oseberg (pl. 15a); three further examples were possibly found at Borre, Tune and By, Løten, Hedmark, all in Norway. Such indications as survive suggest that saddles were made of wood and leather. The Oseberg saddle was presumably placed fairly far forward on the body of the horse, probably right up to its neck, and it has been suggested that the rider's legs stretched out to the front of the saddle and did not hang down by the side as they do today. The stirrup was introduced into Scandinavia, as into the rest of Europe, in the early part of the Viking Age and – sometimes highly ornamented – becomes quite a common object in Viking graves, sometimes forming a set with the spurs. The stirrups have heavy square loops for the leathers

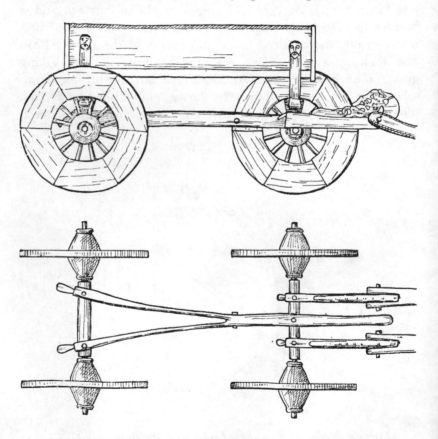

Fig. 36. The method of construction of the Oseberg wagon. Scale 1 : 30.
Viking Ship Museum, Oslo.

and long hoops with elaborate side-plates protecting the deep foot-rests (pl. 14). Spurs had a short, straight prick. Horse shoes are never found but are mentioned in texts as early as *c.* 1100, and spiked points for travelling on ice occur occasionally. Of the horse as a pack-animal we must rely on the sagas and other sources for evidence. The Saga of Grettir, for example, tells of Atli and his companions buying 'much fish and carrying it away on seven horses'; this must have been typical of Iceland, where roads and waterways were unknown.

Fig. 37. Detail of a stone from Alskog, Gotland.

The horse was also used as a draft animal. The only four-wheeled wagon to survive however – that from the Oseberg ship-grave – is a very specialized vehicle and in fact, as at present reconstructed, could not turn corners; it must be considered simply as a ceremonial or even a funerary wagon. The structure of the Oseberg wagon (fig. 36) does however demonstrate certain features which may be taken as indicative of the structure of the everyday cart. Like the typical European carts of a later period, the axle-trees are connected by a beam. The wheels are spoked and are of the same size front and back. It has two shafts connected by a chain and it presumably had outer traces. The fragment of a spoked wheel from Lindholm Høje accurately reflects the structure of the Oseberg wagon wheels. This is the only other major fragment of a wheeled vehicle known from the Viking Age. It is recorded that two wagon frames were used as coffins at the military camp at Fyrkat in Denmark, but these were very fragmentary and are as yet unpublished. Pictures of people riding in carts occur on the Gotland stones (fig. 37) and on the Oseberg tapestry fragments (pl. 13). From such sources it is possible to see that the wheeled vehicles – both carts and wagons – of the period could be quite sophisticated, with single and double shafts and spoked wheels; sometimes drawn by one horse, more rarely by two. Oxen were also used as draft animals, either singly or in pairs. It is not perhaps without interest that the Gotland Law distinguishes between *oyc oc wagn* (draft animals, oxen, and wagon) and *rus oc kerra* (horse and cart). Wood-paved streets and even roadways, found mainly in towns and camps of the Viking period, show that wheeled transport was a not unimportant element in the commercial life of the Viking Age. Wheel marks, or ruts, were revealed by excavation at Lindholm Høje in Denmark, but this does little more than emphasize the presence of wheeled vehicles in minor civil settlements in Scandinavia. Horses and oxen were also used to pull sledges.

Our knowledge of the physical appearance of sledges of the Viking period comes exclusively from the great Norwegian ship-burials, but by the use of comparative material certain tentative conclusions can be reached concerning their typology. Four main types of sledge are known from pre-Viking Europe, the first of which is represented by a single dated example: it is a simple dug-out, made at the beginning of the first millennium A.D., found at Högstale, Bokenäs, Bohuslän, Sweden. It is 2 m. long and consists of a hollowed-out tree-trunk with a hole at the slightly pointed front to take a rope. Of the second type, the keeled sledge on a single runner, we have little or no evidence from an early period. The third type of sledge has a runner with

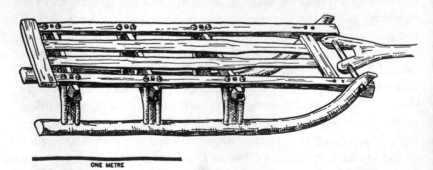

ONE METRE

Fig. 38. The base of the 'simple' sledge from Oseberg. Viking ship Museum, Oslo.

three grooves on the upper face which are pierced for the passage of cord bracing which supports the struts to the platform of the sledge above: it was probably drawn by dogs or men. The fourth type seems to have developed during the first millennium and the Gokstad sledge and the 'simple' sledge from Oseberg belong to this class (fig. 38). It consists of a vehicle in which the horizontal members of the frame and the runners are supported by vertical struts which are morticed into the runners. This particular sledge also had a plain, box-like body which could be fitted onto it if necessary (this is not illustrated in fig. 38). Without the body the sledge could have been drawn by a man; but the presence of what seems to be the body and a shaft show that it was certainly drawn by animals. It has only one parallel in the Viking Age and this is incomplete – it comes from the Gokstad ship-burial. The other known sledges, which also come from Oseberg, are much heavier, but basically only their weight differentiates them from the 'simple' sledge. The struts and body are elaborately decorated, as are the shafts (which indicate that they too were drawn by horses or other animals). Sledges would be used throughout the year for carrying goods, but the elaborate Oseberg sledges can only have been used during winter for transport over snow.

The climate in the north naturally conditioned the development of certain specialized aids to movement. Skis and skates were obviously much used in Scandinavia and in winter it would often have been much quicker to move across country than in summer, when a man had to travel laboriously by horse or on foot. Although skis, and more especially skates, were used for sport, there can be little doubt that they had a more practical application. Despite the fact that they are mentioned frequently in early Scandinavian literature, skis are only recorded in one archaeological find that is certainly of the Viking Age – in the Tune ship-burial. A general ethnographic study of skis suggests that various types of ski were used from the Stone Age onwards, their form being influenced by the normal conditions of the snow. A more tapered ski was used in the north on the hard snow, while a broader ski with a foot-rest was used on the softer snow of south Scandinavia. Two types seem to have been introduced in the course of the first millennium. The first is known as the Bothnic type and has a concave foot-rest and a convex sliding surface. In the south, the Scandic type appears; it had a foot-rest and free-standing borders on either edge of the underside; it developed, possibly in the Viking period, into a ski with a central groove on the sliding surface, to give more security to the skier. There seems little doubt that a single ski-stick was used.

Skates must have been very important aids to movement, particularly on the windswept lakes of eastern Scandinavia. They are first recorded in north Europe in the Migration Period, at Sorte Muld in Bornholm and Vallhagar in Gotland, but they may well have been known at an earlier period (in the Bronze Age in central Europe). In the Viking period they have been recognized in two Swedish grave-fields – at Ihre in Gotland and at Birka (fig. 39) – but they have also been found in large numbers in the *Black Earth* at Birka and in what may be Viking contexts in Arctic Norway. They are made from the long bones of animals, usually the metacarpals of horse, ox or deer (the Norse word for skate, *ísleggr*, means literally 'ice leg-bone') which have been smoothed on the underside and cut away above (fig. 39). They are often pierced at either end for fastening to the feet, while the front of the Birka examples is bevelled. Skates are not often mentioned in the literature but there is a vivid passage in *Heimskringla* where, in a boasting match between the two brothers, Sigurd and Eystein, kings of Norway, the latter is made to say, 'I was so skilful on skates that I knew no one who could beat me, and you could no more skate than an ox.'

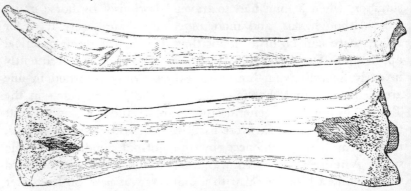

Fig. 39. Bone skate from Birka grave 573. Scale: ½. Statens Historiska Museum, Stockholm.

PLATES

LIST OF PLATES

Plate 2. (a) *Oval brooch from near Egersund, Rogaland, Norway.* Universitetets Oldsaksamling, Oslo.
(b) *Jug of Tatting ware from Birka, Sweden.* Statens Historiska Museum, Stockholm
(c) *Pin-head from Klinta, Köping, Öland.* Statens Historiska Museum, Stockholm.

a

b

Plate 3. (a) *Aerial view of encampment at Gråborg, Öland, Sweden.*
(b) *Foundations of a house at Fuglafjörður, Faroes.*

Plate 4. Marks of ploughing and of carts at Lindholm Høje, Jutland, Denmark.

Plate 5. Cooking utensils of soapstone and iron from Norway.
Universitetets Oldsaksamling, Oslo.

a

b

Plate 6. (a) *Fragment of a carved ston* from Kirk Michael, Isle of Man.
(b) *Initial letter 'D' from Cambridge University MS. Ff. 1. 23.* (c) *and*
(d) *Coins of Viking kingdom of Dubli* (c) *dated* c. 995, (d) *dated* c. 1000. British Museum.

c

d

Plate 7. Ornamented sockets of spearheads. All from Norway.
Universitetets Oldsaksamling, Oslo.

a

b

Plate 8. (a) *Birka from the air.* (b) *Hedeby from the air.*

a

b

Plate 10. Hog-backed tombstones from Brompton, Yorkshire.

Plate 11. Prow of Oseberg ship. Viking Ships Museum, Oslo.

Plate 12. Stone from Tjängvide, Alskog, Gotland.

Plate 13. Reconstruction of a tapestry from the Oseberg ship-burial.

Plate 14. Stirrups from a grave at Nørre Longelse, Langeland, Denmark.
Langeland Museum.

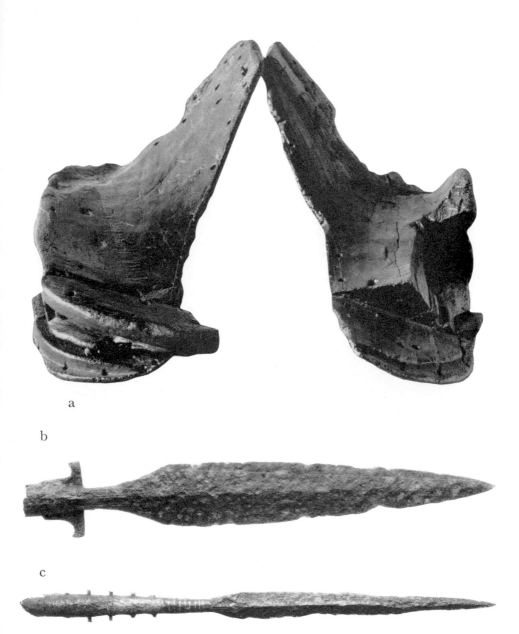

a

b

c

Plate 15. (a) *Wooden base of a saddle from the Oseberg burial.* Viking Ships Museum, Oslo. (b) *and* (c) *Spearheads from Birka, Sweden.* Statens Historiska Museum, Stockholm.

Plate 16. (a) – (c) *Gold mounts from the hoard from Hon, Norway.*
Universitetets Oldsaksamling, Oslo. (d) *Gold mount from Lackalänge,*
Skåne. Statens Historiska Museum, Stockholm. (e) *Silver brooch*
from Finkarby, Södermanland, Sweden. Statens Historiska Museum,
Stockholm. (f) – (h) *Bronze-gilt mounts from Borre, Norway.* Universitetets Oldsaksamling, Oslo. *All scale 1/1.*

a

b

Plate *17*. (a) *Silver-gilt cup from Fejø, Denmark*. National Museum, Copenhagen. *Scale 1/1*. (b) *Silver brooch from Ödeshög, Östergötland, Sweden*. Statens Historiska Museum, Stockholm. *Scale 1/1*.

a

b

c

Plate 18. (a) *Gold spur and mounts from Værne Kloster, Rød, Norway.*
Universitetets Oldsaksamling, Oslo. (b) *Detail of horse-collar from
Mammen, Denmark.* National Museum, Copenhagen. (c) *Detail of
horse-collar from Søllested, Denmark.* National Museum, Copenhagen.

a

b

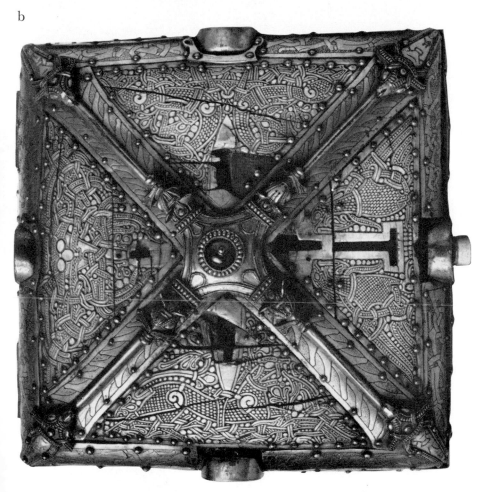

Plate 19. (a) *Silver and niello plate from lid of a house-shaped casket of unknown provenance.* British Museum. *Scale 1/1.* (b) *The Bamberg casket.* Bayerisches Nationalmuseum, Munich.

Plate 20. Axe-head from Mammen, Jutland, Denmark. National Museum, Copenhagen.

Plate 21. The Jelling stone.

Plate 22. The Academician's animal-head post from the Oseberg ship-burial.
Viking ship Museum, Oslo.

a

Plate 23. (a) *Piece of carved panelling from Flatatunga, Iceland.* National Museum, Reykjavík.
(b) *Runestone from Ala, Vassunda, Uppland, Sweden.*

b

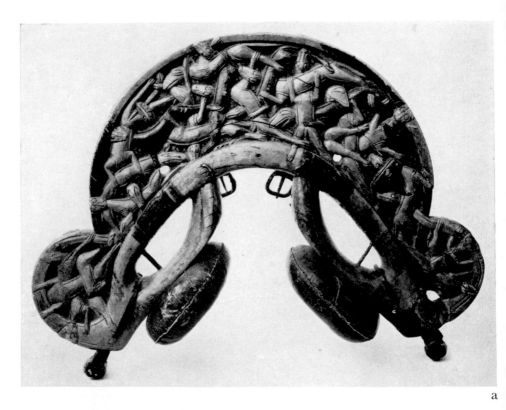

a

b

Plate 24. (a) *Horse-collar from Lom,
Norway.* Nordiska Museet, Stockh...
(b) *Bronze plate from Holycross, Ire...*
National Museum, Dublin. *Scale*

a

b

Plate 25. (a) *Hilt of a sword from the River Lea.* British Museum.
(b) *Shield from Oseberg, Norway.* Universitetets Oldsaksamling, Oslo.

a

b

Plate 27. *The portal of the first stave-church at Urnes, Norway.*

Plate 28. Head of the Virgin from Giske, Sunnmøre, Norway. Historisk Museum, Bergen.

8

Warfare

The Vikings were warriors as well as farmers and traders and the arts of war loomed large in their lives. In Scandinavia, and particularly in the Baltic lands, communities were liable to attack from the sea and an indirect record of these attacks is revealed in the hoards of precious metal laid down in times of threatened trouble and never recovered because the trouble supervened. In early times the Scandinavians often seem to have sited their settlements without thought for protection, but some few Viking Age sites were fortified and it is to these we shall first turn our attention.

Defensive works

Purely military fortification was rare in Scandinavia in the Viking Age. Towns, where they existed, were often protected by a ditch and bank with a palisade and perhaps even interval towers (see pp. 203–24). At Birka (pl. 8a) and Hedeby a citadel commanded the town and the one at Birka was certainly contemporaneous with the town itself. Such a sophisticated fortification probably presupposes regular troops, but most towns would rely on the temporary services of the inhabitants in times of danger. The towns would also form a natural place of refuge for the surrounding population; in some areas – particularly in Sweden – they replaced fortified encampments which had earlier been used for temporary defence by scattered agricultural communities. The idea of the town as a refuge is familiar elsewhere in contemporary Europe. In England, for example, King Alfred established a chain of fortified boroughs to which the agricultural community could flee at the time of Viking invasion.

Smaller settlement sites with major defensive works are rarely encountered in Scandinavia, but since 1964 Mårten Stenberger has been excavating a site at Eketorp, in southern Öland, which

263

is surrounded by a bank of stone which may well once have been as much as six metres in height. This rampart is circular – 80 m. in diameter – and enclosed, at a distance of 10 m., by an outer palisade of timber. The site was a permanent settlement – an agricultural and, in its later phase, a merchant community – in use from about 450 to 750 and from the beginning of the eleventh to the end of the thirteenth century. It had a main entrance towards the south which may have been crowned by a tower. About the year 1200 it was besieged and sacked by the Wends. Throughout the greater part of the Viking period, however, Eketorp was deserted and presumably only served as a place of refuge in times of immediate danger.

Camps were prepared specifically to serve as temporary refuges. In the barren interior of Öland, a limestone region known as Alvaret, a series of circular or approximately circular fortifications were built in the late Roman Iron Age, of which the most famous are Gråborg and Ismantorp. Inside these forts are radially placed house foundations. At Gråborg (pl. 3a), which is the largest (120 m. in diameter), the defences were strengthened in the thirteenth century, but a number of finds demonstrate that it was also used in the Viking Age. It is likely, therefore, that at least some of these pre-existing stone-built forts were used by the local inhabitants in times of danger; just as in the Isle of Man certain single dwellings were placed by the Vikings inside semi-circular banks on cliff-top promontories.

One of the most extraordinary defensive fortifications is undoubtedly Bulverket, 'the bulwark', in the middle of a shallow fresh-water lake in the parish of Tingstäde in the north of Gotland. Here survive the complicated wooden foundations of a lake-dwelling which can only have been used as a temporary defensive position in time of piratical attack. The platform is roughly square, with sides 170 m. long enclosing a central 'harbour' which is entered on the south side. Each side of the square is 7 m. broad and consists of square-cut timbers interlocking with each other; this base carried a floor of split tree-trunks on which, it is presumed, light structures were placed. It has been calculated that the construction of this elaborate platform used up some 10,000 tree-trunks, indicating what was certainly an enormous communal work for the whole of the north of the island. Radio-carbon dating indicates that Bul-verket was built at the end of the Viking period, probably *c.* 1100, when Gotland coin-hoards demonstrate a period of in-stability. It is possible that Bulverket came to a sticky end, for there is a local saying, 'It smokes as it did when Tingstäde lake burnt'. This monument is without parallel in Scandinavia, although Borgarvirki in northern Iceland bears some resem-blance to it in that it is surrounded by marshy country which would form some sort of barrier to an attacking force. The date of this fortification is obscure, though it would seem to fit best in the settlement period.

The idea of linear defensive earthworks was familiar in western Europe of the Viking Age. In England, for example, the great Anglo-Saxon ditches – Wansdyke and Offa's dyke particularly – were famous and formidable landmarks. Only one major ditch survives in Scandinavia; the so-called Danevirke (fig. 40) which defined the southern border of Denmark. It was built, according to the *Annales Regni Francorum*, about 808 by the Danish King Godfred as a defence against threatened attack by the armies of Charlemagne; it stretches from the Schlei fjord, across the neck

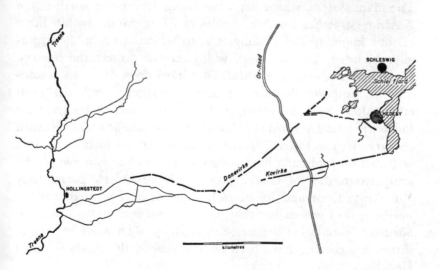

Fig. 40. The Danevirke, Hærvej (Ox-road) and Hedeby.

of Jutland, to the river Treene. It is not a continuous defensive system, but, like the great English dykes, it links impassable stretches of country, the natural barriers being mostly marshland. Various additions and modifications were made to it from time to time; the most important was apparently that of Valdemar I of Denmark (1157–82), who faced part of the rampart with brick.

In its original state the Danevirke consisted through most of its length of a bank (faced with timbers and crowned by a palisade) and ditch; it varies in height, but at its most important point, where the great road called the Hærvej passes through it, it stands today as much as five or six metres high. It appears a complicated structure, with various stretches of wall joining other sections at an angle or standing isolated from the rest, but basically it consists of two main structures, whose history is controversial. The most reasonable explanation seems to be that of Herbert Jankuhn, namely that the Kovirke (German *Kograben*), which extends from the Schlei for some seven kilometres to the west, was the original fortification built by Godfred in 808. It would protect Hedeby from attack and would also control access to Denmark along the stretch of the Hærvej called the Ox-road. The main system, which lies a few kilometres to the north of the Kovirke, stretches from the Schlei to Morgenstern within three or four kilometres of Hollingstedt, to which it probably originally extended. This northern wall does not protect the town of Hedeby, but the southern wall (Kovirke) does. It seems reasonable to suppose, therefore, that the northern wall was built either after the fortification of Hedeby or after its desertion for the newly founded town of Schleswig in the middle of the eleventh century. In this latter case the repeated repairs to the northern wall can be explained by a constant need to keep an eye on the southern frontier of the kingdom. Other scholars, particularly Vilhelm la Cour and Johannes Brøndsted, have argued that the northern wall was earlier than the Kovirke and that it protected *Sliesthorp*, a putative precursor of Hedeby. The Kovirke would, if they are correct, have been built to defend the newly founded Hedeby.

Camps

The most impressive fortifications of the Viking Age are undoubtedly the Danish military camps at Trelleborg on Sjælland, Nonnebakken in the town of Odense on Fyn, and Aggersborg and Fyrkat Mølle in Jutland (fig. 41). Not since the days of the Roman Empire had military encampments in northwest Europe been laid out with such regularity. Even so, they were not the first military camps built by Vikings before the end of the tenth century, the period when the Danish series was apparently inaugurated. Anglo-Saxon sources, for example, record fortifications at Milton Regis and Appledore in Kent, Benfleet and Shoebury in Essex, Burrington in Montgomery, Bridgnorth in Shropshire, on the River Lea, north of London, and in a number of other places. All these were temporary, thrown up by a raiding army for use during a single winter and only constructed when a more easily defended site – a deserted town (like Chester in 893), an island (like Thorney on the River Colne in 893), or a captured town (like York in 867) – was not available. These temporary camps have not yet been recognized on the ground.

Such camps were presumably entirely different from the permanent structures in Denmark which are among the most remarkable remaining phenomena of the Viking Age. Traditions concerning such garrison camps are perhaps preserved in the Icelandic *Jómsvikinga saga*, first written *c.* 1200. The saga tells how a *borg* was founded on the south Baltic coast by a man called Palna-Tóki from the Danish island of Fyn. This *borg* and its inhabitants are described in some detail: it was a fortified place with a harbour which, according to the oldest manuscript (AM 291 4to), held three warships inside it (other versions say that it held 300 ships). The saga says that the harbour was entered by a stone arch crowned by a tower which could be closed with iron gates; the walls of the fort were built out into the water. Such description suggests that it may have been a fort for a small but effective body of professional soldiers. According to the saga, the fort was maintained for a warrior society which fought in summer and stayed in Jómsborg under stern discipline in the winter. Its members were enrolled voluntarily, without nepotism, from men between the ages of 18 and 50; once enrolled they lived under strict rules of loyalty and vengeance. All booty

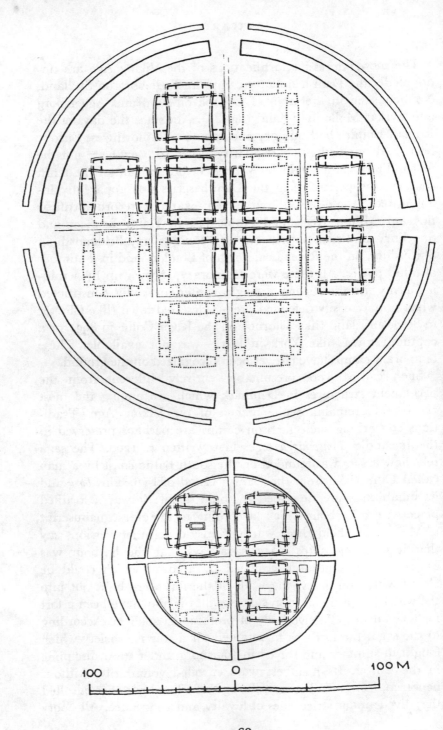

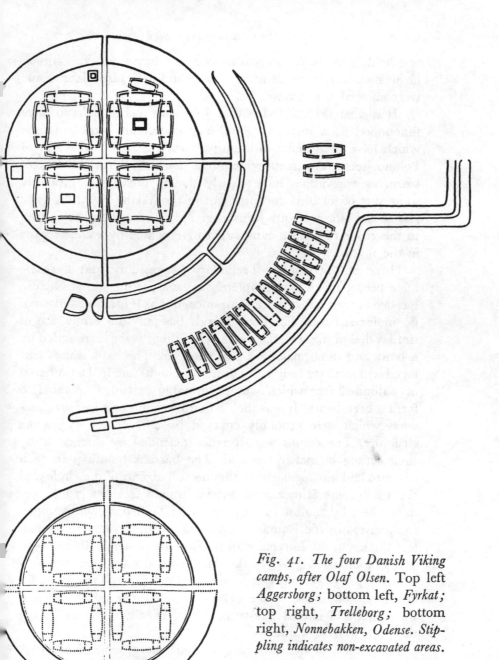

Fig. 41. The four Danish Viking camps, after Olaf Olsen. Top left *Aggersborg;* bottom left, *Fyrkat;* top right, *Trelleborg;* bottom right, *Nonnebakken, Odense. Stippling indicates non-excavated areas.*

was held in common and was shared on return from expeditions; no women were allowed in the camp and only three days' leave were allowed at one time.

It is clear from the saga that Jómsborg was thought to have functioned as a mercenary military community and attempts which have been made to identify it with the town of Wolin in Poland (see p. 219) seem wide of the mark. Wolin was a market town, as excavations have clearly shown, but it was probably some sort of fortified encampment of the Viking Age that gave rise to the stories about Jómsborg. It has often been compared to the group of Danish camps first investigated by archaeologists in the 1930s.

Three of the camps – Trelleborg, Aggersborg and Fyrkat – have been partially or completely excavated; the site at Odense has been investigated more than once, but as it is a built-up area, no major structure has been found. Basically the camps are of similar design (fig. 41), the barrack buildings being surrounded by a bank and ditch making a perfect circle. The bank was of turf laced with timbers (originally some 7 m. high) and had a timbered or palisaded face which was presumably extended upwards to form a breastwork. It was pierced on the main axis by four gateways which were probably covered by a roof or a tower-like structure. The camps were further defended by ditches or by their setting in marshy ground. The barrack buildings in each case are laid out regularly in the four quadrants of the circle and the whole plan is measured out in Roman feet (29.57 cm., reduced here by 24 mm. to 29.33 cm.). At Trelleborg, for example, the houses are 100 Roman feet in length, the bank is 60 Roman feet thick and the internal radius of the bank is 234 Roman feet. The houses (fig. 10) are of the curved-sided type described elsewhere (pp. 151–3) and vary in size and design. At Trelleborg, for example, the houses were of stave construction, the wooden walls made of halved tree-trunks set vertically, while at Fyrkat the walls were of wattle.

The largest of the four camps, Aggersborg, comprised fortyeight houses, twelve in each quadrant; but in the other two excavated examples, and presumably also at Nonnebakken, there were only four houses in each quadrant. All the houses are laid out in groups of four round a square courtyard, but at

Trelleborg fifteen further houses were discovered within an outer defence-work which was concentric with the main line of the bank but with an additional enclosure opposite the main entrance. At Aggersborg there is a further complication in that the camp was built on the site of an earlier Viking settlement of some size.

The finds from the camps undoubtedly demonstrate that they should be dated to the late tenth or early eleventh century. Any attempt to date them to the middle of the eleventh-century must be rejected because of the complete lack of finds to support such a statement. There seems little doubt that the camps had a short life, for the post-holes show no evidence of the replacement of rotted timbers – repairs that would have been inevitable within thirty or forty years of erection. That they were military barracks seems unquestionable, despite the fact that they are without adequate parallel. They were useless as strong points for the defence of the Danish kingdom, but are well situated for the gathering of troops by means of the main lines of communication and must therefore have served some aggressive military purpose. The fact that, at the rate of fifty men per house, accommodation was provided in them for some 5500 men at the beginning of the eleventh century suggests that they were the bases from which Sven Forkbeard and Knut the Great operated in their invasion and conquest of England and in their expeditions to the rest of Scandinavia. Only at this period could such an immense project as the building of these camps be undertaken – a period when money was flowing into the Danish kings' coffers.

The problem of the origin of the camps is puzzling. No satisfactory parallel exists in western Europe and any idea that they had their origin in the standardized Roman military camps must be dismissed on the grounds that the separation of six centuries in time would have stifled any real memory of their existence. A Byzantine origin has been postulated on the grounds that the camps were measured out in Roman feet and because we have hints of camps of foreign nationals in the service of the Byzantine Empire. Such an argument carries little weight, especially since the use of the Roman foot is attested among Germanic peoples in Europe at an earlier period – at Yeavering in Northumberland in the seventh century, for example – and may well have been a standard unit of measurement in the North. Is it too much to suggest that these camps were a Danish invention, based on long experience of building temporary structures in England and elsewhere? Their form may originate in the circular fortifications long known on the Baltic islands (p. 264). What is certain is that they went out of use during the eleventh century and that the next military structure that appeared was the motte with its strong tower, so familiar in feudal Europe in the second half of that century. The end of the camps must be coincident with the death of Knut in 1035 and the subsequent collapse of the Danish Empire.

Weapons

The personal armament of a man was as important to him as his clothes and the wealthy expended enormous sums and the craftsmen enormous ingenuity on the embellishment and decoration of their weapons. But weapons are functional and to this end the Scandinavian weapon-smith – the aristocrat among craftsmen – bent all his skill to produce objects of both beauty and efficiency.

The laws lay down what weapons an adult able-bodied man should own. These were the so-called 'folk-weapons' (the word *folk* probably being used in an original sense of 'war-band') and they were inspected annually by the local royal official. The basic Swedish requirements were shield, sword, spear and iron hat for each man, while a mail-coat or protective jerkin and a bow and three dozen arrows had to be provided for each rowing bench. Elsewhere an axe might be used instead of a sword, and each man, not each bench, might be expected to own defensive armour and bow and arrows. In Norway sword or axe, shield and spear were required, with one bow and two dozen arrows to a bench. In Denmark the ordinary man needed sword, iron hat, spear and shield, while the *styræsman* (pp. 123–4) had to provide, with his neighbours' help, a horse, a coat of mail, and a crossbow and bolts, along with a man to use this if he himself was not a marksman. The *Hirðskrá* of thirteenth-century Norway (p. 101) has elaborate regulations for the armament of the different ranks in this body of courtly retainers, and enjoins the hirdmen to have their weapons at hand and in good condition. The king should often have weapon-inspection and weapon-training. It says: 'Weapons in war are trust and protection, in peace honour and distinction, and they represent good capital investments available for whatever need may arise in any emergency.' These were considerations that must have applied throughout the Viking Age. It may be noted that the Gulathing Law says that weapons in perfect condition might be paid in atonement for a slaying (but not the weapon the victim was killed with!), but swords should only be included in the payment if they were adorned with gold or silver.

The most important of all weapons was the sword. Swords were celebrated in poetry and remembered in the sagas; a vast number of kennings were invented for them – 'fire of battle', 'lightning flash of blood', 'snake of wounds', 'icicle of the baldric'. Many were given names, often based on the quality of the swords themselves: *Brynjubítr* (Byrnie-biter), *Fótbítr*, (Leg-biter), *Gramr* (Fierce), *Gullinhjalti*, (Gold-hilt), *Hvati* (Keen), *Langhvass* (Long-and-sharp) or *Miðfáinn* (Ornamented-down-the-middle). Sometimes their names celebrated a deed, as for example King Hákon's sword *Kvernbítr* (Quern-biter), 'the best that ever came to Norway', which cut a quernstone to the centre. Perhaps a sword from Norway with the name *Rex* inscribed on its blade may have been called by this name by its owners, but usually the smith inlaid his name or mark in the blade during manufacture. Many stories are told of the making of swords, more fabulous than factual in most cases, but they at least tell us something of the craft-mystery of the weapon-smith. Some swords were of magical origin, made by dwarfs, given by Odin, or found in a mound, like the sword *Skǫfnungr* which is mentioned in several sources and which was said to have been removed from the grave-mound of a famous king in Denmark by the Icelandic settler, Skeggi of Midfirth.

The surviving swords tell a more prosaic story for many of the richest have imported blades. Rhenish swords bearing the name *Ulfberht* are found in some numbers in ninth- and tenth-century northern graves, as well as throughout Europe and Russia (cf. the 'Frankish swords' in the verse quoted, p. 323). Not all these swords were made by one man or in the same workshop, as is demonstrated by the Sword of St Stephen in Prague which has the name etched and not inlaid into the blade, but the original *Ulfberht* workshop must have produced high-quality swords to have been imitated in such fashion. There is evidence that some of the blades were given their hilts at Birka, while a Viking sword found in the Isle of Man was undoubtedly carried in a British scabbard and slung from a British baldric. Five sword-blades found in one deposit at Skärlöv, Hulterstad, Öland were presumably imported for mounting in Sweden. Rich swords were imported into Scandinavia like *Kvernbítr*, mentioned above, the sword given to King Hákon of Norway by King Athelstan of England; but many other silver-mounted English swords, with their curved guards and pommels, found their way to Norway, and many formidable Carolingian weapons came to Sweden. Some of these must have been booty but some will have come by trade. Many swords were however made in Scandinavia.

The most important part of a sword was, of course, the blade. Including the tang a sword of this period was usually just over 90 cm. in length – a sword as long as 95 cm. is a rarity – and the tang was about 10 cm. long. The normal sword was sharply shouldered at the tang and the blade was gently tapered towards the slightly blunted tip – the weapon was a slashing implement. Although single-edged swords occurred in the early Viking Age, the vast majority were two-edged. Down the middle of the blade on either side was a shallow round-bottomed channel or 'fuller' which reduced the weight considerably. The blades were often elaborately constructed by a process known as pattern-welding, described above on pp. 183–4. Experiments have shown that it may well have taken a smith nearly a month to make a really fine sword.

Various reasons have been put forward to explain the pattern-welding method of making a sword-blade, varying from the idea that such a structure gives greater pliability – a much desired quality to judge from passages in the sagas – to the idea that at this period it was difficult to obtain a bar of this length free of major carbon inclusions. That the pattern on the blade was important to the customer may be seen from names of swords and kennings used for swords which indicate this feature, especially those that emphasize the similarity of the sword to a snake. There is also some reason to think that the pattern on the blade was believed to have had magical properties.

The hilt consisted of three elements – guard, grip and pommel. The guard of metal, bone, horn or ivory was often ornamented and if of iron sometimes inlaid or encrusted with precious metals. Scandinavian swords usually had a straight guard. In the tenth century, however, drooping curved guards begin to appear, perhaps in imitation of Anglo-Saxon hilts. The grip, which could be of metal, wood, horn or bone, was sometimes covered with leather. All Viking swords were intended for use in one hand and the grip was little longer than the width of a man's hand. The pommel varied greatly in form, from period to period, and it is largely on the basis of this feature that they were set into typological order by Jan Petersen. The pommel was often made up of a short bar and a knop, but sometimes it was a single piece of metal of triangular or D-shaped form (pl. 25a). In the poem called *Sigrdrífumál* we are told that victory runes should be cut on the guard or pommel, and as late as the twelfth century we find a runic inscription on the mounts of a sword-hilt from Korsøygården, Tangen, Hedmark, Norway, where the inscription reads, 'Audmund made me, Asleik owns me'. The sword was usually carried in a scabbard suspended from a baldric or, less certainly, from a belt.

As a weapon grew older it gained in value and virtue. St Ólaf's sword *Hneitir,* for example, was already old when it came into his possession. After his death in battle it was picked up by a Swede and retained in his family for at least three generations, until in the twelfth century it finally ended up, or so we are told, over the altar of St Ólaf's church in Constantinople.

No other weapon had the glamour of the sword – the aristocrat among weapons and the worthy gift of a king. But other weapons of offence were certainly used, particularly the spear (*spjót*), the iron head of which is the commonest weapon found in Viking Age graves (pl. 15); the spear was used both in the chase and in battle. Two main types of spear were used, the throwing spear and the thrusting spear which the warrior retained in his hand. Battles often started with a shower of spears and other missiles, before the real business of hand-to-hand fighting was reached. It is usually said that throwing spears, being lost by their owners, were not as elaborate as those which were kept in a man's hand. We may presume that many of the small plain iron points found on Viking sites belong to this class; some such spears may not even have had heads. But the long slender points found in many graves may show that this theory may be wrong. Their shafts can be reconstructed and it seems that they would be ideally suited for throwing. Because some of these spearheads are so rich we might accept Johannes Brøndsted's suggestion that such spears 'would be carefully returned to their owner after battle'. Certain broader-bladed spears could not have been thrown and must have been used for thrusting; one wonders whether in fact these were not used primarily for hunting and only secondarily as weapons of war. All Scandinavian spears have sockets, and the blades usually have a more-or-less pronounced midrib, giving a lozenge-shaped cross-section. Blades vary in form, but are usually leaf-shaped, with shoulders towards the socket. The sockets are often elaborately encrusted with other metals (pl. 7) in the manner described on p. 185: in western Scandinavia this pattern tends to take the form of a herring-bone pattern, while in the south and east a geometrical, square interlace pattern is more commonly found. Other spearheads have sockets with more easily recognizable patterns which can be dated on the basis of their style. The rivets which attached the spearheads to the shaft often formed additional ornaments to the socket. Heavy spearheads with strong wings on the socket were probably imported from the Carolingian Empire in the ninth century (these might be the 'western' spears mentioned in the verse quoted on p. 323). Halberds were probably used during the twelfth century, and may have been introduced earlier.

The other chief weapon of offence was the axe, in some ways the most emotive of all Viking weapons. It was with an axe, for example, that a Viking, called Brodar in the Irish source, killed King Brian Boru at the Battle of Clontarf outside Dublin in 1014. Long-handled axes are portrayed on a tombstone from Lindisfarne (pl. 1a), a picture which surely represents a Viking attack. According to the twelfth-century writer, Sven Aggeson, gold-adorned axes and rich-hilted swords were required as a condition of admission to the immediate military entourage of Knut the Great. In western countries one form of battle-axe was known as the 'Danish axe', while in Scandinavia itself miniature axes were popular amulets. There can be no doubt that many of the richly-ornamented axes found throughout the Viking world were used as battle-axes. They take various forms (fig. 42) – some, like the Mammen axe (pl. 20), are extremely practical weapons, others, like the bearded axe (*skeggøx*), must have been rather clumsy, having been adapted directly from what was undoubtedly a woodworker's tool. The terminology of the axe is very difficult to disentangle, and since some words like *handøx*, 'hand-axe', and *breiðøx*, 'broad axe', are capable of many interpretations, hard-and-fast definitions are impossible. Ornamented axes were used for display and were almost certainly used as battle-axes; other axes probably fulfilled a dual role as

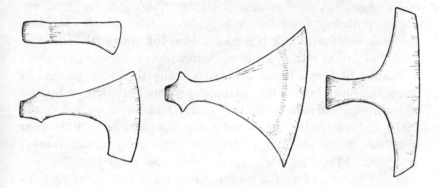

Fig. 42. Axe-heads of the Viking Age.

tools and weapons as occasion required. T-shaped axes, for example, occur exclusively as tools on the Bayeux tapestry, yet some contemporary examples of approximately similar form bear the most elaborate inlaid decoration, one of which (without provenance) can be seen in the University Museum at Lund, while another example was found at Trelleborg. Similarly, a rather miserable wedge-shaped axe from Hadbjerg, Randers, Jutland, which has practically no flare to the blade and which in any other context would be taken as a carpenter's tool, is most elaborately decorated on the blade. An axe wielded with power would be a most satisfactory weapon whatever its origin and normal function, and it is certain that the Vikings used them with skill.

Bows and arrows were also used in battle, and are mentioned frequently in the literature. Saxo, for example, speaks of the Norwegians as famous bowmen. Arrows were carried in a quiver, a portion of a cylindrical example of which was found in Gunnarshaug in Norway, while another example has recently been found at Hedeby. Bows are rarely found and where they do occur they are incomplete. One composite bow strengthened with iron bands has recently been recognized in Norway, but a fresh description awaits publication. Three fragments of long-bows have a good claim to be Viking. One, bearing runes, was found at Staraja Ladoga; a second, tentatively dated to the late Viking Age on the grounds of its ornament, was found in the far north of Sweden at Vibbymyren, Överluleå, Norrland; a third example, probably from the Viking Age (on the basis of pollen analysis), was found in a bog near Sikån, Jokkmokk, also in Norrland. But unfortunately none of them can be regarded as typical.

Bundles of arrow-heads are occasionally found in graves. In one of the Birka burials for example (possibly grave 519) a bundle of twenty-one arrow-heads was found forming a cylinder, the shafts and quiver having rotted away together. Sometimes even more are found together, forty-five, for example, at Ladby, Denmark. Many of the arrow-heads are tanged. Some are socketed and a few have a trefoil cross-section with three cutting-edges. Normally they have long leaf-shaped blades and their overall measurements vary between 10 and 15 cm. There was apparently also a barbed arrow-head (krókr), but these are not found in graves. Not all the weapons found in graves would be used in war, for the bow was a popular weapon in hunting, particularly in fowling when blunt-headed arrows were used. Bows seem to have been little used in Iceland. The cross-bow was probably not generally introduced until the twelfth century.

The chief means of defence was the shield (pl. 25b), and the circular iron shield boss is one of the commonest of all Viking antiquities. The shield boss is almost always hemispherical and has a rim by which it is attached to the board, being locked in place by an iron grip on the underside of the board. The board was normally circular with a central hole for the boss and those found in the Gokstad ship-burial measured nearly a metre in diameter. In the eleventh and twelfth century there is some evidence that kite-shaped shields were introduced. Shields were often painted, sometimes (according to the poets) with scenes (pp. 360–1), but often left in their natural colours. Some, like those from Gokstad, were bound with leather at the rim; others, like that from grave 736 at Birka, were bound at the rim with small bronze plates.

The mail-shirt is rarely found in Scandinavia. The earliest example found belongs to the pre-Roman Iron Age; examples of Viking Age date are fragmentary, the best documented being from the rich Gjermundbu grave from Ringerike in Norway. Here there were many fragments of a mail-shirt made up of inter-locking rings; the rings are formed with overlapping ends, like a modern key-ring, but are not riveted. The form of the shirt is unknown but one may presume that it was a sleeved knee-length garment, like both earlier and later shirts discovered in Scandinavia. It is well documented in poetry in words like *hringserkr, hringskyrta* ('ring-shirt'). It was, however, probably only worn by the wealthy, and they found it hot and heavy to wear.

Another piece of armour which in the early Viking period was probably only worn by the wealthy was the helmet, for although there are many representations of helmeted warriors on the Got-land stones and elsewhere, helmets themselves are rarely found. Many helmets are known from the Vendel period, but only a few fragments survive from the Viking Age, although in the twelfth century they were numbered among the 'folk weapons' (p. 272). Of these the most remarkable again comes from the tenth-century Gjermundbu grave. This helmet consists of a simple rounded cap with four ribs and a band round the fore-head, a spike at the crest, and a sheet metal rim to which was attached a heavy spectacle-like nose- and eye-guard. Its pre-cursors are to be found in the helmets of the rich pre-Viking Swedish graves at Vendel and Valsgärde. The iron eye-brow ridge of a helmet encrusted with copper and silver comes from Lokrume in Gotland. It has a nose-guard and is decorated with interlace ornament which ought to be of tenth- or eleventh-century date. This ornament is so close to that of the so-called helmet of St Wenceslas in Prague Cathedral that one might con-sider this national treasure of the Czechs as a Viking product, despite the representation of a crucifixion on the nose-guard, although the latest scholar to study this object, Dagmar Hejdova, denies such a thesis.

These were the chief weapons with which the Vikings fought. Other weapons were also used. Clubs are sometimes mentioned in the northern sources, and stones were normally used as missiles. The French poet Abbo mentions a machine of war, the catapult, in his almost contemporary description of the Vikings' siege of Paris in 885.

The weapons were on the whole efficient and ideally suited to the irregular mêlée that was battle in this period.

An old Irish triad says: 'Three that are hardest to talk to: a king bent on conquest, a Viking in his armour, and a low-born man protected by patronage.' There is other Irish evidence that the superiority of the war-gear of the Norsemen, not least their coats of ring-mail, made a deep impression on the Irish, who failed against them, says the author of the *Cogadh*, 'because of the excellence of their polished, ample, treble, heavy, trusty, glittering corslets; and their hard, strong, valiant swords; and their well-riveted long spears'.

National military organization in Denmark, Norway and Sweden was based on the *leidang* (WN *leiðangr*, OD *lethang*, OSw. *leþunger*). The etymology of this word is not entirely clear. The first element is *leið*, 'going, passing; sea-way; accompaniment, following (of men); expedition'; the second element may be from *gangr*, 'going, movement', or from *gagn*, 'equipment, supplies'. The *leidang* was a levy of ships, men, armaments and provisions, called out by the king, the supreme military leader, and supplied by the population on a proportional basis. The military needs behind the levy were responsible for the division of the provinces into the small units that provided one man, and the collections of these units that provided one ship for active service. In the twelfth century, when the levy was gradually transformed from a contribution in men, equipment and supplies into a form of cash taxation, existing levy divisions provided a ready-made organization that could be used on a nation-wide scale for the monarchy's administrative and fiscal purposes. The age of the levy system is not known, but it probably began a full, regular existence in the tenth century. There are notable differences in the arrangements and terminology found in the different provincial laws of the thirteenth century, and this variety suggests an ancient origin.

The levy was essentially a naval force. Men who took part in the levy were said *at róa leiðang*, to row *leidang*, and some of the names used for the district divisions under obligation to supply members of the force reflect its seafaring nature: in Sweden *hamna* 'rowlock loop', in Denmark *hafnæ*, 'man's shipboard station', were names for the unit providing a single man for the fleet; in west Norway *skipreiða*, 'ship-providing (district)', was used for the larger unit that fitted out a warship. Similarly, the local officer called *styræsman* in Denmark (pp. 123-4) got his title of 'skipper' (literally 'helmsman') from his function as commander of the local levy vessel.

If an attack was made in a district, every man was under obligation to turn out and even thralls might serve to fight off invaders (p. 70). The *leidang* was, however, a levy, a selection of the able-bodied members of the population. It is thought, for example, that the regions called Tiundaland, Attundaland and Fjädrundaland in Sweden, got their names because they contained 10, 8 and 4 districts called *hund*, and such a district supplied 100 (*hund* and 'hundred' have the same origin) men in four 24-oared ships, probably on an original basis of one oarsman from each estate. In the west-coast regions of Norway, three farms together sent out one man; while later one man was supposed to join the levy for every seven inhabitants. We can make some estimate of the number of ships and men a full levy ideally produced in Denmark and Norway. A contemporary poet says that about 1050 King Sven Estridsson of Denmark had 720 ships; while later sources show that the levy was expected to produce about 900 ships in the twelfth century, with probably about 36,000 men all told, although it is of course doubtful whether so many were ever actually mustered. The figures given for Norway in the thirteenth century show that something over 30,000 men were supposed to be available, but in far fewer ships than were used in Denmark. This is because the Norwegian levy-ships were by then in many cases bigger, specified as 25-bench vessels, and the average crew was reckoned at about 100, while the Danish average seems to have been about 40 (cf. pp. 249-52 on typical warships).

It became the accepted custom, at least in Norway, that a full levy could be called out for defensive purposes, a half-levy if aggression was intended. The summoning of the levy needed advance notice – intelligence that it was being called out would soon reach foreign ears and, depending on the political situation, give warning that defences were mobilized or that an attack might be expected. Once the levy fleet was assembled for defensive purposes, it could only wait for news of an enemy's arrival, and its essential function at this stage was as transport for quick concentration of forces wherever they might be needed. Sudden attacks by smaller or larger forces might be made, however, at almost any time from the spring to late autumn, and we gather that Swedish guard-vessels cruised coastal waters, while in Norway and elsewhere there were elaborate and expensive systems for carrying warnings by means of bonfires sited on high points. All districts had means of hasty communication by messages and tokens which every householder was obliged to carry on to his neighbour. These were used both in peace and war. In the latter case the Norwegian phrase was *at skera upp herǫr*, 'to cut up a war-arrow', a symbolic arrow of wood or iron which demanded immediate response from the yeomen.

Sea battles

Adam of Bremen said it was the custom of Norsemen to fight at sea and, if the enemy materialized, then the levy-ships turned into warships. All the same, they made a naval battle as much like a land battle as possible, by roping their ships close together in line abreast, so as to make one or more floating lines which then opposed the enemy battle-line head-on. As the lines moved towards each other, missiles were exchanged, especially stones, which made particularly useful and cheap ammunition, and arrows. *Sverris saga* has this description at the onset of a naval battle in 1184: 'They saw King Magnús's fleet bearing down on them, and saw too that in front of the fleet the sea looked as it does in heavy rain in still weather. This shower came quickly on, and it was arrow-fall. Then shields were needed.' Once joined, hand-to-hand fighting was concentrated about the prows and forward parts of the ships, while the men in the after parts shot at the enemy and took the places of those who fell in the bows.

To be made a *stafnbúi*, 'stem-dweller, focsleman', was a mark of distinction and a sure sign of reputation as a fighting man. Victory came when resistance on a ship had been so worn down that it was possible to board and clear it; after a time it gradually became obvious throughout the fleet who had the upper hand. This mode of fighting meant that the fleet as a whole had little manoeuvrability, while individual ships could only retire or pursue by cutting themselves loose. It was not until the late twelfth century that more open, mobile methods of sea-fighting were used.

Land battles

In a pitched battle on land the forces were also drawn up in opposing lines, with a centre and wings. A chief might have a so-called *skjaldborg*, 'shield-fort', around him, a tight group of men whose duty was defence rather than attack. Close by him was his standard-bearer, a man of strength and courage for the enemy's attacks were naturally aimed at the banner he carried. Banners were chiefly of the labarum type and we hear of some famous examples. The English captured a 'Raven' banner from the Danes in 878, and Earl Sigurd of Orkney, who fell at Clontarf in 1014, is also supposed to have had one so shaped that when the wind took it it looked like a raven in flight; Harald the Hard-ruler's was called *Landeyðan*, 'The Land-waster', and King Sverri's *Sigrflugan*, 'The Victory-fly'. Trumpets and horns were used for signalling in warfare, as they also were for peaceful purposes in townships. Men might sometimes wear a mark to distinguish them from their enemies, and by the end of the twelfth century heraldic devices were beginning to be used on shields.

Before the battle began it was customary for a leader to incite his men with a speech – there are many examples in the historical literature, some of them very fine, but whether they were actually delivered is another matter – and sometimes spirits were roused by the declamation of a poet or minstrel. In heathen times it seems that an enemy host might be formally dedicated to destruction by hurling a javelin over their heads, an action taken to imply that they were consigned to Odin, the god of war and gatherer of slain men. War-cries were certainly used, shouts intended to inspire confidence on one side and terror on the other.

Slogans were doubtless used as well. Sverri's men at the end of the twelfth century chanted something like, 'Onward Christ's men, cross-men, holy King Ólaf's men', while one source, which we cannot verify, says that Saint Ólaf's followers at Stiklestad in 1030 gave tongue with, *Knýjum, knýjum, konungs liðar, harðla, harðla, bóanda menn* – 'Press on, press on, prince's fighters, hard and hard on farming men!', which sounds good, though it was the farmers who actually won.

Once the lines clashed the battle became a series of isolated fights and it must have been very hard to discover its general progress until the death of leaders or general flight on one side marked the beginning of the end. Men might ask for quarter and it was honourable to stand by mercy that was given. Churches offered a place of sanctuary, but they were not always respected. When the fighting was finished, the slain and wounded were inspected and arrangements made for burying the one and tending the other. The booty was collected and shared out. We have no real notion what the casualty rate in battle was. It was probably higher at sea than on land, because of the difficulty of escape, but it was not necessarily very high and of course depended on varying circumstances. In 1181 a naval battle between Sverri with sixteen larger ships and Magnús with thirty smaller ships ended with a loss of over 300 men on each side; but in the battle of 1184, in which Magnús was killed, his side alone is said to have lost over 2000 men from a total of twenty-six ships. This is an estimate but it is one made by a contemporary and may not be a great exaggeration. Such figures are however notoriously difficult to interpret: there is an ancient Irish poem on the Battle of Sulcoit, an Irish victory over the Norsemen in 968, in which the number killed is put at 'little less than one hundred heads' – two later sources have 3000 and 7000 respectively.

Horsemen were not much used in fighting in the Viking Age. The Irish poem just mentioned says that the Norsemen had a battalion of horsemen among them at Sulcoit, and Adam of Bremen a century later says that the Swedes were 'very great warriors both on horses and on ships'. A cavalry arm was developed in Denmark in the twelfth century as part of the contribution made by superior men to the levy forces (p. 126).

Tactics generally were simple and elemental, consisting largely of bashing hell out of the opposing side. Various stratagems and military formations were, however, known to the Norsemen, although the descriptions we have in the Icelandic histories of feigned flights, ambushes, encirclements, and the pretence of greater forces than were actually present, are of course not necessarily accurate in the contexts in which they appear. The phrase *at hamalt fylkja* means 'to adopt a wedge-shaped battle formation', and this is also called *svínfylkja*, from *svínfylking*, 'swine-order', apparently a calque on the Late Latin *porcinum caput*, 'swine-snout', used of the same array. There are many literary references to the devastating impact this was supposed to have on an enemy line, but what relation they bear to reality we cannot tell. Its famed efficacy was so great that the secret of its origin was supposed to have come from Odin himself. A piece of military advice offered in one poem is not to fight with the sun in your eyes, but other means of ensuring success in battle were less prosaic: it could be learnt from Odin, for example, how to blunt sword-edges and stop the flight of javelins. Abilities of this kind were believed to exist in the fighters called *berserkir,* 'bear-shirts', who probably looked on the bear as a kind of totem animal. They were men who fell or worked themselves into a frenzy which gave wild increase to their strength and made them indifferent to blows. They howled savagely as they went into battle (cf. the verse quoted on p. 323). This form of running amuck probably had its roots in a state of paranoia, related to lycanthropy. It may sometimes have been induced by alcohol (but other drugs are not likely to have been used) and in individual cases it may have been an epileptic response. Such men were prized as warriors and were evidently regarded with awe as manifesting supernatural powers. It was not considered simple or innocent possession, however, for the Icelandic Christian law says that anyone who fell into a berserk frenzy was liable to minor outlawry, thus classing it with other heathen and magical practices. In the Icelandic sagas berserks are stock figures, rather stupid bullies who meet unsympathetic retribution at the hands of heroes.

9

Art and Ornament

The maturity of Viking culture is decisively betokened by the attention paid to the ornament of functional objects. Finds of imaginative art for its own sake are extremely rare. It is the ornament on weapons, brooches, grave-stones, sledges and ships which offer us almost our only clue to the quality of the visual judgement of the Vikings. The surviving material probably gives an unbalanced picture, for little remains of certain types of art which we know to have existed – narrative scenes portrayed in tapestries and painted on shields, secular architectural carving and three-dimensional religious images. We are left with applied art. To the student of the Viking period this art, when set in a sequence, is a useful tool: it can be used as a basis for dating archaeological material and in the interpretation of certain social and economic factors. The meaning and emotional content of the art, however, are at best obscure. There was apparently a need for art in daily life – even the humblest brooch would be covered with ornament – and decorative restraint is rare. One can recognize a certain flashy trait in Viking taste: the glittering surfaces and opulent gilding of much of their metalwork seem to indicate a craving for ostentation both for its own sake and as a sign of wealth and rank.

Viking Age ornament has been divided into a number of different styles which mostly take their name from the find-places of important objects. The terminology is summarized in the table on the facing page to form a framework against which the direct description of this chapter can be placed.

The table brings the story down to the early twelfth century, when the art of western European Christianity was making itself felt in Scandinavia. From about 1090 the true Scandinavian styles gradually gave way to European Romanesque art: the art of the North broke away from its barbarian tradition, and it only

occasionally re-emerges in the folk art of the countryside in later
centuries (pl. 24a).

Style	Notional dates
Style III	– 850
Borre style	840 – 980
Jellinge style	870 – 1000
Mammen style	960 – 1020
Ringerike style	980 – 1090*
Urnes style	1050 – 1170*

*The terminal date in these two cases only applies to Ireland.
Both styles cease rather earlier in Scandinavia.

The table shows that the styles do not simply succeed each
other; they overlap chronologically and sometimes, as in the
case of the Jellinge style and the Mammen style, influence each
other very considerably, so that occasionally it is difficult to say
whether an object is decorated in one style or in another. The
story which is to be told is not a simple one, and is further complicated by the fact that it is often difficult to separate a motif
from a style. Thus the gripping beast occurs both in Style III
and in the Borre style, and only minute analysis of the ornament
can determine to which style the motif belongs.

The earliest Viking art

Scandinavian art of the Viking period has its roots in animal
ornament of an abstract and involved form which was found
throughout northwestern Europe in the period of migrations
which followed the collapse of the Roman Empire. In Scandinavia, as in the rest of the Germanic world of the Migration
Period, there was an abhorrence of naturalistic ornament. The
animals which form the chief elements of the art were twisted
and contorted until, in some cases, it is only possible to see a few
parts of the creature – an eye or a snout, a leg or an arm. Other
motifs – the human figure for example – are hardly to be found

in a naturalistic form outside the Christian areas, and even the introduction during the seventh century of ribbon interlace ornament merely added another dimension to the possibilities of contortion and abstraction in the art. Plant ornament, so common in the Mediterranean and (after 800) in the rest of Christian Europe, is rarely found in Scandinavia until the middle of the tenth century. Representational art does occur, but usually in *graffiti*-like contexts, as on the underside of planks from the Viking ship found at Oseberg, or in specialized contexts such as on the Gotland picture stones which appear to portray mythological or historical events (pl. 12).

The animal art of the Viking Age stems directly from the art of pre-Viking Scandinavia (the Styles I and II of the Migration Period). No new artistic style heralds the arrival of the Vikings on the western European scene; the style which flourished in Scandinavia in the ninth century was merely a more developed form of the art of the earlier centuries in that area.

The earliest Viking decorative style – Style III – contains a number of different motifs, most of which occur in the find from Broa, Halla, in Gotland.

This find consists of a series of gilt-bronze bridle-mounts, which were discovered together with a bridle bit, a sword-hilt and various other objects. The technical quality of these mounts is as fine as that of any collection of metalwork known from contemporary Europe. Most of the objects, although bearing widely

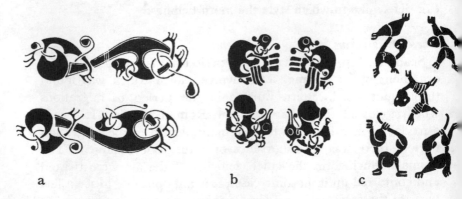

a   b   c

Fig. 43. The three main ornamental motifs from Broa, Halla, Gotland.

different motifs, were the product of a single workshop – probably indeed the products of a single man. This jeweller, a man of high creative genius and eclectic in the motifs he used, produced one of the most brilliant series of objects of the Scandinavian Viking Age.

Three distinct animal motifs occur on the Broa mounts. The first (fig. 43a) has a double-contoured body, usually, but not always, broken in places by the framework which overlies the face of the mount. The head is small in proportion to the size of the animal, while the contour of the body is often broken at the neck or the hip, whence tendrils and limbs are produced to interlace with themselves and with the animal's body. At the point where the contour is broken there is often a heart-shaped opening in the body. The head frequently has a long, frond-like, three-element lappet or pigtail. The second motif (fig. 43b) is very similar to the first, but has no double contour and often takes the form of a bird. These motifs are usually distinguished as Style E. The third type of motif (fig. 43c) – the gripping beast – occurs on only a few mounts. The name of the design is taken from its chief feature, the hands or paws of a creature or number of creatures which clutch the borders of the field or the nearest available limb.

The motifs of the Broa mounts are all native to Scandinavian art. Although certain stylistic details can be compared with what is found in contemporary west European art, all the elements of this style were present in Scandinavian art before the Viking period. Only one group of early Viking Age material is decorated with ornament influenced in any major fashion from the Continent. This ornament – sometimes known as Style F – occurs on a number of bronze mounts and brooches and is derived from an art developed on the Continent under Anglo-Saxon influence. The most important object of this Continental style is the Tassilo Chalice, which was made for the Austrian monastery of Kremsmünster between the years 777 and 788. Objects decorated in this style were imported in some quantity into Scandinavia, the most famous example being a cup from Fejø in Denmark (pl. 17a). A typical example of Scandinavian ornament influenced from this source is on a brooch from Råbylille, Møen, Denmark, (fig. 44), which with its spiral hip and its general technical treatment, closely resembles the Anglo-Carolingian style of the Tassilo Chalice. This style, however, had only a minor influence on early Viking art and was very soon absorbed into, or submerged in, the mainstream of Scandinavian art.

It is evident then that at the beginning of the Viking Age there already existed a sophisticated art indigenous to the North. This art, typified in the Broa mounts, is found – if rarely – throughout the Viking homelands. Its most splendid expression is in the material from the great grave mound at Oseberg, which must be dated to the early ninth century.

Fig. 44. Detail of the ornament of a rectangular brooch from Råbylille, Møen, Denmark. Scale 1/1. National Museum, Copenhagen.

Most of the ornament of the Oseberg grave is carved in wood and this fact is of some importance both for our understanding of the art of the Viking Age and for our judgement of it. Wood is the natural raw material of mainland Scandinavians, to whom large quantities of timber are and have been immediately available. Towards the end of the Viking period we read of houses with elaborate ornamental carvings and when, in the eleventh century, we encounter the first churches in Scandinavia they are also of wood – some, like the church at Urnes (pl. 27), most elaborately carved and ornamented. Wood rots away to nothing in most soil conditions and it is only good fortune that brings wooden objects to light. The few important finds of wooden objects must not cloud our judgement of the art of the Viking period as a whole. It would be wrong, for example, to disparage the art of the Borre style in comparison with that of Style III, because it did not achieve the heights found in the Oseberg ship burial. For we know the Borre style almost exclusively on metal objects, and wood carving in this style is rarely, if ever, found. Stone carving in this style is likewise unknown – indeed, until the late tenth century there was (with the exception of a group of monuments on the island of Gotland) virtually no stone sculpture in Scandinavia.

From the Oseberg burial come a ship, sledges, a cart, bed-posts and many other things decorated with various versions of the three basic animal motifs found on the Broa objects. Certain other facets of the style also occur, but are mostly of trivial importance. Probably the most splendid ornament is that on the stem and stern posts of the ship itself, where interlocking animals are carefully and deeply carved within the strict limits of the available space (fig. 45). The animals have all the features of the Broa mounts: the small weak head, the frond-like feet, the

Fig. 45. Detail of the ornament of the stem of the Oseberg ship (cf. pl. 11).

double-contoured body and the pierced, heart-shaped hips all occur here. Once again the legs are of minor importance, appearing as mere stalks from which hang the useless feet. An element of the gripping beast motif is also present in that the animals' feet occasionally clasp the border of the field in which they are placed. The same artist used elements of the same motif on the tingle (the cross member inside the ship which joins the rising gunwales towards the tip of the prow), which is decorated with comic little men, each of whom has some of the attributes of a gripping beast (fig. 46).

Fig. 46. Ornament of the tingle of the Oseberg ship. After Simpson.

Another sculptor, who in his incidental ornament kept rigorously to the patterns of Style E and has consequently been christened 'the Academician', carved what are probably the most sophisticated objects in the find – a sledge-pole and one of a number of posts carved in the form of an animal head (pl. 22). This latter is one of the most remarkable objects found at Oseberg. The back of the head is covered with Style E animal ornament in the form of a series of fantastically intertwined birds, their limbs coiled inextricably with each other in a completely coherent pattern. But the splendour of the carving as a piece of sculpture resides in the overall design and execution of the post itself: the massive character of the open-mouthed animal head, the restraint of the simple pattern at the base and the unadorned neck, achieve a beauty that is more satisfying to modern eyes than almost any other piece of Viking art.

The normal Style E animal dominates the art of Oseberg, but other motifs also occur. Gripping beasts can be seen in profusion on the misnamed 'Carolingian' animal-head post (fig. 47) and, with bodies normally associated with Style E, on two of the sledge-poles and on a number of other objects. A strange series

Fig. 47. Detail of ornament of the 'Carolingian' animal-head post from Oseberg. Viking Ship Museum, Oslo.

of designs embellish the great ceremonial cart (fig. 36). They include a band of interlacing snake-like creatures, some of which are reminiscent of certain pre-Viking forms and yet have attributes more closely related to the art of the ninth century, such as feet which grip each other in the manner of the gripping beasts. Elsewhere on the cart are panels of ornament which may illustrate a heroic story: in one place a man is entangled in a fantastic mêlée of snakes – perhaps the legendary hero Gunnar in the snake-pit; in another place a horse and rider figure in an enigmatic scene with a man, a woman and an animal.

Processions and scenes which probably depict cult activities also occur on textiles from Oseberg (pl. 13). They are executed with great skill but in a highly conventional, almost naive, manner. Woven in yellows, reds and blacks, they give a spirited rendering of scenes and legends which were familiar to the audience for which they were made, but the meaning of which is nowadays unknown or, at best, doubtful.

Similar scenes are to be seen on a series of memorial stones from the island of Gotland, which are perhaps also of ninth-century date (pl. 12). Carved in the grey local limestone, these objects vary in size from about eighteen inches to nine feet in height. Few of them still stand *in situ*, but there is some evidence that they stood in pairs, as they still do at Änge in the parish of Buttle. The scenes are represented two-dimensionally, against a sunken background which varies in depth from stone to stone: the Hunninge stone, for example, is so shallowly carved that its scenes are hard to make out and have been interpreted in different ways at different times. Other stones may be more deeply carved, the background being hacked away to the depth of a centimetre or more.

The Gotland stones of the early Viking Age have prototypes in the island from the sixth, seventh and eighth centuries. The earliest examples have highly individual abstract designs, shallowly incised in the surface of the rock. By the beginning of the Viking Age, however, more positively sculptural characteristics had been developed and the scenes had become more representational. The most popular motif (pl. 12) on the Viking Age stones is a ship in full sail, often filled with armed warriors. It is depicted in great detail, with prow and stern posts, not dissimilar to those on the Oseberg ship, with elaborate rigging, steering oar and even the weather-vane at the top of the mast. On the more elaborate stones are scenes which have been interpreted in the light of our knowledge of Scandinavian mythology. Loki, Odin, Sleipnir, Nidud, Wayland, Sigyn and others have been tentatively identified, some more plausibly than others. The style of the ornament is only marginally useful in dating these stones. The only uniform well-paralleled feature is the trailing skirt worn by the women; it is a detail which is seen, for example, on the Oseberg tapestry (pl. 13), but which also occurs in tenth-century contexts (cf. pl. 6a). The formal animal and interlace ornament, seen particularly in the bordering panels, is difficult to date. Neither are the runic inscriptions which occur on some of the stones sufficient to date them. On the basis of the interlace patterns they have sometimes been dated to the late eighth century or later. But the parallel between the scenes on the stones and on the Oseberg textiles is an indication of a ninth-century date, as is the treatment of certain ornamental details. For example, the chunky interlaced animal on the upper panel of the Tjängvide stone (pl. 12) is obviously a well-developed Style E creature, the slight modifications of form being due to the intractable nature of the material in which it is carved.

It is difficult to construct a chronology of this early Viking art. The dating of Style III must be based on rough appraisals of foreign influences and on the better-dated styles which succeed it. Available evidence, however, suggests that Style III was introduced in the second half of the eighth century and had begun to give way to its successors before the middle of the ninth century. The rarity of Style III ornament in the Birka graves, which start c. 800, suggests that it was not a very long-lived style in Sweden.

The Borre style

The next style to be considered, the Borre style, is named after the bridle mounts found in the rich barrow burial at Borre in Vestfold, Norway. The Borre style first appeared towards the end of the first half of the ninth century and continued in use until well into the second half of the tenth century. For much of its life it was used alongside the Jellinge style (see pp. 299 – 303) which, as far as we can judge, first emerged c. 870 and continued in use until practically the end of the tenth century.

Three main motifs are represented in the art of the Borre style. The first and most important is a simple form of interlaced ribbon (pl. 16f). The interlaced pattern is a symmetrical two-strand plait, the intersections of which are bound by a ring which encloses a hollow-sided lozenge. The motif is most often found on strap-ends, where it often terminates in an animal mask. The second motif (pl. 16h) is derived from the gripping beast of Style III. It consists of a quadruped with a mask-like face, the ribbon-like body of which curves below the head in an arc between the

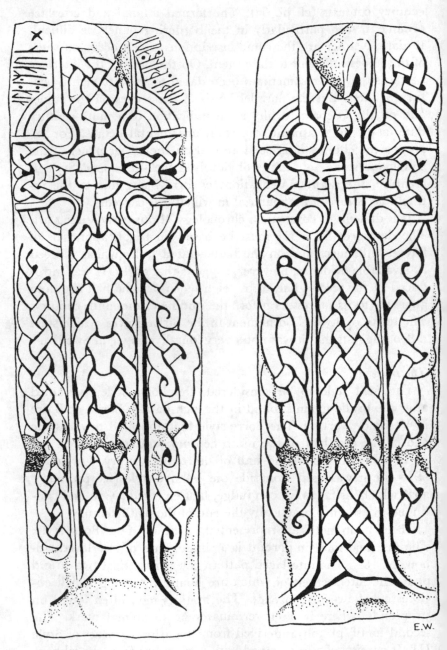

Fig. 48. Gaut's Cross, Kirk Michael, Isle of Man.

two hips. The legs grip the body of the animal or the border of the field in which it is placed. The third motif (pl. 16g) consists of a backward-looking animal of more-or-less normal proportions, with spiral hips and a pigtail or lappet. Its claw-like feet sometimes grip the border of the field in which it stands.

All the Borre bridle mounts, and indeed most of the objects which are decorated in this style, are made of cast bronze or silver. The linear elements of the ornament are often embellished with a series of transverse nicks, a feature which suggests that the style was first developed in filigree wire, the nicked bands imitating in a less expensive medium the appearance of beaded wire. Indeed, it may be claimed that the style is best represented on objects embellished with gold or silver filigree, although it should be noted that the backward-looking animal rarely occurs in this medium. A typical Borre gripping beast executed in filigree is to be seen on the silver brooch from Finkarby, Taxinge, Sweden (pl. 16e), where the heads of four animals are placed in the centre of the object with their bodies disposed regularly round the rest of the field. A happy elaboration of the interlace motif is on the gold filigree mount from a ship-burial at Lackalänge, Skåne (pl. 16d), while there is a more luxurious form of it displayed on the gold spur and strap-end from Værne Kloster, Rød, Norway (pl. 18a), where the bands of the interlace terminate in animal heads of a type that reflects some influence from the contemporary Jellinge style.

The Borre style is found throughout Scandinavia and the eastern Viking world. It is well known in Viking Age finds from Russia, where some splendid examples have come to light. The richest of these is the silver brooch from Jelets, Voronez, with its heavily elaborate three-dimensional animals, in form not unlike the two-dimensional, backward-looking animals of the Borre find itself. Some Swedish brooches exhibit a similar baroque treatment of the ornament and this suggests that the Jelets object was made in Central Sweden.

The Borre interlace pattern is also found in Britain, particularly on certain crosses from the Isle of Man, of which the cross carved by Gaut Bjǫrnsson at Kirk Michael (fig. 48) is a typical example. This motif, often known as Gaut's ring-chain or the Manx ring-chain, is merely an insular development of the

Borre interlace pattern. The same motif occurs throughout the Viking areas of Britain in the tenth century – in Ireland, in Wales, in Cumberland and even in the southwest of England. The motif often occurs in stone sculpture, but it is also known in other materials – on a bone trial piece from Dublin, on a wooden gaming-board from Ballinderry, and on a metal sword-guard from Hesket in Cumberland. It is one of the most easily recognizable early Scandinavian elements in the art of the British Isles and one which is of great importance in dating the insular material.

The dating of the Borre style is complicated by a lack of firmly-established, early chronological horizons. There is, however, one firm peg on which to hang a date. This is the richest of all the Norwegian gold hoards, that from Hon, which contains a necklace consisting of Borre style pendants and mounted coins (pl. 16a–c). Numismatists have shown that the necklace could not have been assembled later than c. 860 and, as the Borre style pendants were not new when they were adapted for use in this necklace, it seems reasonable to suppose that the style was already developed by the middle of the ninth century. As a number of objects decorated with Borre motifs occur in Danish and Swedish coin hoards which are firmly dated to the last half of the tenth century and as they do not occur in eleventh-century hoards, we may conclude that objects decorated in the style ceased to be produced in the last quarter of the tenth century.

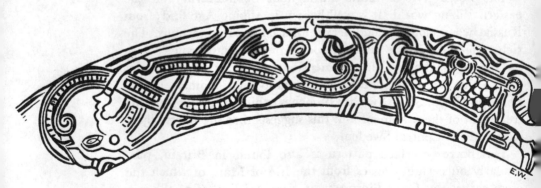

Fig. 49. Ornament of a silver cup from Jelling, Jutland. Scale 1/1.
National Museum, Copenhagen.

The Jellinge style

For much of its history the Jellinge style was contemporaneous with the Borre style. This is adequately demonstrated by the fact that a certain number of objects are decorated in a mixture of both styles. One such, for example, is a brooch from Ödeshög in the Swedish province of Östergötland (pl. 17b). In the centre and at the ends of this brooch are Borre interlace elements, while at the sides can be seen typical Jellinge animals with ribbon-shaped bodies, heads in profile and pigtails interlacing with the body of the animal. The true Jellinge animal takes its name from the ornament of a small, silver, pedestal cup found in one of the mounds at the royal burial site at Jelling in Jutland (fig. 49). The body of the animal is ribbon-like, defined by a double contour enclosing a billeted central panel; the head is in profile and the upper jaw is embellished with a curlicue known as a lip-lappet; it nearly always has a pigtail, and often has a well-defined spiral hip. Jellinge style animals are often surrounded by, or involved with, ribbon interlace, while leaf-like tendrils spring from the lappets or the limbs to add to the rich confusion of each motif. Such a florid style can be seen on the crest of a wooden horse-collar found at Søllested on the Danish island of Fyn (pl. 18c).

The Jellinge style is in the mainstream of Scandinavian art; it has its source both in the gripping beast of the Borre style (from which the ribbon-like body is presumably derived) and in Style III. The open hip of Style III can be seen, for example, on the animal on the crest of another Danish horse-collar from Mammen in Jutland (pl. 18b). The ribbon-like animal, which is merely a normalized version of the animals of the Borre style and Style III, probably had its origins in the pre-Viking ornament called Style D.

Although in Scandinavia it only survives in metalwork, the Jellinge style is best seen in the colonies in stone sculpture. In the generation which followed the initial settlement of Yorkshire *c.* 875, craftsmen in northeast England began to produce carvings, usually memorial crosses, in a version of this Scandinavian style. The Viking settlers took over the idea of stone sculpture from the Anglo-Saxons who had long been erecting stone memorial crosses over their dead. We do not know whether the Vikings attempted to carve the stones themselves or whether, as seems more likely, they commissioned Anglo-Saxon craftsmen to carve ornamental detail in the Scandinavian idiom. At first the products were not particularly successful. They bodged the style and produced poor quality, misunderstood ornament of the type found on the cross-shaft from Middleton in East Yorkshire, illustrated in fig. 50. At Middleton and at a number of other villages along the northern edge of the Vale of Pickering is a series of sculptures probably produced by a single craftsman, which portray animals with bodies more like amorphous sausages than ribbons. These animals, however, fall completely outside the mainstream of

Fig. 50. Ornament of a stone cross from Middleton, Yorkshire.

Anglo-Saxon ornamental tradition and, after a few years, craftsmen carving funerary monuments for the Vikings of northeast England produced a competent, but rather heavy, version of the Jellinge style. It is perhaps best represented on a cross-shaft from Collingham (fig. 51). Occasionally the artist fused Viking and Anglo-Saxon styles, introducing creatures which, while basically Anglo-Saxon in form, have Scandinavian traits. An example of this can be seen in a fragment of Anglo-Saxon metalwork – a nielloed silver plate from the lid of a house-shaped casket (possibly a reliquary) in the British Museum (pl. 19a). Here the layout of the object is completely Anglo-Saxon, as is the material used – silver and niello – and as are the details of the ornament, such as the animals forced into triangular fields between billeted borders, with speckled, triangular bodies. The animals, however, betray Scandinavian influence in their double contour, the free-ring of interlace at the neck, the interlaced ribbon, which clutters up the field, and even in the form of the leg and foot.

From about the year 900, and perhaps earlier, the relatively deserted lands of northwest England were settled by Vikings, many of whom came from the Norwegian settlements in Ireland. Their sculpture is completely different from that of the pre-dominantly Danish settlers of eastern England. It includes elements of the Borre style together with figural scenes derived from the great sculptured 'high-crosses' of Ireland. Ultimately the western and eastern elements coalesced to produce a uniform Viking-influenced style common to much of the north of Eng-

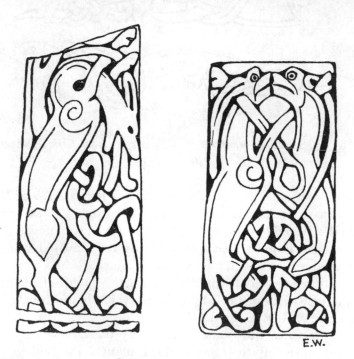

E.W.

Fig. 51. Ornament of a stone cross from Collingham, Yorkshire.

301

land, but in the initial phase of settlement a very distinctive north-western style can be recognized. It is seen at its best on the tall stone cross from Gosforth in Cumberland. The main decorative element on this shaft is a series of interlace patterns, each of which terminates in animal heads. Prominent among them is the Borre ring-chain ornament (which, incidentally, occurs on a fragment of another cross from the same place). Between the lengths of interlacing are panels containing scenes plausibly interpreted as drawn both from the Bible and from pagan Scandinavian ideas about Ragnarǫk. Similar decoration also occurs on other crosses from Cumberland and the northwest of England, sometimes associated with Jellinge style elements. Although there are many completely Scandinavian traits in this art, taken as a whole

E.W.

Fig. 52. Detail of ornament of a stone cross from Kirk Michael,
Isle of Man.

the style seems to be produced outside the mainstream of Norse art, perhaps because it was executed by people at one remove from the Scandinavian stylistic influences – people who drew their models from the secondary Viking styles available in Ire-land, the area from which they chiefly came.

Closely related to this northwest English group of sculptures are the cross-slabs of the Isle of Man, which have already been mentioned in discussing the Borre style. The earliest phase of Viking crosses in this island, typified by those carved by Gaut (fig. 48), gave way to a series which adapted the Jellinge style as one of its main elements. Jellinge animals, which might have come straight off the Søllested horse-collar, can be seen for example on a cross-slab from Kirk Michael (fig. 52). But one of the most extraordinary phenomena of this Manx series, and one that is present throughout the Viking period, from the era of Gaut until the beginning of the eleventh century, is the remarkable group of slabs decorated with scenes from Scandinavian legends and myths. Here Sigurd, Gunnar, Loki, Heimdall and other gods and heroes have been identified. These scenes are firmly rooted in Scandinavian representational art, for the long trailing cloak and the pigtail of a figure like that illustrated in pl. 6a, are very close in form to similar small features in the Oseberg tapestry, the Gotlandic picture stones and certain silver brooches of Swedish origin.

The Jellinge style first appeared in England in the last quarter of the ninth century. This date, together with evidence of associated finds in Norway, seems to indicate that the Jellinge style must have been in existence as early as 860 – 870. Tenth-century hoards containing objects decorated with Jellinge motifs seem to show that it was still in use towards the end of the tenth century (pls. 12, 13).

The Mammen style

It is often extremely difficult to distinguish between the Jellinge style and the Mammen style, for they overlap each other both in time and, to a certain extent, in appearance. The Mammen style is, in effect, an elaboration of the Jellinge style. The animals have more substantial bodies, which are no longer ribbon-shaped, and the spiral hips are strongly emphasized. The bodies are often filled with billets, a development of the single line of billets which often formed the body of the Jellinge animal. An important new element of this style is the extravagant use of tendril ornament as a background to the main ornament. The tendril motif is ultimately derived from the florid acanthus ornament, so commonly found in Carolingian and Ottonian art, which was introduced into Scandinavia on imported objects like the gold trefoil brooch from Hon in Norway. The style takes its name from an iron axe with an inlaid wire pattern excavated at Mammen in Jutland (pl. 20); this, however, is hardly typical, for the style is more usually found in bone, ivory and stone carving.

Fig. 53. Ornament of a stone erected by Thorleif, Kirk Braddan, Isle of Man.

One of the most remarkable objects decorated in this style is a casket of walrus ivory (pl. 19b) which was originally in the treasury of the cathedral church at Bamberg, but is now in a museum in Munich. A tradition first recorded in the nineteenth century says that it was the jewel box of Kunigunde, the wife of the German Emperor Henry II. It is splendidly suited for such a purpose, giving an impression of solidity and safety. The box is low and squat, square in plan with a slightly pitched roof rising to a central point; the ridges of the roof are strengthened by cast bronze bars and there is a key-hole in one panel. The sides are bound by and panelled in bronze. Within the bronze framework is a series of ivory panels floridly decorated in the Mammen style. The animals which occur in most of the fields have heavily billeted bodies and foliate offshoots. The casket belongs to a late phase of the Mammen style and the restlessness of some of the fields is perhaps closer to the ornament in the succeeding, but closely-related, Ringerike style. A more stolid, and certainly earlier, expression of the Mammen style can be seen on the stone erected, according to the runic inscription, by a man named Thorleif at Kirk Braddan in the Isle of Man (fig. 53). Here a clear contact with the Jellinge style can be seen, especially on the decorated edge, where ribbon-like animals occur.

The Mammen style is universal, occurring throughout the Viking sphere of influence from south Russia to the British Isles. But undoubtedly the most historically important – though not stylistically typical – monument decorated in the Mammen style is the famous royal memorial stone (pl. 21) raised by the Danish king, Harald Blue-tooth, certainly before 985 and probably between 983 and 985, in memory of his parents, Gorm and Thyri. This huge semi-pyramidal boulder of red-veined, grey granite stands in the royal cemetery at Jelling in Jutland. It is about eight feet high and is carved on one face with a long runic inscription telling of the circumstances of its decoration (p. 14). The other two faces carry scenes carved in low relief: one bears a figure of the crucified Christ carved in an extremely stylized fashion, while the other depicts a rather ponderous and formal lion entangled with a snake. In style it is closely allied to Mammen art, but its heavy quality removes some of the life from the lion scene of which a more vivacious variant can be seen on the

Fig. 54. The Alstad stone. Universitetets Oldsaksamling, Oslo.

Bamberg casket. As well as being an important manifestation of the art of the Mammen style this stone is significant in that it was probably the direct inspiration for much of the stone sculpture which now begins to appear on mainland Scandinavia for the first time. The king's initiative in creating a carved stone memorial gave a direct impetus to the development of stone sculpture in Scandinavia in the late tenth and early eleventh centuries.

The Mammen style can be dated on the basis of the Jelling stone, for it must have already been well developed when the stone was carved in the 980s. A date somewhere about the middle of the tenth century for the beginning of the fully-fledged Mammen style seems likely. In this case the style was directly succeeded by the Ringerike style, which first appeared early in the first quarter of the eleventh century.

The Ringerike style

The Mammen style links two styles – Jellinge and Ringerike. Ringerike ornament is in effect little more than a logical development of the two earlier styles. It takes its name from a rich district of Norway to the north of Oslo where a number of carved slabs decorated in this style have been found. The main attribute of the style is the subordination of animal ornament to plant ornament. In certain cases the tendrils have completely taken over from the animal and fill the whole field with elegant curves, as on one face of the Alstad stone (fig. 54), which comes from the Ringerike district. All that remains of the animal ornament is the pair of heavy spirals at the base of the design which have their origin in the heavy spiral hips found in earlier Viking art. But the Ringerike artists also understood animal ornament. Consider, for example, the lion and snake motif on the weather vane from Källunge, Gotland (fig. 55a). Here the motif that appeared so pompously on the stone from Jelling is a graceful and lively design; the heavy foliate elements have been elongated, there are more of them, and the curves are much more graceful. One scholar has said of the Ringerike style that it is as though a wind has blown through the turgid animal ornament of the preceding period to produce a design full of movement and life.

The reverse face of the Källunge vane (fig. 55b) exhibits another motif popular in the Ringerike style, a pair of inter-

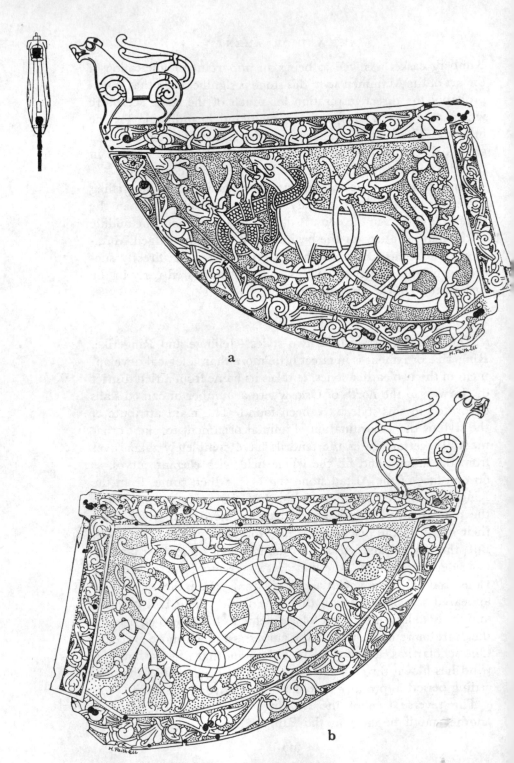

Fig. 55. The two faces of the Källunge vane. Statens Historiska
Museum, Stockholm.

laced looped snakes. This motif was already known in the Mammen style and is here taken to a logical conclusion. It is probably from such designs as this that the rune-masters received the inspiration which turned the snake's body into a band to confine the runic inscription.

The Ringerike stone-carvers did not use finely-drawn snakes. They had not yet achieved complete mastery in the medium and were, in any case, more interested at first in drawing tendril ornament and the much more substantial Ringerike animals. These creatures, which occur most frequently on stones in the south of Sweden, are often of lively character but clumsily placed in the field. Occasionally the Ringerike artist ventured to portray scenes of Christian or heroic significance – there are scenes from the Nativity, for example, on the Dynna stone in Norway.

The Ringerike style also occurs in jewellery. As Christianity began to gain hold in Scandinavia the practice of accompanied burial ceased and objects are consequently found much less frequently in graves. However, at this period many more coin hoards were laid down and these often contain objects of personal adornment. The quality of the objects thus tends to alter, fewer ornaments of base metal are found, more of silver. Excavation of settlement sites and casual finds still provide, of course, a good deal of decorated material.

The Ringerike style was particularly popular and particularly successful in the British Isles. For here, in a period when the English were having their own artistic revival, when masterpieces of manuscript illumination and stone-carving were being produced in the Winchester style, a kingdom was established under a Danish king, Knut, who was surrounded by men with an inbred taste for the Scandinavian ornamental tradition. Although the highly sophisticated Winchester style, with its origin in Carolingian and Ottonian art, remained predominant in England, the two styles, Anglo-Saxon and Viking, were easily reconcilable. The lushness of the early Winchester style acanthus ornament was being replaced in the early years of the eleventh century by a more ragged, tendril-like plant ornament, very similar to, and perhaps influenced by, that of Ringerike tradition. In some of the manuscripts, the two styles blend harmoniously together. An initial letter D, for example, in the Cambridge University Library manuscript Ff.I.23, perhaps painted at Winchcombe, Gloucestershire, in the first quarter of the eleventh century, is, with its elongated tendrils, almost completely Ringerike in appearance (pl. 6b). Such elements of Scandinavian design creep into a great number of what are otherwise Winchester style manuscripts of the same period. Purely Ringerike ornament was also produced in the British Isles. One of the most remarkable examples of it was found in the churchyard of St Paul's Cathedral in London (pl. 26a). It is a stone panel from a sarcophagus, inscribed on one edge with Scandinavian runes and decorated on its face with an animal which is a pure and successful Ringerike interpretation of the lion and snake motif on the Jelling stone. The decoration is executed with extreme competence to produce a classic Viking rendering of a purely Scandinavian motif. The ornament was painted, mainly in blue or black, and the lion was covered with white dots. Such a tombstone as this could only have been carved during the reign of Knut the Great, for before his accession St Paul's was an Anglo-Saxon church which had received, for instance, the bodies of the martyred Archbishop Ælfheah (pp. 66, 103) and of Æthelred the Unready. Another tombstone from St Paul's and a fragment from the church of All Hallow's, Barking, demonstrate the presence of a highly developed Ringerike style in London.

The Ringerike style is also common in the Viking colonies of Ireland, where some of the greatest ecclesiastical treasures of that country were embellished with an almost pure Scandinavian version of this style. The list of such objects is long, but mention must be made of the Shrine of the Cathach (a book shrine), the Shrine of the Crozier of the Abbots of Clonmacnoise, (fig. 56), and the Misach (a book shrine). Together with a group of stone sculptures and a few manuscripts, the ornament of these objects reflects the enormous influence of the Ringerike style on the ecclesiastical art of Ireland, an art apparently controlled by Scandinavian taste and one which was apparently introduced into the country towards the middle of the eleventh century, comparatively late in the history of the style.

The dating of the Ringerike style rests largely on evidence from British sources. Coin hoards and reliably-dated manuscripts, together with the probability that in England the style flourished mainly in the years when the Danish kings were on the throne, suggest that it should be dated to the first half of the eleventh century. It seems likely that in Ireland the style survived in a fully-fledged form until the last quarter of the century and it is an undoubted fact that Ringerike elements were still appearing on Irish objects in the 1120s.

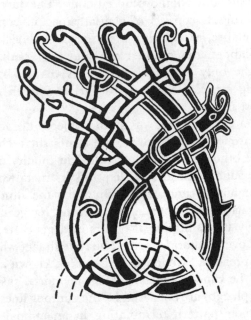

Fig. 56. Detail of the ornament of the Shrine of the Crozier of the Abbots of Clonmacnoise. National Museum, Dublin.

The Urnes style

A feature of the development of the Ringerike style is a gradual refinement of the tendril ornament, a refinement which led to the emergence of the last truly barbarian art of Scandinavia, the Urnes style. The style takes its name from the stave church at Urnes, Sogn, Norway (pl. 27). Here, about 1060, on fertile land by the side of a lake, a rich landowner built what is now one of the most famous churches in Scandinavia. The most exciting surviving portion of the first Urnes church is part of the west wall, which was re-used in the twelfth century in the north wall of the church, as we see it today. There are other remains of the first Urnes building – particularly important is the western gable – but it is the deep carving of the original west portal and wall that reflects the true brilliance of the style to which the church has given its name. The gables are carved in low, flat relief, but the high, round carving of the wall and portal is in places nearly 12 cm. deep. This carving portrays a series of sinuous animals and zoomorphic ribbons. The most distinctive of the Urnes motifs consists of a quadruped in combat with a snake-like creature, each biting the other at the neck. The spiral hip, the lip-lappet, the pointed eye and the combat motif are practically the only features which survive at Urnes itself of earlier Viking art. For the rest, the art is smooth and self-sufficient, almost slick.

Although a fair number of minor objects decorated in the Urnes style are found in Norway, the Urnes stave church stands above all the others and is only rivalled in quality and achievement by the rune stones of Sweden and by metalwork found in hoards throughout Scandinavia. On the rune stones the style is seen in all its facets: it occurs with strong Ringerike overtones or with purely Urnes motifs; it occurs in degenerate, in vivid, in restrained or over-elaborate form. The style in fact was so popular and so widespread in Sweden that it is often known after its chief medium as 'the rune-stone style'. The memorial inscriptions on these stones (pl. 23b) are bordered by the contour lines of a snake's body, the whole pattern terminating in an animal head, often achieving remarkable elegance. Such stones are also found in Norway but it is in Sweden that they occur most frequently.

Once the art of carving stone had developed in southern Scandinavia, Swedish sculptors and rune-masters experimented to bring it to fruition in the high period of the Urnes style. But the story had started earlier, in the period when the Ringerike style still flourished. Transitional motifs are of such frequent occurrence that it is often difficult to attach a distinct stylistic label to the art of a stone or a brooch found in Sweden. It is, however, possible to demonstrate a clearly-defined typological development of the ornament of the Swedish rune stones from the florid Ringerike style to the final flaccidity of the late Urnes style. Because these transitional steps are most easily recognizable in Sweden, it might be concluded that the Urnes style developed in Sweden rather than in Norway. But such a judgement might be false in view of the fact that rune stones are also found in Norway – the country which has produced some of the finest wood-carving of the Urnes style.

For the first time we begin to learn a little about the artists who carved the stones, for they begin to sign their work. Some stones even record that the inscription was coloured. A stone from Nybble, Överselö, Södermanland, for example, has an inscription which is translated thus:

> Äsbjörn carved the stone,
> coloured as a memorial,
> he bound it with runes.

Gylla erected it in memory of her husband Gerbjörn and Gudfrid in memory of his father.

> He was the best yeoman
> in Kil.
> Let him read who can.

Sometimes the runes were carved by one person and the colour added by another, as on another Södermanland stone apparently by the same carver as the Nybble stone, from Gerstaberg, Ytterjärna:

> Äsbjörn cut and Ulv painted.

Occasionally we have records to show that the runes were carved by a man other than the sculptor.

Colour rarely survives on Scandinavian stones, but two recent finds show the colours in reasonably good condition. At Köping, on the Baltic island of Öland, a number of stone fragments were discovered, painted in black, red and white. The black is usually made from soot and the red is red lead. The same colours – together with blue – were found on a gravestone from St Lars church in Linköping. Similar colours have been found painted on wood carved in the Urnes style from the excavations at Hørn-

313

ing church in Denmark, and at an earlier period on Mammen style wooden fragments from Jelling in Jutland.

The Urnes style was soon to die in Scandinavia, but it survived for some time in the British Isles, where it did not finally disappear until after the middle of the twelfth century. It occurs on a few English pieces, most interestingly perhaps on a crozier found in what was perhaps the tomb of Bishop Ranulf Flambard of Durham (died 1123). It also occurs in English sculpture but its most remarkable blossoming is in the art of the metalworker and the scribe in Ireland. Some of these objects are reliably dated as, for example, the Shrine of the Bell of St Patrick's Will which is inscribed:

A prayer for Domnall Ó Lachlaind [King of Ireland 1083 – 1121] under whose auspices this bell was made. And for Domnall, successor of Patrick [abbot of Armagh 1091 – 1105], in whose house it was made. And for Cathalan Ó Mael-Challand, steward of the bell. And for Cu Duilig Ó Inmainen and his sons who covered it.

The shrine must therefore be dated between 1091 and 1105. Similarly, one of the most important of all pieces of Irish metalwork, the Cross of Cong, can be dated by inscription to c. 1123. But perhaps the most attractive piece of metalwork executed in this style is a slightly damaged rectangular plate from Holy Cross (pl. 24b) which shows various animals strikingly similar to those on the portal of the Urnes stave church. This is typical of a whole group of objects of Irish origin which show the final flowering of the true Urnes style – all produced in a country with a strong Norwegian colonial element.

The dating of the style depends on a large series of hoards and inscribed objects, which indicate that it flourished in Scandinavia between, say, 1050 and 1140, while in Ireland the period may well have extended down to about 1160 or 1170.

This is the end of the formal history of Viking art, for in the twelfth century it was replaced by a true Romanesque art (cf. pl. 28) derived from various west European and insular schools, but it is by no means the end of the story. In the late medieval folk-art of the North some of the styles which have been discussed in the course of this chapter are clearly seen. The medium used by the folk-artist was the traditional medium of the North – wood. The stone sculptors, like those who carved the fine capitals of the chapter house or vestry of Trondheim Cathedral, about 1175, drew their inspiration and technique from western Europe, but the sculptors of a wooden horse-collar (pl. 24a) from Lom, Gudbrandsdal, Norway, in a roughly contemporary or even later period, were using a gripping-beast motif which was obviously based on an ancient monument. The twelfth-century artists who carved certain stone fonts in Norway and Sweden, embellished altar frontals in Denmark and carved wooden objects in Norway with the Borre style ring-chain motif, were using old and familiar patterns many centuries after they had gone out of fashion. The same conservatism is also apparent in some of the scenes of pagan myth and legend which appear in Norwegian Christian contexts, like the scenes from the Sigurd cycle on the church portal from Hylestad, Setesdal, Norway (frontispiece).

In the deep and isolated valleys of Norway and on the farms of late medieval Iceland, traditions of the Viking Age lingered on. Stories were told and written and read, old poetry and old customs survived, and alongside them, the peasant artist was happy to continue to use the motifs developed by his distant Viking ancestors. Perhaps the motifs never died out, for in the great resurgence of decorative art in Scandinavia at the end of the nineteenth century, under the influence of *art nouveau* and in a period of romantic excitement about the Viking past, the northern artist blended into his repertoire many of the legends and art forms of the Viking Age.

More than any other single feature of their material culture, the art of the Vikings gives us some insight into the cultural achievement of Scandinavia in this period. The skill of the craftsman and the intricacy of his ornament add to our understanding of the Viking North. Social and other factors, which might otherwise have remained hidden, are illuminated in this part of the archaeological record. From the great carvings of the Oseberg ship we gain some idea of the power and wealth of a royal or aristocratic family. From the standard ornament of the Borre style we gain some impression of the vast area over which Viking taste held sway.

Viking art cannot, however, allow us to enter into the mind of the patron, nor of the craftsman who produced the objects decorated in these strange styles. The psychologist might try to make something of the intricate twists and turns of some of the patterns, but only from poetry and runic inscriptions can we obtain any confident knowledge of the mentality of the Scandinavians of the Viking Age. The artists were working in a period when western Europe was producing ornaments of a uniquely high quality and they must have seen, even owned, objects exemplifying this art; indeed they used some such objects in their own daily life. They were influenced by them – the acanthus leaves of the florid Mammen style illustrate this point – but they never felt it necessary to plagiarize. The Viking artist saw and understood the ornament produced by his continental contemporaries, he tore the heart out of it and then adapted it without self-consciousness to his own vital idiom.

The artist in society

Although the quality of the craftsmanship of the Viking period is so accomplished, it is difficult to gain any real idea of the social position of the artist. There is no single word in the old Scandinavian languages for an artist. The maker of any object was called a smith, and he can be distinguished as a goldsmith (*gullsmiðr*), a sculptor or stone-smith (*steinsmiðr*), an iron-smith (*járnsmiðr*), silversmith (*silfrsmiðr*) or woodworker (*trésmiðr*). A skilful man was called *hagr*, and such a word was used as a nickname; its basic meaning is 'handy' or 'dexterous'.

In the literary sources, the weapon-smith is looked on as a much more important man than the jeweller. There is a story in Saxo to illustrate this. The old warrior-retainer, Starkad, derides a goldsmith who was arrogant enough to make Helga, the sister of Ingeld, his mistress. The goldsmith is described as base-born but wealthy, and Starkad calls him a 'cinder-blower'. His mouth reeked of ashes, his hands were filthy with charcoal and his palms hardened by use of tongs. Starkad distinguished two kinds of smith: the weapon-smith, of whom he approved, and others who were mere jewellers. He condemns these latter by saying they are of a softer temper and that 'Nature has crushed with cowardice the hands that she has gifted with skill'. Saxo cannot resist the age-old dig at the goldsmith for stealing the precious metal with which he worked.

It would seem that most artists were men. It is interesting to note, however, that just after 1200 there is a reference to a crozier of walrus ivory, 'made with such skill that no-one had ever seen one so well made in Iceland', which was carved by a certain Margaret, the 'most point, skilful-(*oddhǫgust*) in all Iceland. The same woman also carved part of an altar piece for Skálholt. We know the names of a number of other artists. Thórd hreda, for example, who lived in the tenth century, was credited with great skill as a builder and carver and has even had the well-known Flatatunga panels attributed to him (pl. 23a), although these were carved long after his death. About 1050 we hear of a man called Gyllingar-Kali (Gilding-Kali), who was skilful with gold and silver. A class of craftsmen who begin to emerge by name in the eleventh century are the moneyers: it is interesting to see that some of them were foreigners, men like Ælfric of Wallingford, Berkshire, who struck coins for Olaf, 'king in Sigtuna', c. 1000. Jewellers are mentioned quite often in the period after 1100, and from this time forward there are a number of references by name to craftsmen working on reliquaries and shrines.

Very few signed objects survive from the early Viking period. The Swedish rune stones are the only major exception. In the eleventh century it is possible to identify certain schools of sculpture in Sweden dominated by craftsmen who sign their names on their work: Asmund, Fot, Balle and Öpir. Not all carvers painted or carved their own stones, as we saw, for example, on the Gerstaberg stone (p. 313). But in most cases we can be fairly sure that both runes and ornament were carved by the same people, as for example in the Isle of Man where both inscription and ornament on some stones were carved by Gaut.

It seems likely that artists were normally free men. One finds implications of such a status in the *Rígspula*, for example, where Smiðr figures as one of Karl's sons (p. 81). It was quite possible to make money as a craftsman, as appears for example in the story from Saxo quoted above, and perhaps one can quote here the case of Thorstein Skeggjason, who round about 1200 was the most skilful goldsmith in Iceland. He earned a lot of money in a short time, but he spent it all and finished up with no more than

enough for food and clothing. Eventually the chief called Gudmund the Precious invited him to come and live with him and
later arranged for him to marry a woman who owned a farm.

We may presume that many craftsmen, like the moneyer
Ælfric, were itinerant, travelling from one patron to the next.
This is obviously true of some of the rune-stone carvers, whose
work is found over a wide area. On the other hand the jeweller
produced more easily portable goods and may well have led a
settled existence. The jeweller's workshop at Helgö, for example,
(pp. 203–5) has produced moulds and waste material which indicate a permanent and long-lived establishment. The jeweller
would presumably prefer to live in a town, if that were possible,
in order to protect his wares and to be available to his various
patrons. It is likely that precious metal for manufacture into
ornaments was provided by the patron and we have hints of this
in the literary sources. We must imagine however that many
objects of base metal would be produced in bulk and perhaps
sold to middlemen.

Poetry

Eddaic and scaldic verse

Norse poetry is conventionally divided into two kinds, one called 'eddaic', the other 'scaldic'. The first gets its name from the word *Edda*. This is properly the title of a thirteenth-century handbook of poetics by Snorri Sturluson (p. 320), but in the seventeenth century it was also applied, erroneously, to the Icelandic codex in which most early verse of this kind has been preserved. Poetry of a related kind is also to be found in the Icelandic *fornaldarsögur*, written stories from the thirteenth century and later about Norse heroes who were believed to have lived before the settlement of Iceland about A.D. 900. Some of this verse was composed by the writers of these sagas, but some of it also came to them through tradition. It has been published under the convenient title of *Eddica minora*.

The term 'scaldic' is derived from *skald*, 'poet', a word of uncertain etymology. It often implies a kind of professional status, as is already apparent in the first certain record of its use, when a poet, about A.D. 965, referred to a king's treatment of the scalds he kept in his service.

Eddaic verse is anonymous and is composed in relatively simple language and metres. The themes are mythological or drawn from heroic legends, some the property of the Germanic world as a whole, others of purely Norse origin. Scaldic poems are usually attributed to named poets and many of them are in praise of named princes. Scaldic metres have strict rules and may be elaborate in structure, while typical scaldic diction is much richer and remoter from everyday speech than that of eddaic verse. Lines of demarcation between the two kinds cannot, however, be rigidly maintained, nor need we suppose that their making and transmission were in different hands. We do not know under what circumstances of inspiration and patronage the anonymous verse came into existence. The anonymity seems related to the fact that the subject-matter was looked on as public property and perhaps the freer verse-forms were also regarded as a common inheritance. Yet the individuality of much of this poetry is also clear, and it seems unlikely that it was the work of entertainers who regarded themselves as fundamentally different from scalds. Scalds were professional eulogists and 'recorders' in the service of great men, but we know too that they were entertainers who might travel from lord to lord and who, if called on for pastime, could recite other verse besides their own. They must have been able to provide poetry of the eddaic kind, and they doubtless modified and improved it and made more like it to suit current tastes. This does not mean that they necessarily thought as highly of it as of their own skilful art.

In the years about 1220 the Icelandic chieftain and historian, Snorri Sturluson, composed the handbook of poetics which he called *Edda*. It comprises a prologue and three parts: one, beautifully written, on the mythological stories which provided much of the subject-matter and diction of early poems; one on the language of poetry, with a wealth of example; and one on prosody, in the shape of a long laudatory poem whose stanzas illustrate different metrical forms. Snorri can be mistaken or misleading but his book is an outstanding piece of medieval scholarship and without it our understanding of Norse poetry would be harshly crippled.

The metres

Rēð Þiōðrīkʀ	*Ruled Thjodrek*
hinn þurmōði,	*the thought-daring,*
stilliʀ flutna,	*lord of seamen,*
strandu Hraiðmaraʀ;	*land of Hreidmarish;*
sitiʀ nu garuʀ	*sits he now chafing*
a guta sinum,	*on charger surely,*
skialdi umb fatlaðʀ,	*buckler on shoulder,*
skati Mæringa.	*best of Mæringar.*
Ár var alda	*Early ages*
þar er Ymir bygði,	*there that Ymir settled,*
vara sandr né sær	*was not sand nor sea*
né svalar unnir,	*nor sea-waves chilling,*

jǫrð fannsk æva	*earth was never*
né upphiminn,	*nor up-heaven,*
gap var ginnunga	*ginnung-gap was then*
en gras hvergi.	*but grass nowhere.*

The first of these verses is part of the runic inscription on the Rök stone in Östergötland, written about 800. The second is from the Icelandic *Vǫluspá*, composed about the year 1000. (The translations given here and elsewhere in this section, on metre, are intended as imitations of the alliteration and verse movement. As will become clear later, pp. 362–4, adequate English renderings of much Norse verse can generally only be given in prose.)

These verses show the Norsemen's inheritance of the two chief elements in the Germanic prosodic system. One of these is the basic metrical unit in which a pair of strongly stressed, long syllables, are set among other syllables of weaker stress and indifferently long or short. Metrically long syllables were essentially those in which a short vowel was followed by two or more consonants (*stilliʀ, strandu*) and those in which a long vowel (one written with a length-mark in the first stanza, elsewhere those with an acute accent in the orthography adopted here and the digraphs *æ* and *œ*) or diphthong was followed by at least one consonant (*Reð, æva, Hraið-*). Two short syllables could stand for one long one (*Ýmir, svalar*); this is called 'resolution'. Distribution of stressed syllables among weaker ones was made in accordance with certain established patterns, but it was usual to mix these patterns, not constantly to repeat the same one. The other traditional element is the combination of these smallest units in pairs (so-called *a*- and *b*-lines) by the use of alliteration. This is done in the Rök verse by initial *þ-, st-, g-, sk-*, found in one word in the *a*-line and repeated, as is usual, in the first stressed syllable in the *b*-line. In the *Vǫluspá* example the alliteration is found in two words in the *a*-line as well as in the first stressed syllable of the *b*-line (e.g. *sandr – sær – svalar*). It also has two instances of vowel alliteration, in lines 1 – 2 and 5 – 6. The rule was that all vowel sounds alliterate with each other, and also with words beginning with *j-* (pronounced like *y* in 'yes').

Organization of the paired *a*- and *b*-lines in longer sequences could produce, as in Old English, Old Saxon and Old High

German, paragraph structures that were rhetorical, not prosodic, units. But we see at once from the above examples that the Norse poets composed in stanzas; and their further innovations were all based on stanza structures that provide combined prosodic and rhetorical units.

The changes in the Norse language in the so-called Syncope Period (p. 2) were more or less over by the beginning of the Viking Age. They must have had a strong influence on metrical developments. In seventh-century Danish runic inscriptions we meet, for example, the proper names *HariwolfR* and *HaþuwolfR*. Two hundred years later these names of three syllables had become *Herjolfr*, with two syllables, and *Hálfr*, with only one. The general reduction in the number of unstressed syllables (prefixes were affected as well as medial and final sounds) naturally produced a shorter line, and the process was carried farther and regularized by influential poets who produced metrical varieties with a fixed number of syllables in the basic two-stress unit. Other major innovations are mentioned below.

Of the five chief metres found in early Norse verse one, *fornyrðislag*, is composed both with and without a fixed number of syllables to the line; its weightier variant called *málaháttr* normally has a regular number; two others, *kviðuháttr* and the *dróttkvætt* metre, which are never used for eddaic verse, are rigorously syllable-counting; while the fifth, *ljóðaháttr*, shows no tendency towards a fixed number of syllables.

Fornyrðislag, 'metre of ancient words', is exemplified in the two stanzas given above. In syllable-counting form it has normally four syllables to the line (or five when a permissible 'resolution', like *Ymir, svalar* mentioned above, stands in place of a long stressed syllable). About 950 Egil Skalla-Grímsson composed his 'Head-redemption' in *fornyrðislag* with end-rhyme, mostly in couplets but sometimes with fourfold repetition. It is a most impressive achievement, and it saved his life, but the form found few imitators.

In the following stanza from the old poem *Atlakviða* (p. 350), we find heavier lines than in the stanzas given above, with more syllables in them and more three-syllable compounds carrying both prime and secondary stress.

Drukku þar dróttmegir,	*Courtmen there caroused with*
en dyljendr þǫgðu,	*(but cunning spoke not)*
vín í valhǫllu,	*wine in walls stately,*
reiði sáz þeir Húna;	*wrath they dreaded Hunnish;*
kallaði þá Knéfrøðr	*Knéfrød he then called out,*
kaldri rǫddu,	*cold his voicing,*
seggr hinn suðrœni	*spoke the southerner,*
sat á bekk háum.	*sat on bench lofty.*

Like *Vǫlundarkviða* (p. 347), which is of comparable age and also shows much metrical variety, *Atlakviða* must belong to a time and milieu in which poets did not find it tasteful to use only one predominant variety of line in their work. It is also significant that in these poems the stanzas vary from two to fourteen lines in length and so represent an intermediate stage between an uneven paragraph structure and the strict stanza construction of later Norse poetry.

The weightier type of line with five syllables (more with 'resolution') was regularized as *málaháttr*, 'metre of speeches', a name we cannot confidently explain. The first example here is from the early *Haraldskvæði*, composed about 900, and is part of the description of ships at the Battle of Hafrsfjord (p. 41). The second is from the Greenlandic *Atlamál*, probably composed in the eleventh century, maybe later, and describes Gudrun fighting on the side of her brothers.

Hlaðnir oru hǫlða	*Full they were of fighters*
ok hvítra skjalda,	*and flashing bucklers,*
vigra vestrœnna	*western war-lances*
ok valskra sverða;	*and wound-blades Frankish;*
grenjuðu berserkir,	*cried then the bear-pelted,*
guðr var þeim á sinnum,	*carnage they had thoughts of,*
emjuðu ulfheðnar	*wailed then the wolf-coated*
ok ísǫrn dúðu.	*and weapons brandished.*
Sá þá sælborin	*Splendid spectator*
at þeir sárt léku,	*of their sport grievous*
hugði á harðræði	*courage she called forward*
ok hrauzk ór skikkju;	*and cloak abandoned,*

nøkðan tók hon mæki	*bared a sword she lifted*
ok niðja fjǫr varði,	*and brothers' life guarded,*
hæg var at hjaldri	*hurt-full the harming*
hvars hon hendr festi.	*where her hands battered.*

The metre called *kviðuháttr* is a syllable-counting development of the regular *fornyrðislag*, in which the *a*-line has only three syllables, the *b*-line the usual four. It is interesting to discover what stately measures such a terse form can produce: with four stressed syllables in every seven, a deliberate effect is attained which emphasizes for us that the poet is in command of metre and matter alike. The oldest poem in this metre is *Ynglingatal* from about 900, but the stanza below is from *Glælognskviða*, made in 1032 by the Icelandic poet, Thórarin Praise-tongue. He is addressing Knut the Great whose allies had defeated and killed King Ólaf Haraldsson of Norway only two years earlier – but for Thórarin and his friends Ólaf was a martyr whose favour Knut required if he was to hold Norway:

Bið Áleif	*Pray Olaf*
at unni þér	*he unto you*
(hann's goðs maðr)	*(he's God's man)*
grundar sinnar;	*grants his country;*
hann of getr	*he now gets*
af goði sjǫlfum	*from God truly*
ár ok frið	*bounty, peace,*
ǫllum mǫnnum.	*bless'd for mankind.*

We come to the two metres remotest from the Germanic forms represented in English and German sources and from the *fornyrðislag* we started with. They are both independent Norse creations – interesting suggestions that have been made about possible foreign models are not compellingly persuasive – and both are subject to metrical laws that enable us to observe, without understanding, something of the keenness of ear of the Norse poets and their audiences. Both metres were also so nearly perfect in their kind that no basic alteration was made in them in the four hundred years or so that we are considering. The more complex one was much the more productive, but there were special reasons for this.

Ljóðaháttr, 'metre of chants', may well have developed as a special form for magical or cult delivery. Marked features of composition in this metre are repetition and parallelism of expression, also reminiscent of magic charms. A variant of the metre is specifically called *galdralag*, 'magic spell metre' (see below). In all the surviving poems *ljóðaháttr* is used to give somebody's words: these may describe action, but the metre is not used for impersonal narrative.

The metre is made of a pair of *a*- and *b*-lines, each of two stresses and bound by alliteration, as in *fornyrðislag*, followed by a third single line, called the full line, which has its own alliteration and either two or three stressed syllables. The full line completes in a forceful but flexible manner the preceding pair of lines. Normally two such segments of three lines are then combined to form a six-line stanza whose first and second half balance. All lines show great variety in number of syllables and stress distribution patterns, but a long stressed syllable followed by an unstressed syllable was not permitted at the end of the full line. In this position we usually find a short stressed syllable followed by an unstressed syllable or alternatively a long stressed syllable with nothing following (cf. *mikit* and *ǫls* in the stanza on p. 326).

We do not know how old this metre is, but lines of a related kind have been found in the runic inscription on the Eggjum grave-stone from Sogn, Norway, which is dated to not later than about A.D. 700. Among them is a *galdralag* stanza which has been reconstructed thus:

> *Hverr of kom Heráss á*
> *hí á land gotna?*
> *Fiskr ór fjanda vim svimandi,*
> *fogl á fjanda lið galandi.*

'As whom came War-god hither to the land of men? A fish from the torrent of enemies swimming, a bird against troop of enemies screaming.'

This shows the miniature 'incremental repetition' which is normal in the additional line of this metre, echoing and varying the full line of the regular *ljóðaháttr* triplet.

Ljóðaháttr is found in a number of the mythological poems of the *Edda*, including *Hávamál* and *Grímnismál* (pp. 342–4, 338), both of which are of ancient, perhaps even ninth-century, origin. The first instances of the metre that can be dated with some accuracy, because they are in poems in honour of known kings, are from the first half of the tenth century. The following example of the metre is from *Hávamál*:

Byrði betri	*Burden better*
berrat maðr brautu at	*bears none abroad with him*
en sé mannvit mikit;	*than a cool discretion;*
vegnest verra	*picnic poorer*
vegra hann velli at	*packs no departing one*
en sé ofdrykkja ǫls.	*than a big load of beer.*

The glory of Norse metrical art is the stanza form called *dróttkvætt*, the lordly metre fit for the *drótt*, the élite body of warriors in the king's personal following. The only original 'document' from the Viking Age itself containing such a stanza is the runic inscription on the Karlevi stone in Öland, carved in the late tenth century or about 1000. In normalized form it reads thus (a prose translation is found on p. 329):

> *Folginn liggr hinns fylgðu*
> *flestr vissi þat mestar*
> *dæðir dolga Þrúðar*
> *draugr í þeimsi haugi;*
> *munat reið-Viðurr ráða*
> *rógstarkr í Danmarku*
> *Endils jarmungrundar*
> *ørgrandari landi.*

The basic unit of the metre is a three-stress line, normally of six syllables, always ending with a long stressed syllable followed by an unstressed one (the kind not permitted at the end of the full line in *ljóðaháttr*). It is this three-stress line with its distinctive cadence which is the real innovation in Norse poetry, but we do not know its origin. These units are linked as *a*- and *b*-lines by alliteration, two initial sounds in the *a*-line matched by the start of the first stressed syllable of the *b*-line. There is also a system of internal rhyme; in each line the last stressed syllable must contain vowel and consonant that chime with those in an earlier syllable. In the *a*-line a half-rhyme should be found, as in *folg-* and *fylg-*, *dæð-* and *Þrúð-*, *reið-* and *ráð*, *End-* and *-grund-* in the *a*-lines above; while in the *b*-line the rhyme should be full, as above in *flest-* and *mest-*, *draug-* and *haug-*, *-stark-* and *-mark-*, *-grand-* and *land-*. The technical term for the half-rhyme is *skothending*, which means something like a 'glancing hit', and for the full rhyme, *aðalhending*, a 'main hit'. In the oldest *dróttkvætt* poetry these rhymes appear as much embellishments as constituents of the metre, and their regular usage only became established in the course of the tenth century. The stanza contains eight lines, and there is normally, as here, a marked syntactic division at the end of line four to make the whole two balancing halves. The sense is spread over the quatrain, in one, two or three clauses, separate or related by subordination, but a single line seldom holds a self-contained statement.

Of a quatrain's twenty-four syllables twelve must be metrically long and stressed; six of them must bear alliteration, three and three; four of them must give half-rhyme and four full rhyme, each two and two. The poet has no choice in the disposition of four of the rhyming syllables and of two of the alliterating syllables. It is no wonder that such verse-making ranked as an *íþrótt*, a skilled feat, and that the poets looked on themselves as craftsmen, *smiðir*, 'makers, smiths', *hagir*, 'dexterous', like the artists in wood and metal. In the appreciation of this poetry one cannot avoid an elementary admiration for the sheer accomplishment of it, but this is nothing to the pleasure we get from seeing how a good poet weds meaning to the music as he moves gracefully, forcefully, wittily amid the great formality.

The only important development on the basis of the *dróttkvætt* stanza was *hrynhendr háttr*, 'flowing metre'. All the rules of *dróttkvætt* applied but the basic unit was extended from a three-stress, six-syllable line to a four-stress, eight-syllable line. This lengthening of the line resulted in a less flexible movement, with statement and line coinciding more often in extent and with a tendency to regular falling rhythm with marked caesura after the third or fourth syllable. It can be ponderous, solemn and expressive; but the regularity can also become wearisome and trivial to modern ears. The following quatrain is from the first long poem we know in this metre, composed about 1045 by the Icelander, Arnór Thórdarson, in honour of King Magnús of Norway (the italicized words in each couplet go together):

Ungan frák þik, eyðir, *þrøngva*	*Boyish you were,* bane of, *staying,*
ulfa gráðar, *þeira ráði;*	barest wolf-greed, *men unruly;*
skyldir *stǫkk með skæðan þokka*	helmsman *ran with hostile thinking,*
skeiðarbrands *fyr þér ór landi.*	high-ship-front's, *from you and country.*

When stanzas occur singly or in small groups, they are called *lausavísur,* 'occasional verses'. A sequence of stanzas in scaldic metre making a poem on one theme is usually called either *vísur,* 'verses', or *flokkr,* 'flock' of stanzas. The most respected form was called *drápa,* a sequence of at least twenty stanzas interspersed with the same or varied refrain stanzas at regular intervals. The meaning of this name is not entirely certain. The best suggestion is that it got the name because such a poem was *drepit stefjum,* 'fitted with refrains'.

The usual verb meaning 'to utter in verse' is *kveða* (cognate for example with archaic English 'quoth'). This verb, however, also means 'say, declare', without reference to verse, so that it does not seem likely that the delivery of poetry was markedly different from that of other speech before an audience. We have no evidence of musical accompaniment of any kind. From the same root as *kveða* come *kvæði,* the usual general term for 'poem, sequence of stanzas', and *kviða,* 'poem'; the latter gives its name to the metre, *kviðuháttr,* but as a separate appellative it is not restricted to verse in this form.

The diction

In the verses quoted above a number of words occur that are either not found in prose sources or, if found, have a somewhat different sense. Thus, the plain meaning of a word *goti* is 'Goth', but in the Eggjum lines on p. 325 it means 'man' in general (*gotna*, gen. pl.), and in the Rök verse on p. 320 the same word means 'horse' – from an original sense of 'horse of Gothic breed' it has come to be used of any fine animal. A word like *mækir*, 'sword', used in the *Atlamál* stanza on p. 324, is an ancient Germanic word, common also in Old English poetry, for example; while *hjaldr*, used to mean 'battle' in the same stanza, is an obvious metaphorical transfer from the word's etymological sense of 'noise, tumult'. Such words as these, proper in poetic diction but otherwise seldom used, are called *heiti*, 'appellations'. They exist in great number as substitute terms for objects that need constant mention in Norse poetry – princes, men, women, ships, horses, weapons, and so forth.

A kenning is the form of circumlocution exemplified in a phrase like OE *hranrād*, 'whale-road', for sea. Such expressions are not much used in eddaic poetry and those that occur are simple in structure. (It may be noted that identification of an individual by a statement of family relationship, as when Thor is called 'son of Earth', for example, is not counted a kenning.) The scalds however make such extensive and elaborate use of kennings in their verse that these are regarded as the prime feature of 'scaldic' style.

A kenning at its simplest comprises two terms, one of which is the 'base-word', while the other is a word to which the 'base-word' is made to relate, so that taken together the terms offer a meaning neither has independently. The base-word and the second term may be expressed by substitute terms, like *heiti* but only usable within kennings, or they may themselves be expressed by other kennings. The Karlevi stanza quoted on p. 326 says this:

Tree of Thrúd of hostilities, the man whom the greatest virtues accompanied – most men knew that – lies buried in this mound; a more upright chariot-Vidur of wondrous-wide ground of Endil will not rule, strife-strong, land in Denmark.

According to the mythology, Thrúd was Thor's daughter, but in this verse her name is used unspecifically for 'goddess, divine female figure'. The 'goddess of hostilities' is a kenning for the valkyrie, who in pagan times was thought to attend battles to select those who were to die, and the valkyrie's 'tree' is the warrior. It was in fact the convention in poetry to regard valkyries themselves as personifications of strife, so that one could equally well read the kenning here as 'tree of strife' – this particular 'tree' is the warrior in either case.

The elements of a kenning are normally related in this genitival way. The word in the genitive may be broadly attributive or strictly possessive or it may express the object of the verbal idea contained in the base-word. The elements of a kenning may also be combined in a compound. Some of these points are exemplified in the kenning for 'man' in the second half of this Karlevi stanza: 'chariot-Vidur of wondrous-wide ground of Endil'. Endil is the name of a legendary sea-king, and the sea-king's 'ground' is the ocean. That leaves us 'chariot-Vidur of ocean', the same as 'Vidur of the chariot of ocean', or 'Vidur of the ship'. Vidur is one of Odin's names, and the ship's 'god' is its captain.

A kenning like the first one for warrior here is said to be 'doubled' but when a kenning is built up further, as in the second example, it is said to be 'extended' (*rekin*). The two comparatively elaborate kennings in this verse have many parallels and could be counted mere stereotyped periphrases for 'man'. We cannot judge their full import, but in this context it does not seem likely that they were felt to be empty of meaning. They made explicit the dead king's achievements as a warrior and a leader at sea; and depth is added by the way in which the poet uses the second 'extended' kenning to parallel the statement about the man who ruled 'land in Denmark' by adding the notion that he also held sway over other 'ground' – ground that was not land at all, but just the opposite, 'sea'. Kennings may thus both add dimensions and have something of the wit of a conceit, so they need to be considered closely before they are dismissed as merely conventional.

Besides divine names, common base-words for 'man' include many *nomina agentis* and words for 'tree'. Of the former kind are *eyðir ulfa gráðar* in the *hrynhent* verse above, p. 328, 'destroyer of hunger of wolves', the feeder of carrion beasts, the victorious warrior; and the common type, 'diminisher of gold', the generous man. When a base-word 'tree' is found, it is usually in expressions like 'tree of battle', as in the Karlevi stanza above; and for 'tree' may be used both generic names like *viðr*, 'wood', *lundr*, 'grove', and specific names like *almr*, 'elm', *pollr*, 'fir'. Occasionally a tree-word is homonymous with a *nomen agentis*, so that *reynir*, 'rowan', for example, is hard or impossible to distinguish from *reynir*, 'tester'. (Snorri thought that such homonymy explained the use of tree-words in kennings, but they doubtless have much older origins.) Tree-words (of feminine gender) are also used in kennings for women, along with names of goddesses and other supernatural beings.

Battle, ships, weapons, armour, gold and silver are usual in completing man-kennings; base-words for women are linked with clothing, gold and jewellery (things they wear), drink and drinking-vessels (things they serve). These objects themselves were also frequently expressed through kennings. Here for example is Snorri's preliminary description of how gold may be described by their means: it may be called fire of Ægir, leaves of Glasir, hair of Sif, headband of Fulla, tears of Freyja, speech and voice or words of giants, drops of Draupnir and rain or shower of Draupnir or of the eyes of Freyja, otter-atonement, dire atonement of the gods, seed-corn of Fyris-fields, mound-roof of Hǫlgi, fire of water of any kind and fire of the forearm and hand, and stone and skerry and gleam of forearm and hand. The last of these kenning types may be termed 'natural', while all the others are explained by myths or legendary stories, many of which Snorri tells in his *Edda*.

Another subject constantly referred to by poets is their own art, and Snorri tells an elaborate story to explain the chief kennings used for it. The gods made a truce with their enemies called Vanir and, as a symbol of the truce, members of each side spat into a tub; out of this the gods later made a being called Kvasir, whose wisdom and knowledge no man could plumb. He was killed by dwarves who mixed his blood with honey, and from this came the mead of poetry. They kept it in three vats, all with names of their own. The dwarves had to pay the precious drink to a giant called Suttung in order to save themselves from drowning on a skerry where he had put them. After seducing Suttung's daughter, Odin stole the mead and flew back to the home of the gods in eagle shape, carrying the mead in his gullet. On account of all this, poetry is called Kvasir's blood, the dwarves' drink, liquid of the vats in which it was stored, the dwarves' ship (because it ferried them to safety), Suttung's mead, sea of Hnitbjǫrg (the place where Suttung kept it in his daughter's care), Odin's catch or discovery or drink or gift, and the drink of the gods, since Odin shared it with his fellows as well as with men capable of creating poetry.

Kennings like these for gold and the scaldic art could be readily varied by the use of *heiti* and extended by 'doubled' and 'extended' kennings, so that the poets had an extremely rich and adaptable diction at their disposal. Kennings, however, have substantive function and must necessarily be construed as subjects or predicates. It will be obvious that if a poet calls a ship 'horse of the sea', he can then continue with a verb appropriate to the movement of a horse or with one appropriate to the movement of a ship or with some neutral verb that might be used of either – 'gallop' or 'glide' or 'rush', perhaps. We often find coherency of the first kind, and it may be extended over the whole clause (so that the 'horse of the sea gallops over the field of the sail', for example), or even further. Snorri thought this coherent style (*nýgervingar*) showed the best taste, and the stanza he composed to illustrate it offers an extreme example:

The wise prince makes battle adders crawl the scabbard's way; the mighty snake of strife goes quick from the straight baldric-nest; the serpent of the squabble of swords can seek the brook of blood; the worm of the slain moves by thought-paths to the warm slaughter-river.

The image throughout is of the snake leaving its nest and making for water. Snake figures as the base-word in four expressions for sword, its nest is the base-word for scabbard; the snake-sword crawls from and by way of the scabbard and goes by way of the enemy's breast ('thought-paths') to the water it seeks, which is blood.

Snorri says that when this congruence is lacking the verse is called 'monstrous' (*nykrat*). It is clear, however, that many poets did not object to and some must have preferred baroque juxtaposition of unlike kennings and neutral or incongruous verbs in their verse. Examples of both kinds of style are found in the verse discussed on pp. 362–6.

The passage above on the origin of the poet's inspiration will have shown that scaldic art was closely associated with pagan ideas and divinities, especially with Odin, the chief of the gods. We know that some tenth-century scalds were devotees of Odin, while others used their verse to celebrate the deeds of the popular god, Thor. It is also clear that heathen lore figured largely in all kinds of kennings, not least in those for battle and carnage. It was inevitable that the conversion of the Norsemen to Christianity should affect their poetic diction. A poet would have to be careful not to suggest in his verse that he was deferential to the devils which the pagan gods had now become. It is illuminating to compare the poems made by the Icelander, Hallfred Ǫnundarson the Troublesome Poet, in praise of Earl Hákon the Great (died 995) and King Ólaf Tryggvason (died 999). Hákon was a pagan and so was Hallfred when he composed in his honour; out Ólaf was a Christian and had brought about Hallfred's conversion and stood godfather to him at his baptism. In the 36 extant lines of his poem on Hákon there are two kennings with names of Odin in them, one with the name of the god Ull and one with the name of a valkyrie; in addition the goddess Earth is twice referred to through her sister and father. But in the two poems on Ólaf, in a total of 264 lines, the only name of a god is Tý, used in two kennings for men, the race of giants is once called the family of Surt, the sky is once called the burden of Nordri the dwarf, and the wolf is twice referred to as the troll-woman's horse. None of these would suggest active belief in the pagan gods. We then find that for a century or more after the Conversion poets generally avoided 'mythological' kennings. This did not mean, however, that they ceased to learn and transmit the poetry of their pagan predecessors; and it seems likely that poets at all times who were composing in eddaic style on stories from the far past did not hesitate to introduce the pagan gods and related notions into their work as part of the historicity of the subject-matter. In the twelfth century there was a sort of scaldic revival, and poets began once more to use elaborate kennings and antique mythological references without inhibition. By this time such things had become mere poetic ornament and carried no heathen stigma, but it sounds undeniably odd when in a scaldic poem on the story of St Eustace we find this

Christian martyr, Roman general though he was supposed to be, described as 'Baldr of the horse of the wide-ground of the sea-king' and 'Thrótt (i.e. Odin) of the flame of the assembly of points', god that is of the ship and sword respectively. But this fashion did not last long.

Danish poetry

We do not know what country the poet of the Karlevi stanza (p. 326) came from, but he must have belonged to a Danish circle which appreciated *dróttkvætt* style, and it is hard to think that Danes did not practise such composition themselves. But we have no more of it, and all the rest of our Danish vernacular poetry down to about 1200 is found in a few simple *fornyrðislag* verses in other runic inscriptions. Danish poetry on heroic themes certainly existed, but we can only come at it through some of the West Norse eddaic verse, for which in some instances a Danish stage has been more or less plausibly suggested, and through the Latin of Saxo Grammaticus, the great chronicler of Danish history, who wrote about 1200. He based some of his narrative on vernacular poetry, and in some cases he renders a native poem in florid hexameters. Occasionally, a West Norse parallel is extant. It is interesting to see the contrast between the Norse and the Latin in the following extreme instance. We have a fragment of a lay in Icelandic sources which is called the 'Old lay of Bjarki'. In it the speaker calls on men to wake and prepare for battle. He says, 'I wake you not to wine, nor to woman's whispers' – there is harder entertainment at hand. Saxo's Latin, in Elton's translation, has this:

I do not now bid ye learn the sports of maidens, nor stroke soft cheeks, nor give sweet kisses to the bride and press the slender breasts, nor desire the flowing wine and chafe the soft thigh and cast eyes upon snowy arms. I call you out to the sterner fray of War.

The matter is the same, but the style could hardly be more different. But elsewhere we see that behind the ample descriptive flow of the Latin, detailed and repetitive, there was heroic vernacular expression of typical Norse, indeed Germanic, kind:

334

'Sweet it is to repay the gifts received from our lord'; 'it beseems us to receive equably difficult and delightsome days'; 'let us do with brave hearts all the things that in our cups we boasted with sodden lips'; and in *Certamina prima fronte gerunt aquile* Saxo renders a valiant native proverbial expression, *Ǫndurðir skulu ernir klóask*, 'Front to front shall eagles claw each other', which we know in a scaldic verse from the early eleventh century.

Poetic taste in Denmark doubtless changed earlier than else-where in Scandinavia, perhaps in part under Saxon influence, and in the twelfth century Latin rather than vernacular literature was encouraged at the court. Native poetry of the old kind did not survive, but its early disappearance made way for the early rise of the Danish ballads in the thirteenth century, and in their new forms some of the primitive values and heroic responses of older ages continued to abide.

Swedish poetry

There was no Swedish Saxo to transmit the legends and poetry of his people and their neighbours in Götaland and Gotland. Our only compensation is a large quantity of verse in runic in-scriptions. One of these is on a copper box found at Sigtuna which contained a merchant's pair of scales for weighing precious metals; it is dated to the beginning of the eleventh century. The verse here is a pair of lines in *dróttkvætt*, difficult to interpret but fully regular in metre. This must at least show that this kind of poetry was also appreciated among the Swedes, as does also the fact that some Icelandic scalds composed poems in honour of Swedish kings. It is of interest to note that three men who signed them-selves as rune-carvers, two in Uppland and one in Västergötland, gave themselves the cognomen of 'scald', but unfortunately we cannot tell exactly what this signified in eleventh-century Sweden.

The remainder of the runic verse is in *fornyrðislag*. Much of this commemorative poetry rings out proudly in the tale of a man's virtues and falls off gently in the remembrance of his death. One good sequence was quoted on p. 101, and here is another noble one, from the inscription on the Gripsholm stone, Söder-manland:

Þeir fóru drængila	They fared like men
fiarri at gulli	far after gold,
ok austarla	and in the east
ærni gáfu.	gave the eagle food.
Dóu sunnarla	They died southward
á Særklandi.	in Serkland.

Our regret at the total loss of other Swedish poetry of this early age is made the keener by the existence of a few pictures on rune stones and the rich illustrations on the peculiar picture-stones of Gotland (p. 294). Occasionally, chiefly with the aid of West Norse poetry and Snorri's *Edda,* it is possible to identify with some degree of probability the figures depicted in their scenes and relate their groups and sequences to myth or legend. The stories of Sigurd the dragon-slayer and of Vǫlund (pp. 347–50) are clearly attested, for example. It is almost certain that the lore on which such illustrations were based – both the few we can and the many we cannot interpret – was in poetic form. We glimpse a fascinating world, but must resign ourselves to the fact that it is surrounded by an impenetrable wall of silence.

It is sad that when we finally get Swedish verse by the thousand lines, a century after Saxo, it is in octosyllabic couplets, rhymed history and chivalric romance, almost as remote as we ourselves are from the Viking Age and the age of the Conversion.

West Norse poetry

Thanks to the Icelanders, we have much poetry preserved from Norway and Iceland and the Atlantic settlements, especially Orkney and Greenland. There was certainly literary exchange between Norseman and Anglo-Saxon and between Norseman and Celt in this western world, but the whole nature and significance of this have still to be clarified – and perhaps never will be, for we deal with haphazard details and have no poetry from a true mixing-area, comparable to the art we possess from East Yorkshire, for example. In the following it will only be possible to describe a few examples of poems drawn from the three main groups, eddaic poetry about gods, eddaic poetry about heroes, and the vast and varied corpus of scaldic verse. The sketches are not all made from one point of view, for the aim is to emphasize the excellent without failing to illustrate the typical. It is also obvious that there will be no room for discussion of the great problems of textual transmission and restoration. Most eddaic verse, for example, exists in only one source, and we must, as far as we possibly can, take the poems as they are, although it would often be easy for us to 'improve' them by imposing a tidier logic upon them. Scaldic verse often exists in several sources but they may all show textual corruption. It will not be possible to present the considerations that have led to the adoption of particular readings in the translations given here.

Mythological poems

The characters who appear in these poems are chiefly gods and associated other-world beings, giants and dwarves. Eleven such poems are in the *Edda* codex, but the one called *Hávamál* (p. 342) is a collection of five or six poems, most of which have no connection with myths. Of the others three are proper narrative poems, while the remainder have a narrative frame or introduction but a monologue or dialogue as their main constituent. Some of these are like little plays, but it has not been possible to substantiate a theory that they represent ritual drama. It is in fact only rarely possible to detect some connection between these poems and any practices of heathen cults – they are certainly not hymns. They are imaginative descriptions, sometimes humorous, sometimes philosophical in the comments they imply, and they are often didactic in that they contain much old lore, some of which must have been of specific interest because of its relations with the language of poetry or because of its usefulness in charms of healing or other wizardry.

One such 'didactic' poem is *Vafþrúðnismál* in which Odin contends in knowledge with a wise giant. The giant is doomed to die if he cannot answer any question of Odin's, and die he must because Odin can ask: 'What did Odin himself say in his son's ear before he mounted the funeral pyre?' – a secret only he and Baldr share. But the consequence of the failure is no part of the poem; it is simply in prospect. In another poem of this kind Thor asks questions of a dwarf, who has come to demand the god's daughter in marriage. He keeps him talking till sunrise: to catch a giant or dwarf with the dawning day was to turn him to rock, so Thor

337

saves his daughter and learns a good deal of charming diction into the bargain. This is found in the dwarf's answers to his questions about the names of things among the different classes of beings. In these names we get some impression of the Norseman's awareness of the world of nature, some delight and tenderness which we seldom meet in other sources. The sky is called wind-weaver, up-world, the lovely roof, the dripping hall; the sun is the ever-glowing, the bright wheel, the all-sheer; night is the shadow-mask, the obscure, sleep-fun and dream-goddess.

Another poem full of information about the world of the gods is *Grimnismál*. It makes part of a story told in prose and without the prose it would be hard to understand. It concerns dealings between gods and men and is savage and uncomfortable: we can feel at home with many things in the Norse world, but not with this. The text of the story is not long and is in a typical style:

King Hrǫdung had two sons, one called Agnar, the other Geirrǫd. Agnar was ten, Geirrǫd eight. The two of them went out in a boat with their lines fishing small fish. A wind drove them out to sea. In the darkness they were wrecked on some shore and they went up and found a smallholding; they stayed the winter there. The housewife fostered Agnar, and the man fostered Geirrǫd and taught him things. In the spring the man gave them a boat. And when he and the woman walked down to the shore with them, the man spoke privately to Geirrǫd. They got a fair wind and came to their father's harbour. Geirrǫd was forward in the boat; he jumped ashore and pushed the boat off and said, 'Go where trolls can have you!' The boat drifted out to sea. But Geirrǫd went up to the houses, he was made welcome there; and his father had died. Geirrǫd was then made king and he became famous.

Odin and Frigg sat in Hlidskjalf and looked over all worlds. Odin said, 'Do you see Agnar, your foster-son, where he is getting children with an ogress in the cave? While Geirrǫd, my foster-son, is a king and now rules his country.' Frigg says, 'He is so mean with food that he tortures his guests, if he thinks too many are coming.' Odin says that this is the biggest lie; they have a bet on it. Frigg sent her maid Fulla to Geirrǫd. She told the king to take care that a warlock who had come to the country did not bring him to ruin; and said that a mark to know him by was that there was no dog so fierce that he would jump at him. But that was quite baseless, that King Geirrød was not free with food; and yet he had the man arrested that dogs would not go for. He was in a black cloak and gave his name as Grímnir and, though asked, said nothing more about himself. The king had him tortured to speak and had him put between two fires, and there he sat for eight nights. King Geirrød had then a son, ten years old, called Agnar after his brother. Agnar went to Grímnir and gave him a full horn to drink and said his father did wrong to torture this man for no reason. Grímnir emptied the horn; the fire had come so near that the cloak was burning off him.

It is at this point that the verse begins. Grímnir speaks as if he were experiencing visions induced by his sufferings. He describes the world of the gods, the homes, rivers and horses of that other world, with everything centred on the great ash-tree which upheld the cosmic order. The description goes on for forty-four stanzas and then comes this: 'Before the sons of the victory-gods I have raised up scenes – with that the longed-for saving will start – '. The scenes are those he has called up in his speech so far and the moment of rescue began with Agnar's approach to him. Now he begins to recite the names of Odin – 'never by one name was I known since I came among men' – and the final revelation is at hand. He tells Geirrød that he is drunk and has lost his favour, that he sees his sword lying blood-covered. 'Now the Terrible shall have sword-wearied slain – I know your life is over. The *dísir* (p. 392) are hostile, now you can see Odin: come near me if you can. Now my name is Odin, just now I was called the Terrible –.' So the poem ends and is followed by this:

King Geirrød sat and had a sword across his knees, half-drawn. And when he heard that Odin had come there, he stood up and meant to take Odin away from the fire. The sword fell from his hand and the hilt went downward, the king tripped and pitched forward, the sword went through him and he died. Then Odin disappeared. And afterwards Agnar was king there for a long time.

339

None of the other poems suggests such awareness of that injustice of circumstances which can be interpreted as the cruelty of divine powers towards their favourites; none of them is concerned with the divine irresponsibility which wilfully seems to set limits to what it will know and do; none of them leads to such terror as this poem does. It is difficult to relate *Grímnismál* with any certainty to palpable facts of heathen faith and ceremony; but it is also hard to believe that it does not give us a smell and taste of pagan atmosphere and pagan awe. When we know this poem, we may see some of the more savage Oseberg carvings in a new light.

The attitude to the adventure of Thor told in *Hýmiskviða* is quite different. The poet's respect for the god is indubitable, but it was a funny story and he both relished the comedy of the situation in it and added to it by bringing in ironic touches of scaldic diction which clearly invite a smile. The matter is as follows:

The gods want an ale-feast and the prophetic ritual points to the giant Ægir as the one to give it. He is 'childishly cheerful' until he is forced to work by Thor. He gets his own back by demanding a cauldron big enough to brew beer in for them. Tý tells Thor that his father, a giant called Hýmir, has a great cauldron which they might get from him with guile. They set off and find Tý's beautiful mother, Hýmir's mistress, as well as his nine-hundred-headed grandmother. She welcomes them and puts them under the cauldrons that hang at the end of the hall. Hýmir returns – it is the classical 'fee-fy-fo-fum' situation – coming in from the mountain snows, apparently, for the poet says: 'He walked in, icicles rang, the old chap's cheek-forest was frozen.' The lady points out the visitors, modestly sitting at the end of the room with a pillar in front of them. Merely at Hýmir's glance a beam breaks, the pillar springs apart and seven out of eight cauldrons are smashed. Three oxen are taken and despatched, not casually but with a certain incongruous formality: 'each was made shorter by a head.' Thor ate two of them, which seemed excessive to Hýmir, who says that next evening they must sup off what they catch. Thor asks about bait, and Hýmir directs him to his oxen, but is then upset when Thor snaps off the 'lofty settlement of a horn-pair', the head, of a jet-black bull. They row out to sea, but not as far as Thor would like. Hýmir catches two whales on one hook; meanwhile Thor is preparing his line in the stern, using the ox-head as a bait. He is fishing for the monstrous snake, who lies in the outer sea girdling the earth until Ragnarǫk, when he does battle with the gods (pp. 345–6). And sure enough, the bait is gaped over and taken by the 'hater of the gods', the 'belt of all lands', and he is swiftly pulled as far as the boat's side by Thor, who then brought his hammer down on the 'too ugly high hill of the hair of the battle-brother of the wolf'. ('Hill of hair' is a kenning for head, the wolf is Fenrir, another monster, born of the same parents as the great serpent, who is chained up until the last battle.) All the ancient earth shuddered at the blow, and 'that fish' took itself down into the deeps. Moody and silent, Hýmir rows back. He carries the whales ashore, while Thor carries the whole boat, the 'surf-swine', home to the giant's house. But Hýmir is stubborn and mean-minded: he said that just because a man could row powerfully, it did not mean he was strong – not unless he could also break a particular goblet he had in his possession. Thor tried to break it, and failed. But he learnt a trick from Tý's handsome mother, who advised him to try it on Hýmir's skull:

> Grim rose on knee
> goat-beasts' master,
> wholly gathered
> his god's might then:
> whole the old man's
> helm-stub topmost,
> but round goblet
> reeled split-sided.

(Thor's chariot was pulled by goats; 'helm-stub' is 'helmet-stump', head.)

Hýmir cannot now refuse Thor the cauldron he has come to get. Tý tries to move it but cannot, so Thor gets it up on his head, and the rings by which it could be hung up jangled at his heels.

It was a big cauldron. Pursued by Hýmir and his friends, Thor pauses to despatch with his 'death-eager' hammer the 'rock-whales', as the giants are called. And so he comes home and the gods can have their party.

The poet moves abruptly from scene to scene, and skilfully joins the cauldron-seeking to one of the best known of Thor's adventures, his fishing for the monstrous serpent, a theme treated with much more graphic detail in other poetry and known from stone carvings as well (pl. 26b, c). The poet appreciates the absurdity of the situations, pointed here and there by the playfulness of his language, and is clever at suggesting, without being laboriously consistent, extravagance of size and strength. An essential source of the poem's liveliness also lies in the contrast between Thor, who merely acts and has no thoughts or feelings, and Hýmir, who responds with enough stupidity, stubbornness and vanity to make him a recognizable human character.

A sequence of 164 stanzas of *ljóðaháttr* is given the general name of *Hávamál*, 'High-one's speech', i.e. words of Odin, from the occurrence of this phrase in the last part of the collection. The different parts must originally have been separate poems, but they have been put together because they all amount to advice from some fount of wisdom. Odin is explicitly identified as the source in some parts, but elsewhere we do not know for sure who the speaker is.

Of particular interest is a short sequence of stanzas (138 – 45), which begins:

I know that I hung on the windy trunk all of nine nights, wounded with a spear and given to Odin, myself to myself, on that trunk sprung from the roots of what tree nobody knows. They refreshed me with neither loaf nor horn. I peered down, I took up runes, screaming I took them, and fell back from there. I learnt nine mighty chants from the famous son of Bǫlthorn . . . and I got a drink of the precious mead, dipped out from Ódrœrir [of the mead of poetry, from the vat called 'Spirit-mover']. Then I began to grow fecund and wise, to grow and prosper: one word from another sought a third word for me, one deed from another sought a third deed for me.

The other stanzas speak of mighty runes and refer enigmatically to heathen practices of sacrifice and perhaps of divination.

These few verses have a pagan authenticity comparable to that of *Grímnismál*. They start in exposure, wounding, hunger and neglect, but we learn that this is voluntary and purposeful – although the poet words it as if Odin himself wondered at what he had done – and wild agony becomes wild triumph at the moment Odin grasps the runes and, instead of the ordinary drink from the horn that might have refreshed him, gets a drink of the mead of poetry. People have pointed out the similarity between this solitary hardship, followed by instruction in secret knowledge and consequent jubilation, and forms of tribal and cult initiation known in other cultures.

Approximately the first half of *Hávamál* is taken up with good counsels of various kinds, without reference to the sacred or magical. Sometimes the verse is in the first person; at one point the 'I' appears to be Odin but elsewhere it is an unidentifiable voice we hear, perhaps Odin's, perhaps simply the poet's.

This first part begins as if it were going to be a 'situation poem'. The point of view is that of a traveller, who arrives at a house and, as a visitor should, looks carefully around because he does not know what company he will be keeping. He greets the hosts, asks for a place, speaks of a guest's need of warmth, water for washing, and a good welcome. This thought of what a man needs leads into a long disquisition on how a man should behave. In this the idea of man as a wayfarer and guest often recurs: 'The wary guest when he comes to a meal keeps silent with a keen silence'; 'A man bears no better burden on his way than great good sense'; and in the first-person voice of experience: 'I used to be young, I journeyed alone, then I lost my way; I thought myself rich when I met someone else – man is man's delight'; 'Much too early I came in many places, and too late in others; the ale was drunk, elsewhere not ready – the man ill suffered seldom comes at the right time'. Many prescriptions are given for conduct, and the sensible and foolish man are defined by example and contrast. The poet speaks of the value of wide experience and of knowledge of men, of industry, independence, health and the cultivation of friendship; it is foolish to worry overmuch and dangerous to use a scornful tongue. Moderation is needed, in speech, in eating and drinking, in the use of power, even in the gifts which found and promote friendship: 'A man should not give anything big, he often buys himself good words for little; with half a loaf and a jug that needed tilting I gained a companion.' Health and prosperity are best, but even without them life is to be recommended – even the maimed man can achieve something. It is the dead man's case which is hopeless. But everything dies in the end, with one exception – a man's reputation (see pp. 431–2).

The bulk of this is wisdom literature of high value for the information it gives about social and ethical attitudes, for its quick-chiselled aphorisms, and for its flexible verse and easy and witty phrasing. The full line of the *ljóðaháttr* triplet, with its internal alliteration, functions well as a 'punch-line' and often has a proverbial ring: 'everything is easy at home', 'much goes worse than expected', 'a return should render the gift', 'timid is a naked man', 'nobody benefits from a corpse'. Sometimes it is the whole triplet, alone or in a variant pair, which offers a well-shaped, wise saying, sometimes cynical and merciless, usually hard-headed, blossoming most in warm words about friendship, in feeling for the man who has lost his independence, and not least in remembrance of the creature comforts and civilized pleasures – speech and silence – that hospitality and human society can give. But fundamentally life is good, empty only for the man without affection.

The poet is a serious man, with at best a wry humour; he might become sentimental if it were not for the wide experience which has so confirmed him in his relative values – 'when he comes among the valiant a man finds that no one is boldest of all'. He speaks like a man of the yeoman class, cautious and sober, who can see daring as rashness and idealism as folly. Yet he knows that, although a maimed man can get something out of life, it is the man morally blemished who irredeemably suffers death.

The *Vǫluspá*, 'Sibyl's prophecy', stands rightly at the beginning of the *Edda* codex. It is the poem we could least well be without for the nobility of its language and for the knowledge it gives us of the man who composed it, by far the greatest of the few religious thinkers we know from pagan Scandinavia. He was concerned to describe the whole history of the gods from their creation, through their innocent age, to their corruption and downfall. That downfall meant the end of a world order, to be succeeded, as he believed, by a new and better order under the governance of a power superior to the old gods. The poet had to compass both past and future in his poem, for he lived and composed in the midst of the cosmic process. He manages this with bold craft, relying on his auditors to make an imaginative leap at the right moment, seizing and holding them with his urgency from start to finish. It goes like this.

The sibyl calls for silence: her audience is world-wide, gods and men. Then she speaks to Odin alone: does he wish her to rehearse ancient lore, the remotest she can remember? She demonstrates her age and powers: she can remember the world-tree a seedling below the ground. She goes on to describe the creation of the world, moon, sun and stars; the creative, civilizing activity of the gods; how powers of greed and sorcery came to them and how they provoked violence and forswearing among them. Now the gods must worry about their future and the future of the good things they have made. And at this point in time Odin, the chief of the gods, seeks wisdom: and it is from herself, the sibyl, that he seeks it. Suddenly she addresses him directly and intimately, and we realize that this is also the real beginning of the poem, the moment in the whole of time which is now, actual, present. These stanzas describing Odin and the sibyl face to face give the setting which explains the first stanza with its call for universal silence. The poet is both remarkably imaginative and remarkably systematic.

Thereafter the sibyl's utterance is almost entirely prophetic, describing what is yet to come. There is graphic mixing of tenses. Sometimes she uses the past because it is what she has seen in her trance; sometimes the prophetic future; sometimes future action lives urgently in the present tense; and sometimes the present tense conveys the real, menacing present, for some signs of the doom to come are even now visible and audible.

The major steps of the future are war in the world, the death of Baldr, the vengeance on his slayer, Hǫd, and the punishment of Loki; monsters are ready to destroy the sun, decay and terror fill the world of nature and of men; monsters are let loose, giant forces with weapons of fire and venom gather, they fight the battle in which Odin and Thor and their enemies, the wolf and the giant serpent, are killed; the sun is darkened, earth sinks into sea. Then a new earth arises; innocent gods, Baldr and his unwitting slayer, Hǫd, return; there is a hall where righteous men who have survived the disasters enjoy content for ever. And a single mighty ruler will come.

But there is one more stanza, and it brings us back to the present, the situation now in the world, quiet but menacing. Before the sibyl sinks down, she points to a dark-winged monster, with corpses in its plumage, flying up from pitch-black mountains and over the level ground.

The poem is a personal reinterpretation of stock mythological themes. The language seems fresh, not derivative, though even here the tendency to use poetry as a vehicle for information has led to the inclusion of a list of dwarves' names at the place where their origin is spoken of – something we should like to think was not in the poem's first form. The poet makes relentlessly effective use of refrain: the spiteful unwillingness of the sibyl, squirming and hostile though fixed by force and flattered by gifts from Odin, the rational but futile discussions of the gods, the baying of the great hound, Garm, are all repetitive themes which serve a structural as well as emotive purpose.

Nothing in the poem is more impressive than the description of the chaos and violence as the natural order collapses and the last battle is fought. There are tremendous earth-shaking shudders and din from all quarters; then suddenly these are followed by swift, single, silent movements, as the sun is extinguished, the stars disappear from the sky, the earth slips into the sea. Even the rushing vapour and flame leaping as high as heaven seem quiet; the fire that now consumes the world is made abstract in a simple ironic kenning – it is called 'life-nourisher' – and with this the poet seems to detach himself and us from the horror of the ruin and makes it easier to bear. Now, with the cosmic stage empty and dark, there comes for the last time the sound of the baying of the great hound Garm, which belongs to the present and the future, and we move to the last part of the vision. A new earth rises as silently as the old earth sank; and the sounds now to be heard do not destroy the peacefulness but set it off – the sound of cascading water, where the eagle (not now the carrion bird screaming in anticipation of battle) finds fish for food; and the voices of the young gods, Baldr and Hǫd, once the victims, now the inheritors, who find in the grass the golden play-pieces of their earliest existence and talk of the past's mighty events. With such sure touches the poet moves from dark immensity to a corner in a sparkling landscape.

Heroic poems

The oldest and most impressive of the four poems in the *Edda* collection that are not connected with legends of Sigurd the dragon-slayer and Gudrun, his widow, is *Vǫlundarkviða,* the lay of the famous metal-worker, Vǫlund. The language of the poem shows unique connections with Old English and continental Germanic, and it may depend in part on a foreign source. Yet it does not give the impression of being a relic. Its chief difference from other poems in the *Edda* lies in the doubtful nature of Vǫlund, who is called at one place 'prince of elves' and whose marvellous skill as a craftsman seems not of this world. In spite of this, however, Vǫlund and other figures in the story suffer and inflict suffering in the truest human fashion. We are drawn into a barbaric world where, astonishingly, the outcome is compassion.

The story is simple. Vǫlund and his brothers take three women to wife. These had come flying from the south, and the inference is that the brothers held them as beloved captives by hiding their 'swan-shapes'. In the ninth year they escaped – it was their destiny for they were not beings who belonged to people or places. Two of the brothers go in search of their wives, but Vǫlund stays at home and makes rings and waits. A king called Nídud, apparently inspired by greed, carries Vǫlund away captive along with his treasures; Vǫlund is hamstrung and put in an island to be the king's goldsmith. Nídud's sons go to see him; he entices them with promises, so they come again and he kills them. From their eyes he makes jewels for the queen, brooches from their teeth for Bǫdvild, the princess, and from their skulls silver-plated bowls for the king. Now Bǫdvild has broken a ring, once Vǫlund's, and she brings it to him to mend. He gives her strong drink and seduces her. He is now in a position to escape because he is somehow in possession of wings. He completes his vengeance on Nídud by telling him, at a safe distance,

what he had done, and that Bǫdvild is with child. The poem
ends with Nídud's asking Bǫdvild whether what Vǫlund has
told him is true. It is true, she says: 'I did not know how to resist
him; I did not have the power to resist him.'

The poet leaves us to finger the regret, grief and pain, and
takes no sides. (Only the malevolent wife of Nídud is dismissed
as bad and of no real account.) The sense of tragedy is there
because the poet starts one story – Vǫlund and his strange wife
who leaves him – and then moves into another. This second
story finds a bitter end for Nídud and Bǫdvild, but there is no
end to answer to the opening of the poem – that loss remains as
it was. Some people have thought the first story was grafted onto
the second, but they cannot now be separated and seem not to
have been for the poet. And without the first story Vǫlund would
leave the scene laughing, as he does, but we should not feel for
him. The poem is more complex and more satisfying as it is.

It is a poem more of shadows and metal-glints, flame, white
flesh, white bone, than of colours and daylight. The poet is bold
and brief; with a picture, for example: 'Men-at-arms went by
night, their coats of mail were studded, their shields gleamed
against the pared moon'; or with a tone of voice, eager, boyish:
'Early one called to another, brother to brother, "Let's go see
the bangles" '; or with deliberate precision of movement: 'And
they took them off, and they put them on, all save one which
they kept off'. The same superb calculation is found in the repetition of whole stanzas, when action is repeated, or when Vǫlund
tells Nídud what has happened to his sons in just the same words
as the poet used when he originally described Vǫlund's actions.
The poet is sure of his technique and has an unerring feel for his
pattern.

Sixteen poems in the *Edda* codex are linked in some way to
the stories of Sigurd and Gudrun, although the former figures as
a protagonist in little more than half of them. Some of the poems
are narratives that include talk between the characters. Others
are 'situation poems'; these often lead into a monologue by one
of the women in the story (p. 357).

Only a dull, late poem surveys the whole legend, in the form
of a forecast. The other poems presuppose the legend or parts of
it. A brief reconstruction of the bare story as it might have been

told in Iceland about the year 1200 is given below. Some of the matter is certainly late and local accretion, and exactly how much of the rest a Norwegian poet of the ninth century would have recognized is hard to say. The oldest and youngest of the heroic poems differ greatly in mood and outlook, but there are others between them that are much more difficult to place. It is not surprising that we find the older poems – vital, savage and often enigmatic – keener whips to the imagination than the younger poems, which have their beauties and some fine lyrical passages, but which also tend to a certain obtrusive sentimentality. The three poems discussed below throw some light on the changes that came over Norse taste and Norse life between the ninth and the twelfth century, but they by no means fully illustrate the range and quality of this heroic verse.

The story of Sigurd began when the gods forced a dwarf to give them his gold because they needed it to pay atonement for a man in otter-shape whom they had killed (cf. the kennings for gold on p. 331). The dwarf put a curse on the gold before he parted with it. The man who took the atonement refused to share it with his two remaining sons, Fáfnir and Regin, so they killed him. Then, however, Fáfnir alone took the gold and went to live in a wasteland, guarding the treasure in the shape of a dragon. Regin was a marvellous blacksmith. He fostered young Sigurd, forged him a sword, and arranged for him to attack Fáfnir. Sigurd killed the dragon, took the treasure, learnt Regin planned treachery and killed him.

While travelling Sigurd came upon Brynhild, a valkyrie, and woke her from a charmed sleep. Sigurd married Gudrun, sister of Gunnar and Hǫgni. In the shape of his brother-in-law, Gunnar, he then wooed Brynhild, also identified as sister of King Atli, fulfilling conditions that Gunnar could not fulfil and deceiving Brynhild who thought he had. Brynhild learnt of the deceit and played on Gunnar and Hǫgni to kill Sigurd, their brother-in-law and sworn friend. In the end Sigurd was killed. Brynhild stabbed herself and joined Sigurd on his funeral pyre.

Gudrun was married to Atli, king of the Huns, whose greed for the treasure of his brothers-in-law led him to invite them to visit him. They came in spite of warning, having hidden their gold; and they were killed at Atli's command because they would not reveal its whereabouts. Gudrun avenged their deaths horribly on her husband, whom she finally killed with her own hands.

Gudrun made a third marriage to a king called Jónakr. Her daughter by Sigurd, Svanhild, had been given in marriage to King Jǫrmunrekk. Jǫrmunrekk had Svanhild killed – she was trampled to death by horses – and his own son hanged because of an accusation of love between the two. Gudrun incited her sons by Jónakr, Hamdir and Sǫrli, to avenge their half-sister. They attack Jǫrmunrekk, mutilate him and are killed themselves.

The ancient poem *Atlakviða* is to do with the death of Gudrun's brothers and the end of her second marriage. It has many archaic features in metre and vocabulary, and scholars generally think it was composed in Norway, perhaps about A.D. 900.

Atli sent a messenger to Gunnar to invite him and his brother, Hǫgni, to visit him; with the invitation were promises of rich gifts in goods and land. Gunnar is not moved by this – his horse, sword, bows, armour, helmet, shield are better than the best owned by Huns – and he asks Hǫgni what he advises. Hǫgni replies with a question: 'What do you think the woman – Gudrun – meant when she sent us a ring wound round with wolf's hair?' – and he answers himself, 'I think she offered a warning – our way is wolfish': we shall meet fangs and merciless ferocity. No one at all urged Gunnar to go, but in the face of this opposition and his sister's warning, voiced by Hǫgni, Gunnar then spoke 'as a king ought to speak' and made plain his intention of accepting the invitation, though without putting it directly into words. He calls for drink to be served and then paints a picture of what will happen if he does not return, a picture of elemental savagery, closing in on the civilization which he appears to think is maintained by his presence. These glimpses of Gunnar in command and representative of his people give him a stature and responsibility which other characters in the poem do not have. The heroic single-mindedness and self-confidence he later displays do not make us impatient, for they only come up to the standard that has been set for him.

The invitation has become a challenge and, as a king must, he accepts it. The lurking menace and suspicion of the beginning must now come into the open. Their 'shame-free' followers bid them farewell, with tears, and we learn that Hǫgni leaves a son. The journey is told with such haste that the men seem to be driving themselves to meet what they must meet – the faster the better. The poet describes their view of Atli's land and guarded citadel, but their arrival is seen through their sister's eyes. She tells Gunnar he is betrayed – he should have come armed and put Atli into the snake-pen that lies in wait for him. Gunnar's reply is light – it is too late, and too far to look for a following of 'shame-free' warriors over the hills of the Rhine – the adjective takes us back to the regretful men who had seen him on his way. Gunnar is immediately seized and bound; Hǫgni defends himself but is overcome.

They ask Gunnar if he would buy his life with gold. His reply shocks them and us. He will first have his brother's heart in his hand: the apparent explanation is that he proposes to reveal the secret to save his life but is unwilling to face Hǫgni's reproach if he does so. There follow these stanzas, with their play on a few simple words:

> They cut the heart from Hjalli's breast [we are not told here who Hjalli was], bloody, and put it on a platter and brought it to Gunnar. Then Gunnar, lord of men, said, 'Here I have the heart of Hjalli the timid, unlike the heart of Hǫgni the valiant, which trembles fast as it lies on the platter, trembled twice as much when it lay in his breast.' Then Hǫgni laughed as they cut the living warrior to the heart – farthest from him was any thought of weeping; they put it bloody on a platter and brought it to Gunnar. Gunnar, glorious spear-Niflung, said: 'Here I have the heart of Hǫgni the valiant, unlike the heart of Hjalli the timid, which trembles little as it lies on the platter, trembled not so much when it lay in his breast.'

Gunnar goes on to address Atli directly – until now we did not know he was present. Gunnar is triumphant: Atli will never get the treasure, the secret depends on him alone, and he makes clear the real reason for his demand for his brother's death: 'Doubt was ever in me while we two were alive – now I have none when I alone am living!' He dwells lovingly on the picture in his mind of the gold consigned to the keeping of the Rhine: 'The blood-red rings will gleam in the dashing water rather than be gold shining on the arms of Huns.'

This is the end of the first act. From now on Atli and Gudrun (now mentioned by name for the first time) are the chief figures on the stage. Atli orders Gunnar's execution. Gudrun kept back tears and reminded him of the oaths he had sworn to her brother, to no avail.

A host of warriors put the living prince in the pen crawling inside with serpents. But Gunnar, alone, savage-minded, struck the harp with his hand, the strings rang: this is the way a valiant ring-giver should keep his gold from men.

The poet enjoys stressing this one instance where it was fitting for a king to be niggardly and returns to it in the next stanza when he describes Gunnar as 'treasure-guardian'.

On the return of Atli and his men from the murder, Gudrun presents a cup of drink to her husband and makes what appears to be a conciliatory speech. They go in to the feast she has prepared for them, and she serves them with drink and choice food. Now in this stanza the poet suddenly uses epithets to describe Gudrun, which he has not done hitherto, and prepares us for the explicit horror of what is to come: her face is of a luminous pallor, she is strange and acting under compulsion. Then she tells Atli that he has eaten the hearts of his sons – she emphasizes the disgust – he has chewed them, carcase-bloody, sweetened with honey, now he can digest the slaughtered human flesh. Then she plays on the poignancy – 'You will never call the boys to your knees again'. Her words are greeted with wailing, the Huns wept, but not Gudrun, who 'never wept for her brothers, fierce as bears, and for her sweet boys, young, untutored, whom she got with Atli'.

This quieter moment of marvel at the implacable Gudrun is followed by swift, relentless movement as she prepares the final vengeance. She stabs Atli in his defenceless drunkenness and with the aid of servants she has richly bribed beforehand, she sets fire to the house and burns to death all who had come from the moorland where Gunnar had died. 'That was the atonement she took for her brothers.'

352

The poem moves swiftly but despite the speed the impression gained is rich and complex. This is chiefly due to the constant use of adjectives and compounds, some metaphorical, some kennings of traditional kind. They range from the naturalistic and pictorial to the forcefully dynamic; some seem suggestive of splendour, even though we cannot fully grasp their import. Thus, the beer is mellow, Knéfrød's voice is cold, horses bite on bits, helmets are gold-adorned, bears are dun-coated, fields are all-green, days are sun-bright, corpses 'need-pale', fire is hot, rings are red, gold is bright metal, house-timbers are ancient. The wolf is a moor-dweller, the hall a mead-house, Gunnar and Hǫgni are the hard-minded ones, their horses the whip-shy ones, benches are seat-trees. Gunnar is described as the friend of the Burgundians, the battle-governor; Hǫgni is the powerful rider, the forger of wounds; the horse is the shaker of the bridle, swords are strife-thorns, gold is strife-metal. Many of the epithets are conventionally naturalistic, only a little heightened for the occasion. They make a background of the expected and normal against which the extraordinary conduct of the protagonists is set.

And what was truly extraordinary was the behaviour of Gudrun. The title of the poem in the codex, 'Atli's Lay', its subtitle, 'Atli's death', and a brief prose preface, 'Gudrun, daughter of Gjúki, avenged her brothers, as has become famous . . .', all show that it was the second act of the poem which was regarded as of greatest moment. For the poet and his audience Hǫgni and Gunnar were behaving as kingly heroes were expected to behave; we are kept in suspense but finally they had no choice; neither were they the only examples in history of supreme defiance, the ultimate proud loneliness of the hero, even to be bought if need be with a brother's life. But Atli's fate was unparalleled. The poet describes Gudrun's actions with fascinated precision, in part horror-struck, part moved by sad respect. He is aware of the pathos, but comes at it indirectly to emphasize her stern tearlessness. He is not astonished that men can reach the limits Gunnar and Hǫgni reach, but he marvels that a woman, wife and mother, can go as far as Gudrun goes. For the poet and his audience this story must have been history, and he does not present Gudrun as a paragon so much as a unique fact, almost beyond emulation: he ends with, 'Full told is this: since then no woman in coat of mail goes about vengeance for brothers in such a way . . .' That blood-ties could be as strong as Gudrun makes them stirred the poet deeply, and it is true that, although we get near the heart-beat of close kin in other ancient Norse poetry, nowhere is the thud of it so overwhelming as in the Lay of Atli.

The poet of *Atlakviða* does not query the wisdom of Gunnar's acceptance of the invitation and its menace or the wisdom of Gudrun's relentless regard for dutiful vengeance. But the poet of *Hamðismál* allows the notion to intrude that perhaps there is folly and waste in his tale; unlike *Atlakviða* his poem also deals with supernatural forces, inspiring irrational behaviour and giving magic protection.

Hamðismál begins with stanzas (which are partly shared with another poem called 'Gudrun's urging') in which Gudrun incites her sons to avenge their sister Svanhild, the girl whom Jǫrmunrekk 'trampled with horses, white and black, on the public way, grey, trained to pace, horses of the Goths'. The accumulation of adjectives suggests appalled fascination at the fact of the execution and a deliberate removal of attention from the figure of Svanhild to these animals, in themselves peaceable and serviceable, who had killed her. Gudrun recalls her lonely state, only Hamdir and Sǫrli are left to her – 'I have become solitary like an aspen among the evergreens; deprived of kinsmen, like a fir of its branches . . .' Her son Hamdir answers her roughly, but his brother Sǫrli joins in to prevent their useless altercation. But he is equally hard and asks her what she wants from them – something very terrible so that she can make a virtue of not weeping over it? Then he bids her fiercely, 'Weep for your brothers and your sweet sons . . . and you shall weep for both of us, Gudrun, who sit here doomed on our horses – we shall die far off.' They left the courtyard, nearly howling out loud with rage: rage not at Jǫrmunrekk, the ultimate cause, but at the duty which sends their young lives to doom. In this mood they have no sense of proportion left, and from some obscure lines we learn that they took offence at Erp, their half-brother, son of Jónakr by a different mother, and killed him. He had offered his help, and by his death they diminished their strength by a third.

Their journey is soon over. West of the township they met a

grim sight – their sister's son wounded on a tree, 'wind-cold outcast-tree', a gallows – this must be Jǫrmunrekk's son whose death he had ordered because of the accusation against him and Svanhild. As in *Atlakviða*, the point of view is abruptly switched from them outside the settlement to the men inside the hall. Here they were cheerfully drinking and did not hear the horses until one of the young men sounded his horn. Jǫrmunrekk was told of their coming and was contemptuous: 'Then Jǫrmunrekk laughed, clapped his hand to his moustache . . . shook his head of brown hair, looked on his white shield, made the golden goblet revolve in his hand.'

The young men come in and are inexplicably successful in the fighting, so that bodies lie around them sprawled in Gothic blood. Then Hamdir spoke: 'You, Jǫrmunrekk, wanted us brothers, sons of one mother, to come into your fortress: you see your legs and your arms, Jǫrmunrekk, thrown into the hot fire.' 'Jǫrmunrekk roared, as if a bear were roaring, "Stone the men, if spears, edges, iron will not pierce the sons of Jónakr".' We now understand that the boys have some kind of extraordinary protection, but also that there is no prospect of their escape. Sǫrli told Hamdir that he had done ill to make Jǫrmunrekk speak, but it is not made clear how Hamdir's words had given Jǫrmunrekk the solution to the problem of their invulnerability. As it stands, Hamdir's words are no more than a pointed taunt to Jǫrmunrekk, prompting a desperate last command, but it is easy to speculate on other reasons that may have been fully apparent to the poet and his audience. Silence is often made a condition if magic is to work successfully.

The action is now effectively over, but the poem would not be as moving as it is without the exchange between the brothers that follows. Sǫrli continues with a reproachful reflection on his brother's rashness: courage you have, if only you had sense with it! This links the end with the beginning, the opening scene with Gudrun, where Hamdir is impetuous, Sǫrli deliberate. Hamdir in his reply takes us back to the second stage in the poem; he says, 'His head would be off if Erp were alive, our war-valiant brother, whom we slew on the way, the slaughter-bold man, the battle-sacred.' He regrets not that they killed a man and a brother, but that they wasted such a fighter. But this he says was prompted by *dísir*, malevolent supernatural women (p. 392) – he can apparently find no other way to explain it. Sǫrli speaks last and, practical and calm, strikes a note of reconciliation and just pride in their achievement. He says they should not tear at each other, like greedy wolves, unrestrained wasteland beasts. 'We have fought well, we stand on corpses of Goths, above the sword-edge-weary ones, like eagles on a branch. We have won good fame, whether we die now or tomorrow: a man sees no evening out after the Norns have given their verdict.'

This is a poem more stark in style but less stark in sentiment than *Atlakviða*. Epithets are sparingly used, while sententious comment in the speech of characters, though somewhat heavy, is not otiose. Explanations are few and we have to leap from part to part – we cannot be sure whether this is because the parts are only remnants of a larger whole or whether the effect is nearly as the poet intended it. As a heroic poem it is better without some explanations. It is good, for example, that the poet makes nothing of the charmed protection the boys apparently have and of the way in which the charm is broken. If he had been elaborately explicit, the heroic human stature of the young men would not be the same. Sǫrli's last words would be unthinkable in a folk-tale.

In spite of the obscurities, there is no doubt what the poem is about: how duty must be done, no matter anger and anguish and mindless cruelties, inexplicable save as the work of malicious powers, and how indifferent a thing death is if it comes when duty has been done. Indeed, there is at the end of the poem a hint of the immortality which fame confers – an answer given by the heroic attitude in all ages but with particular force in the Norse world (cf. p. 432).

Atlakviða and *Hamðismál* are old poems, harsh in outlook and, as far as we can see, representative of the tales surrounding Gudrun in relatively simple form. As time went on, the legends were elaborated, to some extent by additional incidents but more especially by the revaluation of old characters and the introduction of new ones, as the poets sought to provide explanations of the often enigmatic conduct of the people in the early poems. They often chose to do this by describing a situation, usually with dialogue which leads to a retrospective monologue, sometimes a kind of *apologia,* by one of the central women characters, especially Gudrun and Brynhild. We have some powerful romantic poetry as a result, with pathos and passion taking the place of the iron-willed response to duty which so dominated the thinking of the older poets.

Men might shed tears of grief in early Scandinavia but it was not counted manly. The Danes are not allowed to weep for their dead, said Adam of Bremen. Similarly, the old poets did not ask us to have pity for Gunnar and Hǫgni, Hamdir and Sǫrli. In some of these other poems, however, we are asked to share the sorrows of women, and the softness seems indicative of a later age. Perhaps we are to see in this an effect of Christianity, whose pastoral care required contrition and confession and encouraged people both to feel and to exercise compassion.

One example will suffice to illustrate the sort of novelties in plot, technique and sentiment that are common in much of this poetry.

Oddrúnargrátr, 'Oddrún's lament', starts with mingled narrative and dialogue, but the last 21 of its 34 stanzas contain a monologue by Oddrún. She is identified as Atli's sister. She hears that a certain princess called Borgný is unable to give birth to the child she is carrying, and Oddrún goes to see her. She learns that the father of the child is Borgný's lover, and that the two have been making love in secret for five years. With the aid of suitable magic chants Oddrún helps her in the delivery. She is blessed by Borgný for her assistance but says that she has not aided her because she deserved it but because of a vow she has made to help every being. Borgný reminds her of old faithful friendship, but Oddrún says she remembers that when she entertained Gunnar, Borgný had said that no other girl in the world would behave in such a way. We must presume that this reproof had distressed Oddrún, and now she finds Borgný in just the same state. Why Oddrún should think she was beyond reproach becomes clear in the following monologue in which she rehearses her sad story. Before his death her father had decided that she should be put in the care of her brother, Atli, while the other sister, Brynhild, should have a helmet and be a valkyrie. Three rapid stanzas refer to the wooing of Brynhild by Sigurd in Gunnar's place: 'It was not long but a woefully short while after-

357

wards that she knew all those deceits. She had hard vengeance exacted for it, so that we all suffered enough in consequence. It will be known in every land that she killed herself with Sigurd.'

Oddrún speaks of herself: 'I loved Gunnar as Brynhild should have done.' Atli would not accept Gunnar's honourable offer of marriage (apparently because of Brynhild's fate, though this is not clear) but Oddrún and Gunnar could not resist love's power. Atli was warned of their meetings but said he trusted Oddrún's discretion – she says, 'One should never deny the possibility of transgression where love is in question.' They were finally discovered in bed together, and it was apparently because of this that, when Gunnar and Hǫgni rode their 'hoof-gold' horses into Atli's courtyard, they were seized and put to death in the traditional ways. Oddrún was absent at the time but Gunnar played his harp to attract her help. She heard it and came but was forestalled by Atli's mother, who burrowed in serpent-shape to Gunnar's heart.

She says: 'I often marvel how I can hold onto life since then, since I thought I loved the battle-brave sword-dealer as myself . . .', and her last words are, 'Everyone lives according to his affections' – we are all decisively swayed by our emotions, they control us, not we them.

It is clear that the old story has been modified in important details. Oddrún is an entirely new character, and it is the forbidden love between her and Gunnar which brings about his death and Hǫgni's. He plays his harp not as an act of defiance, royal and dignified, but to summon aid. (In other young forms of the story he plays to soothe the snakes, and it is his success in this which causes the intervention of Atli's wicked mother; this was probably assumed by the poet here too. He does not, however, have the other variant in which Gunnar, because he was bound, had to play the harp with his toes – a pathetic instance of un-generous consistency on the part of some plodding imagination, but one which evidently increased some people's admiration for the indomitable hero – cf. frontispiece, top left).

The vocabulary is generally unobtrusive, occasionally unusual and inflated; there are numerous echoes of other poetry; the metre has a certain regularity, but its smoothness does not become trivial. It would be difficult to date the poem very closely on the basis of its style, but one may speculate about its background on the basis of its sensational ideas. A first consideration is that its attitude to love answers closely to what is found in foreign literature of the twelfth century (but hardly before that period). This could be typified in the famous story of Tristram, where the situation is not the same as in *Oddrúnargrátr*, but where the outlook is entirely comparable. If we went on to guess that the poem had social as well as literary relevance, we might conclude that its wholehearted acceptance of the idea that sexual passion cannot be denied would perhaps have special appeal in a society where women had, in fact or in prospect, husbands selected for them by their fathers with a main eye on social standing and money. (The poet in fact could not avoid using words which express social disapproval of illicit love: *vamm*, 'shame, blot', *lýti*, 'blemish', *lǫstr*, 'fault, failing'.) But it might follow that, if a poet could compose like this chiefly to please women, the fixed marriage customs must have existed side by side with notable female freedom. On the other hand, the poem might also be symptomatic of a protest, in which both men and women could share, against the Church's strict refusal of marriage within the forbidden degrees, a denial of love between men and women in various situations entirely artificial from the point of view of the 'family society'. (It is doubtless only a coincidence that the case here is one of a deceased wife's sister!) A background in which all these hypothetical factors were valid could be provided without difficulty by twelfth-century Iceland, and the poem is more likely to belong there than to one of the other northern countries, although we lack the detailed information to make a decisive comparison between them in such a matter.

Scaldic poetry

Scaldic metre and style were fully established in the course of the tenth century and scaldic poetry remained strongly traditional thereafter. It was extensively cultivated and the poetry of the past was remembered both for its own sake and because of the historical facts it might preserve or corroborate. Young poets naturally took the old poems as their models. Despite changes in the use and composition of kennings, noted above (p. 333), and much metrical experiment in the twelfth century, the kenning style lived on and the *dróttkvætt* stanza never fell from general favour. We know most about Icelandic poets, who from soon after the Conversion seem to have displaced Norwegians almost entirely as the official scalds of Norwegian kings. This does not mean that Norwegians stopped making and appreciating scaldic composition, but it does mean that their work is not preserved in the twelfth- and thirteenth-century histories of the kings of Norway, almost all written by Icelanders, where much of the scaldic verse is to be found. (Recent finds of rune-sticks in Bergen suggest that *dróttkvætt* poetry was still very common there *c.* 1200 and later; the obscurity of some of the diction might imply that Norwegian kenning conventions had perhaps developed in ways different from those of the Icelandic poets.)

Recognition of the basic homogeneity of the poetry over a long period must not, however, blind us to the variety and quality of the scaldic achievement. In an attempt to convey some notion of these a brief review will be given of the chief kinds of scaldic poetry, with some illustration of scaldic style and a final description of two typical but contrasting examples of scaldic excellence.

The oldest authentic scaldic poetry we possess is a fragment of a poem by Bragi, *Ragnarsdrápa*, in which he describes scenes painted on a shield – the subjects treated include Thor's fishing for the great snake and the death of Hamdir and Sǫrli (cf. above). It has been suggested that it is in such poetry, perhaps in this very poem, that we are to seek the birth of the kenning style. The poet was forced to compete with the lines, planes and colours of the graphic artist, and found in complex and heavily laden kennings a concentrated verbal means of conveying the pictorial detail, dynamic gesture and symbolic value of the scenes framed within the shield-segments. As a theory of origin this does not seem adequate, but it remains a telling analogy. Many people find illumination in considering scaldic styles and the styles of ornamental art described in Chapter 9 as products of a common taste, however hard it is to demonstrate concrete relationship between them. At the most superficial level it is at least possible to say that both kinds of art were made for audiences appreciative of craftsman's skill and not afraid of intellectual endeavour. However this may be, kennings were used to brilliant effect by Bragi in putting his shield-pictures into words, and equally brilliantly by Thjódolf in his *Haustlǫng* from about A.D. 900, a shield-poem in which he provides longer, more elaborate narratives of myths. A poem of a related kind is the *Húsdrápa*, composed in Iceland in the late tenth century, describing the scenes carved on the panels in a newly-built chieftain's hall.

We have a few poems in praise of royal dynasties, composed as a form of eulogy offered to a single ruler. Thjódolf's *Ynglingatal*, on the Uppsala dynasty from which the kings of Vestfold in Norway traced their descent, is the best known. Many poems are laudatory of living princes, in whose service the poets were or from whom they looked for reward: a helpful Icelandic list, *Skáldatal*, from the thirteenth century arranges the poets in groups according to the kings and earls they had composed about. These poems are descriptive and narrative, emphasizing the king's eminence as governor and warrior and lauding his generosity. A special kind of panegyric poem is one offered by a poet to save his life – a 'head-redemption'. Egil Skalla-Gríms-son's rhyming poem of this kind, presented to King Eirík Blood-axe in York about 950, is the most famous. Another kind of poem presented to a king was the 'Frank-speaking verses' composed about 1035 by Sigvat Thórdarson, in which he told King Magnús Ólafsson of unrest among his people, unrest for which he put the blame squarely on the king's shoulders. The king took heed of his words.

Some poems of praise are elegies, usually on kings but some-times on a kinsman or friend. Egil's great poem, *Sonatorrek*, a deeply personal and most unconventional expression of feeling, was occasioned by the death of his son (cf. p. 403). Among such commemorative poems *Eiríksmál* and *Hákonarmál* stand out be-cause of their experimental form and pagan philosophy (p. 391). The first was composed after the death of Eirík Blood-axe in England soon after 950. It is in mixed *málaháttr* and *ljóðaháttr* and the setting is Valhall, before and at the arrival of the dead king there. The second, composed about 965, is much more elaborate though in a similar mixture of metres. It describes with kennings and word-play the battle in which King Hákon was mortally wounded, and this is followed by conversation between the king and a valkyrie and more speech as they arrive at Valhall. The poem ends with four stanzas in which the poet makes his personal comment on the significance of Hákon's welcome to Valhall, the king's pre-eminence and the sadness of his loss.

There are poems in scaldic style on divine subjects, both pagan and Christian *Haustlǫng,* mentioned above as a shield-poem, belongs with these, and we have fragments of *drápur* (p. 328) in honour of Thor. Twelfth-century Christian poems show much variety. They include *Plácitúsdrápa,* a versification of the legend of St Eustace; *Geisli,* a poem in praise of St Ólaf by the Icelandic priest, Einar Skúlason, composed for delivery in Nidaros Cathedral in 1153; and *Harmsól,* by an Icelandic Augustinian canon, called Gamli, a personal confession of sin and a moving plea to others to repent.

There are many verses and a few longer poems in praise of or connected with beloved women. Other poems are satirical or scurrilous. Both kinds of poetry were believed to inflict personal and social damage and in Iceland they were banned by law.

Occasional verses, generally attributed to named characters, exist in great quantity in the Icelandic sagas and histories. These may be witty, boastful, threatening, defiant, sentimental, obscene, triumphant, pained – whatever indeed the Icelanders generally avoided saying in their laconic prose might find expression in verse. Needless to say, the problems of detecting what is authentic and what spurious among such poetry are enormous.

We may take one such *lausavísa,* whose authenticity can hardly be doubted, to illustrate problems connected with the interpretation and appreciation of such verse. It is in *Egils saga* and was made in the tenth century when Egil heard of the death of his kinsman by marriage, dear friend and protector, the Norwegian nobleman, Arinbjǫrn Thórisson. Egil praises him as a generous man; we know from other poems of his that silver meant much to Egil.

> *Þverra nú þeir's þverðu*
> *þingbirtingar Ingva*
> *hvar skalk mildra manna*
> *mjaðveitar dag leita,*
> *þeira's hauks fyr handan*
> *háfjǫll digulsnjávi*
> *jarðar gjǫrð við orðum*
> *eyneglða mér heglðu.*

Reduced to essentials Egil says this: 'The men who used to give their gold away are getting fewer. Where shall I look for generous men? Men such as those who, beyond the sea, lavished silver upon me because of my poetry.' This is not particularly impressive, and we must look more closely at the kennings and construction of the stanza in order to appreciate the challenge and beauty of the style.

The first half-stanza is not difficult to follow if put more or less straight into English, once we have grasped the kennings and understood – as is grammatically obvious in the Icelandic – that the italicized words are construed together:

> *Diminish now who diminished*
> *moot-summoners of sea-king*
> where shall I generous men
> *mead-horn's daylight* look for.

The moot of the sea-king is battle, whose summoners are warriors; mead-horn's daylight is the gold that adorns it, so gold in general. The mood is quiet, but there is emphatic word-play in the first line's repetition of the verb: those warriors who once diminished gold – by giving it away – are themselves being diminished – by death. The universal *Ubi sunt* motif is given a personal note in 'Where shall I look for generous men?' This is carried over into the second half-stanza, which is another subordinate sentence describing the past actions of the generous men Egil now looks for in vain. If we put this straight into a virtually uninflected language like English, the result is a mere jumble:

> *those who of hawk beyond*
> *high mountains with pendant snow*
> *earth's girdle against words*
> *isle-studded to me hail-covered.*

But it has to be construed like this: 'Those who, beyond isle-studded earth's girdle – the sea – made pendant snow – silver – fall like hail on my high mountains of the hawk – my hands – in return for my words – my poetry.' The 'earth's girdle' is qualified by a congruent metaphorical compound, 'isle-studded'; and in the rest there is a most pleasing kenning-cluster, again with a coherent verb, so that silver poured into his hands or silver rings slipped over his wrists are a storm of snow on mountains.

The literal version given above, is , of course, not a fair transfer, any more than a literal translation of Latin verse would be. For the native speaker interpretation was eased by the inflectional endings, which could show indubitable connections between words, by the initiation they had in the conventions of the poetic language, by the existence of certain preferred, but by no means regular, patterns for the distribution of sentence-parts, and possibly in some way by the manner of delivery, some system of pointing which we do not understand but may one day rediscover. There was, of course, no question of absolutely simultaneous comprehension, any more than in hearing a periodic sentence in German and English. Thus, in Egil's stanza, the audience could associate the adjective *eyneglða*, 'isle-studded', only with *gjǫrð*, 'girdle', because of its grammatical termination; and they knew that *jarðar gjǫrð*, 'earth's girdle', was a kenning of common type for the sea. Similarly, they would naturally connect *hauks*, 'hawk's', with *háfjǫll*, 'high mountains', because this makes a variant of a common kenning for hand or forearm, the 'hill' where the trained hawk rests. But the exact distribution of words in the second half-stanza only becomes quite clear when the last word is reached. Momentary ambiguities must have arisen – sometimes, indeed, it is evident that a poet relies on them himself, as he seems to be keeping options open as to ways in which he may complete a particular kenning. In the lines here a listener could bear in mind the possibility of construing *fyr handan*, 'beyond', with *háfjǫll*, 'high mountains', which follows hard upon it, at the same time as the association of *háfjǫll* with *hauks* would make it less likely that this collocation was intended. What doubt there was would be resolved only when the obvious completion of *fyr handan* came in *jarðar gjǫrð*, 'earth's girdle', the sea. It would also be natural for an auditor to link *digulsnjávi*, 'pendant snow' (in the dative case), with the 'high mountains', both because of their contiguity and because of their natural association. In fact, this connection was intended by the poet, but the precise way in which the two are to be joined is not clear until the verb finally appears.

364

There has been occasion to mention the poem *Vellekla* else-where (pp. 136, 138–40). It was composed by Egil's younger contemporary and friend, Einar Helgason, called 'scales-tinkle', in honour of Earl Hákon the Great (died 995). We now have thirty-seven stanzas and half-stanzas that are believed to belong to the poem, and it is certainly not complete. We may look at the open-ing verses, comprising the poet's call for silence and his preliminary description of his poetry and his subject. They are among the most vivid, forceful and pompous of all scaldic stanzas. The move-ment of the verse, the elaborate kennings, the swift succession of images, natural and unnatural, all combine to catch us up in the poet's exhilaration.

Hugstóran biðk heyra,	*Great-heart, bid I listen – listen,*
heyr jarl Kvasis dreyra,	*earl, to Kvasir's blood – earth-*
foldar vǫrð á fyrða	*warden, to men-of-firthbone's*
fjarðleggjar brim dreggjar.	*surf of lees.*

Kvasir's blood, we remember, is poetry (p. 331), and the earl is told to *hear* the blood (an example of the 'monstrous' style, cf. p. 332). Blood is a fluid, and the poet moves from it into a related kenning for poetry, 'surf of lees', i.e. strong drink or beer, of giants (p. 331). These beings are called 'men of the bone of the firth', 'men of the rock' – crags and mountains are giants' homes. But in this imagery the poet is also talking about the sea (surf, firth), and this shift is introduced by his description of the earl as *foldar vǫrðr*, 'earth-warden', which in Norway meant first and foremost one who looked seaward. And from now on the poet, while making verse about the art of poetry, is also making verse about the sea and seafaring. At the outset he uses striking rhyme, *heyra – heyr* (this repetition is called *dunhent* and is effectively used by Einar here and elsewhere) – *dreyra*, thudding like a pulse-beat, while in the last line we hear the heavy crash of the breakers in *leggjar – dreggjar*.

Ullar gengr of alla	*The fierce rock-lagoon of dwarves*
asksǫgn, þess's hvǫt magnar	*goes over the ship's crew of the*
byrgis bǫðvar sorgar,	*god who makes potent the urging*
bergs grymmilá dverga.	*of the grief of the fort of battle.*

In the first stanza the earl was told to listen. Now the poet says that his poetry – described this time as the water that was kept in a rock and had belonged to dwarves (cf. p. 331) – breaks over the warrior's crew, washes over the men in the hall like a wave over a warship. 'Grief of the fort of battle' is a 'doubled' kenning for sword, the thing that causes pain to the shield, man's defence or fort in battle.

Hljóta munk, né hlítik,	*I shall have to bail (nor do I*
Hertýs, of þat frýju,	*need to be urged to it) the brine*
fyr ǫrþeysi at ausa	*of the wine-ship of the War-god*
austr vingnóðar flausta.	*for the urgent driver of ships.*

The sea of poetry that broke over the men in the hall leads the poet to his next image. He has to bail, but not the ship he has been talking about, but rather the ship which contains the wine of Odin, i.e. the god himself who had carried the mead of poetry. It is appropriate that he should be bailing out the brine of that ship, pouring out his poetry, for the earl – his men know all about bailing for he drives his ships furiously on.

In the next half-stanza Einar makes a tentative start at praising Earl Hákon directly, but he is still preoccupied with his identification of poetry and sea. Now he is back to his own recital: the sea of Odin foams before me; the wave of the ocean of Odin roars over the flat rock of charms – his verse surges over his tongue. And in the next half-stanza, which completes the introduction, he calls again for a hearing, now that the 'wave' of poetry begins to heave. He ends here with a striking discordancy, as he began, telling men to *hear* 'the boat of the rock-men' – poetry, which can be called 'the ship of the dwarves' in accordance with the story told above on pp. 331–2.

By now his audience must have been riveted. The men in Hákon's following who first heard this poem were Norwegian warriors and yeomen, but they were also born seamen. With great skill Einar makes his demand for silence an evocation of the Viking's way of life, a coast of fjords and skerries, stormy weather, dangerous sailing, the drenching weight of the wave breaking over the ship, the labour of bailing. The idea of poetry as a mighty liquor could not be exploited more richly. The tales of the origin of poetry, remote from everyday reality but not from the poet's mind, and his actual poem, its circumstances and moment of recital, meet in the sea-imagery, into which the flood of inspiration can be transmuted. We analyse these things as separate factors, but in the poetry they are fused in an over-whelming concentration, a compounding that produces not a smooth-surfaced, indistinguishable alloy but a nuggety amalgam in which the elements gleam jagged here and there. When with patience and sympathy we achieve some awareness of this em-bracing identification of the sensuous and intellectual, at once natural and baroque, we realize that we have learnt something of a Norse artist's assimilation of experience, his mode of percep-tion of life.

Thirty years or so after Einar composed *Vellekla*, another Ice-landic poet, Sigvat Thórdarson, a devoted follower of King Ólaf Haraldsson of Norway, went to visit Earl Rǫgnvald, most prob-ably in Västergötland, on the king's business. He described his successful but uncomfortable journey in a sequence of verses called *Austrfararvísur*, 'East-journey verses'. We are fortunate in having much other poetry by Sigvat, whose verse was deservedly popular and an authentic source of information about people and events in the time of St Ólaf and his son, Magnús. He was a man of firm character, a bold and loyal friend, good-humoured and tactful by temperament. What distinguishes his composition are a distinctly personal ease and good taste. He fills his 'East-journey verses' with pleasing matter in a prevailing mood of gentle, rueful comedy at his own expense; there are noteworthy touches of natural description and sparing use of kennings, none of many elements and of course without the introduction of pagan terminology. The following four stanzas give some im-pression of his range. They flow like a limpid stream and make a good contrast to the superb sea-crashing of the opening of *Vellekla*.

We must remember that Sigvat is making a hard and toilsome journey through wasteland and forest. In the first stanza he remembers with nostalgia the speed and freshness of sailing. The second pair of stanzas find him close to the journey's end.

Kátr var ek opt þá er úti
ǫrðigt veðr á fjǫrðum
vísa segl í vási
vindblásit skóf Strinda.
Hestr óð kafs at kostum,
kilir ristu haf Lista,
út þá er eisa létum
undan skeiðr at sundi.

I was often cheerful in sea-toil
when out in the fjords the hard
wind ripped round the weather-
blown sail of the prince of men
of Strinda. The horse of the deep
moved finely, keels furrowed the
sea of Lister, out where we let
ships rush on through the sound.

Snjalls létum skip skolla
skjǫldungs við ey tjǫlduð
fyr ágætu úti
ǫndurt sumar landi;
en í haust, þars hestar
hagþorns á mó sporna,
ték ýmissar ekkjum
iðir, hlýtk at ríða.

At summer's start we let the
ships of the bold king gently
sway under awnings way out by
an island off the famous land;
but this autumn I must ride,
where horses tread over haw-
thorn's moorland; I tell ladies of
my varied occupations!

Jór renn aptanskæru
allsvangr gǫtur langar,
vǫll kná hófr til halla
– hǫfum lítinn dag – slíta.
Nú er þat er blakkr of bekki
berr mik Dǫnum ferri.
Fákr laust drengs í díki
– dægr mœtask nú – fœti.

The steed runs in the gloaming,
famished, over long paths. The
hoof can wear out the ground
that leads to houses – we have
little daylight. Now the black
horse carries me over streams,
distant from Danes. My swift
one caught his leg in a ditch –
day and night converge.

Út munu ekkjur líta
allsnúðula prúðar
– fljóð sjá reyk – hvar ríðum
Rǫgnvalds í bý gǫgnum.
Keyrum hross svá at heyri
harða langt at garði
hesta rás ór húsum
hugsvinn kona innan

The stately women will look
out in all haste – the ladies see
the dust-cloud – where we ride
past in Rǫgnvald's town. Drive
on our horses so that from indoors
the wise woman may hear from
far off the coursing of steeds
towards the courtyard.

Such verse requires no commentary but it may be helpful to
point out some obvious ways in which the style achieves its

fluency, unlike the encrusted, pompous style of Einar's. Sigvat's stanzas have, for example, more clauses with finite verbs in them, and these shorter sentences are easily picked out, even where the word-order is complicated. The kennings are few and simple, and there are few compounded words of the substantial trisyllabic type, like *vindblásit* in the first stanza above. Small adverbs and conjunctions occur in stressed positions and may carry rhyme such as *úti*, *út* and *fyr* in the first two stanzas. The poet uses adjectives like *ágætr*, 'famous', of the land of Norway in the second stanza, and *hugsvinn*, 'wise', of a lady in the fourth; while they are not entirely empty of meaning, they produce a diffuse not concentrated effect, more like the tone of everyday speech.

The inimitable poetry of the scalds is of value to the student of religion because of the authentic pagan heritage it transmits. It is valuable to the historian because it offers first-hand comments on people and events in periods from which primary sources are otherwise rare. But its greatest value is in the introduction it gives us to the poets themselves, their personalities and their strivings as craftsmen. We gain unique glimpses into the ancient Norse world through their verse, but their poems are also sources of living excitement and delight. It is infinitely regrettable that they are bound to appear so stiff and pallid in translation and paraphrase.

Justice

In this chapter we shall give brief consideration to the most important procedures by which one man maintained his rights against another by law in the ancient Scandinavian world. The written laws that we have were not codified until the twelfth and thirteenth centuries (p. xix), a busy time of legal creativity and adjustment, occasioned especially by the extension of the power of the monarchy and the influence of canon law. The difficulties of disentangling new and old vary in different parts of the corpus, but some main lines of older customary law can be distinguished, revealed sometimes by comparison with other Germanic or primitive law (an aspect that cannot be developed here) and sometimes by features that emphasize collective, family responsibility as opposed to individual, personal responsibility. The following description is necessarily in broad terms and when, for example, a legal rule is said to exist 'in Sweden', it is not to be taken as implying that it is attested in every province of Svealand and Götaland.

To be a legal man one needed to be free, to belong to a family and to have a residence – the last were doubtless often synonymous in early times. The status of the family within the free yeoman society could affect the legal rights of the individual, particularly in Norway (cf. pp. 84–5), and general legal responsibility rested with next-of-kin. Domicile was essential for legal procedure to take formal effect, because in order to bring a charge against a man it was normally necessary to summon him to appear at a particular *thing*, and both the correct delivery of the summons and the location of the assembly depended on the man's residence. Some part of procedure in a case might depend on the testimony of neighbours, whose identification also obviously depended on where a man lived. One reason why vagabonds were looked on with such disfavour was doubtless their nonlegal status in respect of residence: they were free men but it was more difficult for other free men to obtain legal redress against men without homes. It should be added that in Iceland a man had no legal existence who was not 'in *thing* with' a *goði* (p. 134). This contract with a chieftain dictated the assembly within the Quarter he was supposed to attend; and his *goði* might also be needed in court procedure.

A general notion of the free man's legal nature was expressed by the adjective *heilagr,* used in the laws with a sense of 'inviolable; in which a man has exclusive right'. The word is cognate with English 'holy' and has this sense in religious contexts, certainly in Christian and probably in heathen times; but how far a religious sanction was felt to exist behind the legal sanction implied by its use in the laws is hard to determine. It has been forcefully argued in recent studies that the word's profane sense was originally dominant, perhaps exclusively so, among the Norsemen and that it only gained its sacral connotation with the conversion to Christianity, but we lack the authentic pagan evidence to be entirely sure of this. Corresponding to the adjective are the verb *helga* and the abstract nouns, WN *helgi,* EN *hælgh,* the former meaning to impose or claim the inviolable status indicated by the second. This legally guaranteed security of the free man's person is made explicit in the compound *mann-helgi, manhælgh.* To disturb or destroy this inviolable state is naturally an offence for which legal penalty can be exacted. It also follows that a natural, automatic consequence of some illegal acts – malicious attack, adultery, acts classified as deeds of a *níðingr* (p. 426), for example – was loss of inviolability; and if a man were killed under such circumstances, nothing could be claimed for him. The same result could follow as a penalty after a legal case had demonstrated a man's guilt, so that he was deprived of his inviolable status, either as an enemy of the public or of an individual; he had forfeited his rights to legal consideration and could obtain no legal redress for injuries done him. The extreme application of this is in sentences of outlawry (p. 382). A limited application is found in Danish law which says that a man who failed to abide by a judgement of a court could lose his *manhælgh* in respect of his prosecutor who, if he caught him within the *herred,* could ill-treat him as he wished short of maiming or killing him. A man without *manhælgh* in this restricted sense was also denied certain of the ordinary public rights of a free man – he could not appear as a plaintiff or as an oath-helper.

In the West Norse world a further expression of the freeman's legal status was to be found in his *réttr*, 'right', the claim he had to treatment of a certain kind from his fellows which found expression in a monetary value put on his status by society (cf. p. 85). This was made a standard price payable to him as personal satisfaction for certain offences committed against him. Halved or doubled amounts were prescribed in certain cases. Thus, an insult was called *fullréttisorð*, 'full-right's saying', and an ambiguous remark, one that could be taken in a good or bad sense, was *halfréttisorð*, 'half-right's saying', indicating the degree of satisfaction to be made in each case.

Procedure

The *thing*, the public assembly of free men, was the forum for complaints made by one man against another. There were *ad hoc* procedural *things* summoned in respect of a single case, but the regular assemblies ranged from those for a *herred*-quarter to the general assembly of a province, or in Iceland from the local *thing*, superintended by three *goðar*, to the Althing, the assembly of the whole nation where forty-eight *goðar* functioned. As courts these assemblies were originally all on one level, and those for larger areas merely gave people from different localities a formal opportunity to do legal and other business together. Cases could be transferred from one *thing* to another if difficulties were encountered. In Trøndelag, for example, a suit might move from the one-*fylke* assembly to the two-*fylke* assembly, from there to the four-*fylke* assembly, and from there to Eyrathing, the assembly for the eight *fylke* of the region, or to Frostathing, which had jurisdiction in Trøndelag and the other provinces associated with it (p. 46). Larger *things* tended to become regular rather than optional courts of second instance, and in time this gave rise to a pyramidal structure, ultimately with the king at the apex. In Iceland some cases involving minor penalties had to be initiated before the local *thing*, and the Althing then provided a court of second instance; in other cases a man might choose where he would bring his suit.

The assembly as a whole was originally responsible for giving a verdict in favour of one side or another. We know little about the manner of judgement in early times, but assent to a decision and hostility to a condemned man were expressed by the custom called *vápnatak*, 'weapon-taking', when arms were clashed and brandished (in Iceland the term came to mean the end of the *thing*-proceedings in general). In some places suits were presented before a restricted number of judges, representative of the public; they could generally be challenged and replaced if there was reason to doubt their impartiality. For the most part they had little scope for the exercise of discretion, for the laws were explicit in prescribing both procedures and penalties. In Norway and Sweden cases must have been argued before such men as lawmen and *herred*-leaders (p. 127). These were originally elected by local yeomen, but in later times (in Norway by about 1200) these became royal appointments, and the general tendency was for judges to be state officials with a duty to investigate a case as well as listen to the pleading.

In a closely-knit local society there was often little doubt about the nature of an offence and the identity of an offender, and the prime need was to demonstrate that a man's responsibility for a wrong was notorious. A man had right on his side if he had the community on his side. The point of view of the public was not necessarily dictated by abstract notions of justice but could depend on hard-headed expediency. This is reflected at one extreme in certain provisions in Norwegian law, where responsibility for killing or starting a fight has to be decided. Thus, if three men were together and one was killed, both the others were counted guilty if neither one of them confessed or absented himself from the assembly. If four men were together and one was killed, the slayer was odd man out of the remaining three – even if he was a slave. If a man was killed in a company of five or more and no single man made himself responsible for it, the prosecutor could pick out the best man among them as the one to be charged. 'If men are fighting and people see their fight from across a river or impassable ground and cannot recognize them, and one of them is so cut about that his head is off or his brains on the ground or his spine severed or both his hands off, then he is the one who started the fight, for he could never again

373

strike a man down; the other man has inviolable security' [i.e. full legal rights in case of attack, an avenger has no superior right]. The dead or seriously maimed man can take no personal vengeance or cause death in the future, and it is better to do what may protect public peace than to attempt an investigation into the truth whose outcome is bound to be doubtful.

A man bringing a case against another was required to demonstrate his notorious guilt through the testimony of witnesses, in some places with the aid of oath-helpers. If public conviction of his guilt was substantiated by prescribed legal means, no defence was possible, judgment was given against him and he was obliged to abide by the judgment or suffer further penalties. Where the case was not entirely self-evident, the accused had the right to clear himself, usually by oath-helpers, sometimes also with witnesses. In every case the law laid down which side had to provide the major demonstration of public knowledge, represented by witnesses, or public faith, represented by compurgators.

The people who were called as witnesses were seldom casual observers of an incident whose testimony was expected to give others a true view of what had happened. They were rather people formally called on by a principal in a suit to take note of facts that affected him and his case. The law prescribed the presence of witnesses, usually two free men who had come of age, at certain important contracts, such as marriage settlements and agreements on terms of truce, property sale and division. In other cases a man had to make public before witnesses the nature of an injury received or loss incurred. Witnesses had also to be present at every stage in the legal procedure, from the formal summons to the actual proceedings at the assembly's court, and at each successive stage they gave their testimony that the correct procedure had been followed. A name given in the Frostathing Law to the neutral men, who were called by either party to stand by and hear the actual pleading of a case, is *dómstaurar*, 'judgement-or court-props', and the essential function of many of the witnesses formally required by law was the same as is now fulfilled by written minutes of meetings.

When the law allowed a man the right to clear himself, straightforward denial was inadequate even where, for whatever reason, the accusation itself depended on little more than one

374

man's word. A denial had to be supported in some way by public opinion, and this was effected by the use of compurgators. The number of oath-helpers varied. Twelve was a common number, but could be doubled or trebled in some places, especially when oath came against oath and it was a question of seeing which side could do better in producing such public support. In Norway the number was graded according to the seriousness of the case: the accused swore with one oath-helper where property valued at two *aurar* was involved, with two (*lýrittareiðr*, 'common-law-oath') for property of three *aurar* or more and for minor criminal cases, with five (*séttareiðr*, 'half-dozen-oath') in cases where the penalty was outlawry compoundable by atonement, and with eleven oath-helpers (*tylftareiðr*, 'dozen-oath') for unatonable crimes.

We know very little of pagan oaths but they could be sworn on sacred objects and with invocation of gods (p. 403). In Christian times the oath was solemnly sworn, after due preparation, on a Gospel or other sacred book inside a church. After the man accused had made his statement on oath, then each of his oath-helpers swore that they believed his oath to be honest. Their oaths thus had no direct bearing on the facts of the case at all. Originally the co-swearers were generally selected by a man from his own kindred, and this may have been seen as a safeguard in that a whole family's good fortune was put at risk. But the religious sanctity of the oath was not always equally strong – abuses arising from false swearing were one cause of clerical opposition to compurgation in the thirteenth century – though family loyalty tended to be, so that the system did not necessarily produce a clear-cut conviction, public or private, that justice had been done. The laws of the different countries show various modifications of the system which are aimed at achieving a more evidently fair assessment of right and wrong.

In Norway we find a distinction made in the Frostathing Law between two kinds of oath-helpers. In the one sort (*fangavitni*) the members were freely selected, but in the other (*nefndarvitni* – the only sort known in the Gulathing Law) a 'dozen-oath', for example, comprised the principal, two close kinsmen, seven men freely chosen by him, and two men selected from a group of twelve, six of whom had been nominated by each side. In Jutland we meet what is probably a thorough mixing of old and new in the so-called *kyns næfnd*, 'family panel' (cf. *nafn*, 'name', *nefna*, *næfnæ*, 'to name'), which consisted of twelve members drawn from one party's family but nominated by his legal opponent.

It is in Denmark and Sweden that we find the fullest development of a distinctly neutral panel, called *næfnd*, 'nominated group', as in the Norwegian *nefndarvitni* and Jutlandic *kyns næfnd* just mentioned. Its origin is uncertain and it perhaps did not come much into prominence until the thirteenth century, after the abolition of the ordeal (see below). This panel differed decisively from the oath-helpers of the old system in that its members did not simply testify to their faith in a man's honesty but delivered a verdict on oath as to their view of the truth of a case. This could entail an examination of facts and a weighing of evidence, so that their function was more like that of a modern jury. It is probable that unanimity was at first expected of such a panel, but later a majority decision was counted acceptable There was a tendency to make the *næfnd* a kind of standing committee. In Västergötland, for example, such a panel was established at the outset of each assembly to act when required, while in Jutland it came about that the king appointed some such 'jurymen' to serve for life, while others were locally elected for a year at a time.

In Iceland there is practically no trace of compurgation, probably because under the circumstances of colonization the normal family aid that was expected in such a system was simply not to be had. Procedure in a case required, however, in addition to witnesses, a panel of farmers, whose identity was dictated by their economic status (liable to *þingfararkaup*, p. 86) and by their domicile in immediate proximity to the scene of the offence or other vital place as prescribed by the law. Emphasis was thus placed on the theoretical likelihood that the neighbours who made up the panel would know the facts and circumstances of the matter at issue. The panel had nine members in more serious cases, five in less serious, and was called *nábúakviðr*, 'neighbours' utterance'; the word *kviðr* is related to *kveða*, 'to say, declare' (p. 328). Their *kviðr*, or verdict, followed the decision of the majority and generally applied to single facts or points of procedure; it allowed progress from stage to stage of a suit and the means of meeting legal objection from the other side. The overall duties that the *næfnd* came to have in continental Scandinavia were in effect performed in Iceland by the judges. At the Quarter Courts at the Althing thirty-six judges were appointed, one by each *goði* (pp. 132–4). When a case had been pleaded and defended before these men, one of the judges rehearsed the process of the prosecution and one the process of the defence, and the judges then gave their verdict. If six or more of them disagreed with a verdict, two judgements were entered, one in favour of each party. No resolution of this legal deadlock was thereafter possible in the courts before the so-called Fifth Court was established *c.* 1005 (p. 58), but it may sometimes have happened that a duel was proposed to reach a settlement at such a juncture. In the Fifth Court a decision was reached by a simple majority, and chances of deadlock, though not entirely removed, were practically negligible.

Ordeal

Testimony could be strengthened by swearing an oath, and even more by submitting to ordeal to justify it. Appeal to divine judgement revealed through the results of ordeal was especially made in cases where evidence was hard to come by or in certain instances as a form of final test after compurgation had failed. Among the former kind, to take examples from Norwegian law, may be counted the opportunity of ordeal given to a woman to prove her assertion that her child's father was a man who was dead or abroad, or the ordeal offered as the only means of clearing a man named by the victim as his slayer. Among the latter kind were incest, unnatural sexual behaviour and witchcraft.

A form of ordeal used for women was *ketiltak*, 'cauldron-taking', when stones had to be plucked from the bottom of a vat of boiling water. The commonest type was *járnburðr*, 'iron-carrying', known throughout the North and given a detailed description in the Skåne Law:

> If a man is to carry iron, he must wash his hand and afterwards touch nothing with it, neither hair nor clothes nor anything else, until he touches the iron and takes it up. If a man

carries 'throw-iron', he must go nine paces before he throws it. If he throws it sooner, he is condemned. If some say he is condemned and some say he is not, let two men testify that he carried it fully and not falsely. If a man carries 'trough-iron', the trough is to stand twelve paces from the posts and the man who is to carry it must throw it into the trough. If it falls outside the trough, the man must pick it up and throw it again into the trough . . . As soon as the iron has been carried, a mitten is to be placed over the hand and a seal placed on it and it shall be opened on Saturday [the ordeal took place on a Wednesday]. The hand is not to be freed until the accuser arrives, and he shall be waited for until the end of the appointed assembly-time. If he does not come, then the men who are present are to release the hand and judge whether he is guilty or not guilty of the charge. If he is clean . . . then he shall pay the priest his fee; if he is not clean, then the accuser shall pay it.

Bandaging and subsequent inspection of the wound were the normal procedure, and the decision was based on the relative cleanness of the wound. The priest's fee was for the liturgical ceremony prescribed by the Church in connection with ordeal.

As a form of evidence or proof the ordeal must have been introduced under Christian auspices – it was well known in England and among the Franks, for example. Saxo thought the ordeal by hot iron which Bishop Poppo underwent to convince the Danish king of the superiority of Christianity was an ultimate cause of its introduction, and it is possible that it was adopted all the more readily because of Norse admiration for Christian ascetics who, because of their faith, did not fear or feel pain. It was well meant in that it gave a last chance to people in a perilous situation unable to use or profit from the normal system of compurgation, but the possibility of falsification of the result, for example, could not be ruled out, and doubt was not infrequently cast on its efficacy. Such doubts were confirmed by the Church itself at the Fourth Lateran Council of 1215, when ordeal was generally forbidden; and its use in the Scandinavian countries came to a gradual end after that date.

The duel

Two men could settle their differences by fighting, and rights of conquest were awarded the victor, either in general terms or in accordance with a specific agreement made before the duel. As far as that went, single combat might partake of the nature of a wager. It also seems to have been accepted that recourse could be had to a duel to settle a legal case, but as a procedure it was extra-judicial, even though the result was legally binding. In Christian times it might be regarded as an ordeal, but it is unlikely that it had this character among pagans. It is true that some ritual or sacrificial practices probably accompanied a formal duel in heathen times, but these are more likely to have been precautionary measures or an expression of personal gratitude than an indication of public belief in divine intervention.

Duelling was abolished early in the North; it is uncertain when it disappeared in Denmark and Sweden, but it was forbidden soon after 1000 in Iceland and Norway. Saxo knew it was an ancient custom in Denmark but, while he regretted its replacement by ordeal and compurgation, he was not happy to report an attempt to reintroduce it *c.* 1150 under Sven III. A brief legal text, which shows that in Sweden the duel was an accepted means of making good the most serious kind of verbal injury or its denial, is the so-called Pagan Law (*Hednalagen*), extant in modern copies but ultimately from a thirteenth-century lawbook of Uppland origin. It says this:

A man uses an unutterable word to another: 'You are not a man's equal and not a man at heart.' [He answers:] 'I am as much a man as you.' They are to meet at a place where three roads join. If the one comes who gave the insult and the other who received it does not come, then he will be what he is called: he cannot swear a legal oath or bear witness on behalf of either man or woman. If he comes who received the insult and not the one who gave it, then let him shout three *niðing*-shouts and mark the other man in the ground. Let him who spoke what he did not dare maintain be so much the worse a man in consequence. If they meet both fully armed, and the one falls who received the insult, atone for him with half-price for manslaughter. If he falls who gave the insult – the crime of

379

words is worst, the tongue a prime slayer – let him lie in the valueless field [i.e. no atonement is paid for his death].

(On the name of *niðingr*, see p. 426.) The mark in the ground must have been some visible token of the man's disgrace, perhaps comparable in some degree with the *niðstǫng* 'shame-pole', described in *Egils saga* as a post with a horse's head on it raised against a man with hostile runes and poetry, or the *tréníð*, 'wood-shame', forbidden in Norwegian laws, which most likely consisted of a wooden figure, or figures, representing the man against whom it was directed in some disgusting posture. The phrase *Tunga hovuðbani*, 'the tongue a prime slayer', varies a proverb found also in *Hávamál* (pp. 342–4), *tunga er hǫfuðs bani*, 'the tongue causes the death of the head'. It is finally interesting to note that if the man who was insulted is killed in the duel, he is only atoned for with half the usual price, even though he had shown his manliness by responding to the insult in the proper way. This suggests that the duel was to some extent considered to share the nature of an ordeal: the fact that he lost the fight presumably occasioned doubt as to whether he was entirely worthy, and so caused the reduction of the atonement.

We are given more information about duelling procedure in some Icelandic texts. The usual West Norse word for the formal duel is *holmganga*, 'island-going', because islets must have been favoured as sites for such fighting: they had ready-made barriers which made interference and escape difficult, and possibly it was felt that they were neutral ground where blood might be shed without danger. The most detailed description we have is in *Kormáks saga*, ch. 10, where it is said a kind of duelling ring was made of a piece of cloth about seven and a half feet square fixed on the ground by pegs at the corners. Around the square three furrows, each a foot wide, were cut and outside these were four hazel posts, possibly joined by a rope. The two duellists met on the cloth, each accompanied by a second. The principals inflicted the blows turn and turn about, with the challenged man striking first, and the seconds protected their principals with a shield. A new shield was substituted for one hacked useless, and up to three shields might be used on either side. If blood was shed on the cloth, the fight could be called off; the man worse

wounded could buy himself off then, or at some subsequent stage
of the fight, by payment of three marks of silver. A man who set
foot outside the hazel-post boundary was said to retreat, but if
he went outside with both feet, he was said to be running.

Penalties

The penalties imposed by the courts were of three main kinds:
atonement in cash; outlawry that could be compounded or
limited by payment of atonement (WN *bótamál*, EN *botæmal*);
outlawry that could not be compounded (*óbótamál, orbotæmal*).
In the monarchies many penalties required additional fines to
be paid to the king. Physical punishments, like whipping and
mutilation, were inflicted on slaves but not generally on free men,
though in time they came to be used as penalties for minor theft.
Beheading was counted a decent mode of execution for the free
man. Hanging was the usual punishment for theft, while stoning,
drowning or sinking in a morass might be used for people guilty
of witchcraft. The execution of criminals was properly the duty
of those who had prosecuted them, although this function was
later taken over by the local royal official. Thieves and warlocks
were especially regarded as dangers to society as a whole, requiring public action to destroy them, but otherwise it was
normally family against family, man against man, and legal
condemnation of an outlawed man still left execution in private
hands.

A man's right to immediate vengeance was recognized in
certain instances, especially where close kinswomen were taken
in adultery or where a killing straightway provoked an attack
on the slayer. In the latter case a formal offer of atonement required the avenger to stay his hand and give his enemy the chance
of legal defence at an assembly. For many kinds of offence atonement was the fixed legal penalty and if a man chose or was
obliged to proceed by law he had no option but to accept the
payment, and forcible distraint to obtain it was legal. In some
places, as in Norway and Gotland (see below), it was legally
permissible to refuse atonement offered for manslaughter. The
'levelling oath' (p. 428), known in Denmark and to some extent
elsewhere, reflects the fear of being accused of 'turning honour
into money' by accepting atonement in place of vengeance.

A name for the man condemned to outlawry was *skógarmaðr*, 'forest-man'; it became the standard term even in Iceland where refuge in forest was hardly possible. In general, outlawry must have often amounted to a sentence of banishment from the district, province or whole country. It also entailed the confiscation of the outlaw's property (but not usually land), from which came payment of compensation to the prosecutor, debts and sometimes an allowance for the maintenance of dependents; the residue must have originally gone to the local inhabitants, but in the monarchies it came to be looked on as the king's due. This may have been chiefly because of increasing recognition of the need for official co-operation in achieving the execution of justice on an outlawed man, especially when both court and confiscation were superintended by royal agents. As the king came to be looked on as the ultimate arbiter, rights of pardon were also granted him, and he might allow an outlawed man to rejoin society, although in Denmark, for example, a man sentenced for killing could only be pardoned with the consent of the victim's family.

The full, irredeemable outlaw 'is as if he were dead', said the Eidsivathing Law. It was criminal to feed him, harbour him, help him on his way. He lost all goods and all his rights – his children illegitimate, his body buried in unconsecrated ground. In its full rigour the sentence of outlawry required the rejection of the condemned man not only by indifferent society but also by his own family. Such total rejection can only have become possible where social authority, doubtless chiefly exercised by superior men (see Chapter 4), had achieved a notable strength. It may not have come about until the early Viking Age itself.

A condemned man might be given a chance to escape. In Norway, for example, a man who failed to produce the oath-helpers he required had 'five days from the church-door' in which to get to safety. Elaborate rules for asylum were applied in manslaughter cases in Gotland. Three churches there had special asylum sanctity. When a man killed another, he had to retire forthwith to one of these, accompanied by his closest kinsmen, and stay there for forty days. Thereafter he should go to the place where he intended to draw his *banda*, 'band, ribbon, enclosing line'; this should encircle three farms and a certain surrounding area – it might contain a church but not a market or assembly place. Within that perimeter the man had inviolable status, though if he were killed on this ground only half the usual atonement was payable for him. He could only safely leave the area in order to go abroad on pilgrimage and he went back to it on his return. Once inside the *banda*, atonement should be offered on his behalf. If the principal on the other side wished, he could accept atonement at once and be 'a man without shame'; but he could also refuse it at the outset and twice more at yearly intervals, in the hope of waylaying the slayer and exacting vengeance. The culprit had to stay within the *banda* the full three years, but thereafter the case was invalid against him if atonement was not accepted. The penalties imposed on a man who made no offer of atonement were full outlawry and fines to the public purse.

Somewhat similar rules existed in Iceland for the man condemned to the compoundable outlawry called *fjǫrbaugsgarðr*, 'life-ring fence'. He bought his life – i.e. he bought himself off from full outlawry – by payment of a silver ring (later an equivalent sum in kind) and was supposed to leave Iceland for three years. While in Iceland he enjoyed normal rights at three specified farms and on the direct roads joining them and on the road to the ship that was to take him abroad. Elsewhere he could be killed without redress. He had to attempt to get abroad in three successive summers and if he failed he automatically became a full outlaw; the same penalty was incurred if he returned before his three years' banishment were out. Once abroad the 'life-ring' man enjoyed normal security, unlike the full outlaw who was everywhere open to attack without any legal redress.

From the Västergötland Law

The ancient laws of Scandinavia are generally framed in casuistic fashion: a man does so-and-so, then the procedure and the penalty are such-and-such. This often means close description of people's behaviour and offers welcome information to a social historian. Sometimes, above all in the Swedish laws, the statement of a hypothetical case is presented in vivid, dramatic terms, with passages where rhythm and alliteration may produce an effect like that of verse. But this kind of framing also means that the laws are often unsystematically presented and show great variety and complexity of detail. Brief and cogent quotation is consequently difficult, but the following passage from the Older Västergötland Law may give some idea both of how law might be framed (here in plain, sometimes cryptic terms) and how legal procedure might work.

On manslaughter. – If a man is killed and deprived of life, then the slaying is to be announced at one assembly and the death reported to the heir, and [the announcement] repeated at the next. And at the third assembly he must bring his case, or else the suit is of no avail. Then the slayer must go to the assembly and stand outside the assembly place and send men to the assembly to ask for safe conduct (*grip*). The *thing*-men shall allow him to appear at the assembly. He is to admit the killing.

Then the heir is to give the name of the slayer. It is in his power to allot the slaying to whom he pleases if there are many slayers. With a child as heir, then the man nearest related to him on the father's side shall name the slayer with him. If a wife has [so young] a child [that he is] on her knee, she is to name the slayer. Then the men who laid hands on the dead man and the men who were present at the slaying are to be named. There shall be five of them [at most], and one man accused of plotting the man's death.

Then a meeting shall be decided on by judgement at the home [of the accused] on the day agreed by all at the assembly. Then at that meeting *thing*-men's witness is to be given: 'I was then at the assembly and six of us together. The judgement in your case was that you should stand here today and make good the charge of manslaughter against him on oath with two dozen helpers. May God be gracious to me and my witnesses in as much as judgement in your case was given as I now testify.'

Then the heir shall swear, 'So may God be gracious to me and my witnesses that you laid on him point and edge [of weapons] and you are his true slayer, and such was the name I gave you at the assembly.' Then the heir shall stand before the second dozen [of oath-helpers] and swear the same oath. Twelve men shall stand in each dozen, and each dozen shall use the same expression. This expression shall be used in each 'dozen-oath': may God be gracious or angry towards him.

Then the heir shall go to the following general assembly (*sægnarþing*) . . . and testify with men who had been present, praying God be gracious to him and his witnesses in as much as he had at the home-meeting done everything in respect of the accused's security as the law prescribed. Then he is to go before the assembly again and have him judged to be without security at the hands of heir and prosecutor and unatonable. Then he [the condemned man] shall flee from peaceful conditions (*friþær*) – at the morning-meal eat at home on that assembly day and at supper-time eat in the forest. The *herred*-leader [p. 127] is liable to pay twelve marks if the outlaw stays where he is and he does not concern himself about it, and forty marks are payable by the *herred*, and three marks by the man who eats and drinks with him and meets him . . . If on the other hand he has atonement offered on his behalf, he may eat supper guiltless [at home].

If they are willing to take atonement, then there shall be nine marks in heir-atonement and twelve marks in kindred-atonement. [Of this twelve] six shall be paid by the [slayer's] heir, six by the family, three on the father's side, three on the mother's. [That six is made up thus:] the closest kinsman shall pay 12 ounces, the next closest 6 ounces, the next 3 ounces, the next thereafter $1\frac{1}{2}$ ounces. So all shall pay and so shall all receive, always reduced by half at each remove, until the sixth degree is reached [i.e. normally a fifth cousin, who would be liable to pay $\frac{3}{8}$ ounce].

Old and new

Instances have been noted of the growing influence of royal authority in the judicial sphere, with the use of officials in the administration of justice and the king's new rights to fine, confiscate and pardon. A notable departure from the old system of family support was the institution of the more neutral *næfnd*, the 'nominated group', with functions approaching those of a jury. Such developments were sometimes instigated and always aided by the influence of the Church because of the stress Christian teaching laid on individual responsibility. It opposed the idea of collective family responsibility expressed in older forms of compurgation and in the wide kindred's share in payment and receipt of atonement. Canon law maintained that a wrongdoer was solely responsible and attached more importance than native law to the circumstances and degree of wilfulness of a man's offence. This attitude of the Church could only be finally effective when some system of public law and order gave the individual the protection which membership of a family had previously provided. This came slowly with the gradual extension of royal authority, and had by no means been achieved by the end of the period we are describing. Consequently we find that in the thirteenth century churchmen had to continue to accept vengeance as a just form of retribution, while insisting that only the guilty should suffer from it (cf. p. 430).

Legal developments plainly reveal the ways in which the ancient family societies of Scandinavia were gradually transformed into nations of individuals. The elaborate achievements in the field of customary law, built up by agreement among the yeomen of the Viking Age and still clearly visible in the provincial laws that have come down to us, finally gave way before canon law and national, king-made codes. But a stubborn, inherited regard for law and the ability to balance the rights of individuals against the claims of society continued to play a part in the formation of the new states of the North.

12

Religion and Conduct

The religious ideas and practices of a pre-Christian farmer in the heart of Norway, living close by the burial mounds of his forefathers and familiar with the spirits that resided in his hearth and fields, could hardly be exactly the same as those of the Swedish merchant making his way through Russia or of the Viking cruising in the Irish Sea or even of the emigrant yeoman in Iceland who came to live in a vast, strange land, where he had no ancestral dead. The Viking Age represents the last two centuries of paganism among the Scandinavians, and it was characterized by shifting emphases within the heathen cults, by the influence of Christianity, and by the fostering of a profane self-reliance as a result of success in war, exploration and sea-faring. In this chapter we can only look at some of the elements that might occur in the many blends of religious ideas and many kinds of religious attitudes possible in such a period. The pan-theistic religion tended to be fluid and tolerant, but we may assume that most heathens leading settled lives in ninth- and tenth-century Scandinavia would be brought up with similar ideas about the behaviour and function of the gods and other supernatural powers and with similar experience of cult ritual. We may look first at the divine figures and then at the ways in which men sought contact with them, although the two themes cannot always be separated, because the gods become most real when they touch the life of human beings. After that we may consider the conversion of the Scandinavians to Christianity and the creeds by which men lived.

The gods

The gods were looked on as a related group of beings called *Æsir* (sg. *Áss*), to whom were added some who had come from another divine tribe called *Vanir* (sg. *Vanr*). The etymology of both names is uncertain. Other words that are used for the gods are more transparent in sense: *regin*, 'deciding powers', *bǫnd*, *hǫpt*, 'binding powers', all neuter plural words, indicate age-old ideas of the divinities as the upholders and arbiters of existence. The word *goð, guð*, 'god', was also grammatically neuter, but when it came to be used of the distinctly personal God of the Christians it was turned into a masculine name. As a group the gods were believed to exist in their own world, where they had splendid houses and possessions and joined together at assemblies for discussion, ritual and games, just as men did in their world.

Many divinities are named in the sources but a number of these had either lost or were fast losing their importance in mythological narratives and cult activities – some of them perhaps had never had any. Among such figures were Tý and Ull, both once imposing sky-gods, while Njǫrd, looked on as the father of Frey, did not retain the significance he had previously had as a god of fertility but had some popularity as a god of seafarers. Heimdall is another god frequently mentioned in mythological sources but whose significance is extremely enigmatic. He was born of nine mothers (which presumably meant that he had nine lives) and at some stage was mysteriously killed by somebody's head; he appears as the watchman of the gods and is identified with the Ríg who became father of mankind according to the poem *Rígspula* (p. 65). Baldr is the famous son of Odin whose death was brought about by the machinations of Loki – he gave Hǫd, Baldr's blind brother, a stick of mistletoe to throw at him, the one thing that had not promised to do Baldr no harm. In revenge the gods took Loki and bound him with the guts of his own children. Little else is known about Baldr, but Loki figures in many stories about the gods, as their clever helper and as their prospective enemy. He is the father of the World-snake and Fenrir the wolf, monsters who will fight with him against the gods in the last battle at Ragnarǫk (cf. pp. 345–6), and of the lady called Hel, the ruler of the gloomy world to which most dead were assigned. Loki has an essential narrative function in the myths but it is not surprising that neither he nor Baldr should have real relations with mankind; the one was chained up until Ragnarǫk, the other was in Hel's keeping and if he returned at all, it would not be until Ragnarǫk was past.

About 1070 Adam of Bremen wrote that in the temple at Uppsala there were three images, one of Thor, the most powerful of the gods, one of Wodan, and one of Fricco. The last-named must be Frey, whose name simply means 'lord'. The Swedes sacrificed to Thor when there was threat of dearth and disease, to Odin if war was at hand, to Frey at weddings. Frey was particularly associated with the Swedes and was believed to be the ancestor of the Yngling dynasty of Uppsala and Vestfold in Norway. He originally belonged to the Vanir and stood especially for powers of fertility and peaceful increase. His image at Uppsala had a gigantic penis. Animals associated with him were the boar and the stallion, both urgent symbols of animal potency, and fat land was looked upon as his – a certain field in North Iceland, for example, was called 'Giver of the assured crop' because of Frey's favour. The eddaic poem called *Skírnismál* tells how Skírnir goes to woo the giant-girl, Gerd, on behalf of Frey who had fallen in love with her at first sight. He tries to bribe her with promises but finally only wins her unwilling consent by threats and terrifying curses. Ultimately behind this episode lies a myth in which sunshine and summer take the maidenhead of frost and winter, and perhaps a ritual of sacred marriage to ensure fecundity and fresh crops. But the poem itself is instinct with sexual passion and masculine wish-fulfilment and conveys a compelling idea of the powers associated with Frey.

His sister, Freyja, is his counterpart in name and function. She is voluptuous and stands for fertility and wealth. She also represents the mysteries of women and wizardry, an art she is thought to have introduced among the gods and imparted to Odin. She was the great *dís*, the head of the otherwise unindividualized female beings who represented powers of fruitfulness in nature and man (p. 392). She and her brother were widely venerated and invoked.

Adam's informants told him that Thor ruled in the sky and 'governed thunder and thunderbolts, winds and rain-storms, fair weather and the fruits of the earth'. His name is cognate with English 'thunder', and other sources equip him with the hammer Mjǫllnir, which means 'lightning' or perhaps 'the crusher', and a chariot drawn by goats. In West Norse sources there is little indication of his role as a divine promoter of fertility but all the more emphasis on his function as the protector of the world against the primeval powers of chaos, the giants. A widespread myth tells of his attempt to fish up and destroy the World-snake (cf. p. 341), and according to Vǫluspá (p. 345) these two will be adversaries at Ragnarǫk and kill each other. Thor's popularity is shown by many things. His name occurs commonly in place-names and in personal names. We hear of his worship in England and Ireland as well as in the northern countries; and from Norse religion he passed into the religion of the Lapps. Scalds made poems in his honour, he was invoked in Danish runic inscriptions, and when a Christian missionary in Iceland was discomfited by the wreck of his ship, it was Thor who had the praiseworthy responsibility. All in all, there seems little reason to doubt that he was the god chiefly revered by the yeomen of early Scandinavia, both as farmers and as warriors. He was reliable.

Nevertheless it is Odin who appears as the chief god in the West Norse poetic sources, in the myths Saxo tried to turn into history and in the thirteenth-century writings of the Icelanders. 'Wodan, id est furor', said Adam, and he is a wild and amazing figure, by no means reliable. He appears as the experimenter and adventurer: there is nothing he will not dare to explore the depths and bounds of existence. He suffers torture, perhaps even death, for the mysteries of runes and poetry (p. 342); he gives an eye for a drink at the well of wisdom; he learns all that happens in the world through his scouting ravens, and he learns still more by communing with hanged men and forcing prophecy from wise women. He learnt the magic called seiðr (p. 404) which involved such practices as to make people believe that he played the woman's part in the sexual act. In the Norse world such an invert was regarded with disgust but also with apprehension, for it seems to have been believed that unknown knowledge and perilous psychic force might be gained by playing such a role. Odin's powers were beyond those of other gods, and his devotees must have believed that they could attain similar powers themselves.

All the gods are warrior gods and Thor is pre-eminently the god of physical strength. Only Odin, however, is the god of strife. He encourages battle and gives victory, he is the lord of the dead, the valkyries are his servants. The Viking Age was a turbulent time and it must have often been seen what unlikely chances swayed the outcome of battle. The unpredictable in war was attributed to Odin, the fickle god who had his favourites but did not keep them for ever: he was openly regarded as one whose oath could not be trusted. Poets and thinkers in the tenth century found an answer to the problem presented by Odin's unreliability. There was one event that Odin could foresee but not prevent: the destined threat to the order maintained by the gods, like the destined death of every individual, was bound to come. The monsters now kept at bay were only biding their time, and their attack was in real prospect. In the poem called *Eiríksmál* (p. 361), composed soon after 950, Odin in Valhall is asked why he deprived King Eirík of victory, seeing he thought him valiant: 'Because it is hard to know for certain', said Odin – 'the grey wolf looks at the homes of the gods.' So Odin gathers dead warriors and the cream of men – bitter and unjust their defeat – because he must collect his host for the final battle. In Valhall, 'slain-hall', the select warriors fight and feast without regard to old enmities. This is not an ignoble explanation of the brutal accidents of war.

In Denmark and Götaland there seems to have been an official public cult of Odin, but in Norway there is little evidence of general worship of him and still less in Iceland (cf. fig. 57). The best explanation of this is that, although Odin had long existed in the pantheon of Norse gods, his cult only spread through west Scandinavia in the Viking Age itself, when it answered particularly to the needs of warrior-kings and their retinues, of the scaldic poets they patronized, and of Viking mercenary soldiers cut off from the secure regularity of the family farming community. The warriors called berserks (p. 285) and the ruthless men who employed them were alike Odinic initiates.

Other-world beings

The major gods were clearly differentiated as persons, even though their functions might overlap. Other figures from the world of the gods were not individualized in the same way. The valkyries, Odin's emissaries who conduct the slain to Valhall, are differentiated by name but have all one character. In romantic stories they turn into princesses who for one reason or another have taken up this particular career, but originally they were demons of carnage and death. Other women, the Norns, represent powers of destiny, to which both gods and men are subject. Success and failure are attributed to them alike, but particularly failure and death. They may thus become grim figures of unmotivated malice. Neither valkyries nor Norns were objects of cult-worship, but a third group of female figures, the *dísir*, were celebrated in some form of public cult in Sweden proper and in Norwegian Oppland and apparently in domestic festivals elsewhere. With Freyja, the great *dís*, they were thought to have power over the forces of natural increase. The well-being of land and family depended on their favour. If an individual suffered, it could be interpreted as the result of the hostility of the *dísir*, who from well-disposed spirits could turn into malevolent and merciless enemies. It is sometimes difficult to keep the *dísir* distinct from valkyries or harsh Norns on the one hand and the spirits called *fylgjur*, 'accompaniers', on the other; and it is probable that the Norsemen themselves had notions about these beings that varied from time to time and place to place. *Fylgjur* were attached to families or individuals, but had no local habitation or individual name. They appear to have represented the inherent faculty for achievement that existed in a family's offspring. Everyday observation of consonant or discrepant facts of heredity would confirm that it was possible for a *fylgja* to desert an individual or to be rejected by him. As family 'fetches' *fylgjur* were normally manifested in female form, but as personal 'fetches' they might appear in animal shape.

Dead kinsmen were buried near the homestead and were believed to live on in their grave-mounds or keep each other festive company inside some local 'holy' hill, an idea probably associated in origin with the practice of communal family burial. In the influence they were believed to have on the thriving of crops, beasts and household, it is hard to separate them entirely from the elves, who lived in the ground itself and whose favour was ensured by sacrifices. When the settlers arrived in Iceland, they found it empty of men, but they were not so rash as to assume that it was empty of spirits, encroachment upon whom needed care and ceremony. These spirits lived independently of human habitation but were not by nature hostile as the giants were. Giants lived in a land of their own, in earth's outer ring, and existed also among desolate crags and mountains. They were the enemies of the gods and hurtful to men. Other rock-dwellers were the dwarves, who were wise and cunning and great craftsmen. Contact with giants and dwarves was not made through sacrifice and veneration, though they might be bargained with, tricked or caught.

Relations between men, divinities and supernatural powers

Valuable evidence of veneration of gods in early Scandinavia is to be found in place-names compounded with divine names or containing words that refer to cult activity. Such names have been intensively studied, but the enthusiasm of some scholars is still being tempered by the caution of others and much remains inconclusive while more material and fresh consideration are awaited.

Almost all theophoric place-names have come down to us as farm-names. In these a god's name, normally in the possessive case, is combined with some kind of other name: words for natural features such as woodland, stony outcrop, hill, island, headland, lake; words implying human use of a place, such as pasture, crop-field, haven; words implying human habitation, like home, farmstead; and words that appear to refer specifically to a cult-place. This last kind will be discussed separately below after a brief survey of the other main types.

In Danish names the gods Tý (Ti) and Thor occur most frequently. Tý – whose name elsewhere occurs only once, in west Norway – is compounded particularly with words for wood or grove, -with, -lund. Thor's name is compounded with -lund and also with -akær (WN akr, cf. English acre), which early came to have the meaning 'cultivated land'. Odin's name is found with names of natural features like grove, hill, stream, bog. Names of other gods, Njǫrd, Frey and Freyja, are found occasionally with habitation-names, such as Nærum from *Niarthar-rum*, 'Njǫrd's site', and Frøs Herred in South Jutland which means 'Frey's *herred*'.

In Sweden names in -lund and -aker (modern Sw. lunda, åker) are found particularly with names of Odin, Ull, Thor, Frey, and Freyja. Njǫrd occurs in some names, with -*lund* and -*ö* (island) for example. A number of theophoric names are compounded with -*tuna,* an element peculiar to Sweden meaning a farm-settlement of some special but undefined type (possibly it was fortified). This is found with Ull, Njǫrd, Thor, Frey and Freyja, but not with Odin – a fact which has been taken to show that the cult of Odin came to the country after the cult of the other gods, though still well before the Viking Age began. The appearance of Thor's name with -*aker,* as in Denmark, bears out Master Adam's words about his role as a god of fruitfulness (p. 389); this compound is unknown in western Scandinavia.

The names of Norway agree with those of Sweden in giving prominence to Ull, whose name is frequently compounded with -*vang,* 'pasture', and -*akr* (modern Norw. *åker, aker*). Thor, Njǫrd, Frey and Freyja are also common, but Odin is very rare. Usual second elements, besides *vang* and *akr,* are -*nes* (headland, particularly common with Thor's name), -*vin* (meadow), -*heimr* (home, dwelling-place), and -*land.* The absence of names with an element meaning woodland is notable, and presumably implies that sacred groves did not play the same part in the religious practices of the Norwegians as they did in Denmark and Sweden.

Iceland has few theophoric names. Njǫrd occurs twice with -*vik,* 'bay, inlet'; Frey twice with -*nes,* 'headland', once with -*hólar,* 'hillocks'; but there are eighteen certain examples of Thor names, including five in -*nes* and five in -*hǫfn,* 'haven'; the other eight have elements denoting natural features. The assembly-place for all the Faroe Islanders was at Thor's harbour, the modern capital Tórshavn, on Streymoy; and presumably their central cult-place was there too, although a case has been made for locating it a few miles away at Velbastaður.

Thor's headland, Frey's field, Ull's pasture – on the most literal interpretation such names imply a recognition of the god's ownership, but the significance of this attribution in the Viking Age is problematical. A prime difficulty is one of chronology, for most of the names are older than the last centuries of paganism, and the continued use of a place-name does not necessarily mean the continued flourishing of a cult (many of the names are still in use today, after 1000 years of Christianity).

Place-names compounded with Tý in Denmark and Ull in Norway and Sweden can hardly be of much significance for Viking Age religion. The most positive evidence for the religion of that period would be the occurrence of divine names in combination with elements that were much used in making new names in the ninth and tenth centuries, but unfortunately the mainland evidence of this sort is far from unambiguous and the evidence from a new settlement like Iceland is, as seen above, very meagre. There is no doubt, on the other hand, that the distribution of theophoric place-names gives valuable information about cultural groupings within Scandinavia, emphasizing the distinctions between Götaland and Svealand, for example, or between east and west Norway. Another difficulty in interpreting theophoric names lies in our ignorance of what degree of public veneration is implied by them. The answer is straightforward where they contain elements referring specifically to cult-places. Some theophoric nature-names and use-names may imply that the divinity was thought to be immanent or resident (of course not uniquely so) in some particular field or grove or cataract, but this need not have meant more than at best domestic veneration and local caution. In other cases a theophoric name may have arisen because a man gave land to the god with some form of dedication, a move to establish friendship with its typical bargaining nature, maintained and balanced by gifts (cf. p. 423), but this too need not imply a widespread public cult.

There must be similar doubt as to the significance of a number of names in which a natural feature or inhabited area is compounded with the word guð- (goð-), 'god', or with a form of the adjective heilagr, 'holy'. An original guð-heimr, 'god-habitation', is well attested throughout Scandinavia, and in Norway for example we find others like 'god-pasture', 'god-dale'. In Iceland names such as Goðaborg and Goðafoss are most probably compounded with the same word and mean 'hill of gods' and 'waterfall of gods'. The adjective heilagr is used with island, fell, headland, land, river. There are several examples of Helgafell, 'sacred mountain', in Iceland, and we are told that one or two of them were treated as holy ground by the first settlers, but we can do little more than surmise the nature of their veneration.

Two nature-names that have especially been thought to indicate active cult are *lundr*, 'grove', and *hǫrgr*, 'stone outcrop, bald rock'. The first, as we have seen, is often compounded with gods' names in Denmark and Sweden. These must show that a grove held sacred to a particular divinity was in the neighbourhood of the farm, and this grove was probably an object of veneration to the local society as a whole. It may be noted, for example, that the Gotland Law forbids veneration of groves, and the pagan importance of the wood at Uppsala is shown in Adam of Bremen's description (p. 400). We cannot assume, however, that the many examples of *Lundr* as an uncompounded name all have cult significance. The word *hǫrgr* is much less informative, for an Odin's *hǫrgr* and a Thor's *hǫrgr* in Sweden are the only instances we know where it is compounded with a god's name. It is clear from literary sources, however, that this word could indicate some sort of structure. The likely development is that such rocky outcrops began as places where offerings were made; they might then have been fenced off and sometimes provided with wooden statuary, over which a roof may have been erected. Such cult-places were probably for more strictly local or domestic worship. The Christian law of Gulathing said that neither mounds nor *hǫrgar* were to be venerated; and that people must not make mounds, or make a building and call it a *hǫrgr*.

We come finally to the two place-name elements whose general significance for pagan cults seems certain, but whose precise significance is harder to define. The word *vé* (OD *vi*, OE *wīh*) means a sanctuary, a place marked off as sacred; the related verb is *vígja*, 'make sacred, hallow'. One of the instances of the word *goði* outside Iceland (pp. 132–3) is on the tenth-century Glavendrup rune stone in Fyn, where the dead man is described as *kuþa uia*, '*goði*, priest, of the sanctuaries'. In place-names it occurs as a simplex and in compounds with nature-and habitation-names – Vä, 'sanctuary', in Skåne, Viborg, 'sanctuary hill', in Jutland, Vestad, 'sanctuary-place', in Norway, for example, and many more. In Sweden it is found compounded with the names of all the chief gods, Thor, Odin, Frey, Freyja, Njǫrd and Ull; in Norway it is never connected with a divine name in this way. In Denmark the only five reliable examples are compounded with Odin, including the best-known, Odense in Fyn. It has been plausibly suggested that this place-

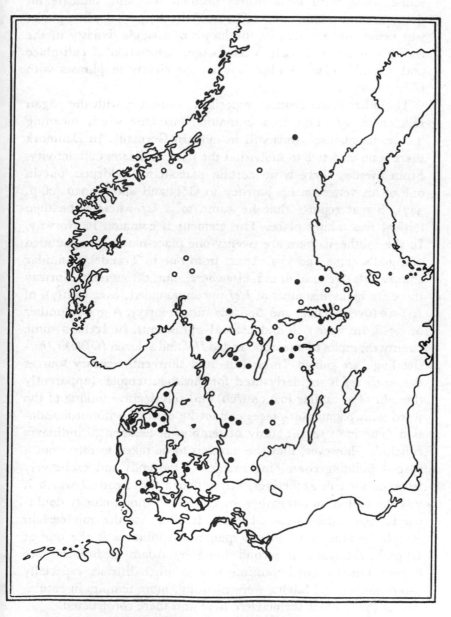

Fig. 57. Place-names with Odin in mainland Scandinavia. After de Vries.

● nature-names; ○ names in *-akr, -vin, -lundr, -land, -hǫrgr, -hof, -vé, -salr.*

name, along with some others peculiar to Odin, indicate his dominance in public cult in Denmark in the period when power was being concentrated in the hands of a single dynasty in the eighth century and early Viking Age. Association of cult-place and assembly-place is also shown most clearly in phrases with *vé* (see below).

The other name element especially connected with the pagan religion is *hof*. This is a common Germanic word, meaning 'house, farmhouse' (thus still in modern German). In Denmark there is no evidence to show that the name indicates cult activity. From Sweden there is no certain place-name evidence, but in one of his verses on his journey to Götaland about 1020 (cf. p. 367), Sigvat reports that he came to a *hof* where a heathen festival was taking place. The element is common in Norway. In the southeast there are twenty-one place-names compounded of a god's name and -*hof*. Apart from one in Trøndelag, similar compounds are not found elsewhere, but throughout Norway there are many instances of *Hof* uncompounded (over eighty), of *Hof-vin* (over twenty) and *Hof-land* (about forty). A good number of *hof* farms were rich and central settlements. In Iceland some twenty examples of uncompounded *Hof* and a dozen *Hofstaðir*, 'hof-steading', are known. In twelfth- and thirteenth-century sources the word *hof* is regularly used for 'heathen temple' (apparently thought of as similar to a church) and this decisive linking of the word with pagan cult-places cannot be entirely without foundation. The most recent study of temples in heathen Scandinavia concludes, however, that the name is to be taken to mean not a special building containing images of the gods and exclusively reserved for cult gatherings, but rather a farmstead at which it was the custom to foregather for cult celebrations, chiefly doubtless for the regular seasonal feasts. In that case the only certain temple building we know in pagan Scandinavia is the one at Uppsala described at second hand by Adam of Bremen (see below), but it is not impossible that in other districts, especially where timber and labour were plentiful, more temples in emulation of that famous shrine were here and there constructed.

It seems otherwise certain that a major part of the cult-celebrations normally took place out of doors, at a place regarded as sacred and where images of gods might be located. It consisted of sacrifice of animals, and sometimes human beings, invocation of the gods, oracular observations, probably joined, at least in some places, with processions, dramatic shows of mythical episodes and competitive games. That the gods were held to visit places kept sacred for them is suggested by the poem *Vellekla* (p. 365), where it says that the gods 'turn to the sacrifices' and that Earl Hákon 'made real to men the lands of Thor's *hof* and the sanctuary of the powers'.

Ibn Fadlan, as well as describing the funeral of a leader among the Rus (p. 408), tells how these merchants of Norse origin behaved on their arrival at a trading-place on the Volga. The account is not clear in all details, but he says that each merchant went ashore from his boat to a tall wooden pillar with a human face, which was surrounded by small figures, and behind them all were other tall, wooden posts. The principal figure was addressed as 'lord', while some or all of the others were representations of the wife and children of the 'lord'. Each man asked for rich and ready customers for his wares, and laid before the post bread, meat, onions (of some kind), milk and strong drink. If things went badly with his trading, he might return with more offerings and a separate gift for each of the smaller figures; and if he was successful, he came back with a thank-offering, sheep or cattle, which were killed – some of their flesh was given away but the remainder was cast down among the wooden posts and the heads were hung on the pillar. Ibn Fadlan adds that the dogs ate this meat by night, but the Rus merchant was content to think that the 'lord' had shown that he was well disposed by consuming his sacrifice.

Ibn Fadlan's journey was made in 922, and it is interesting to set the crude images and primitive ritual described in his account beside the contemporary scaldic poetry we have from Norway. In the poetry we discover highly elaborate myths and an approach to the stories about the gods which is not always serious. It may be that a more refined ritual had been developed in some circles (in keeping perhaps with the idea, attested in *Grímnismál* (p. 338), that Odin lived on wine alone, for example), but in general there is little reason to suppose that the basic elements in the cult acts of the farming society throughout Scandinavia were much different from those described of the Rus on the Volga.

There are many references to images in later Icelandic writings but the only early authentic descriptions are those given by Ibn Fadlan and by Master Adam, writing of the temple at Uppsala. Given the abundance of wood, Norse skill in carving, and the individual anthropomorphic characteristics of the main gods, it seems likely that images were common. In Iceland we hear of objects of domestic veneration of a related kind, the so-called 'high-seat pillars' (cf. p. 160), which settlers are said to have brought with them from their Norwegian homes. Probably their original value was as symbols of the world-tree upholding the universe – nails in them were called *reginnaglar*, 'nails of divine might' – but it appears that they may in some cases have been carved with the figure of a god and thus possibly represented an individual divinity.

An account of much more elaborate cult behaviour is given by Adam of Bremen a century and a half later than Ibn Fadlan in his description, at second hand, of the temple at Uppsala. There the greatest festival is held for nine days at the vernal equinox every ninth year. Everyone in the country must send gifts and attend, but Christians can buy themselves off from this duty. Nine head of all kinds of male animals are offered, 'with whose blood it is the custom to placate the gods', and the carcases are hung in the grove beside the temple. 'The grove is so holy that each single tree is regarded as sacred because of the death and corruption of the sacrificial victims.' Adam speaks of dogs and horses hung up there as well as human corpses; and a Christian informant had told him he had counted 72 carcases there. Here there is clearly no suggestion that the flesh of sacrificial victims was expected to be consumed by the gods to whom they were dedicated. It is probable on the other hand that they and their images were given a share of the blood that flowed.

Verbs meaning 'to sacrifice' are *sóa, senda, fórna*; *sóa* probably first meant 'stab' and came to be used for 'kill' in exclusively religious contexts; *senda* is 'send, consign'; *fórna* means 'present, give', and it and its associated noun, *fórn*, were adopted by the Church to translate *offero, oblatio,* used especially of Judaic sacrificial rites. The most generally used word for 'worship, sacrifice', however, is the verb *blóta* and its cognate noun *blót*, unfortunately of obscure etymology. The verb is normally construed with the god in the accusative and the thing sacrificed in the dative – the divinity was thus possibly thought to be honoured or influenced by the offering. In West Norse the verb later came chiefly to mean 'curse, swear', presumably because the invocation of old gods (or new devils) stayed strong in it (Swedes were still using Odin as a name for Satan in the fifteenth century). The noun *blót* meant the act of worship or sacrifice, and was later used of any object or practice designed to give someone supernatural power – a clay image of a human being used in witchcraft, for example, could be called *blót*.

Generally there were three major religious festivals each year, one in autumn after harvest, one in midwinter, sometime after the solstice, and one at the beginning of summer. They were all designed to promote security and fertility, but in some circles the feast at the outset of summer was particularly associated with sacrifice for victory in the campaigns or raids planned for the following months. It was doubtless not least in these circumstances that systematic attention was paid to oracles. The best attested means of foretelling the future was by casting lots. Pieces of wood, for which the name *blótspánn*, 'sacrificial chip', *hlautteinn*, 'lot-twig', are recorded, were marked, possibly with sacrificial blood, shaken and thrown down like dice, and their positive or negative significance then decided. In the course of war the gods might be called on for aid. The enemy might be dedicated to Odin (p. 283), and the slain were regarded as an offering to him. 'Odin saw (with approval) where the dead lay' are words of Egil's in praise of Eirík Bloodaxe.

The other main part of the cult gathering was the feast that followed and continued the sacrifice. Here communion with the divinities and among men was established by sharing food, including meat from animals offered in sacrifice, and drinking strong drink in honour of the gods. The Saga of the Gotlanders describes large religious gatherings for the major divisions of the island, 'but smaller *things* had smaller sacrifices with animals, food and ale, and members of these assemblies were called *supnautar*, "seethed-meat-sharers", because they boiled food all together'. The feasting apparently took place indoors, doubtless to the accompaniment of ceremonies of dedication and possibly with poetry, shows and games – Adam of Bremen refers to lewd

401

singing at Uppsala, but we cannot be sure at what stage in the celebration this took place. In districts where most households lived and worked in comparative isolation – especially in the long winters amid all the sameness of snow, when food was not always plentiful – we can imagine that the crowded warmth of the hall where the cult feast was held, dim save for the flare and blaze of the big fires in the centre, the gorging of beef, horsemeat and pork, rich with blood and fat, rank with garlic, the draining of horn upon horn of thick ale, must have led to a rapid break-down of reserve, a jovial relaxation of defences, a mutual revela-tion of the same human instincts and needs. The god-given elation and feeling of communal solidarity must have lasted, consciously or unconsciously, beyond the ceremony itself. The importance of the party as an element in religious life is reflected in an odd way in the Christian customs of Norway. Farmers in the Gulathing, in groups of at least three (save remote dwellers who had to act on their own), had to brew beer by All Saints' Day, 1 November, and again for Christmas, and then drink it at a party for peace and prosperity after consecrating it 'so that it might be pleasing to Christ and St Mary'. In Trøndelag the feast of St John Baptist, 24 June, Midsummer's Day, was a time for an obligatory ale-feast. Failure to comply with these laws was punishable by a fine paid to the bishop, and repeated neglect could lead to outlawry.

The divine powers were also involved with the conduct of the public assemblies for discussion, legislation and justice. An assembly was hallowed in some way at the outset, presumably by sacrifice and invocation, and its sanctity prevailed over the defined area within which it took place and for the length of time it lasted. The phrase *vargr í véum*, 'outcast in the sanctuaries', is used of a man who killed at a hallowed assembly; and the ropes surrounding the place at Norwegian assemblies where the *lǫgrétta* sat (p. 130) were called *vébǫnd*, 'sanctuary ropes'. The Althing in Iceland was hallowed by the so-called *allsherjargoði*, 'priest of all the host', the chieftain who held the *goðorð* in the family of Ingolf, the first settler. Otherwise it appears that a cult gathering was also made the opportunity for a public as-sembly, which apart from the transaction of public business might turn into a kind of fair. Games, contests, dancing might all be more or less closely connected with the cult celebration. Horse-racing and horse-fighting seem to have been particularly usual at heathen feasts – possibly they played a part in the selection of victims for sacrifice, possibly a victorious beast was looked on as especially favoured by the gods.

In the legal process much use was made of the solemn oath (p. 375). We hear of a sacred arm-ring among Norsemen in England and Ireland as well as in Scandinavia, and oaths might be sworn on such a ring. One form of oath called on the gods to be genial or angry according to the truth or falsehood of the statement a man made. The gods could thus be expected to inter-fere in individual lives on behalf of the group, their vengeance was a benefit to society. The oath continued to play an essential part in judicial life after the conversion to Christianity, rein-forced by swearing on relics and the Bible and by the other-world sanctions the Church could impose.

Remarkable evidence of an individual's beliefs concerning the influence of the gods is found in Egil Skalla-Grímsson's moving poem, *Sonatorrek,* which he composed about 960 after the death of his promising son. The boy was drowned, and Egil speaks of the impossibility of vengeance on the gods of the sea, however willing he would be to exact it. He thinks of his solitarinesss and loss, and he blames Odin for what he suffers. He says (the ken-nings are simplified): 'I was on good terms with the lord of the spear; I made myself confident in trust of him; until he ripped our friendship apart. It is therefore with no eagerness that I worship (*blóta*) him, but yet, if I count them up better, the god has fur-nished me with things that atone for evils. He gave me the unblemished skill of poetry, and such a mind that I made deceitful men into open enemies.' The gods could be held responsible for life and death, but it is the idea of friendship and gifts which appears typical of the Norse religious outlook. Egil 'worships' Odin through *blót* – we do not know exactly what that meant – this is his part of the bargain; and Odin has given him gifts worth more even than kinsmen's lives. The concept of poetry as an immaculate divine gift is illuminating (cf. pp. 331–2).

Not all pagans were devout. Some may have been atheists, others may have believed in the existence of gods but put no trust in them. We read in the Icelandic stories of people who gave up sacrificing or put their trust in their own 'might and main'. Such attitudes were probably particularly fostered among unsettled mercenary fighters. But even such men were unlikely to be free of belief in the power of magic. Witchcraft for good or ill, faith in talismans and ways of achieving prophetic insight, flourished outside the major cults and changed little with the introduction of Christianity, which brought its own superstitions, some innocent, some less so, to the northern peoples.

The most striking form of sorcery in early times was that called *seiðr*. Norse descriptions of the rite have no overt sexual elements in them, but the practice was regarded as perverse for men to perform, and it was probably because of this that it was apparently regarded with disfavour by orthodox pagans, while it seems to have been successfully suppressed in Christian times. It was performed by a wizard aided by a group of other people. The wizard mounted a platform, where he was presumably free from undesirable influences, and there fell into a trance, helped in this by the chanting of the group. In his trance his spirit was freed, and if the purpose was evil, it could beset and harm a human mind or body; if the purpose was divinatory, the freed spirit seems to have been thought to learn from other spirits what the future held. The spirit might meet many difficulties before it regained its body, and the wizard, usually exhausted, might be helped out of his trance by a special song. Given the beliefs attendant upon the ceremony, we can only be impressed by the daring of the performer in casting himself into a world of shadowy, perilous forces; and we understand why the terrifying god, Odin, was credited with the same aberrant urge.

Talismans might take the form of small images of divine figures. One or two such, identified as representations of Frey and Thor, have come to light in Iceland and Sweden; they could be carried in a purse and were doubtless personal tokens of the god in whom a man put most trust. Amulets in the form of Thor's hammers have been found in graves and elsewhere. Some information about superstitious practices can be gleaned from the laws and penitentials. Such Christian texts all have a literary history and it is possible that prohibitions in them have simply been carried over from one country to another, irrespective of their relevance in the new context. Generally there seems little reason to doubt the validity of evidence from such northern writings, although of course some things – like malevolent magic using hair, nails, clothes, and images in clay or dough – are universally condemned. Genuine relics of Norse paganism are certainly to be found in the Norwegian ban on erecting what is called a 'penis-pole' (though the precise purport of this symbol is not clear) and on believing in 'land-spirits' in groves, mounds and waterfalls; and in the Gotland prohibition of veneration of 'fences', presumably fenced-off places that may have been or resembled pagan *vé* or *hǫrgr*. We further learn from the laws that 'sitting outside' in special places by night, waking up dead men and 'mound-dwellers', and applying to Laplanders, were regarded as ways of winning knowledge of the future. Health and long life might be ensured by special stones, which could be filled with magic power, perhaps by invocation of gods; and roots of curious shape might have special significance in witchcraft. Women might be accused of biting off a baby's finger or toe 'for long life'; and a child might be kept unbaptized to the same end. In Iceland farm animals might be looked on, for whatever reason, as given over to some unnamed supernatural power; they were left unmarked and thought to bring good luck. Runic charms of all kinds, active and prophylactic, were well known, and much store was set by dreams, in Christian times no less than heathen.

If we read accounts of beliefs and customs among isolated Scandinavian farming communities in the nineteenth century, we may get the impression that there was hardly a day or action without its moment of fearful deference to the supernatural powers that beset man's existence. Such a dead weight of apprehension may have existed in some districts in the Viking Age as well, but it does not seem to be typical of the period. The voyage of Ohthere to the White Sea and the ventures across open ocean to Iceland and beyond were enterprises that seem to have hardly been thought daring. Danes besieging Paris in the ninth century might spare churches outside the walls and others in Ireland might send a votive gift to St Patrick's shrine, but in 1006 the Danish host in south England showed little regard for superstition when they went on purpose to Cuckhamsley Knob on the Berkshire Downs 'and there awaited the great things that had been threatened, for it had often been said that if ever they got as far as Cuckhamsley Knob, they would never again reach the sea.' But, as it was, they then beat the English in a fight nearby and made their way to the sea with their plunder, 'an arrogant and confident host', passing under the eyes of the helpless inhabitants of Winchester.

There were mysteries in nature and humanity over which men sought fumbling control, forcing themselves even to obscene limits. But against such a dark background we can also set the sane and cheerful scorn of the tenth-century poet who said:

> *I lived a long time,*
> *I let the gods rule,*
> *I never wore*
> *moss-red stockings,*
> *I never tied*
> *at my neck a bag*
> *full of herbs –*
> *yet I am still alive!*

The dead

More than anything else, death confirmed the existence of another world. Sooner or later every household had a corpse on its hands, and we learn a good deal about the religious ideas of the ancient Scandinavians from the ways in which they treated their dead. On this point we are fortunate in having first-rate literary and archaeological sources, although of course there are always many things hard to understand.

When someone died, the first act was to close the nostrils and mouth, possibly the eyes as well; the body was often washed and the head might be covered with a cloth. A corpse might be carried from a house by a special route, and generally it was treated with great care. This was not least because of a common belief in 'dead walkers', people who appeared dead and were certainly buried, but who retained their physical form and could return to plague the living, usually with an increase in brute strength and malevolence. Various measures might be taken to help fix a dead person in his grave or in the other world or to aid him on the journey he had to undertake – sometimes both kinds of measures were taken at the same time, since the ancient Scandinavians did not necessarily find the two aims inconsistent. We hear of tying special shoes to a dead man's feet for the march he had ahead of him, and of adding a special mooring stone to the boat used as a resting-place for the man to be buried. It may be noted that the Oseberg ship was securely moored by a cable round a great boulder in its mound. Ship-burials and ship-shapes reflect an original notion of an other-world voyage, but they can also express an opinion as to what a man might need in his new life after death – comparable to the horse or weapons or tools that also accompanied him. It is hard to relate grave-finds to ideas we meet in literary sources of a shadowy underworld ruled over by the goddess Hel; and when we meet a rich grave furnished both with weapons and farm implements, we cannot say that it provides a precise pointer to the Valhall of Odin as depicted by poets, where the warlike objects would certainly be useful, but sickle and leaf-knife less so. From the best furnished graves it is difficult not to get the impression that the people who filled them with all kinds of useful and decorative objects were making sure that the dead man got all that he was due and all that might – not necessarily would – be useful to him, at the same time as they displayed an ostentation that would impress their neighbours in this world and put the dead man one up in the company he was to keep in the next.

Inhumation and cremation were both practised, and, although cremation was apparently more common in Denmark than in the rest of Scandinavia, and is only once found in a Viking grave in Western Europe (at the Île de Groix, Brittany), the basic rite in a particular cemetery tended to follow a local pattern. Solitary burials in single graves or mounds are often encountered, while abroad, in England and the Isle of Man, for example, burial might take place in the Christian cemeteries the Norsemen found there. The practice of burying objects of daily use with the dead is almost universal. Men, especially if they were rich, would be buried with weapons and war gear, horses and trappings, and often laid in a boat or ship. Women were also furnished with some tokens of the worldly wealth of their families, and one of the richest of all Viking burials, that at Oseberg in Norway, was the burial of a woman, probably indeed of a queen.

It is generally agreed that the Arabic traveller Ibn Fadlan

was describing a Norse funeral when he wrote of an encounter with the people called Rus on his visit to the Volga in 922. He writes as an eyewitness, and although there is no reason to doubt his general accuracy, we must bear a number of factors in mind before generalizing on the basis of his account. It is the funeral of a rich and important man; it is a funeral by cremation; it took place in Russia (and many Russian scholars do not accept it as a description of a Scandinavian ceremony), where the Norsemen had certainly been subject to foreign influence, perhaps especially from the Volga Turks; finally, some things in the account can only have been obtained by Ibn Fadlan through an interpreter. Ibn Fadlan writes this:

I was told that when their chieftains died one of the least things which was done was cremation. I was therefore greatly interested to find out about this, until I heard one day that one of their chief men was dead. They laid him in his grave and roofed it over for ten days while they cut out and made ready his clothes. What they do is this: for a poor man they make a small boat, place him in it and then burn it; but if he is rich, they gather together his wealth and divide it into three – one part for his family, one part to provide clothes for him, and a third part for *nabidh* [a fermented drink], which they drink on the day that the slave woman is killed and burned together with her master . . . When a chief has died his family asks his slave women and slaves, 'Who will die with him?' Then one of them says, 'I will.' When she has said this there is no backing out . . . most of those who agree are women slaves . . .

[When, in this case, a girl had volunteered] two female slaves were appointed to guard her wherever she went so that they even washed her feet with their own hands. Then they began to get things ready for the dead man; to cut out his clothes and do all that should be done, but the slave drank and sang every day happily and joyfully.

When the day came that the dead man should be burned together with his slave, I went to the river where the ship lay. It had been hauled up on land and supported by four posts of birch and other wood. Around it was arranged what looked like a large pile of wood. The ship was then drawn up and placed on the wood. People began to go to and fro and spoke words which I did not understand, but the corpse still lay in the grave from which they had not yet taken it. They then brought a bier which was placed in the ship, they covered it with Byzantine brocaded tapestries and with cushions of Byzantine brocade.

Then an old woman, whom they call the Angel of Death, came and spread these hangings on the bier. She is in charge of embalming the dead man and preparing him and it is she who kills the girl. The one I saw was a strongly-built and grim figure. When they came to the grave they removed the earth from the wood and removed the wood as well. They then removed the loin cloth which he was wearing when he died. I noticed that the body had turned black, owing to the coldness of the ground. They had put with him in the grave *nabidh*, fruit and a lute, all of which they now took out. The corpse did not smell at all and nothing but the colour of his flesh had changed. They then clothed him in drawers and trousers, boots and tunic, and a brocade mantle with gold buttons on it. They placed a cap made of brocade and sable on his head. They carried him into a tent which stood on the ship, and laid him on the tapestry and propped him up with the cushions. Then they brought *nabidh*, fruit and sweet-smelling herbs and laid these beside him. Next they brought bread, meat and onions and threw these beside him. Next they took two horses which they caused to run until they were sweating, after which they cut them in pieces with a sword and threw their flesh into the ship. Then they brought two cows, which they also cut into pieces and threw them in. The slave woman who wished to be killed went to and fro from one tent to another, and the man of each tent had intercourse with her and said, 'Tell your master that I have done this out of love for him.'

It was now Friday afternoon and they took the slave away to something which looked like the frame of a door. Then she put her legs on the hands of the men and was thus lifted, so that she was above the top of the door-frame, and she said something . . . [this was done three times]. Then they gave her a chicken and she cut off its head and threw it away. Then they took the hen and threw it into the ship. Then I asked what she had done and my interpreter answered: 'The first time they lifted her up she said, 'Look, I see my mother and father'; the second time she said, 'Look, I see all my dead relations sitting together'; the third time she said, 'Look, I see my master sitting in paradise and paradise is beautiful and green, and together with him are men and young boys. He called to me, so let me go to him.' They then took her to the ship. She then took off two arm-bands which she had on and gave them to the old woman who was called the Angel of Death, who was the one who would kill her; she also took off two ankle-rings which she wore and gave them to the two girls who were in attendance on her and who are the daughters of the woman called the Angel of Death. Then they took her to the ship, but did not allow her to enter the tent. Then came men who had shields and staves, and gave her a beaker of *nabidh*. She sang over it and drained it. The interpreter said to me, 'She now takes farewell of her friends.' Then she was given another beaker. She took this and sang for a long time, but the old woman warned her that she should drink quickly and go into the tent where her master lay. When I looked at her, she seemed bemused, she wanted to go into the tent and put her head between it and the ship, then the old woman took her hand and made her enter the tent and went in with her. The men began to beat with their staves on the shields so that her shrieks should not be heard and the other girls should not be frightened and thus not seek death with their masters. Then six men went into the tent and all had intercourse with the girl; then they laid her by the side of her dead master, then two took her legs, two took her hands, and the old woman who is called the Angel of Death put a rope round her neck, with the ends in opposite directions, and gave it to two men to pull; then she came with a dagger with a broad blade and began to thrust it time and again between the girl's ribs, while the two men choked her with the rope so that she died.

Then came one who was nearest related to the dead man. He took a piece of wood and fired it. Then he went backwards towards the ship with his face towards the people and held the torch in one hand, his other hand was on his back-side. He was naked. Thus the wood which lay under the ship was fired after they had laid the slave woman whom they had killed by the side of her master. Then people came with wood and branches – everyone had a piece of burning wood. They threw it on the wood which lay under the ship so that the fire took hold of the pyre, then of the ship, then of the tent and of the man and of the girl and of all that was in the ship ... By the side of me stood a man who was of the Rus tribe and I heard him talk with the interpreter who was together with him. I asked what he had said and was answered: 'He says, "You Arabs are stupid." "Why?" I asked and he answered: "Well, because you take those you love and honour most and put them in the earth and the worms and earth devour them. We burn them in the blinking of an eyelid so that he goes to paradise at that very moment."' . . . [Within an hour] the ship, the pyre, the slave and the master had become fine ashes. Then they built on the place where the ship had stood after it had been hauled ashore something like a round mound. In the middle of it they raised a large post of birch. Then they wrote the name of the man and the name of the king of the Rus on it and so went on their way.

Striking elements in this description, such as the 'Angel of Death', the ritual intercourse, and the wary and naked kindler of the pyre, cannot be paralleled in Norse sources, and other items – the 'door-frame' object and the vision of paradise 'beautiful and green' – are too vague to provide secure links. These things can be neither accepted nor rejected as widespread features of Norse burial rites, but there remain a good many other details that are reflected in our archaeological and literary sources.

Ship-burial, well known in pre-Viking times, is common in Norway and Sweden in the Viking Age itself, but rare in the colonies and Iceland and represented by only three examples in Denmark (where, however, stone settings in the shape of ships are found).

A person murdered to accompany the dead has been noted at Oseberg in Norway, Birka and Valsgärde in Sweden, Balladoole in the Isle of Man, and less certainly at a number of other sites.

A settler in Iceland, Ásmund Atlason, is said to have been buried in a boat, accompanied by a slave who had killed himself after his master's death. Ibn Rustah, writing some time after A.D. 922, says this of the Norsemen in Russia: 'When a leading man among them dies, they dig a grave like a big house and put him inside it. With him they put his clothes and the gold bracelets he wore and also much food and drinking vessels and coins. They also put his favourite wife in the grave with him, while she is still living. And so the entrance to the grave is stopped up, and she dies there.'

Animals are commonly found in graves, though not poultry (which would be hard to recognize in any case) unless we put Oseberg's exotic peacock in this category. Oseberg also contained no less than thirteen horses and an ox. Excavation at Balladoole has shown that animals were sometimes cremated to accompany an inhumation burial. There is, of course, massive evidence of giving the dead person ornaments, weapons and tools. Objects were sometimes 'killed' before being put in a grave – a sword bent in two or wooden furniture broken up. It was presumably thought important to make these things 'different', in the same way as the dead man was 'different'; possibly in some contexts it was intended to discourage or disappoint grave-robbers. Vikings were not above despoiling the dead of their goods, a practice which gave rise to lamentation and wrath in Irish chronicles and scenes of excitement and suspense in Icelandic sagas.

Graves were usually capped by mounds, although flat graves are not infrequent and in some cemeteries, at Ingleby in Derbyshire for example, the mounds are very small, not more than two or three metres in diameter. Some rich graves stood isolated under mounds dominating the skyline, as at Oseberg, Gokstad and Borre. Mounds could also be marked by substantial wooden posts – the custom is known from the Isle of Man and Denmark, for example, and some Swedish runic inscriptions record the erection not only of memorial stones but also of a memorial post or posts.

The normal practice was to bury the dead in a coffin, but in some areas larger burial chambers of wood are known. Graves are found singly or in cemeteries. Many of the latter are family burial places, like that at Valsgärde in Sweden where a succession of fifteen boat-burials, from about A.D. 600 to 1100, provides unique evidence of steady continuity among the conservative yeomen of Uppland. Certain larger cemeteries, at villages and townships like Lindholm Høje, Hedeby, Birka and Gnezdovo (by Smolensk in Russia), contain thousands of graves.

A strange phenomenon recorded at a small number of Scandinavian sites is the existence of empty burial mounds. The largest barrows in Norway and Denmark – the enormous pre-Viking Raknehaug, 19 m. high and 95 m. across, and the biggest Jelling barrow – are among them. Harald Anderson has suggested that these barrows were capped with a mortuary house and, indeed, there is some evidence at Jelling of such a structure on the flat top of the mound. This theory cannot be proved, but the presence of a ship-burial on top of the empty barrow at Ulltuna in Sweden suggests that it is a more satisfactory interpretation of these unusual monuments than a common theory that they are cenotaphs. It is, of course, possible that they were monuments raised by leaders who intended them as their burial places – an intention nullified perhaps by death far afield or at sea.

It is interesting to note that in certain areas where Scandinavians settled in a Christian country they continued their heathen practice of accompanied burial in the existing churchyards. This has been demonstrated in the Isle of Man and the north of England, but has not so far been found elsewhere. At Kildale in Yorkshire a well-furnished Viking grave was discovered beneath the floor of the later parish church. Such rites perhaps show pantheistic Viking respect for sacred ground and a certain preference for keeping the dead in one safe place, but it is more likely that people buried in this way were generally new Christians, whose heirs could not bring themselves to treat their kinsmen so scantly as the Christian custom was – or perhaps they were hedging their bets. That the practice was accepted as normal, at least for some time, is revealed by carved crosses at Middleton in Yorkshire, with pictures of warriors lying in their graves, surrounded by their weapons.

Stone memorials carved with scenes are rarely encountered, outside Gotland, before the Viking settlement of Britain (where the habit was firmly entrenched from the end of the seventh century). After the settlement such stones begin to appear in Scandinavia, but many of the numerous rune stones merely record good works or are memorials not associated with graves. In the eleventh century free-standing stone sarcophagi are encountered, and the famous slab from the churchyard of St Paul's Cathedral in London (pl. 26a) is presumably part of such an object. This type of memorial is also similar to hog-backed tombstones from the north of England (pl. 10). These great slabs, shaped like a house, lay over a grave, partly perhaps in imitation of a sarcophagus and partly to represent the dwelling of the dead. In Sweden, especially in Östergötland, occur the impressive grave monuments generally known as Eskilstuna sarcophagi. They are made of five slabs of stone, two long walls and a roof and two tall gable ends. They are richly ornamented with carving and bear runic inscriptions. They were raised on top of graves from the late eleventh century onwards. Elsewhere in Sweden simpler coffin-shaped blocks of stone were placed over graves, sometimes with decorated stone slabs at either end.

The Christian practice of unaccompanied burial was introduced into Scandinavia in the tenth and eleventh centuries and replaced the pagan custom. From this time forward the burial rite is simple and reveals little to the archaeologist.

Christianity

The bare facts of the introduction of Christianity and the organization of the early Church in the northern countries were given in Chapter 1. Here we may add some remarks on the impact and success of the new faith.

Pantheistic pagans were not necessarily hostile to the idea of a new god. In Birka in the ninth century one response to the preaching of St Ansgar came from a man who claimed he had witnessed a council of the gods, at which they had decided that, if the Swedes wanted a new divinity, they were prepared to accept a recently dead King Erik as one of their number. The question as to whether the Christian cult should be allowed to remain in Birka was then tested by casting lots, but when they fell out in favour of the foreign faith, the people were still not content. In the ensuing argument one man spoke on behalf of tolerance and said that many of them in perilous times at sea or in other tight corners had called on the Christians' god with good results. Helgi the Lean, an important settler in Iceland towards 900, called his farm Kristnes, 'Christ's point'; he is indeed said to have believed in Christ but to have invoked Thor before voyages and hard undertakings. Archaeological evidence of a kind of mixture of paganism and Christianity was mentioned above. The existence of Thor's hammers and Christian crosses side by side point in the same direction – indeed, a single soapstone mould for the production of both kinds of amulets has been found at Trendgarden in Himmerland, Denmark. Norsemen at home might have Christian slaves or concubines or meet Christian merchants, while the many who travelled abroad saw Christian ceremonies and churches, probably had some notion of the powers claimed for God by Christian priests, and might have gone so far as to receive the *prima signatio,* the cross-mark which was the catechumen's first rite of initiation and technically necessary for commerce between Christian and heathen; the phrase was adapted to make the Norse verb, *prímsigna.*

The first missionaries were Englishmen and Saxons, who generally would not find it hard to make their essential message understood, and native priests were taught as quickly as possible. The Christians could argue convincingly enough that their religion was nobler and cleaner than the pagan cults men were used to. They did not deny the existence of heathen gods, but reclassified them as demons, and it was of course easy to demonstrate the impotence of idols. It was a common approach also to maintain that the good things men thought they owed to the gods – rain and sunshine, grass and corn, even victory in war – had always been under the dispensation of the almighty Christian God. Stress was laid on God's potent angelic ministers, especially St Michael, the soul's escort after death, and there were many great marvels to recount and even display – Bishop Poppo was credited with miraculous success in ordeals of red-hot iron and fire to bring about the final acceptance of Christianity in tenth-century Denmark. The Christian account of the Creation and Redemption offered the Norsemen an ordered past, a temporal structure which they did not otherwise possess, for which of them could say when the events of their myths had taken place? No less well ordered was Christianity's view of the future, per-

415

sonal and universal; and its plain logic of moral cause and effect, of virtue rewarded and transgression punished, must have appeared a welcome solution to Norsemen who, like the poet of *Vǫluspá*, were alive to the ethical inadequacy of the pagan gods. This solution depended essentially on the firm answers the Church gave to questions concerning death, life after death and the purpose of it all, problems of concern to Norse pagans like everybody else – we saw above the solution proposed by the Odinic poet of *Eiríksmál*. The single, assured Christian answer linked this world indissolubly with the next, and must have offered novel clarity in the confusion that otherwise prevailed and to which the varying pagan burial rites bear witness. With that clarity went a new consolation, for with its cheerful hope of a better life in the next world, Christian teaching could soothe grief for the dear and innocent dead. (Perhaps in time Christianity's most conspicuous gift to the North was to add a dimension of pity to the lives of a hard people, brought up to admire and condemn but not to sympathize.) Hardest of all to understand, as everywhere else, were the virtues of submission and forgiveness, whatever the provocation. Some opposition to Christianity took the form of scorn for the Christ who suffered without a fight; and it was a long time, as we shall see, before the Church persuaded men to give up the vengeful pugnacity which had not been called in question in heathen times.

Of all the elements in the missionary teaching, it was not unnaturally the lot of the soul after death which was of most concern to the new converts. Early in the eleventh century Hallfred the Troublesome Poet (p. 333), mortally ill, made a touching verse which says: 'I would die now soon and sorrow-free if I knew my soul was safe – young I was sharp of tongue; I know I grieve for nothing – everyone must die – but I fear hell; let God decide where I wear out my time.' Typical prayers on early Christian rune stones in Sweden and Denmark are 'God help his soul', 'Christ and St Michael help his soul', 'God and God's Mother help his soul into light', 'Christ and St Michael help their souls into light and paradise'; and occasionally the prayer begs with true humility that God should be merciful beyond the soul's deserts. Coupled with the idea of retribution and reward in the next world was the teaching of the efficacy of good works in this. Many rune stones bear witness to works undertaken for the benefit of souls in the after-life: a bridge over a stream, a causeway through a quagmire, a shelter for wayfarers. These show the stress laid on improving communications as a public and Christian duty, mainly, it seems, to ensure that all possible paths that led to the new church buildings might be opened.

'All Christians shall believe in Christ, that he is God and there are no other gods beside him. No man shall worship (*blota*) false gods and no one put faith in groves or stones. All shall honour the church: thither all shall go, the quick and the dead, entering the world and leaving the world.' These words from the Uppland Law – found too in the associated laws of Hälsingland and Södermanland – crystallize the early Christian teaching and the essential significance of the church, God's house. Every missionary's first endeavour must have been to get a church built, and many hundreds of Scandinavian farmers of the first Christian generations put up a little wooden house, waited for a bishop to consecrate it, and secured the casual or regular services of a priest. They were mostly intended for household use – and they continued in many places as family property – but it was a meritorious work to provide a church, and an incentive to build a big one was given by a story told in Iceland that a man would be allowed into Heaven with as many people as his church would hold. Gradually it came about that the districts became church-centred, with parish organization and parish life an important element in secular as well as religious affairs.

It is clear from numerous Norwegian examples that an estate which had importance as a *hof* might become the site of the future parish church. It may well be, however, that this continuity depended primarily on the wealth and influence of the family who lived there, and in some cases on topographical convenience, rather than on any kind of deference to the preexisting sanctuary. At present we simply cannot say where the yeomen preferred to build their churches or what advice was given them. Since houses reserved for cult purposes were hardly common in Scandinavia, there can generally have been no question of the adaptation of heathen structures for Christian use. At Jelling, on the other hand, the medieval church was built very near the ancient burial grounds of the royal line, which means continuity of site at this traditional centre. It has also generally been held that the church at Old Uppsala stands on or near the site of the heathen temple described by Master Adam; and a Swedish source of thirteenth-century origin says that in 1138 King Sverker began the cathedral church there and 'joined it to the ancient pagan building of three gods, purified by fire and sanctified by "Yggemundus",' which, if true, means the temple had been cleansed and then consecrated as a church. Recently traces of paganism have been found in a Viking Age level under the church at Mære in North Trøndelag, a place known from literary sources to have been an important cult centre for the region. Around four post-holes in this layer had been deposited some thin gold plates, stamped with two human figures (man and woman), of a kind well known in early and Viking Age Scandinavia and often interpreted as votive offerings connected with fertility rites. It is interesting to note that the four posts once in these holes could have had no structural function, and it has been tentatively suggested that they were pillars of the 'high-seat' type (p. 400). The significance of the finds is under debate and much work remains to be done before a consensus of opinion is likely to be achieved on the nature of the continuity between paganism and Christianity on such a site. The investigations at Mære have, however, certainly given a new impetus to research in this important field.

It seems reasonably certain that the first churches in Scandinavia were not built in stone. There is even some archaeological indication that one of the earliest cathedrals in Scandinavia, Viborg, was originally a wooden church, and it is not impossible that the wooden church excavated in 1961 at Lund was the original cathedral of c. 1060 (preceding the stone church which was started c. 1080). There is unfortunately no space in this book to discuss the stone churches of Scandinavia which are expressions – primitive or otherwise – of the general architectural tradition of medieval Europe: the great cathedral of Lund and the little church at Hove in west Norway both form part of the European corpus of Romanesque architecture. There is, however, one group of ecclesiastical buildings – the stave-churches – which are completely Scandinavian in character and must be considered here.

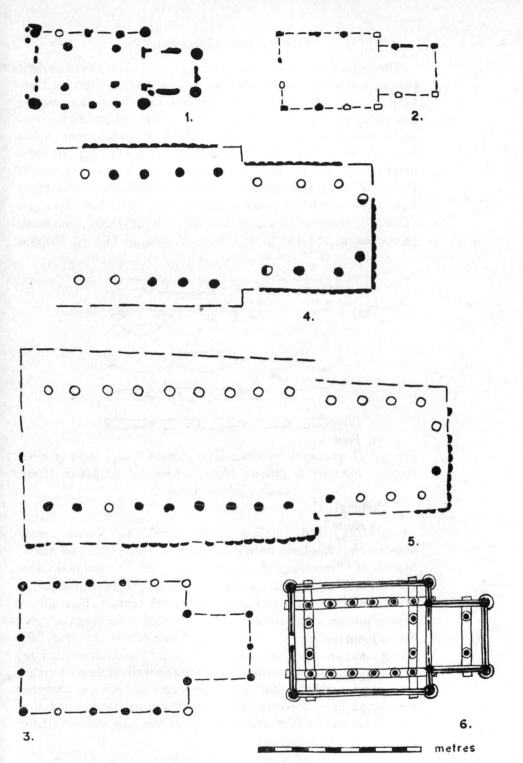

Fig. 58. Ground plans of stave-churches. 1 *Urnes I,* 2 *Hørning,* 3 *Oslo,*
4 *St Maria Minor, Lund,* 5 *church on the 'Thule' site, Lund,* 6 *Urnes II.*

The technique of stave construction, with walls made of upright planks, was known in Scandinavia before the first churches were built (see pp. 152, 212, on Hedeby and Trelleborg). Excavation has yielded a group of eleventh-century stave-churches in Denmark, Sweden, Norway and even England, which bear remarkable resemblance in ground-plan to each other (see fig. 58). In Denmark two stave-churches have been found in the episcopal town of Lund (fig. 58) and descriptions have been published of substantial remains of wooden churches found in Brørup (Ribe), Hørdum (Thisted), Hørning (Randers; fig. 58), Jelling (Vejle), Snoldelev (København), St Ibs in Roskilde, V. Starup (Ribe), Vorgod

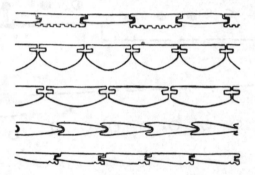

Fig. 59. Diagrammatic representation of sections through walls of stave-churches. From top to bottom: Urnes I, Greensted, St Maria Minor, Lund, Hedared, Urnes II.

(Ringkøbing) and Værløse (København). In Norway early wooden churches have been excavated at Urnes, Oslo and Mære, Sparbu, N. Trøndelag (cf. fig. 58 and p. 418). The original stave-church at Greensted, Essex, as revealed by Anglo-Scandinavian excavations, may also belong to the eleventh century. Basically all these churches are of similar form, consisting of rectangular nave and approximately square chancel. Some of the churches (like Urnes I and the two Lund churches) have an aisled nave and choir, but the majority had no internal posts. The walls of these churches vary considerably in their structure (fig. 59). All the churches mentioned here, however, have one thing in common in that none is set on sills laid on the ground as the later stave-churches were (fig. 58, 6) – all have the planks sunk directly in the ground. As a result of this the planks rotted away at ground level and we find either that nothing remains save the stumps or marks of the posts in the ground or that, as at Urnes and Greensted, the wall planks were re-used in later churches on the same site. This is most strikingly seen at Urnes where the west wall of the eleventh-century church was removed to form part of the north wall of the twelfth-century church (pl. 27). Posts in the nave and choir observed at Lund may have served to heighten the main part of the church and we may see here the origin of the great posts which dominate the interior of many of the later stave-churches. This feature also existed in the original church at Urnes (Urnes I, fig. 58, 1) and was to occur in most of the later Norwegian churches, but seems unknown in Sweden and Denmark except at Lund. In the later Norwegian churches the central area of the church was built to a great height, and the huge posts which carry it caused them to be called mast-churches, a name which, although rarely used nowadays, is perhaps more descriptive of these buildings than the usual term, stave-churches.

In Norway, where all but two of the surviving standing stave-churches are found (the exceptions being Greensted in Essex and Hedared in Västergötland), the great mast-churches occur with every sort of elaboration, but like all the surviving examples the churches are laid on stout timber sills which are often raised off the ground by means of short stretches of dry-stone walling. Typical of an early phase of this technique is Urnes II (fig. 58, 6), erected in the early twelfth century.

The church building with its exclusive functions, its exclusive servant, the priest, and its exclusive language, Latin, were great novelties in the Norse world, and their assimilation led to numerous modifications of approved practices found elsewhere in Christendom – as the account of the position of clergy on pp. 94–7 above, for example, shows. One factor of great cultural importance, especially in Norway and Iceland, was the swift use men made of the vernacular not only for ordinary pastoral instruction, which was inevitable, but also for the creation of a Christian literature, writings that could be circulated, so that wherever one man could read all might benefit.

Around the church was the graveyard where all were welcome

– rich and poor, friends and enemies – and this was a novel idea too in most districts. Men were no longer buried on their own land, their dead shapes no longer lingered near their kinsmen and kept watch over fields and flocks. It took time to get used to, and in some places in Sweden people set up a rune stone on the old family burial place to commemorate their dead kinsmen lying in the churchyard. Consideration of the dead, who were still on the premises as it were, and belief in their influence had been strong in pagan Scandinavia, and now that living and dead were generally separated, a whole change of outlook must have gradually resulted. A Christian farmer as he looked over his land would be unaware of many presences that had been real to his pagan forefathers. This too made a contribution to the slow relaxation of family ties and the emergence of men less trammelled as individuals than they had been in earlier times.

Conduct

The commanding influence of the family was stressed at the beginning of the book (pp. 4–5). Kinsmen were a man's natural friends and allies. In their extensive concern for all kinds of personal injuries, the laws, for example, do not consider the possibility of kinsmen in dispute with each other – if such a thing was not inconceivable, it was still a matter that could not be of public concern – and the most tragic of heroic stories are those involving a clash of family loyalties. The circle of natural kin was to some degree supplemented by the 'adoption' of the freed slave and the relationship between patron and freedman (pp. 72–4), by group connections as in the guilds (p. 99), and by the bonds between foster-parents and foster-children and between people of different families brought up by one foster-father. The term 'foster-brotherhood' was also used of the bond between friends who went so far as to become 'blood-brothers'. The following description of a blood-brotherhood ceremony is from *Gísla saga*; it was written early in the thirteenth century, but is in all likelihood substantially authentic. The chief parts of the ceremony were evidently designed to symbolize a new birth. Two brothers and their respective brothers-in-law go through the ceremony. The pact was supposed to be clinched by a final handshake.

[They] cut and raise up a long sod in the turf, leaving the two ends fast, and they set a spear with a patterned blade under it, so long-shafted that a man could just reach the rivets of the head with outstretched hand. All four should now pass under . . . and now they draw blood and let their blood run together in the earth which was scratched up under the sod, and mix it all together, earth and blood; and then they kneel and swear an oath, that each shall avenge the other as his brother, and they call all the gods to witness . . .

There could obviously be many causes and degrees of friendship, but an established friendship could have a formal aspect which gave it the nature of a contract. Verses in *Hávamál* stress exchange of gifts as an essential element in friendship: 'givers and repayers of gifts are friends longest, if all goes well'; 'a man must be a friend to his friend and render gift for gift'; 'If you have a friend in whom you have good faith and wish to get good from him, you must share your mind with him and exchange gifts, visit him often.' The recipient of a gift was not regarded as one who passively profited but as one who by his acceptance actively bound himself to make a corresponding return. The return could be in service or in the form of another gift. This is even given formal expression in the Gulathing Law: 'A gift is better than payment in that a man still owns his own as long as it is unrequited. No gift is repaid unless as much comes in return as was given.' (The section goes on to enumerate certain irrevocable gifts where this rule did not apply – gifts to king and Church, of freedom to slaves and money to illegitimate children.) An illustration of the nature of giving and receiving is found in this passage from *Þorgils saga ok Hafliða*, written about 1200 but giving an account of events about 1120. Two chieftains, Haflidi and Thorgils, were in dispute over a man's death, and the case reached this stage:

Haflidi said: 'I will give Thorgils eight *kúgildi* [worth about $1\frac{1}{2}$ lbs. of silver] for the sake of his esteem and honour, and I call it a gift and by no means a payment.' And the point at issue between them was that the one thought he had nothing to pay for and the other thought a small payment for the suit better than having to make good a gift. And each thought his honour depended on what name was given to it, payment or gift, and that stood in the way of settlement.

Gjǫf sér æ til gjalda, 'A gift always looks for a return', was the proverb. As we saw above, this fundamental principle for establishing and maintaining friendship was also applied to men's relations with the gods.

The interests and integrity of an individual and his family (or other group which supplemented or replaced it) were expected to be identical. By conducting himself in a proper way a man maintained or increased the prestige of himself and his group. That prestige was expressed by words we usually translate as 'honour': *virðing* (worth, respect for worth), *metorð* (measurement, evaluation), *metnaðr* (esteem, sense of value). The first two normally refer to the external view of a man, but the third often covers an individual's own awareness of his standing and worth. The other common words for 'honour' are *sómi*, *sæmð*, which appear to express an original notion of what was proper for a man amongst men (cf. the cognate English 'seemly, seemliness').

Prized qualities in men find some expression in rune-stone epitaphs of Swedish yeomen. The words 'good' and 'best' (used of father, son, husband, brother, often with *dreng*, seldom with *bóndi*, cf. pp. 81, 105–8) are frequent but vague; *nýtr*, 'useful, worthy', is occasionally found; *snjallr*, 'alert, valiant, able, eloquent', is rather more specific, as is also *úníðingr*, 'the opposite of niggardly'. In Södermanland a grand expression fashionable for a time was *þróttarþegn* – 'a mature and doughty man' – the first element, *þróttr*, refers especially to powers of endurance (it occurs as one of Odin's many names). Liberality with food, eloquence and gentleness of speech also find specific mention in the inscriptions.

Physical bravery was taken for granted but there was also an ideal of self-control. Kings are described as saying little when angry – that offers one expression of it, but it is seen best in a man's equanimity in the face of danger. This equanimity was not regarded as the result of insensibility or stupidity, but depended on a sense of the relative unimportance of everything when set beside self-respect and public respect (in early times these two must have generally been virtually identical). King Harald the Hard-ruler is supposed to have said of the Icelander Halldór Snorrason that 'of all the men who had been with him he was least moved by sudden events. Whether it was danger or relief or whatever peril loomed, he was never in higher or lower spirits, never slept less or more, and never drank and ate save according to his custom.' There was a practical element in such imperturbability, for it was useless as well as unmanly to show concern or fear.

Many verses in *Hávamál* counsel caution and moderation (pp. 343-4), but these are essentially regarded as pragmatic aids to the maintenance of life and a tolerable position of equality within society. The need for effectiveness was naturally stressed where in the end a man had only himself to rely on, so much so that the poet of *Hávamál* also recommends cold guile: you should laugh and speak false with those you mistrust. Doubtless the average man's aim was to attain just such self-preserving efficiency, but in the Icelandic sagas we meet two more prominent types who, though in marked contrast to one another, belong on the same plane. One is *hófsmaðr*, 'a moderate man', the other is *ójafnaðarmaðr*, 'an unjust man'. The former appears as a social ideal, firm but not aggressive, consequently popular. The latter is pugnacious, self-assertive and domineering; he is not popular but he may be respected, even admired, as long as he is actively and openly brave – it was on this point that public assessment finally hinged. Conspicuous success might be achieved in other ways – by skill in law or in the manipulation of other people – and be found impressive but it was not sealed with the nobility conferred by a willingness to risk life in pursuit of one's aims.

Beyond the efficient, however, there was a further ideal. The character most admired was the exceptional one who was magnanimous rather than cautious, uncalculatingly generous rather than shrewd in his giving, open rather than guileful, ready to offer an enemy a fair chance rather than ruthlessly dispatch him. For this cast of mind and kind of conduct the word *drengskapr* came to be used, 'qualities of a *dreng*', with a connotation that must have grown out of the typical virtues of a member of a fighting ship's crew (cf. p. 106). That must have meant bravery, but also a quick eye for the needs of others and a cheerful discipline. Snorri Sturluson put it admirably and succinctly when he said, 'Valiant men who exert a good influence are called *drengs*'. We do not know how old the noun *drengskapr* is, but the adverb *drengila*, 'after the fashion of a *dreng*', found in scaldic poetry and runic inscriptions, shows that the abstraction came early into being. Many episodes in the Sagas of Icelanders illustrate the force of the concept – bravery, nobility, fair play, respect for others, strength to do what is right – but it also becomes a vague, embracing category, with a sense of 'personal honour'. This is matched by the term *þegnskapr*, a parallel abstraction formed on the word *þegn*, 'mature man, seasoned warrior'. In the Icelandic laws, for example, a man may swear an oath on his *þegnskapr*, for which the easy – and perhaps the only adequate – translation is 'on his honour as a gentleman'.

The commonest words for 'dishonour' are *svívirðing*, with the corresponding verb *svívirða*, where the first element is pejorative, so that what is implied is the reduction of esteem to the level of contempt; and *skǫmm*, 'shame, disgrace', a word probably related to the adjective *skammr*, 'short', for what semantic reasons we do not know. A word which has the same force as 'dishonour' is *ámæli*, 'blame, verbal condemnation'; its use emphasizes the essential element of reputation in this terminology. The lowest of men was the *níðingr*, one who was the object of hate and scorn. The word is used in the laws of outcasts, men who had forfeited all their rights. The classical cause for being so branded was wilfully failing those who had reason to trust you, worst was treachery towards a friend. A typical example is in the eleventh-century inscription that was carved on a stone, now lost, at Söderby in Uppland, Sweden, raised in memory of a brother called Helgi: 'And Sassur killed him and did the deed of a *níðingr* – he betrayed his comrade.'

It is clear that a Christian ideal of self-sacrifice could merge with the notions implicit in *drengskapr*, and a Norse kind of chivalry in keeping with these standards can be found among the Danes in their twelfth-century warfare. Saxo tells how on one occasion in the 1170s Esbiorn and Wetheman (cf. p. 23) with four ships met seven Wendish vessels. In the fight Mirok, a Wendish champion, leapt on board the latter's ship and only Wetheman dared face him. Esbiorn came up and saw this but only laughed and said he would not help – it should not be said that he had helped many against one. Mirok was finally overcome but the Danes set him free, because of their admiration for his courage.

It is also clear that the Church could make use of the concept of the *niðingr* – it was used with relish of Julian the Apostate, for example. In the assessment of conduct between the extremes of the *góðr drengr* and the *niðingr*, however, the Christian view and the secular view – already in existence in pagan times but not derived from pagan religious ideas – were much at odds. Christian teaching distinguishes between humility and pride, but the secular attitude between pride and arrogance. Christianity encourages charity and forgiveness, but the other attitude differentiates between the liberality that springs from magnanimity and that which springs from fear. To take from another man is wrong in Christian teaching, but while Norsemen regarded theft as despicable they did not deny the rights a man won by victory in a duel. The Christian has a clear-cut command, Thou shalt not kill, but the Norsemen made a distinction between the killing publicly avowed, which was honourable, and the secret murder which was abominable because it appeared that the killer was not man enough to abide by the consequences of his act. In the stories told in the Sagas of Icelanders this secular ethical attitude is paramount. In them the arbiter of what was fitting is public opinion; and as we shall see, in the essential sphere of vengeance the outlook is given public sanction in some of the ancient laws of Scandinavia, and receives Christian approbation as well.

A sense of moral imperfection was conveyed by words meaning 'blot, blemish, fault', *vamm, lýti, lǫstr* (cf. p. 359). The second of these is also especially used for physical scar or disfigurement. The third could be used in Christian writing as a synonym for 'sin', for which the usual word, *synð*, is a loan-word from Low German. Other Christian moral terms might be native words with forms of meanings modified, sometimes by existing Christian usage in Old English or German – *réttvíss*, for example, 'rightly-knowing; upright', comes to mean 'righteous', like its Old English cognate, and the abstract *dygð*, 'strength, ability', acquires a predominant sense of 'virtue', from use in Christian contexts. It was apparently necessary to introduce a term for 'conscience'

(WN *samvizka*, EN *samvit* – both calques on the Latin), but the idea of regret and repentance could be expressed by old native words, the verbs *iðra(sk)* (not found in Danish) and *angra*. Words for 'grace' are *gæfa, gipt,* from the root in 'give', (cf. e.g. OE *giefu,* 'gift, good thing, divine grace'), and it is probable that these terms also existed in pre-Christian times with the sense of 'fortune, good luck'. The terms and their negatives may be freely used in some of the Icelandic writings, but it is not always easy to disentangle notions of 'grace' and 'good fortune', 'sin' and 'misfortune'.

Honour was a kind of equilibrium which a man could not allow to be disturbed. It was intolerable if you were not on even terms with society at large, if you and your family could be spoken of with scorn. Balance and good name were restored only with successful retaliation for insult or injury. This might be done by law, but because so much stress was put on a man's individual bravery and fighting spirit, it was particularly expected to be done by vengeance, above all if it was a personal insult or injury, or a sexual affront or killing in the family. Talking of atonement for blows and wounds, the Gulathing Law says bluntly: 'Now no one, neither man nor woman, has any personal right to atonement more than thrice if he does not avenge himself in the meantime.' In Danish law a man who accepted money atonement for an injury was also assured by his opponent on oath (the so-called 'levelling oath') that if he were in his position he too would accept atonement – i.e. he would not have spurned it and held out for blood-vengeance.

The matter was straightforward in the case of substantial offence, but the code also bred an alert, tense attitude; it was thought better to be over-hasty than sluggish in detecting the insult or symbolic injury which might lower a man in the eyes of others. The delicacy of the balance can be shown by a story from the thirteenth-century *Reykdæla saga* which may serve as typical:

At a horse-fight a man called Eyjolf accidentally struck another man, Bjarni, when the two of them were goading horses. Eyjolf did not want to make a quarrel of this, apologized and to confirm his regret offered Bjarni 60 sheep when they were rounded up in the autumn. Bjarni accepted the apology and the proffered gift. When the time came Eyjolf took from the fold the sheep he had promised Bjarni, who was standing by to receive them. Eyjolf's father, Thormód, asked why the sheep were being taken out, and Eyjolf told him he was giving them to Bjarni. Then Thormód said, 'I think it must have been a big hit, for it is being well paid for.' Straightway Bjarni cut him down with a death-blow.

It was impossible for Bjarni to tolerate any suggestion that he was being bought off. In the story the quarrel went on but when agreement was finally reached, those fixing the terms decided that Thormód had put himself outside the law by his words and no atonement was to be paid for his death. These terms undoubtedly express accepted public opinion on such a matter.

In states with little or no executive powers vengeance was also justice. It took a long time for Church and monarchy between them to find something effective to put in its place, and indeed, room had to be made for it within Norse Christendom down to the end of our period and beyond. The difficult position of the priest who cannot get redress is spoken of in the Gotland Law: 'If he will not offer atonement to a priest, then the priest must go to the assembly before all the people and there make his complaint, saying: "I am a priest and consecrated to God's service – I cannot stand amid strokes or in battle – I would take atonement if it were offered, but shame I would not willingly suffer".' In Iceland towards 1200 there was a young priest, Gudmund Arason, later bishop of Hólar and regarded by many as a saint. He prosecuted a man and got him sentenced as an outlaw, but Gudmund was then troubled because any attempt to execute further judgement on him would jeopardize his clerical status. But all went well, because in a brawl at a horse-fight the son of a man who had sheltered the outlaw was killed and the outlaw himself was wounded. The bishop's biographer says that in this way God avenged Gudmund, but so guarded him that he contributed to this end by neither word nor deed.

When vengeance was retribution as well as restoration of a man's position in his own and others' eyes, it might seem all the more important that it should be undertaken patiently and deliberately. The devout Christian author of the thirteenth-century Norwegian *Konungs skuggsjá* (it has been suggested that he was an archbishop) regards vengeance under some circumstances as inevitable, but wishes it to be as coolly considered as possible. In his colloquy between Father and Son, the former says: 'Be as peaceable as you can, but only so that you do not suffer injuries or lay yourself open to serious reproach on account of cowardice. And if needful matters force you to violence, then do not make yourself hasty in revenge until you see that it will be successfully achieved and will come down on the man who deserves it; but if you see it cannot be achieved, do not be precipitate; and seek your honour later, unless the other man offers such terms as to make you honourable amends.' The emphatic requirement here, that vengeance should be a punishment justly visited on the man responsible for inflicting the injury, marks the attempt by Church and Crown to control the revenge that was automatically expected. The old savage practice was to take vengeance for a killing by attacking not the slayer but, if possible, a more distinguished, but maybe quite innocent, member of his family. This is expressly condemned as a prevailing 'evil custom' in Norway in a thirteenth-century article in the Frostathing Law.

Family and personal honour, maintained by fulfilling the duty of vengeance, required possession of sensibility, vigour and valour. In the last resort it also required that unyielding courage which is the hallmark of the outlook conveniently termed 'heroic'. As Saxo says, 'Without peril in utmost need, it is not easy to discover whether a man possesses true and solid fortitude', and the hero appears essentially as the man triumphant in the face of death. One knows of a Christian heroism and one can imagine an Odinic heroism, but in both cases the man who suffers with bravery would look into a life beyond death. It is typical of the heroism one meets in the northern poems and stories that there is no concern with what is to come – the hero is strenuously involved only with this world and its secular values. If a man dies cheerfully and defiantly it is for the sake of his own self-respect, for the sake of honour – usually, that is, the esteem of others. He recognizes the likelihood of death as the supreme opportunity, and he is aided in his response to it by the knowledge that this moment was destined. (There is a common pragmatic note to be heard in this: every man is bound to die, so fight boldly.) In many (not all) of the Icelandic sagas there is frequent reference to unavoidable fate, and although it is partly a literary device, one which allows development of telling dramatic irony in the story, there seems no doubt but that many people were fatalistic in outlook, partly deterministic, partly stoic, in the face of human behaviour and natural disaster. The belief must indeed have been an ancient heritage, for words to do with fate in Norse belong to a common Germanic terminology. When death was due, it was thought that a state or condition might be produced in the person about to die so that all he did predisposed him to disaster – he was *feigr*, 'fey'. If a man escaped against odds, it might be said, for example, that it was because he was an active man and not fey. On the basis of such retrospective observation, belief in the power of destiny could grow, as it might also by witnessing the good or bad fortune that came upon individuals. In Christian terms indifferent destiny could be re-written with faith as merciful providence. But in the heroic stories fate is essentially represented by death: the 'verdict of the Norns' in *Hamðismál* (p. 356) is death; in another ancient poem, the so-called *Hlǫðskviða*, the judgement of the Norns is death, but it is there called an evil judgement because the death is that of a brother at the hands of a brother. The idea of an inexorable fate with death as its instrument may exist in any period, but one can imagine that it might acquire paramount force in times of disruption and strife. The Viking Age saw many men plucked out of secure corners and the steady round of toil and ritual, set down in strange places, and bewildered by conflicting notions of the purpose of this life and the nature of the next. There must have been many who gave up thinking and stuck to what was known. And what was known for sure was, on the one hand, the fact of death – and, on the other hand, the witness of brave men in one's own experience and of all the brave men who were famous in poems and stories. The heroic creed was based on this simple correlation:

> *Wealth dies,*
> *kinsmen die,*
> *a man dies likewise himself;*

431

but fame
dies never,
for him who gets good fame.

Wealth dies,
kinsmen die,
a man dies likewise himself;
I know one thing
that never dies,
the verdict on each man dead.

These famous *Hávamál* stanzas are from the ninth century, but they have found no essential modification in the Christian texts of the Norwegian court four hundred years later. *Konungs skuggsjá* says: 'Remember that there are many who themselves live but a little while but whose conduct lives long after them, and it matters much what a man is remembered for, for some become famous for good deeds, and they live on for ever after him, and his honour is always alive, though he himself is dead.' *Hirðskrá* says: 'Remember that once a man dies as a *niðingr*, he will never be a *drengr* again, and his memory must live on with the reputation that goes with the name he had when he died.' The standard for honourable conduct was ultimately set by public opinion, and public opinion provided the reward. The quintessence of past public opinion resided in history and legend and maintained the ideal. Poems like the Lay of Atli not only gave models for heroic behaviour, they also proved the truth of the assertion that a man could win everlasting fame, a secular immortality, in keeping with the emphasis on individual human responsibility and self-reliance.

This ethic has been known at all times, but there are few literatures in which its values are treated with such reverence and in such variety of circumstances as that of medieval Iceland. But for some it was more than literature and entertainment. A supreme expression of the heroic response is in the Lay of Atli in the description of how 'Họgni laughed as they cut him, the living warrior, to the heart'. That theme was taken up and cheapened in romantic stories of the twelfth century. But this next passage is the work of a sober historian describing an event which took place in Iceland in 1244, in circumstances neither romantic nor larger-than-life heroic. Bjǫrn Dufgusson was a stalwart kinsman and supporter of the Sturlungs, capable of brutality but with something of a dash about him. He was cornered by a man called Bersi. 'Bjǫrn asked for quarter and Bersi said he should have it as far as he was concerned. He brought him to Kolbeinn [his leader], and he asked why he did not make short work of Bjǫrn. Then five of them thrust at him at once, and each thrust was mortal. A man called Óttar struck Bjǫrn on the neck. And there he died, and they say that he died laughing.'

To be in Hǫgni's company after seven hundred years is in Bjǫrn's case a kind of vindication of the belief in the immortality of fame. But in admiring the hard, heroic achievement of people in the Norse world, we may well end by recalling what we owe to the poets and historians of ancient Scandinavia. The Icelanders above all created and preserved stories which give us a sense of that achievement in credible, human terms, and express stern and stirring ideals of conduct whose validity must be acknowledged even while their limitations are recognized.

Bibliographical notes

The following highly selective lists of books and papers are given chapter by chapter and some infrequent repetition of titles is unavoidable. The differences that exist between the scholarly situation of the philologist and that of the archaeologist have some effect on the nature of the lists. Most of the archaeological references are to the publications of major importance from which the information given at any point is drawn. The philological sources, on the other hand, are the texts which are enumerated, normally once and for all, in the sections below relating to the Introduction and. Chapter 10. A few outstanding works of older scholarship are mentioned among the other non-archaeological references, but otherwise these are for the most part restricted to recent publications which themselves include useful bibliographies. They generally offer the latest (not the last) word on a subject and make a natural starting-point for a student's own investigation.

INTRODUCTION

xvi   Jones Gwyn. *A History of the Vikings.* 1968.
           Keary C.F. *The Vikings in Western Christendom.* 1891.
           Kendrick T.D. *A History of the Vikings.* 1930.
           Sawyer P.H. *The Age of the Vikings.* 1962.
           Shetelig H. *An introduction to the Viking history of Western Europe* (Viking antiquities in Great Britain and Ireland 1). 1940.

xvi–xviii Two encyclopaedic works of great importance are the series called *Nordisk Kultur,* 30 volumes published between 1931 and 1956, some of which are individually mentioned in the lists below; and *Kulturhistorisk leksikon for nordisk middelalder,* of which 14 volumes (A – Samgäld) have so far been issued, from 1956 to 1969. We have made much use of this latter work, though naturally we do not necessarily agree with all the opinions expressed there on controversial topics, and we warmly recommend readers to profit from the informed comment and up-to-date bibliographies provided by it.

xviii   Brøndsted J. *Danmarks Oldtid* III. 2. Udg. 1960.
           Brøndsted J. *The Vikings.* Trans. Kalle Skov. 1965.
           Shetelig H., Falk H., Gordon E.V. *Scandinavian Archaeology.* 1937.
           Lindqvist S. *Gotlands Bildsteine.* 1941–2.
           Stenberger M. *Det forntida Sverige.* 1964.
           Cleasby R., Vigfusson, Gudbrand. *An Icelandic-English Dictionary.* 1874.
           Fritzner J. *Ordbog over det gamle norske Sprog.* 1883–96.
           Kalkar O. *Ordbog til det ældre danske Sprog.* 1881–1918.
           Söderwall K.F. *Ordbok öfver svenska medeltids-språket.* 1890–1918. Supplement in progress from 1925.
           Falk H.S., Torp A. *Norwegisch-Dänisches etymologisches Wörterbuch.* 2 Aufl. 1960.
           de Vries J. *Altnordisches etymologisches Wörterbuch.* 1961.
           Seip D.A. *Norsk språkhistorie til omkring 1370.* 2. utg. 1955.
           Skautrup P. *Det danske Sprogs Historie* I. 1944.
           Sahlgren J. *Vad våra ortnamn berätta.* 2. uppl. 1963.
           Hald Kr. *Vore Stednavne.* 2. Udg. 1965.
           Hald Kr. *Stednavne og Kulturhistorie.* 1966.
           Olsen M., ed. *Stedsnavn* (Nordisk Kultur V). 1939.

xix   Fischer F. *Die Lehnwörter des Altwestnordischen* (Palaestra 85). 1909.

Kristensen M. *Fremmedordene i det ældste danske Skriftsprog (för omtr. 1300).* 1906.

Thors C.-E. *Den kristna terminologien i fornsvenskan* (Studier i nordisk filologi 45). 1957.

Finsen Vilhjálmur, ed. *Grágás. Codex Regius.* 1852. *Staðarhólsbók.* 1879. *Skálholtsbók.* 1883. The last volume contains a valuable *Ordregister.*

Lárusson Ólafur. *Yfirlit yfir íslenska rjettarsögu.* Pjetur G. Guðmundsson fjölritaði. 1932.

Lárusson Ólafur. *Lög og saga.* 1958.

Larson L.M., trans. *The earliest Norwegian laws. Being the Gulathing Law and the Frostathing Law.* 1935.

Munch P.A., Keyser R., Storm G., Hertzberg E., ed. *Norges gamle Love indtil 1387.* 1846–95.

Robberstad K., trans. *Gulatingslovi.* 2. utg. 1952.

Robberstad K. *Fyrelesningar um rettssoga i millomalder og nytid.* 1964(?)–6.

Holmbäck Å., Wessén E. *Svenska landskapslagar tolkade och förklarade . . .* 1933–46.

Pipping H., ed. *Gutalag och Gutasaga.* 1905–7.

Schlyter C.J., ed. *Samling af Sweriges Gamla Lagar.* 1827–77.

Wessén E., ed. *Äldre Västgötalagen.* 1965.

Wessén E. *Svenskt lagspråk.* 1965.

Brøndum-Nielsen J., Jørgensen P.J., ed. *Danmarks gamle Landskabslove.* Udg. af Det danske Sprog- og Litteraturselskab. 1920–61.

Jørgensen P.J. *Dansk Retshistorie.* 3 Opl. 1965.

Kroman E., Iuul S. *Danmarks gamle Love paa Nutidsdansk.* 1945–8.

Kroman E., Iuul S. *Skaanske Lov og Jyske Lov.* 3 Udg. 1963.

xx   v. Friesen O., ed. *Runorna* (Nordisk Kultur VI). 1933.

Musset L. *Introduction à la runologie.* 1965.

Jacobsen L., Moltke E. *Danmarks Runeindskrifter.* 1941–2.

Bugge S., Olsen M. *Norges indskrifter med de ældre runer.* 1891–1924.

Liestøl A. 'Runer frå Bryggen', *Viking* XXVII, 1963, 5–53.

Liestøl A. 'Sigurd Lavards rúnakefli', *Maal og minne*, 1964, 1–11.

Liestøl A. 'Correspondence in runes', *Mediaeval Scandinavia* I, 1968, 17–27.

Olsen M. *Norges innskrifter med de yngre runer.* 1941–60. To be continued by A. Liestøl.

Olsen M. 'Runic inscriptions in Great Britain, Ireland and the Isle of Man' *Viking Antiquities in Great Britain and Ireland* VI. 1954, 151–233.

Jansson Sven B.F. *The runes of Sweden.* 1962.

Sveriges runinskrifter. In progress since 1900.

Birkeland H. *Nordens historie i middelalderen etter arabiske kilder* (Skrifter utgitt av Det Norske Videnskaps-Akademi i Oslo. II. Hist.-filos. Klasse. 1954. No. 2). Cf. references against pp. 110, 399, 408.

Henrichsen C.L., trans. Adam af Bremen. *De Hamburgske Ærkebispers Historie og Nordens Beskrivelse.* 1930 (reprinted 1968).

Schmeidler B., ed. *Magistri Adam Bremensis Gesta Hammaburgensis Ecclesiae Pontificum.* Ed. tertia. 1917.

Trillmich W., Buchner R., ed. and trans. *Quellen des 9. und 11. Jahrhunderts zur Geschichte der hamburgischen Kirche . . .* 1961.

Helmoldi . . . Cronica Slavorum. In *Monumenta Germaniae Historica. Scriptores . . .* XXI. 1869.

Waquet H., ed. and trans. *Abbo. Bella Parisiacae urbis.* 1942.

Dudonis . . . de moribus et actis primorum Normanniæ ducum libri tres. In Migne, *Patrologia Latina* CXLI. 1880.

Todd J.H., ed. and trans. *Cogadh Gaedhel re Gallaibh. The War of the Gaedhil with the Gaill.* 1867.

xxi   Hollander Lee M. *A Bibliography of Scaldic Studies.* 1958.

Hermannsson Halldór. *Bibliography of the Eddas* (Islandica XIII). 1920.

Hannesson Jóhann S. *Bibliography of the Eddas. A Supplement* (Islandica XXXVII). 1955.

Bekker-Nielsen Hans. *Bibliography of Old Norse-Icelandic Studies.* In progress from 1963.

Holm-Olsen L., ed. *Konungs skuggsiá.* 1945.

Hirðskrá. Published in *Norges gamle Love* II (see against p. xix above).

xxii   Gertz M.Cl., ed. *Vitae Sanctorum Danorum.* 1908–12.

Olrik H., trans. *Danske Helgeners Levned.* 1893–4.

Gertz M.Cl., ed. *Scriptores minores historiæ danicæ medii ævi.* 1917–22.

Holder A., ed. *Saxonis Grammatici Gesta Danorum.* 1886.

Olrik J., Raeder H., Blatt F., ed. *Saxonis Gesta Danorum.* 1931–57.

af Petersens C., Olson E., ed. *Sǫgur Danakonunga.* 1919–25.

Munch P.A., ed. *Chronica regum Manniæ et Insularum.* 1860.

Guðmundsson Finnbogi, ed. *Orkneyinga saga* (Íslenzk fornrit XXXIV). 1965.

Jónsson Finnur, ed. *Færeyinga saga.* 1927.

Halldórsson Ólafur, ed. *Færeyinga saga.* 1967.

Grænlendinga saga. In Sveinsson Einar Ól., Þórðarson Matthías, ed. *Eyrbyggja saga* (Íslenzk fornrit IV). 1935.

Storm G., ed. *Monumenta Historica Norvegiæ.* 1880.

Jónsson Finnur, ed. *Ágrip af Nóregs konunga sǫgum* (Altnordische Saga-Bibliothek 18). 1929.

Hermannsson Halldór. *Bibliography of the Sagas of the Kings of Norway* (Islandica III). 1910.

Hermannsson Halldór. *The Sagas of the Kings . . . [a supplement]* (Islandica XXVI). 1937.

Metcalfe F., ed. *Passio et miracula beati Olaui.* 1881.

Storm G., ed. *Otte Brudstykker af den ældste Saga om Olav den hellige.* 1893.

Johnsen O.A., ed. *Olafs saga hins helga.* 1922.

Johnsen O.A., Helgason Jón, ed. *Den store Saga om Olav den hellige.* 1941.

Jónsson Finnur, ed. *Saga Óláfs Tryggvasonar af Oddr Snorrason . . .* 1932.

Halldórsson Ólafur, ed. *Ólafs saga Tryggvasonar en mesta.* In progress from 1958.

Jónsson Finnur, ed. *Morkinskinna.* 1928–32.

Jónsson Finnur, ed. *Fagrskinna.* 1902–3.

Aðalbjarnarson Bjarni, ed. *Heimskringla* (Íslenzk fornrit XXVI-VIII). 1941–51.

af Petersens C., ed. *Jómsvikinga saga efter Arnamagnæanska Handskriften N:o 291. 4:to.* 1882.

xxiii   Indrebø G., ed. *Sverris saga etter Cod. AM 327 4°.* 1920.

Benediktsson Jakob, ed. *Íslendingabók. Landnámabók* (Íslenzk fornrit I). 1969.

Jóhannesson Jón, Finnbogason Magnús, Eldjárn Kristján, ed. *Sturlunga saga.* 1946.

Biskupa sögur gefnar út af hinu íslenzka Bókmentafélagi. 1858–78.

Hermannsson Halldór. *Bibliography of the Icelandic Sagas and Minor Tales* (Islandica I). 1908.

Hermannsson Halldór. *The Sagas of Icelanders . . . A Supplement* (Islandica XXIV). 1935.

Hannesson Jóhann S. *The Sagas of Icelanders . . . A Supplement* (Islandica XXXVIII). 1957.

Íslendinga sǫgur, Sagas of Icelanders, have normally been consulted in the series *Íslenzk fornrit,* in progress since 1933.

CHAPTER I

1   Sömme A., ed. *The geography of Norden.* 1960.

Mead W.R. *An economic geography of the Scandinavian states and Finland.* 2nd impression. 1964.

6–7 Johnsen A.O. *Fra ættesamfunn til statssamfunn.* 1948.

7 Koch Hal. *Den danske Kirkes Historie* I. *Den ældre Middelalder indtil 1241.* 1950.
Koch Hal. *Kongemagt og Kirke 1060–1241* ([Politikens] Danmarks Historie 3). 1963.
Christensen Aksel E. 'Denmark between the Viking Age and the time of the Valdemars', *Mediaeval Scandinavia* I, 1968, 28–50.

13 The extracts from the Chronicle are from the translation by G.N. Garmonsway: *The Anglo-Saxon Chronicle* (Dent's Everyman's Library No. 624). 1953.

14 Waitz G., ed. *Vita Anskarii auctore Rimberto. Accedit Vita Rimberti.* 1884.
Rudberg G., trans. *Rimbert. Ansgars levnad.* Med historisk inledning av Nils Ahnlund. 1965.
Vita Anskarii is also edited and translated in Trillmich . . . *Quellen*, see against p. xx above.

16 Hansen Fr..C.C. *De ældste Kongegrave og Bispegrave i Roskilde Domkirke.* 1914. 47.

20 *Vita Sancti Wilhelmi* is edited in Gertz, *Vitae*, and translated in Olrik, *Helgeners Levned*, see against p. xxii above.

25 Andersson I. *Sveriges historia.* 3. uppl. 1950.
Rosén J. *Svensk Historia* I. *Tiden före 1718.* 1962.
Ahnlund N. *Jämtlands och Härjedalens historia . . . intill 1537.* 1948.
Sjöberg Åke G. *Historia kring Gotland.* 1963.

28 Jansson Sven B.F. *Svenska utlandsfärder i runinskrifternas ljus.* 1948.

30 Malmer Brita. *Mynt och människor.* 1968. 139–45.

34 Hagen A. *Forhistorisk tid og vikingtid* (Vårt folks historie I). 1962.
Helle K. *Norge blir en stat 1130–1319.* 1964.
Holmsen A. *Norges historie fra de eldste tider til 1660.* 3. utg. 1961.
Joys C. *Hellig Olavs arv* (Vårt folks historie II). 1962.

52 *Færøerne.* Udg. af Dansk-færøsk Samfund. 1958.
Trap J.P. *Færøerne* (Danmark. Femte Udgave. XII). 1968.
Foote P.G. *On the Saga of the Faroe Islanders.* 1965.
Eldjárn Kristján *Kuml og haugfé úr heiðnum sið á Íslandi.* 1956.
Jóhannesson Jón. *Íslendinga saga.* 1956–8.
von Maurer Konrad. *Island von seiner ersten Entdeckung bis zum Untergange des Freistaats (ca. 800–1264).* 1874 (Neudruck . . . 1969).
Þorsteinsson Björn. *Íslenzka þjóðveldið.* 1953.
Þorsteinsson Björn. *Ný Íslandssaga. Þjóðveldisöld.* 1966.

54 Lárusson Ólafur. *Byggð og saga.* 1944.

55 Lárusson Magnús Már. 'Nokkrar athugasemdir um upphæð manngjalda', *Saga*, 1960, 76–91; and in *Fróðleiksþættir og sögubrot.* 1967. 136–48.

56 Jones Gwyn. *The Norse Atlantic Saga.* 1964.
. Ingstad Helge. *Vesterveg til Vinland.* 1965.
Nordal Sigurður. *Íslenzk menning.* 1942.

CHAPTER 2

65 von See Klaus. 'Das Alter der Rígsþula', *Acta Philologica Scandinavica* XXIV, 1957, 1–12.
Sveinsson Einar Ól. *Íslenzkar bókmenntir í fornöld* I. 1962. 287–91.
Turville-Petre G. *Saga-Book of the Viking Society* XVI, 1962–5, 254–7.

66 Gjessing A. 'Trældom i Norge', *Aarbøger for nordisk Oldkyndighed og Historie*, 1862, 28–322.
Landtmanson I.S. *Träldomens sista skede i Sverige* (Skrifter utgifna af K. Humanistiska Vetenskapssamfundet i Upsala. v.6). 1897.

75 The verse here, but not elsewhere, is cited from the translation by Olive
  Bray: *The Elder or Poetic Edda* . . . *The mythological poems*. 1908. 205.

CHAPTER 3
81 Robberstad K. 'Odelsretten'. In *Frå gamal og ny rett* I. 1950. 18–22.
92 Reichborn-Kjennerud I. *Vår gamle trolldomsmedisin* (Skrifter utgitt av Det
  Norske Videnskaps-Akademi i Oslo. II. Hist.-filos. Klasse. 1927. No.
  6; 1933. No. 2; 1940. No. 1; 1943. No. 2; 1947. No. 1).
  Hrafns saga Sveinbjarnarsonar is in *Sturlunga saga* and *Biskupa sögur*, see against
  p. xxiii above. A new edition is to be published by Dr Guðrún P. Helga-
  dóttir.
94 *Monumenta Germaniae Historica. Epistolae selectae* II ii. 2 . . . Aufl. 1955. 498.
  Steffensen Jón. 'Aspects of life in Iceland in the heathen period', *Saga-
  Book of the Viking Society* XVII 2–3, 1967–8, 177–205.
97 Stender-Petersen A. *Varangica.* 1953.
  Stender-Petersen A. 'Varægerspørgsmålet', *Viking* XXIII, 1959, 43–55.
  Blöndal Sigfús. *Væringjasaga.* 1954.
98 For references to guilds on rune stones see especially Jansson Sven B.F.
  'A newly discovered rune stone in Törnevalla church, Östergötland', in
  Early English and Norse Studies presented to Hugh Smith. 1963. 110–9.
99 *Þorgils saga ok Hafliða*, in *Sturlunga saga,* see against p. xxiii above. Also
  edited separately by Ursula Brown, 1952.
  Guild regulations are printed in *Norges gamle Love* v, see against p. xix
  above. See also Storm G. 'En gammel Gildeskraa fra Trondhjem',
  in *Sproglig-historiske Studier tilegnede Professor C.R. Unger.* 1896. 217–26.
101 *Hirðskrá* is printed in *Norges gamle Love* II, see against p. xix above.
102 *Vederlov* in Brøndum-Nielsen J. *Danske Sprogtekster til Universitetsbrug* II.
  1942. 24–5.
  Sven Aggeson's *Lex castrensis* in Gertz, *Scriptores minores* . . . I, see against
  p. xxii above.
105 Aakjær S. 'Old Danish Thegns and Drengs', *Acta Philologica Scandinavica* II,
  1927–8, 1–30.
  Nielsen K.M. 'Var thegnene og drengene kongelige hirdmænd?', *Aarbøger
  for nordisk Oldkyndighed og Historie,* 1945, 111–21.
107 Wessén E. *Historiska runinskrifter* (Kungl. Vitterhets Historie och Antikvitets Akademiens Handlingar. Fil.-filos. Serien 6). 1960.
110 The report of al-Ghazal has been consulted in the translation of Bernard
  Lewis printed by W.E.D. Allen in *The Poet and the Spae-wife.* 1960.
  (Also in *Saga-Book of the Viking Society* XV, 3, 1960.)
114 von Schwerin C.F. 'Die Ehescheidung im älteren isländischen Recht',
  Deutsche Islandforschung I, 1930, 283–99.
117 Steffensen Jón. See reference against p. 94 above.
120 Robberstad K. 'Litt meir um gravgangsmennene', *Historisk tidsskrift* 34,
  1946–8, 609–12.

CHAPTER 4
124 Holtsmark Anne. 'Landsmaðr – landmaðr', *Arkiv för nordisk filologi* 82,
  1967, 147–54.
127 Ljunggren K.G. '*Landman* och *boman* i vikingatida källor', *Arkiv för nordisk
  filologi* 74, 1959, 115–35.
139 Baetke W. *Yngvi und die Ynglingar* (Sitzungsberichte der sächsischen
  Akademie der Wissenschaften zu Leipzig. Phil. hist. Kl. B. 109, Heft
  3). 1964.
  Ström F. 'Kung Domalde i Svitjod och "kungalyckan" ', *Saga och sed,*
  1967, 52–66.

439

30

CHAPTER 5
145–90   Blomqvist R., Mårtensson A.W. *Thulegrävningen 1961*. 1963.
         Hodges H. *Artifacts*. 2nd ed. 1964.
         Petersen J. *Vikingetidens Redskaper* (Skrifter utgitt av det Norske Videnskaps-
         Akademi i Oslo. II. Hist.-Filos. Klasse. 1951. No. 4).
148   Hougen B. *Fra seter til gård*. 1947.
         Gelling P.S. 'Medieval shielings in the Isle of Man', *Medieval Archaeology*
         VI-VII, 1962–3, 156–72.
         Matras C. 'Gammelfærøsk *ærgi*, n., og dermed beslægtede ord', *Namn och*
         Bygd XLIV, 1956, 51–67.
148–9   Hofsten N. von. *Eddadikternas djur och växter* (Skrifter utgivna av Kungl.
         Gustav Adolfs Akademien 30). 1957.
149   Hagen A. *Norway*. 1967. 198.
         Stenberger M. 'Vollmoen och Island', *Fornvännen* 1943, 169–73.
150   Ramskou T. *Lindholm Høje*. 1960.
         Steensberg A. *Den danske Bondegaard*. 1942.
         Steensberg A. *Atlas over Borups agre*. 1968.
         Strömberg M. 'Eine siedlungsgeschichtliche Untersuchung in Hagestad,
         Südost-Schonen', *Meddelanden från Lunds Universitetets Historiska Museum*,
         1961, 123–54.
         Strömberg M. 'Handelsstråk och vikingabygd i sydöstra Skåne. Om
         Hagestadsundersökningen', *Ale* III, 1963, 1–25.
         Strömberg M. 'Undersökningarna rörande Hagestad, Skåne', *Kuml*, 1967,
         117–23.
         Thorpe H. 'The Green Village in its European Setting', *The Fourth Viking*
         Congress, ed. A. Small, 1965, 85–111.
151   Hope-Taylor B. 'The boat-shaped house in northern Europe', *Proceedings*
         of the Cambridge Antiquarian Society, 1961, 16–22.
         Magnusson M. 'Ein frühmittelalterlicher Fischplatz in der Nähe von
         Kivik', *Meddelanden från Lunds Universitetets Historiska Museum*, 1948, 81–94.
         Olsen O. 'Trelleborg-problemer', *Scandia* XXVIII, 1962, 92–112.
         Olsen O. 'Om at udgrave stolpehuller'. *Nationalmuseets Arbejdsmark*, 1968,
         155–70.
         Ramskou T. 'Husbygning i vikingetidens Danmark', *Árbók hins íslenzka*
         fornleifafélags (Fylgirit), 1958, 134–7.
152   Dahl S. 'Toftarannsóknir í Fuglafirði', *Fróðskaparrit* VII, 1958, 118–46.
         Dahl S. 'Bústaður í Eingjartoftum, Sandvági', *Fróðskaparrit* X, 1961, 53–76.
         Dahl S. 'Víkingabústaður í Seyrvági', *Fróðskaparrit* XIV, 1965, 9–23.
         Small A. 'A Viking longhouse in Unst, Shetland', *The Fifth Viking Congress*,
         ed. B. Niclasen, 1968, 62–70.
153   Bakka E. 'Ytre Moa', *Viking* XXIX, 1965, 121–46.
         Cruden S. 'Excavations at Birsay, Orkney', *The Fourth Viking Congress*,
         ed. A. Small, 1965, 22–31.
         Gelling P.S. 'The Braaid Site', *The Journal of the Manx Museum* VI, 1964,
         201–5.
         Radford C.A.R. *The Early Christian and Norse Settlements at Birsay, Orkney*.
         1959.
154   Thorarinsson S. *The eruptions of Hekla in historical times*. 1967.
154–7   Stenberger M., ed. *Forntida gårdar i Island*. 1943.
157   Hamilton J.R.C. *Excavations at Jarlshof, Shetland*. 1956.
158   Hinsch E. *Naust og hall i jernalderen* (Årbok for Universitetet i Bergen.
         Humanistisk serie. 1960. No. 2).
         Thun E. 'Die Wassermühlen', *Meddelanden från Lunds Universitetets Historiska*
         Museum, 1962–3, 224–37.
         Thun E. *Medieval Tommarp, Archaeological Investigations 1959–1960* (Acta
         Archaeologica Lundensia, octavo series 5). 1967.

159   Steensberg A. *Atlas over Borups agre.* 1968.
        Krogh K.J., Voss O. 'Fra hedenskab til kristendom i Hørning',
        Nationalmuseets Arbejdsmark, 1961, 5–34.
163   O'Kelly M. 'An ancient method of cooking meat', *Congresos internacionales
        de ciencias prehistoricas y protohistoricas: Actas de la IV sesion,* 1956, 615–8.
166   Campbell Å. *Det svenska brödet.* 1950.
168   Hoffman M. *The warp-weighted loom* (Studia Norvegica XIV). 1964.
172   Guðjónsson E.E. 'Forn röggvarvefnaður', *Árbók hins íslenzka fornleifafélags,*
        1962, 12–71.
173   Hald M. *Jernalderens dragt.* 1962.
174   Blindheim C. 'Osebergskoene på ny', *Viking* XXIII, 1959, 71–86.
175   Glob P.V. *Ard og Plov i Nordens Oldtid* (Jysk Arkæologisk Selskabs Skrifter I).
        1951.
176   Lerche G. 'The radiocarbon dated Danish ploughing implements', *Tools
        and Tillage* I, 1968, 56–8.
177   Steensberg A. *Atlas over Borups agre.* 1968.
        Steensberg A. *Ancient harvesting implements.* 1943.
178   Berg G. 'A tool chest from the Viking Age', *Universitetet i Bergen Årbok
        1955* (Historisk-antikvarisk rekke I), 77–83.
181   Blindheim C. 'Smedgraven fra Bygland i Morgedal', *Viking* XXVI, 1962,
        25–80.
182   Arrhenius O. *Die Grundlagen unserer älteren Eisenherstellung* (Antikvariskt
        Arkiv XIII). 1959.
183–4   Martens I. 'Jernvinna i Norge', *Teknisk Ukeblad* nr. 17, 1968, 2–10.
        Ohlhaver H. *Der germanische Schmied und sein Werkzeug.* 1939.
        Oldeberg A. *Metallteknik under vikingatid och medeltid.* 1966.
        Thomsen R. 'Forsøg på rekonstruktion af en fortidig jernudvindingsproces',
        Kuml, 1963, 60–74.
        Thomsen R. 'Forsøg på rekonstruktion af fortidige smedeprocesser', *Kuml,*
        1964, 62–85.
184   Nordahl E. 'Till frågan om falukopparens ålder', *Falu gruvas ålder,* 59–79.
185   Theophilus. *De Diversis Artibus,* ed. C.R. Dodwell. 1961.
186   Skjølsvold A. *Klebersteinsindustrien i Vikingetiden.* 1961.
188   Strömbäck D. 'Cult elements in Icelandic dramatic dances', *Arv* IV, 1948,
        132–45.
        Samsonarson Jón. *Kvæði og dansleikir.* 1964.

CHAPTER 6
191–231 Bjernum J.P. 'Vikingetidens handel og dens betydning for Nordens folk',
        Aarbøger for nordisk Oldkyndighed og Historie, 1948, 294–302.
        Schück A. *Studier rörande det svenska stadsväsendets uppkomst och äldsta utveckling.*
        1926.
192   Paulsen P. *Studien zur Wikinger-Kultur.* 1933.
195   Morrison K.F. 'Numismatics and Carolingian trade: a critique of the
        evidence', *Speculum* XXXVIII, 403–32.
196–200 Brøgger A.W. *Ertog og øre* (Vitenskapsselskapets Skrifter. II. Hist.-Filos.
        Klasse. 1921. No. 3).
        Dolley R.H.M. *Viking Coins of the Danelaw and of Dublin.* 1965.
        Dolley R.H.M. *The Hiberno-Norse coins in the British Museum.* 1966.
        Grieg S. 'Vikingetidens skattefund', *Oslo Universitetets Oldsaksamlings
        Skrifter* II, 1929, 177–311.
        Holst H. 'Uten- og innenlandske mynter i norske funn, nedlagt før år
        1100', *Nordisk numismatisk årsskrift,* 1943, 56–112.

Kiersnowski R. 'Coin finds and the problem of hoarding money in early medieval Poland', *Wiadomsci Numizmatyerne* v, 1961, 35–56.

Malmer B. *Nordiska mynt före år* 1000 (Acta Archaeologica Lundensia, octavo series 4). 1966.

Rasmusson N.L. 'Vikingatidens skattefynd: en orientering', *Nordisk Tidskrift* xxxiii, 1957, 241–51.

Skovmand R. 'De danske Skattefund', *Aarbøger for nordisk Oldkyndighed og Historie*, 1942, 1–275.

Stenberger M. *Die Schatzfunde Gotlands der Wikingerzeit.* 1947–58.

200–203 Lewis A.R. *The Northern Seas.* 1958.

201 Hougen E.K. 'Handel og samferdsel i Nordens vikingtid', *Viking* xxix, 1965, 167–90.

Selling D. *Wikingerzeitliche und frühmittelalterliche Keramik in Schweden.* 1955.

202 Helle K. 'Trade and shipping between Norway and England in the reign of Håkon Håkonsson', *Sjøfartshistorisk Årbok*, 1967, 7–34.

203–5 Holmqvist W. 'Helgö, en internationell handelsplats', *Proxima Thule*, 1962, 139–55.

Holmqvist W., Arrhenius B. *Excavations at Helgö* ii. 1964.

Holmqvist W., Granath K.-E. *Helgö, den gåtfulla ön.* 1969.

205–10 Arbman H. *Birka, Sveriges äldsta handelsstad.* 1939.

Arbman H. *Birka* i. 1940–3.

Kivikoski E. 'Studien zu Birkas Handel im östlichen Ostseegebiet', *Acta Archaeologica* viii, 1947, 229–50.

210–13 Aner E. 'Das Kammergräberfeld von Haithabu', *Offa* x, 1952, 61–115.

Eriksson H.S. *Hedeby, en søhandelsstad i vikingetiden.* 1967.

Hübner W. *Die Keramik von Haithabu.* 1959.

Jankuhn H. *Haithabu: eine germanische Stadt der Frühzeit.* 1937.

Jankuhn D. *Die Ausgrabungen in Haithabu.* 1943.

Jankuhn H. *Haithabu, ein Handelsplatz der Wikingerzeit.* 4th ed. 1963.

Schietzel K. 'Die archäologischen Befunde (1963–64)', *Berichte über die Ausgrabungen in Haithabu* i, 1969, 10–59.

213f. Blindheim C. *Kaupang.* 1953.

Blindheim C. 'The Market Place in Skiringssal', *Acta Archaeologica* xxxi, 1960, 83–100.

Blindheim C. 'Kaupangundersøkelsen etter 10 år', *Viking* xxiv, 1960, 43–68.

Almgren B. *The Viking.* 1967.

214f. Floderus E. 'Västergarn', *Fornvännen* xxix, 1934, 65–83.

Nerman B. 'Det forntida Västergarn', *Fornvännen* xxix, 1934, 84–8.

215 Blomqvist R. and Mårtensson A.W. *Thulegrävningen 1961.* 1963.

Christie H. 'Old Oslo', *Medieval Archaeology* x, 1966, 45–58.

Floderus E. *Sigtuna, Sveriges äldsta medeltidsstad.* 1941.

Fritz B. 'Stadshistoria och arkeologi', *Historisk tidskrift*, 1965, 472–98.

216 Andersen H., Madsen H.J. 'Nygade i Århus', *Kuml*, 1966, 7–29.

Klindt-Jensen O., Andersen H. 'Det ældste Århus', *Kuml*, 1963, 75–87.

216f. Herteig A. *Bryggen i Bergen.* n.d.

Herteig A. 'Marknadsplatser-statsbildningar', *Tor* 1964, 93–112.

Liestøl A. 'Runer frå Bryggen', *Viking* xxvii, 1963, 5–53.

218 Cramp R. *Anglian and Viking York* (Borthwick Papers xxxiii). 1967.

Richardson K.M. 'Excavations in Hungate, Yorks', *The Archaeological Journal* cxvi, 1959, 51–114.

Langenheim K. 'Spuren der Wikinger um Truso', *Elbinger Jahrbuch* xi, 1933, 262–83.

219 Gimbutas M. *The Balts.* 1963.

Hensel W. *Anfänge der Städte bei den Ost- und Westslawen.* 1967.

Jankuhn H. 'Die frühmittelalterlichen Seehandelsplätze in Nord- und Ostseeraum', *Studien zu den Anfängen des europäischen Stadtwesens*, 1965, 451–98.

Ludat H. 'Frühformen des Stadtwesens in Osteuropa', *Studien zu den Anfängen des europäischen Stadtwesens*, 1965, 527–53.

Nerman B. *Grobin-Seeburg, Ausgrabungen und Funde.* 1958.

Sturms E. 'Schwedische Kolonien in Lettland', *Fornvännen* XLIV, 1949, 205–17.

Die Zeit der Stadtgründung im Ostseeraum (Acta Visbyensia I). 1965.

219–20   Arbman H. *Svear i Österviking.* 1955.

Arbman H. 'Zur Frage der Verbindungen zwischen Ost und West in IX.-X. Jahrhundert', *Atti del VI Congresso Internazionale delle Scienze Preistoriche e Protostoriche* I, 1962, 221–32.

Arne T.J. 'Sveriges förbindelser med Östern under vikingatiden', *Fornvännen* VI, 1911, 1–66.

Arne T.J. *La Suède et l'Orient.* 1914.

Arne T.J. 'Die Warägerfrage und die sowjetrussische Forschung', *Acta Archaeologica* XXIII, 1952, 138–47.

Chadwick N.K. *The Beginnings of Russian History.* 1946.

Grekov B. *Kiev Rus.* 1959.

Likhacev D.S. 'The origination of independent Russian culture amid Byzantium and Scandinavia', *Nord-Sud, Colloque . . . C.I.P.S.H.*, Copenhagen 1967, 19–28.

Mongait A.L. *Archaeology in the USSR.* 1961.

Rybakov B.A. *Remeslo drevnej Rusi.* 1948.

Stender-Petersen A. *Varangica.* 1953.

Thomsen V. *The relations between ancient Russia and Scandinavia and the origin of the Russian state.* 1877.

Vasmer M. 'Wikingerspuren in Russland', *Sitzungsberichte der preussischen Akademie der Wissenschaften*, Phil-Hist. Klasse 1931, 649–74.

Vernadsky G. *The Origins of Russia.* 1959.

221   Raudonikas W.J. *Die Normannen der Wikingerzeit und das Ladogagebiet* (Kungl. Vitterhets Historie och Antikvitets Akademiens Handlingar XL: 3). 1930.

222   Thompson M.W. *Novgorod the Great.* 1967.

223   Karger M.K. *Drevnij Kiev.* 1958.

224–8   Balodis F. 'Handelswege nach dem Osten und die Wikinger in Russland' *Antikvariska Studier* III, 1948 (Kungl. Vitterhets Historie och Antikvitets Akademiens Handlingar 65), 317–65.

Nerman B. *Die Verbindungen zwischen Skandinavian und dem Ostbaltikum in der jüngeren Eisenzeit* (Kungl. Vitterhets Historie och Antikvitets Akademiens Handlingar XL: 1). 1929.

225   Cross S.H., Sherbowitz-Wetzor O.P. *The Russian Primary Chronicle.* 2nd ed. 1953.

Moora H. *Die Vorzeit Estlands.* 1932.

Constantine Porphyrogenitus, *De administrando imperio.* I Greek text, ed. G. Moravacsik and R.J.H. Jenkins; II Commentary by F. Dvornik, et al. 1949, 1962.

226   Almgren B. 'Geographical aspects of the silk road especially in Persia and East Turkestan', *Museum of Far Eastern Antiquities, Bulletin* XXXIV, 1962, 93–106.

227   Abromowicz A., Gupieniec A., Mlynarska M. *Haut Moyen Age* (Inventaria Archaeologica, Pologne, fasc. 1). 1958.

Arbman H. 'Une route commerciale pendant les X et XI siècles', *Slavia Antiqua* I, 1948, 435–8.

Paulsen P. *Wikingerfunde aus Ungarn im Lichte der Nord- und Westeuropäischen Frühgeschichte* (Archaeologica Hungarica XII). 1933.

443

228   Arbman H. *Schweden und das Karolingische Reich* (Kungl. Vitterhets Historie och Antikvitets Akademiens Handlingar XLIII). 1937.

Arbman H. 'Influences carolingiennes et ottoniennes en Scandinavie', *Settimane di studio del centro italiano di studi sull'alto medioevo* XI, 1964, 355–70.

Braat W-C. 'Les Vikings au Pays de Frise', *Annales de Normandie* IV, 1954, 219–337.

CHAPTER 7
232–56   Brøgger A.W., Shetelig H. *The Viking Ships*. 1951.

Falk H. 'Altnordisches Seewesen', *Wörter und Sachen* IV, 1912, 1–122.

Magnússon E. 'Notes on Shipbuilding and Nautical Terms of Old in the North', *Saga-Book of the Viking Club* IV, 1905–6, 182–237.

232   Campbell A., ed. *Encomium Emmae Reginae*. 1949.

233   Brøgger A.W. *Borrefundet og Vestfoldkongernes graver* (Videnskapsselskapets Skrifter. II. Hist.-Filos Klasse. 1916. No. 1).

Brøgger A.W., Falk H., Shetelig H. *Osebergfundet*. 1917–.

Christensen A.E. 'Færingen fra Gokstad', *Viking* XXIII, 1959, 57–69.

Johannessen F. 'Båtene fra Gokstadskipet', *Viking* IV, 1940, 125–30.

Nicolaysen N. *Langskibet fra Gokstad ved Sandefjord*. 1882.

Olsen O., Crumlin-Pedersen O. 'The Skuldelev Ships', *Acta Archaeologica* XXXVIII, 1967, 73–174.

Olsen O., Crumlin-Pedersen O. *Fem vikingeskibe fra Roskilde Fjord*. 1969.

Shetelig H. *Tuneskibet* (Norske Oldfund II). 1917.

Shetelig H. 'Ship Burials', *Saga-Book of the Viking Club* IV, 1905–6, 326–63.

234   Andersen M. *Vikingfærden*. 1895.

Bersu G., Wilson D.M. *Three Viking Graves from the Isle of Man* (Society for Medieval Archaeology: Monograph Series 1). 1966.

Arbman H. 'En sjökonungs grav', *Arkeologiska Forskningar och Fynd*, 1952, 326–34.

238   Thorvildsen K. *Ladby-Skibet* (Nordiske Fortidsminder VI: 1). 1957.

Thorvildsen K. *The Viking Ship of Ladby*. 1961.

239   Crumlin-Pedersen O. 'Das Haithabuschiff', *Berichte über die Ausgrabungen in Haithabu* III, 1969.

240   Bruce-Mitford R.L.S. *The Sutton Hoo Ship Burial, A Handbook*. 1968.

Marsden P.R.V. *A ship of the Roman period from Blackfriars, in the City of London*. N.D.

241   Åkerlund H. *Nydamskeppen*. 1963.

244–7   Åkerlund H. 'Åss och beitiáss', *Unda Maris*, 1955–6.

Åkerlund H. 'Vikingatidens skepp och sjöväsen', *Svenska kryssarklubben, Årsskrift*, 1959, 23–81.

Bertheussen C. 'Ei gåta frå Gokstadskipet', *Viking* XXI-XXII, 165–174.

251   The translation is a revision of S.Laing, *Heimskringla* I, *The Olaf Sagas* I, 1964, 76–8.

254   Almgren B. 'Vikingatåg och vikingaskepp', *Tor*, 1962, 186–200.

Almgren B. 'Vikingatågens höjdpunkt och slut', *Tor*, 1963, 215–50.

255   Binns A. 'The navigation of Viking ships round the British Isles in Old English and Old Norse sources', *The Fifth Viking Congress*, ed. B. Niclasen, 1968, 103–17.

Sølver C.V. *Vestervejen, om Vikingernes sejlads*. 1954.

256   Marcus G.J. 'The Course for Greenland', *Saga-Book of the Viking Society* XIV, 1953–7, 12–35.

Steen S. *Ferd og Fest*. 2nd ed. 1942.

259   Berg G. *Sledges and Wheeled Vehicles* (Nordiska Museets Handlingar 4). 1935.

Christensen A. E. 'Vognen i nordisk forhistorie', *Viking* XXVIII, 1964, 63–88.

260   Atlestam P.O. and Niklasson N. 'En förhistorisk tragsläde', *Göteborgs och Bohusläns Fornminnesförenings Tidskrift* VI, 1942, 59–66.
261   Berg G. 'Förhistoriska skidor i Sverige', *På skidor*, 1933, 142–69.
        Berg G. *et al. Finds of Skis . . . from Swedish bogs and marshes.* 1941.
        Berg G. 'The origin and development of skis throughout the ages', *Nordiska Museets Handlingar*, 1950.

CHAPTER 8
263   Stenberger M. 'Eketorp's Borg, a fortified village on Öland, Sweden', *Acta Archaeologica* XXXVII, 1966, 203–21.
264   Stenberger M. 'En preliminär undersökning av Ismantorps borg', *Fornvännen*, 1925, 358–75.
        Stenberger M. *Ismantorps borg och Gråborg.* 1934.
        Zetterling A. *Bulverket i Tingstäde träsk.* 1934.
265   Jankuhn H. *Haithabu und Danewerk.* 1958.
        La Cour V. *Danevirkestudier.* 1951.
268–72 Nørlund P. *Trelleborg* (Nordiske fortidsminder IV: 1). 1948.
        Olsen O. *Fyrkat, the Viking Camp near Hobro.* 1959.
        Schultz C.G. 'Aggersborg, vikingelejren ved Limfjorden', *Fra Nationalmuseets Arbejdsmark*, 1949, 91–108.
272–82 Falk H. *Altnordische Waffenkunde* (Videnskapsselskapets Skrifter. II. Hist.-Filos. Klasse. 1914. No. 6).
273   Davidson H.R.E. *The sword in Anglo-Saxon England.* 1962.
        Petersen Jan. *De norske vikingesverd. En typologisk-kronologisk studie over vikingetidens vaaben* (Videnskapsselskapets Skrifter. II. Hist.-Filos. Klasse. 1919. No. 1).
274   Liestøl A. 'Blodrefill og mål', *Viking* XV, 1951, 71–98.
        Anstee J.W., Biek L. 'A study in pattern-welding', *Medieval Archaeology* V, 1961, 71–93.
276   Paulsen P. *Axt und Kreuz in Nord- und Osteuropa.* 2. Aufl. 1956.
279   Grieg S. *Gjermundbufunnet* (Norske Oldfunn VIII). 1947.
        Hejdová D. 'Prilba Zvaná "Svatováclavská" ', *Sborník Národního Muzea v Praze* XVIII, 1964, 1–106.
280   The triad is quoted in the translation of David Greene and Frank O'Connor: *A Golden Treasury of Irish Poetry.* 1967. 105.
285   Grøn F. *Berserksgangens vesen og årsaksforhold* (Det kgl. Norske Videnskabers Selskabs Skrifter, 1929, Nr. 4).

CHAPTER 9
        A full bibliography of Viking art will be found in Wilson D.M. and Klindt-Jensen O., *Viking Art*, 1966, to which the reader is referred for references to important monuments. Since this book appeared the following important works have also been published:
        Anker P. *L'art scandinave* I. 1969.
        Henry F. *Irish Art* II. 1967.
        Holmqvist W. *Övergångstidens metallkonst* (Kungl. Vitterhets Historie och Antikvitets Akademiens Handlingar, Antikvariska serien II). 1963.
316   The quotation from Saxo is adapted from the translation by O.Elton, *The First Nine Books of the Danish History of Saxo Grammaticus*, 1894, 237.

CHAPTER 10
319   Heusler A., Ranisch W. *Eddica minora.* 1903.
        Helgason Jón. *Norges og Islands Digtning.* In Nordal Sigurður, ed. *Litteraturhistorie B Norge og Island* (Nordisk Kultur VIII:B). 1953.
        Jónsson Finnur. *Den oldnorske og oldislandske Litteraturs Historie.* 2. Udg. 1920–4.

Paasche F. *Norges og Islands litteratur inntil utgangen av middelalderen.* Ny utg. ved Anne Holtsmark. 1957.

Sveinsson Einar Ól. *Íslenzkar bókmenntir í fornöld* 1. 1962.

de Vries J. *Altnordische Literaturgeschichte.* 2. Aufl. 1964–7.

320   Jónsson Finnur. *Edda Snorra Sturlusonar.* 1931.

Heusler A. *Deutsche Versgeschichte* 1. 1925.

Sievers E. *Altgermanische Metrik.* 1893.

321   Wessén E. *Runstenen vid Röks kyrka* (Kungl. Vitterhets Historie och Antikvitets Akademiens Handlingar. Fil.-filos. Serien 5). 1958.

325   Nielsen Niels Åge. *Runestudier* (Odense University Studies in Scandinavian Languages 1). 1968. 118–23.

328   Gering H. *Vollständiges Wörterbuch zu den Lieder der Edda.* 1903.

Jónsson Finnur. *Lexicon poeticum* . . . oprindelig forfattet af Sveinbjörn Egilsson. 2 Udg. 1931.

329   Meissner R. *Die Kenningar der Skalden.* 1921.

Lie H. 'Skaldestil-studier', *Maal og minne,* 1952, 1–92.

Lie H. *'Natur' og 'unatur' i skaldekunsten* (Avhandlinger utgitt av Det Norske Videnskaps-Akademi i Oslo. II. Hist.-Filos. Klasse. 1957. No. 1).

334   Gustav Albeck puts the same texts side by side in Albeck G., Billeskov-Jansen F.J. *Dansk Litteratur Historie* 1. 1964. 37.

335   Jansson Sven B.F. 'Forntidens litteratur'. Ståhle Carl Ivar. 'Medeltidens profana litteratur'. In Tigerstedt E.N., ed. *Ny illustrerad svensk litteraturhistoria* 1. 1955.

Jansson Sven B.F. 'Poetry in runes'. In *The Runes of Sweden.* 1962. 118–36.

336   Bugge S., ed. *Norrœn fornkvæði* . . . *Sæmundar Edda* . . . 1867.

Helgason Jón. *Eddadigte* 1. *Vǫluspá. Hávamál.* 2. Udg. 3. Opl. 1964.

Helgason Jón. *Eddadigte* II. *Gudedigte.* 3. Udg. 4. Opl. 1965.

Neckel G., ed. *Edda.* 4. Aufl. von Hans Kuhn. 1962–8.

Olsen M. 'Fra Eddaforskningen. Grímnismál og den høiere tekstkritikk'. In *Norrøne studier.* 1938. 130–49.

342   Jónsson Finnur. *Hávamál.* 1924.

Wessén E. *Havamal. Några stilfrågor* (Filologiskt arkiv 8). 1959.

344   Nordal Sigurður. *Völuspá.* 2. prentun. 1952.

Holtsmark Anne. *Forelesninger over Vǫluspá.* Høsten 1949. [Oslo] Universitetets Studentkontor. 1950.

Ólafsson Ólafur M. 'Völuspá Konungsbókar', *Landsbókasafn Íslands: Árbók* 22, 1965, 86–124.

Ólafsson Ólafur M. 'Endurskoðun Völuspár', *Landsbókasafn Íslands: Árbók* 23, 1966, 110–93.

347   Dronke Ursula, ed. *The Poetic Edda* 1. *Heroic poems.* [*Atlakviða, Atlamál, Guðrúnarhvǫt, Hamðismál.*] 1969.

Helgason Jón, ed. *Tvær kviður fornar. Völundarkviða og Atlakviða.* 2. útg. 1962.

Helgason Jón, ed. *Kviður af Gotum og Húnum. Hamðismál, Guðrúnarhvöt, Hlöðskviða.* 1967.

Helgason Jón, ed. *Eddadigte* III. *Heltedigte.* 3 Udg. 1968.

349   Finch R.G., ed. and trans. *The Saga of the Volsungs.* 1965.

359   Helgason Jón. *Skjaldevers.* 1962.

Jónsson Finnur. *Den norsk-islandske Skjaldedigtning.* 1912–5.

Kock E.A. *Den norsk-isländska skaldediktningen.* 1946–50.

Kock E.A., Meissner R., ed. *Skaldisches Lesebuch.* 1931.

360   Liestøl A., Krause W., Helgason Jón. 'Drottkvætt-vers fra Bryggen i Bergen', *Maal og minne,* 1962, 98–108.

Benediktsson Jakob, Magnússon Ásgeir Bl., Helgason Jón og medarbeidere, Krause W. 'En ny dróttkvættstrofe fra Bryggen i Bergen', *Maal og minne,* 1964, 93–100.

Lie H. *'Natur'* . . . see reference against p. 329.

361   *Skáldatal* is best edited in *Edda Snorra Sturlusonar.* 1848–87. III. 205–752.

362   For verse by Egil see, in addition to references against p. 359 above, Nordal Sigurður, ed. *Egils saga Skalla-Grímssonar* (Íslenzk fornrit II). 1933.

367   For verse by Einar Helgason and Sigvat Þórðarson see, in addition to references against p. 359 above, Aðalbjarnarson Bjarni. *Heimskringla* (Íslenzk fornrit XXVI–VIII). 1941–51.

CHAPTER 11

371   von See Klaus. *Altnordische Rechtswörter* (Hermaea 16). 1964. Kap. 3, Recht und Religion.

379   Nelson A. 'Envig och ära', *Saga och sed,* 1944, 57–94.

CHAPTER 12

387   Briem Ólafur. *Heiðinn siður á Íslandi.* 1945.
Briem Ólafur. *Vanir og æsir* (Studia Islandica 21). 1963.
Munch P.A. *Norrøne gude- og heltesagn.* Revidert utg. ved Anne Holtsmark. 1967.
Ström F. *Nordisk hedendom.* 2. utg. 1967.
Turville-Petre G. *Myth and religion of the North.* 1964.
de Vries J. *Altgermanische Religionsgeschichte.* 2. Aufl. 1956–7.

392   Ström F. *Diser, nornor, valkyrjor* (Kungl. Vitterhets Historie och Antikvitets Akademiens Handlingar. Fil.-filos. Serien 1). 1954.

393   On place-names with possible religious significance see the general works on place-names and religion listed against pp. xviii, 387.

396   Rostvik A. *Har och harg* (Acta Academiae Regiae Gustavi Adolphi XLIV). 1967.

398   Olsen O. *Hørg, hov og kirke.* 1966. (Also in *Aarbøger for nordisk Oldkyndighed og Historie,* 1965.)

399   The passage from Ibn Fadlan is based on the translation given by Birkeland, see reference against p. xx.

403   Cf. note against p. 362 above.

404   Strömbäck Dag. *Sejd* (Nordiska texter och undersökningar 5). 1935.
Eldjárn Kristján. *Kuml og haugfé úr heiðnum sið á Íslandi.* 1956. 362–3.

408   On this new translation from Ibn Fadlan see the Foreword, p. xi. Since writing this chapter our attention has been drawn to the discussion with full bibliography by H.M. Smyser: 'Ibn Fadlan's account of the Rus with some commentary and some allusion to Beowulf'. In [*Franciplegia.*] *Medieval and Linguistic Studies in Honor of Francis Peabody Magoun Jr.* 1965. 92–119.

411   Shetelig H. 'Traces of the custom of suttee in Norway during the Viking age', *Saga-Book of the Viking Club* VI, 1910, 180–208.

413   Andersen H. 'Tomme Høje', *Kuml,* 1951, 91–135.

414   Jørgensen A.D. *Den nordiske Kirkes Grundlæggelse og første Udvikling.* 1874–8.
Kolsrud O. *Noregs kyrkjesoga* I. *Millomalderen.* 1958.
Ljungberg H. *Den nordiska religionen och kristendomen.* 1938.
Maurer K. *Die Bekehrung des Norwegischen Stammes zum Christenthume, in ihrem geschichtlichen Verlaufe quellenmässig geschildert.* 1855–6.
Paasche F. *Møtet mellom hedendom og kristendom i Norden . . .* utgitt ved Dag Strömbäck. 1958.
Palme S.U. *Kristendomens genombrott i Sverige.* 1959.
Sverdrup G. *Da Norge ble kristnet.* 1942.

418   Kumlien Kjell. *Biskop Karl av Västerås och Uppsala ärkesätes flyttning* (Historiskt arkiv 14). 1966.
Lindqvist Sune. 'Uppsala hednatempel och första katedral', *Nordisk Tidskrift* 43, 1967, 236–42.

Lidén H.E. 'From pagan sanctuary to Christian church', *Norwegian Archaeological Review* II, 1969, 1–32.

418–21 Anker P. *L'art scandinave* I. 1969.

Bjerknes H. 'Urnes stavkirke. Har det vært to bygninger forut for den nuværende kirke?', *Foreningen til norske fortidsminnesmerkers bevaring, Årbok* CXIII, 1958, 75–96.

Blindheim M. *Norwegian romanesque decorative sculpture 1090–1200.* 1965.

Blomqvist R., Mårtensson A.W. *Thulegrävningen 1961.* 1963.

Bugge A. 'The origin, development and decline of the Norwegian stave church', *Acta Archaeologica* VI, 1935, 152–65.

Bugge A. *Norwegian Stave-churches.* 1953.

Christie H. 'Urnes stavkirkes forløper belyst ved utgravninger under kirken', *Foreningen til norske fortidsminnesmerkers bevaring, Årbok* CXIII, 1958, 49–74.

Ekhoff E. *Svenska stavkyrkor.* 1914–6.

Møller E., Olsen O. 'Danske trækirke', *Nationalmuseets Arbejdsmark*, 1961, 35–58.

Mowinckel R. 'De eldste norske stavkirker', *Universitetets Oldsaksamlings Skrifter* II, 1929, 383–424.

Phleps H. *Die norwegischen Stabkirchen.* 1958.

421 Turville-Petre G. *Origins of Icelandic Literature.* 1953. Chapter V, Early religious prose.

423 The passage from *Gísla saga* is adapted from the translation by George Johnston: *The Saga of Gisli* (J.M. Dent and Sons Ltd). 1963. 8. For *Þorgils saga ok Hafliða* see reference against p. 99 above.

425 Gehl W. *Ruhm und Ehre bei den Nordgermanen.* 1937.

Nordal Sigurður. *Íslenzk menning.* 1942.

426 On *níðingr* see Almqvist Bo. *Norrön niddiktning* I (Nordiska texter och undersökningar 21). 1965. 73–7 and bibliography.

431 Ström Åke V. 'Scandinavian belief in fate'. In Ringgren H., ed. *Fatalistic Beliefs in Religion, Folklore, and Literature.* 1967. 63–88.

ADDITIONAL BIBLIOGRAPHY, JANUARY 1971

xvi Christensen A.E. *Vikingetidens Danmark.* 1969.

xviii Ståhl H. *Ortnamn och ortnamnsforskning.* 1970.

99 Johnsen O.A. *Tre gildeskråer fra middelalderen.* 1920.

152 Schmidt H. 'Vikingernes husformede gravsten', *Nationalmuseets Arbejdsmark*, 1970, 13–28.

203–5 *Early medieval studies* I (Antikvariskt arkiv 38). 1970.

213f. *Viking* XXXIII, 1969, contains new reports on the Kaupang excavations.

216f. Herteig A. *Kongers havn og handels sete.* 1969.

219–20 Kirpicnikov A.N. 'Russisk-skandinaviske forbindelser i IX–XI århundreder illustreret ved våbenfund', *Kuml*, 1969, 165–89.

227 Żak J. *Importy Skandynawskie na Ziemiach Zachodniosłowiańskich od IX do XI Wieku*, I–III. 1963–7.

Chapter 9 Jansson Í. 'Wikingerschmuck und Münzdatierung', *Tor XIII*, 1969, 26–64.

329 Sveinsson Einar Ól. 'Dróttkvæða þáttur', *Skírnir* 121, 1947, 5–32.

387 Holtsmark A. *Norrøn mytologi.* 1970.

414 *La conversione al Cristianesimo nell'Europa dell'alto medioevo* (Settimane di studio del Centro italiano di studi sull'alto medioevo XIV). 1967.

Index

Abbreviations used in text and index

A.	*archbishop*	OI	*Old Icelandic*
adj.	*adjective*	OIr.	*Old Irish*
B.	*bishop*	OLG	*Old Low German*
D.	*Denmark, Danish*	ON	*Old Norse*
E.	*earl*	ONorw.	*Old Norwegian*
EN	*East Norse*	OSw.	*Old Swedish*
f.	*feminine*	pl.	*plural*
I.	*Iceland, Icelandic*	Q.	*queen*
Ir.	*Ireland, Irish*	R.	*river*
K.	*king*	Rþ	*(occurs in) Rígsþula*
m.	*masculine*	Ru	*(site of, name in, carver of) runic*
MLG	*Middle Low German*		*inscription*
n.	*neuter*	St	*saint*
N(orw).	*Norway, Norwegian*	S(w).	*Sweden, Swedish*
OD	*Old Danish*	vb.	*verb*
OE	*Old English*	WN	*West Norse*
OHG	*Old High German*		

In the Index *æ* and *œ* have the alphabetical position of *ae* and *oe* respectively; *á* and *ä* are treated as *a*, *ð* as *d*, *þ* as *th*, and *ö*, *ø* and *ǫ* as *o*. The rare Greek and Russian terms occupy the position they would have if transliterated (as the Russian words in fact are). We have not found it practical to introduce in either the text or the index the modifying marks used in the transliteration of Arabic words and names.

The names of the northern countries and their inhabitants, which occur on almost every page, and very common names like Baltic, England, Europe, are not included.

451

Eskil, St 31
Eskil, A. 18, 22, 125
Eskilsø 20
Eskilstuna 31, 32, E. sarcophagi 414
Essex 66, 105, 267, 420, 421
Essupi 225
Estonia 33, 226
Estrid, Q. 16
eþsörisbrot 142
Eustace, St 333, 362
Evesham 20
eyðir ulfa gráðar 330
Eyjafjöll 256
Eyjafjörður 54
Eyjolf, I. 428–9
Eyjolf Sæmundsson, I. 63
eyneglða 364
Eyrathing 372
eyrir (pl. *aurar*), ounce 55, 73, 93, 198
Eystein, N. K. 139, 262
Eystein, S. K. 115

Faðir, Rþ 65
fælæghsbryti 87
Færeyinga saga xxii
Fáfnir 349
Fagrskinna xxii
Falster 10, 224
Falun 28, 184
fame 432
family society 4–5, 6–7, 422
fangavitni 375
Faroes, Faroese xv, xix, xxii, 1, 39, 43, 48, 50, 52, 56, 131, 132, 147, 148, 152, 201, 256, 394
Faroese, Saga of xxvi
Färsjö, Ru 84
fate 431
fé, annat fæ 68, *gefin til fjár* 113
feast, freedom- see *frelsisøl*
feasting, in cult-celebrations 401–2
feigr 431
Fejø 289, pl. 17a
félag 97
félagi 97
fences 405
Fenrir 341, 388
ferja 236
festr 234
fetches (*fylgjur*) 392
field systems 176–7
Fifth Court 58, 61, 133, 377
files 182, fig. 20s, t
fimtánsessa 235
fines 382

Finkarby 297
Finland, Finns xv, 33, 38, 205, 221 (Gulf of F.)
Finnish Bight, 28, cf. Finland
Finnish language 87
Finnvid, sons of, Ru 84, 127
fires, fire-places 162
fish 146–7, 164, f. trade 200, 202, 217
Fish-spine, sword 144
Five Boroughs 218
Fjädrundaland 281
fjørbaugsgarðr 383
Fjørtoft 241
Fläckebo, Ru 111
flætføring, flätföring 119
Flambard, Ranulf, B.314
Flanders 66
flannstøng, see penis-pole
Flatatunga panels 317
flax 149, 171
Flekkefjord 39
flokkr 328
floors 162
Flugumýrr 154–5, fig. 11
foldar vørðr 365
folk 272
folk art 314–5
folk weapons 272, 279
fonts 315
food, f. storage 161–7
food trade 195, 201–3
foot, Roman 270, 271
footgear 174–5
Forkun, Ru 106
fórn 400
fórna 400
fornaldarsögur 319
fornyrðislag 322, 324, 325, 334, 335
fortifications 263–6
forts, at Birka 207, Hedeby 210, Novgorod 222
foster-brotherhood 422
fostering 116
fóstra, nurse 108
fostra, fostre, slaves 75
Fot, Ru 318
Fótbítr 273
Foul, Rþ 76
frælse 127
frelsisøl, freedom feast 73, 74
Framlev 163
France xv, 13, 15, 20, 60, 62, 66, 79, 228, 230, 234
Frankish swords 273
Franks xv, 12, 79, 197, 378
Frank-speaking verses 361